Windows Vista® Accelerated

Copyright ©2007 YoungJin.com Inc., 3F Mapo Tower Bldg, 418-1 Mapo-dong, Mapo-gu, Seoul 121-734, Korea. World rights reserved. No part of this publication may be stored in a retrieval system, transmitted, or reproduced in any way, including but not limited to photocopy, photograph, magnetic, or other record, without the prior agreement and written peromission of the publisher.

ISBN: 978-89-314-3438-5

Printed and bound in the Republic of Korea.

How to contact us:
support@youngjin.com
feedback@youngjin.com

Address: YoungJin.com
3F Mapo Tower Bldg, 418-1 Mapo-dong,
Mapo-gu, Seoul 121-734, Korea
Fax: 82-2-2105-2206

Credits
Author: Guy Hart-Davis
Production Manager: Suzie Lee
Editorial Service: Publication Service, Inc.
Developmental Editor: Kenny Chumbley, Publication Service, Inc.
Editorial Manager: Lorie Donovan, Publication Service, Inc.
Book Designer: Design Chang
Cover Designer: Litmus
Production Control: Jay Won, Woong Ki

Notice of Rights
All rights reserved. No part of this book may be reproduced or transmitted in any form by any means, electronic, mechanical, photocopying, recording, or otherwise, without the prior written permission of the publisher.

Trademarks
Windows Vista® is a trademark of Microsoft Corporation. Registered in the United States and other countries.

Many of the designations used by manufacturers and sellers to distinguish their products are claimed as trademarks. Where those designations appear in this book, and YoungJin was aware of a trademark claim, the designations appear as requested by the owner of the trademark. All other product names and services identified throughout this book are used in editorial fashion only and for the benefit of such companies with no intention of infringement of the trademark. No such use, or the use of any trade name, is intended to convey endorsement or other affiliation with this book.

Notice of Liability
The information in this book is distributed on an As Is basis without warranty. While every precaution has been taken in the preparation of the book, neither the author nor Youngjin Singapore Pte, Ltd. shall have any liability to any person or entity with respect to any loss or damage caused or alleged to be caused directly or indirectly by the instructions contained in this book or by the computer software and hardware products described in it.

Windows Vista®

Accelerated

Different Versions of Windows Vista /6

Chapter 1

Getting Started with Windows Vista / 8

Section 01	Upgrading to Windows Vista / 10
Section 02	Starting Your Computer and Logging On / 19
Let's go Pro!	Understanding the Icons at the Bottom of the Welcome Screen / 22
Section 03	Switching Users, Logging Off, and Shutting Down / 24

Chapter 2

Navigating The User Interface and Running Applications / 28

Section 01	Using the Desktop, Start Menu, and Taskbar / 30
Let's go Pro!	Choosing Which Applications Appear on the Start Menu / 34
Section 02	Working with Application Windows / 35
Section 03	Using or Turning Off the Sidebar / 37
Section 04	Running, Installing, and Removing Applications / 42
Let's go Pro!	Understanding User Account Control / 50

Chapter 3

Working with Files and Folders / 52

Section 01	Using Windows Explorer / 54
Section 02	Copying and Moving Files and Folders / 64
Section 03	Deleting Files and Folders / 69
Section 04	Searching for Files and Folders / 74
Section 05	Creating and Using Zipped Folders / 78
Let's go Pro!	Using Shortcuts to Access Files or Folders Quickly / 81

Chapter 4

Customizing Windows to Suit Your Needs / 82

Section 01	Setting Up Your Screen and Desktop / 84
Let's go Pro!	Changing the Theme / 90
Section 02	Customizing the Taskbar, Notification Area, and Toolbars / 92
Section 03	Changing Sounds, Appearance, and the Start Menu / 97
Section 04	Managing User Accounts and Passwords / 109
Section 05	Using Parental Controls and Activity Reports / 114
Let's go Pro!	Setting Up Ease of Access Features / 121

Chapter 5

Connecting to the Internet and Using Internet Explorer / 122

Section 01	Setting Up an Internet Connection / 124
Section 02	Browsing with Internet Explorer / 132
Section 03	Searching, Using Favorites, and Navigating / 137

Chapter 6

Making the Most of E-mail and Instant Messaging / 144

Section 01	Setting Up Windows Mail and Sending Messages / 146
Section 02	Using Signatures and Attachments / 153
Section 03	Getting and Setting Up Windows Live Messenger / 157
Section 04	Communicating via Windows Live Messenger / 162
Let's go Pro!	Set Up Audio and Video / 165

Chapter 7

Enjoying Music, Video, DVD, and TV / 168

Section 01 Starting Windows Media Player and Creating Your Library / 170

Let's go Pro! Changing Your Ripping Settings / 178

Section 02 Playing Music / 179
Section 03 Burning CDs and Sharing Music / 184
Section 04 Playing Videos and DVDs / 189
Section 05 Getting Started with Windows Media Center / 191

Chapter 8

Networking Your Computers and Sharing Files / 196

Section 01 Creating a Wired Network / 198

Let's go Pro! Choosing a Network Technology / 200

Section 02 Creating a Wireless Network / 202

Let's go Pro! Connecting Your Computer to a Closed Wireless Network Manually / 212

Section 03 Specifying an IP Address Manually / 214
Section 04 Browsing and Using Folders on a Network / 217
Section 05 Sharing Files with Other Users / 221

Chapter 9

Managing Hardware, Printers, and Fonts / 226

Section 01 Installing Hardware Devices / 228

Let's go Pro! Providing a Driver Manually / 231

Section 02 Updating a Device Driver / 233
Section 03 Installing a Printer / 236
Section 04 Adding and Managing Fonts / 243

Chapter 10

Securing Your PC and Windows / 246

Section 01 Applying Essential Security Settings / 248

Let's go Pro! Configuring Windows Firewall to Allow a Program to Run / 251

Section 02 Installing an Antivirus Program / 253
Section 03 Keeping Windows Up-to-Date / 257

Let's go Pro! Resetting Internet Security Settings Manually / 261

Section 04 Scanning for Problems with Windows Defender / 262

Chapter 11

Troubleshooting Problems / 266

Section 01 Getting Help via Remote Assistance / 268

Let's go Pro! Giving Help via Remote Assistance / 274

Section 02 Using System Restore / 276
Section 03 Backing Up and Restoring Your Data / 279
Section 04 Finding Solutions for Problems / 283

Let's go Pro! Closing a Program That Has Crashed / 286

Chapter 12

Using the Windows Vista Ultimate Features / 288

Section 01 Using Remote Desktop / 290

Let's go Pro! Getting Windows Ultimate Extras / 297

Section 02 Backing Up and Restoring Your Entire PC / 298
Section 03 Faxing with Windows Fax and Scan / 302
Section 04 Encrypting Your Drive with BitLocker / 306

Let's go Pro! Turning Off BitLocker Drive Encryption / 311

Index / 312

Different Versions of Windows Vista >>>

Windows Vista comes in six different versions aimed at different markets: one for emerging markets, two for home use, and three for business use.

■ Emerging Markets

Windows Vista Starter Edition® is available only in emerging markets, such as India and Thailand. This version has a low price and limited features—for example, it can run only a few programs at the same time. It does not have features such as the Vista Aero user interface or TV recording.

■ Home Computing

Windows Vista Home Basic® is the least expensive and most limited version of Windows Vista that's widely available. Home Basic includes the main Windows features, such as the Windows firewall and Windows defender security features, new search capabilities, and Internet Explorer 7®. Home Basic does not have the Vista Aero user interface and does not include Windows Media Center, which allows you to watch and record TV on your computer.

Home Basic is a good choice for a home desktop computer used for e-mail, Web surfing, music, and creating business or school documents. But Home Basic does not include the Mobility Center or support for Tablet PC features (such as handwriting), so it's not a good choice for laptop computers.

Windows Vista Home Premium® has all the features of Home Basic, but also the Vista Aero user interface, Windows Media Center, Mobility Center, and Tablet PC features. Home Premium is a good choice for home desktop and laptop computers.

Neither of the Home versions can connect to a business network running Windows Server.

■ Business Computing

Windows Vista Business Edition® is designed for use in companies and organizations. It has the Windows Aero user interface, includes powerful encryption, and can connect to business networks running Windows Server. It does not have Windows Media Center.

Windows Vista Ultimate Edition® includes all the features of Windows Vista Home Premium Edition®, but also the business-related features (such as encryption), which allow the ability to connect to a business network. Ultimate Edition is most suitable for professionals who use their computers at work and at home (whether laptops or desktops) with a Windows Server network.

Windows Vista Enterprise Edition® is designed for, and only available for sale to, large businesses with many users.

■ Vista Editions This Book Covers

This book covers the Home Basic, Home Premium, Business, and Ultimate Editions. Most of the screen shots are from Windows Vista Ultimate Edition, since this edition includes all the features of the other editions. Major differences among the versions of Windows Vista (Starter Edition and Enterprise Edition excepted) will be clearly noted.

Chapter 1

Getting Started with Windows Vista

Welcome to Windows Vista! The latest version of Microsoft's market leading operating system, Windows Vista introduces many new features and provides greater security, together with a brand new user interface.

In this chapter you will learn how to log onto your computer, log off, switch from one user account to another, and shut your computer down when you're finished.

If you're upgrading an existing computer to Windows Vista, see "Upgrading to Windows Vista" at the end of this chapter for an overview of how to upgrade. If Windows Vista is already installed on your computer, you do not need to read this section.

SECTION 01 Upgrading to Windows Vista

The normal way to get Windows Vista installed on a computer is to buy a new computer with Windows Vista preinstalled. When you do this, the computer manufacturer handles the installation and takes care of any compatibility problems, so you should receive a computer that runs Windows Vista with no problems.

However, if you have a computer that's running Windows XP©, you may be able to upgrade from Windows XP to Windows Vista.

Preparing to Upgrade

Before you upgrade, make sure that your computer is powerful enough to run Windows Vista. Because of its many new capabilities and its security features, Windows Vista requires a much more powerful computer than Windows XP.

Here are the recommended minimum specifications for a computer to run Windows Vista:

Component	Recommendations
Processor	1GHz or faster. Intel Celeron and AMD Sempron processors are adequate, but you will enjoy far better performance from an Intel Core Duo, Intel Core 2 Duo, AMD Turion, or AMD Athlon processor.
RAM	512MB minimum. Having 1GB to 2GB RAM is much better, as it allows you to use advanced features such as speech recognition as well as running large programs.
Hard Drive	16GB minimum free space. Having far more free space is far better, as you can take advantage of space hungry features such as burning DVDs and recording TV programs (in Windows Vista Home Premium and Windows Vista Ultimate).
Optical Drive	DVD ROM minimum, DVD writer preferred; dual layer DVD writer even better.

Using the Windows Upgrade Advisor

If your computer meets these specifications, use the Windows Vista Upgrade Advisor to make sure that your computer's other components are compatible with Windows Vista. Follow these steps:

1. Start Windows XP as normal. Insert the Windows Vista DVD in your computer's DVD drive. AutoPlay launches the Install Windows window. Click the [Check Compatibility Online] button.

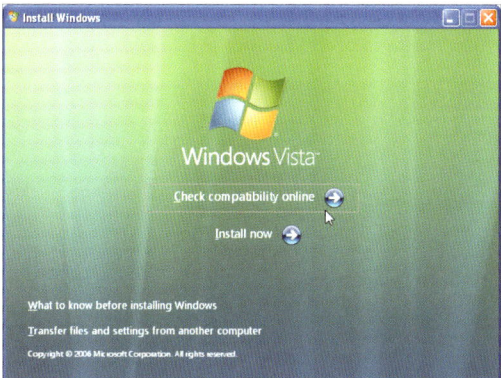

2. Windows opens a browser window (for example, an Internet Explorer window) to the Windows Upgrade Advisor Web page. Click the [Download Windows Upgrade Advisor] link to go to the download page, and then click the [Download] link.

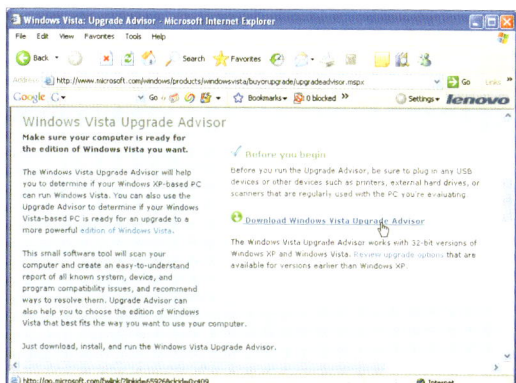

3. Windows displays the File Download - Security Warning dialog box asking if you want to run or save the file. Click the [Run] button.

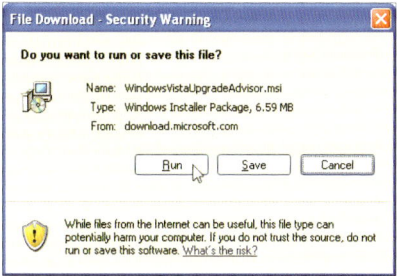

4. Windows downloads the Windows Upgrade Advisor to a temporary folder and then prompts you to run the software. Verify that the software is named Windows Vista Upgrade Advisor and that the publisher is Microsoft Corporation, and then click the [Run] button.

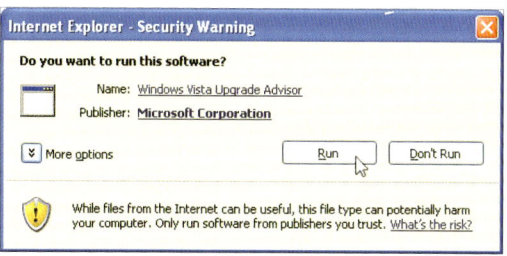

5. The first screen of the Windows Vista Upgrade Advisor appears. Click the [Next] button. The License Agreement screen appears. Read the license agreement, select the [I Agree] option button if you agree, and then click the [Next] button.

6. The Select Installation Folder screen appears. If necessary, change the installation folder (see the nearby Note). Click the [Next] button.

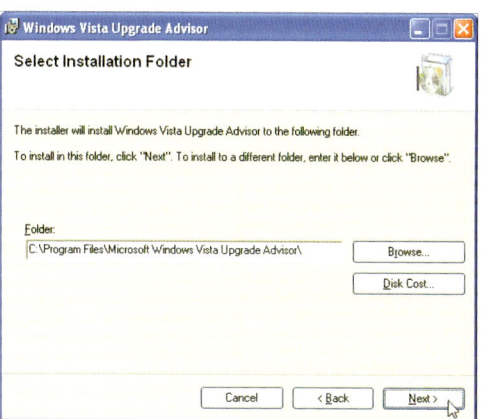

11

7. The Confirm Installation screen appears. Select the [Create Desktop Shortcut] option button if you want to create a shortcut on your desktop for running the Upgrade Advisor. You probably won't want this shortcut, so you may prefer to select the [Don't Create Desktop Shortcut] option button. Click the [Next] button.

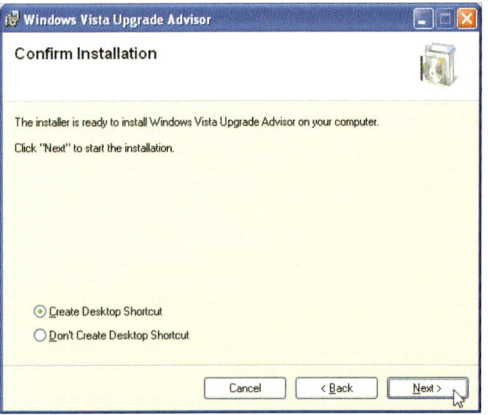

8. Windows installs the Upgrade Advisor and then displays the Installation Complete screen. To run the Upgrade Advisor, leave the Launch Windows Vista Upgrade Advisor check box selected (as it is by default, otherwise, clear this check box). You can then launch the Upgrade Advisor from the desktop shortcut or from the Start menu as needed. Click the [Close] button.

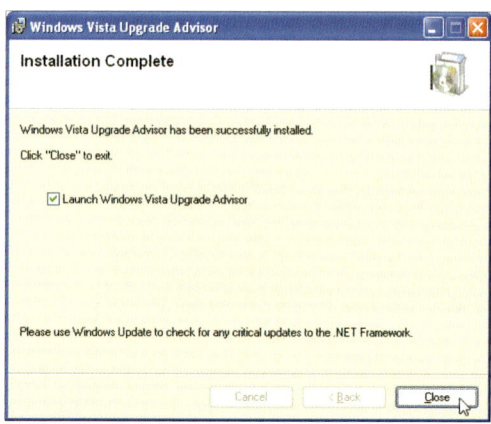

Choosing Where to Install the Upgrade Advisor — Note >>>

Normally, it's best to leave the default installation folder—a folder named Microsoft Windows Vista Upgrade Advisor—in your Program Files folder, but you can change folders if you wish. To do so, click the [Browse] button, select the desired folder in the Browse For Folder dialog box, and then click the [OK] button.

You can click the [Disk Cost] button on the Select Installation Folder screen to check how much disk space the Windows Vista Upgrade Advisor will require. However, because the Upgrade Advisor normally requires only around 30MB, and you need 16GB free to install Windows Vista, the amount of space the Upgrade Advisor consumes is not usually a concern.

9. Windows closes the window and launches the Upgrade Advisor. Make sure you've plugged in all devices you want to use with Windows Vista, such as your printer and scanner. Then click the [Start Scan] button.

10. The Upgrade Advisor scans your computer and then displays a report. Click the [See Details] button.

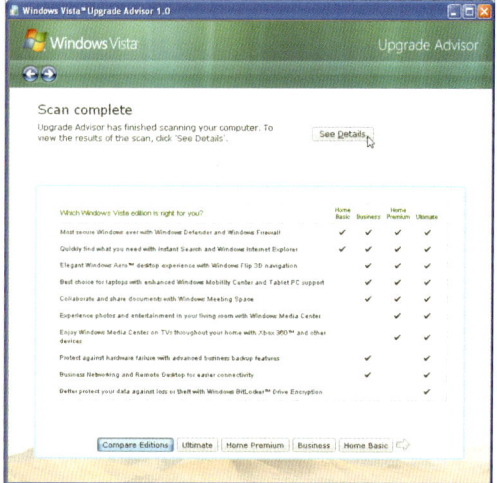

Chapter 01. Getting Started with Windows Vista

11. The Upgrade Advisor displays the overview of a report telling you whether your computer can run Windows Vista, and recommending the version of Windows Vista that seems best suited to your computer. The icons below the description show features in the recommended edition of Windows; click a feature icon for more information. You can view information about another version of Windows Vista by clicking its button in the left column.

12. To see information about the upgrade, scroll down the Upgrade Advisor window. To see details of any of the issues that the Upgrade Advisor has found, click the [See Details] button in the System Requirements area, the Devices area, or the Programs area.

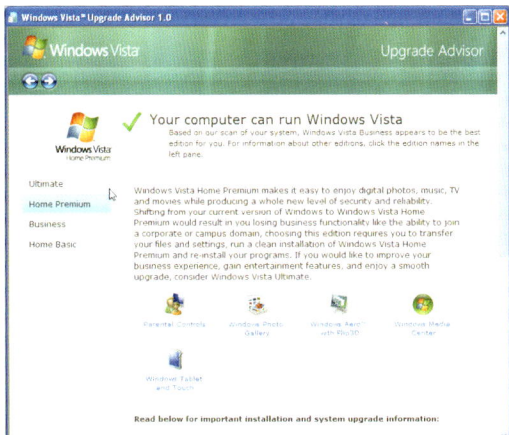

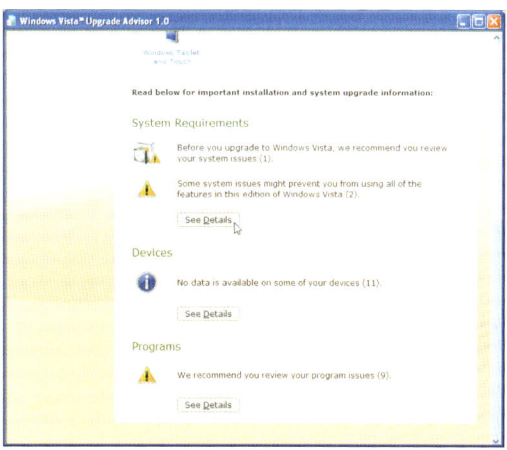

13. The Upgrade Advisor displays the Report Details window for the category of issues you chose. The following illustration shows details of System Requirements issues that need to be resolved before installing Windows Vista on the example computer. To see details on another of the three categories, click the appropriate tab below the Report Details heading.

14. The following illustration shows the Device Details information for the example computer. To review a list of what you need to do before you install Windows Vista on this computer, click the [Task List] tab.

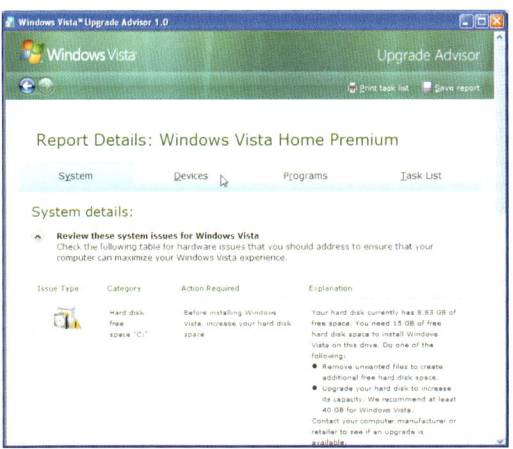

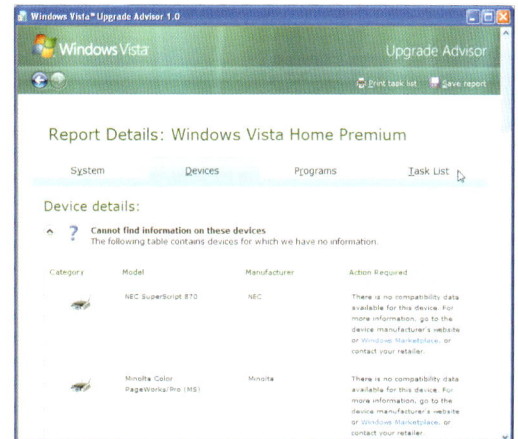

> **Deciding Whether to Ignore a Device Issue**   Note >>>
>
> Some of the device issues the Upgrade Advisor warns you about may not be serious. For example, if you have several printers installed, and Windows cannot find software for one of them, you may choose to proceed even if you end up not being able to use that printer.

13

15. The Upgrade Advisor displays the Task List tab. Work your way through the Things You Need To Do Before Installing Windows Vista section.

Only after you have taken care of all the tasks the Upgrade Advisor has identified, are you ready to perform the upgrade. In case you run into problems, it is a good idea to back up your files before upgrading.

> **Understanding How the Upgrade Advisor Recommends Editions** Note >>>
>
> The Upgrade Advisor recommends an edition of Windows Vista based on the version of Windows XP you have and your computer's capabilities.
> If you have Windows XP Home Edition, the Upgrade Advisor recommends Windows Vista Home Basic for an underpowered desktop computer, and Windows Vista Home Premium for a more powerful desktop computer or laptop.
> If you have Windows XP Professional, the Upgrade Advisor recommends Windows Vista Business.

Performing the Upgrade

To perform the upgrade from Windows XP to Windows Vista, follow these steps:

1. Start Windows XP as normal. If you are running an antivirus program, disable it until you have finished the upgrade. Insert the [Windows Vista DVD] into your computer's DVD drive. AutoPlay launches the Install Windows window. Click the [Install Now] button.

2. The Get Important Updates For Installation screen appears. If you want to allow the installation routine to collect information about how well the upgrade works, and then send that information to Microsoft, select the [I Want To Help Make Windows Installation Better] check box. Then click the [Go Online To Get The Latest Updates For Installation] button if you want to download the latest updates. These updates include hardware drivers that may be required for devices on your computer, so downloading the updates is a good idea if you have a fast Internet connection. Otherwise, click the [Do Not Get The Latest Updates For Installation] button to install Windows Vista using only the files on the DVD.

3. The Type Your Product Key For Activation screen appears. In the Product Key text box, type your Windows Vista product key, and then click the [Next] button.

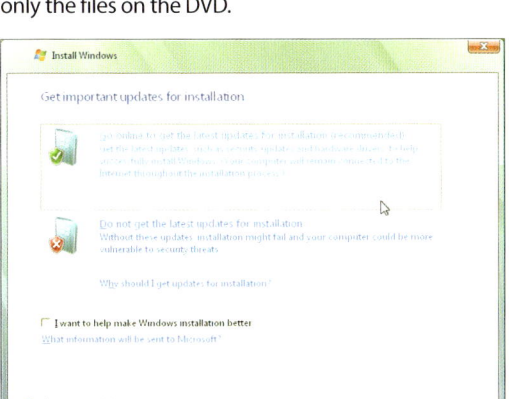

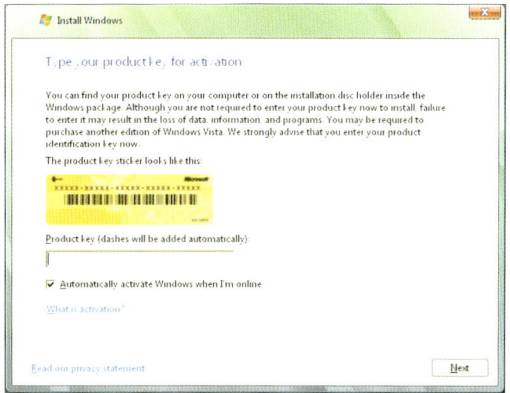

Finding—and Keeping—Your Windows Vista Product Key Note >>>

Normally, you will find the product key on a sticker on the Windows Vista box. It's a good idea to write the product key on the DVD in case the DVD and box become separated from each other.

While you can skip entering the product key during installation, there is little advantage to doing so, since you will have to enter it later. However, you may choose not to activate Windows until you've checked that the upgrade was successful. To prevent Windows from running activation automatically, clear the [Automatically Activate Windows When I'm Online] check box on the Type Your Product Key screen.

4. The Please Read The License Terms screen appears. Read the license (its contents depend on the version of Windows Vista). If you accept the license (as you must to install Windows Vista), select the [I Accept The License Terms] check box, and then click the [Next] button.

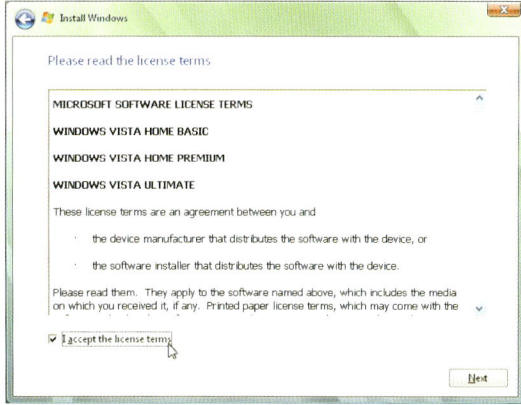

5. The Which Type Of Installation Do You Want? screen appears. Click the [Upgrade] button.

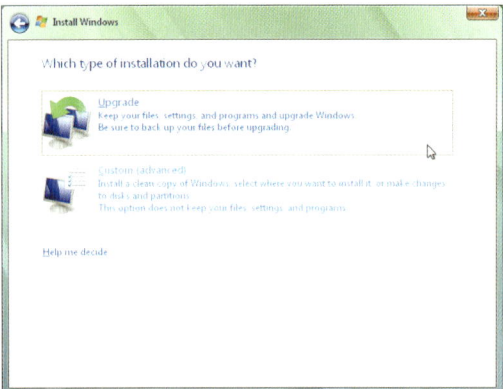

6. The Upgrading Windows screen then appears. This screen shows the progress of the upgrade, which may take up to several hours depending on how fast your computer is. The upgrade process requires your computer to restart several times automatically, so don't be surprised to see it rebooting.

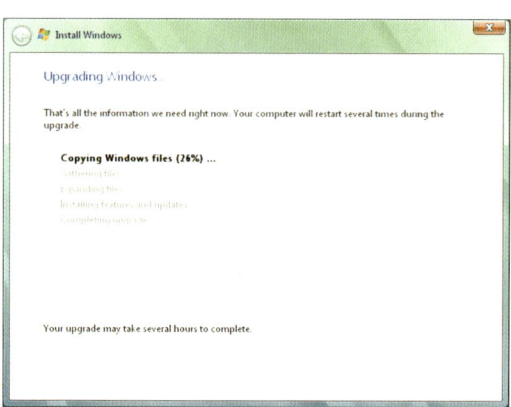

7. When the upgrade is finished, Windows displays the Help Protect Windows Automatically screen. For maximum protection, click the [Use Recommended Settings] button. To install only the most important updates, click the [Install Important Updates Only] button. To defer the issue, click the [Ask Me Later] button.

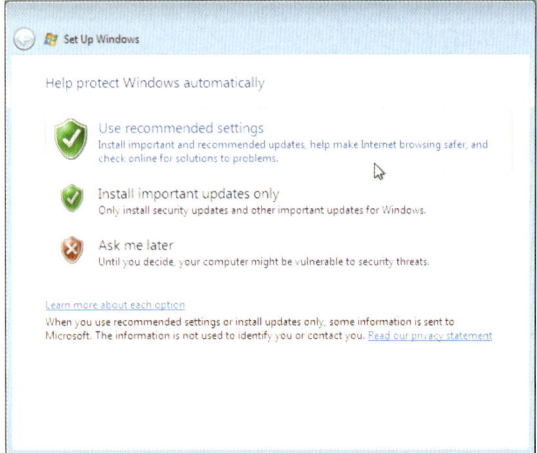

8. Windows notes the button you clicked, and displays the Review Your Time And Date Settings screen. In the Time Zone drop-down list, select your time zone—for example, "(GMT -08:00) Pacific Time (US & Canada)" if you're using Pacific Time. Select the [Automatically Adjust Clock For Daylight Saving Time] check box if you want to use Daylight Saving Time (which most computing systems do). Verify that the Date control shows the current date, and that the Time control shows the correct time. If either is wrong, change the date or time. Click the [Next] button.

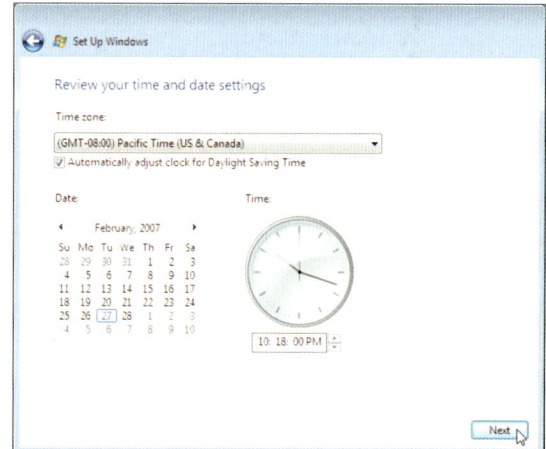

> ### Understanding Windows Update — Note >>>
>
> Windows Update is a feature for downloading and installing updates for Windows, Internet Explorer, and other system software. Microsoft recommends that you accept its default settings, which run Windows Update automatically at 3 a.m. every day to download and install all new updates.
>
> These settings keep your computer up-to-date with the latest features, while protecting it against as much malevolent software as possible, but your computer must remain powered on (or in Sleep mode) to retrieve the updates, and you must be prepared for Windows to restart your computer without your permission—even if you have applications open with unsaved work in them. This means that you should save all your work, and preferably close all your documents, before you leave your computer for the night.
>
> Instead of using the default settings, you may prefer to have Windows notify you of available updates, so that you can decide whether or not to install them. See the section "Keeping Windows Up-to-Date" in Chapter 10 for a discussion of how to set this up. You can also turn Windows Update off and check manually for updates whenever it suits you.

9. If Windows detects that your computer is connected to a network, it displays the Select Your Computer's Current Location screen. If this network is a home network, click the [Home] button. If the network is at work, click the [Work] button. If the network is public (such as a city wireless network or a wireless hotspot in a coffee shop), click the [Public Location] button.

10. Windows applies the appropriate security settings for the network type, and then displays the Thank You screen. Click the [Start] button.

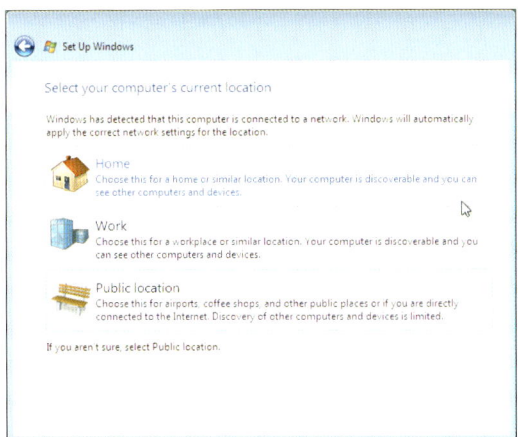

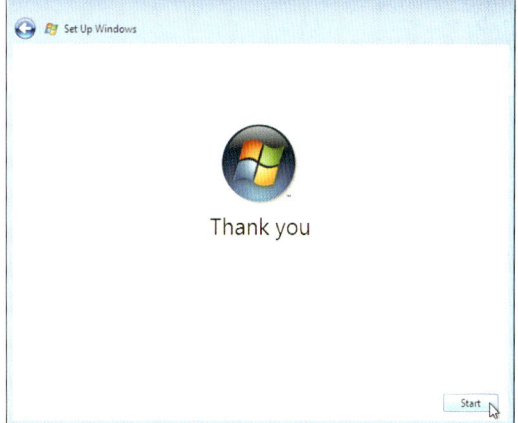

11. Windows displays the Welcome screen if you need to log in. If Windows XP was set to log in automatically, Windows Vista logs you in automatically, and then displays your desktop and the Welcome Center window. The Welcome Center contains icons for tasks you may need to perform after starting Windows Vista for the first time, together with icons for offers from Microsoft.

Activating Windows

If you upgrade to Windows Vista, you will need to activate Windows within thirty days of installation. If you do not activate it by this time, most features stop working—except for the activation feature.

Windows warns you repeatedly that you need to activate it, so it is not likely that you will be taken by surprise.

To activate Windows, follow these steps:

1. Press <Windows Key> + <Break>. Windows displays a System window. In the Windows Activation section at the bottom of the window, click the [Activate Windows Now] link.

2. Windows displays a User Account Control window to ensure that it's you (rather than some malevolent software) that has given the command. Click the [Continue] button.

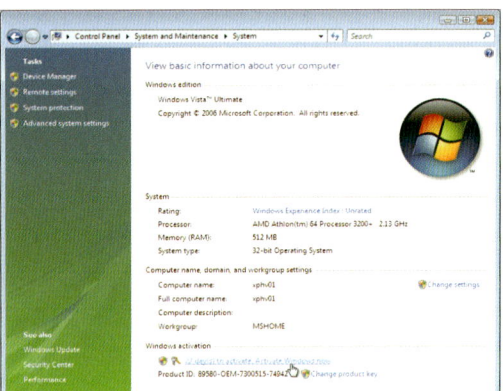

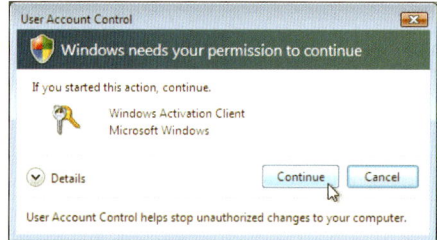

3. Windows starts the Windows Activation wizard (a wizard is a series of steps that walks you through a complicated process). Click the [Activate Windows Online Now] button.

4. The Windows Activation Wizard performs the activation, establishing an Internet connection if you do not have a permanent connection.

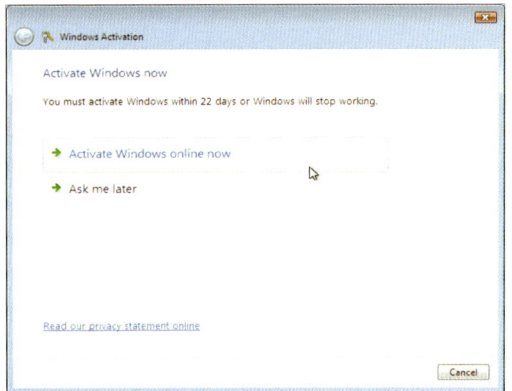

tip>>

Making Sure Windows Is Working Before Activation
Don't rush to activate Windows immediately. Before you activate Windows make sure that all your hardware and software is working the way it should.

SECTION 02

Starting Your Computer and Logging On

Before you can get anything done on your computer, you must start it and log on to Windows Vista.

Starting Your Computer

To start your computer, press the [Power] button. The Power button is usually easy to find, but if you can't locate it, refer to the computer's documentation.

As Windows starts it displays startup information. If all is well, and the computer's only operating system is Windows Vista, the Welcome screen appears after a few seconds.

The appearance of the Welcome screen depends on the Vista edition, but the following screen is typical for a computer that's not part of a Windows Server network. Click your [user name].

If you have a password (as is strongly recommended for security reasons), Windows prompts you for your password. Type your password, and then either press <Enter> or click the [arrow] button. Windows logs you in.

If you enter the wrong password, Windows displays a message telling you that the user name or password is incorrect. (As long as you chose the right user name, it's the password that's wrong.) Click the [OK] button.

19

Windows displays the password box again. If you have a password hint, Windows will display it to help you remember your password. Type your password and press <Enter> or click the [arrow] button.

If you've forgotten your password, you can reset it—provided you've created a password reset disk. See the section "Creating a Password Reset Disk" in Chapter 4 for instructions.

Choosing Which Operating System to Log On To Note >>>

If you see a screen that lists different operating systems you can press <↑> or <↓> to select the Windows Vista item, and then press <Enter>.

Logging On to Windows Vista

From the Welcome screen, you can log on to Windows Vista. To log on:

1. Click your [user name]. If your user account uses a password (as is strongly recommended), Windows prompts you for it. Type your password and then press <Enter> or click the [arrow] button.

2. Windows logs you on and displays your desktop. Most likely, no applications will be running, but the Windows sidebar will be displayed on the right side of the desktop. The sidebar contains small applications called gadgets. Windows typically puts several sample gadgets in the sidebar by default, including the clock and a headline ticker.

The desktop is the area on which you open applications in Windows. You will learn about running applications in detail in Chapter 2, but for now, try opening the WordPad word processing application that's included with Windows. To open WordPad:

1. Click the [Start] button.

2. Windows displays the Start menu. Click the [All Programs] item just above the Start button. Windows displays the All Programs list.

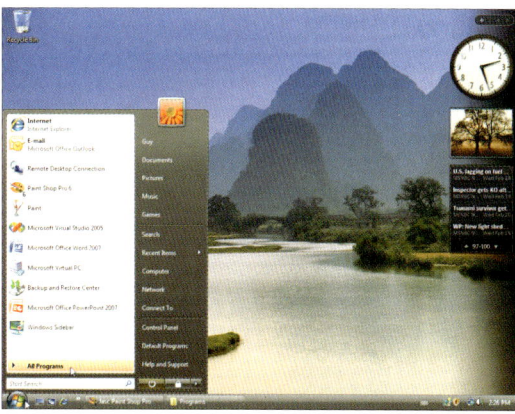

3. Click the [Accessories] folder to expand it, and then click the [WordPad] item.

4. Windows launches WordPad, which opens in a window on the desktop and automatically creates a new document.

5. If you like, try typing in the WordPad window. When you've finished, click the [Close] button (the ⊠ button) at the upper-right corner of the WordPad window. If you've made changes to the document, WordPad asks if you want to save the document. In this case, click the [Don't Save] button, because you don't need to save this document.

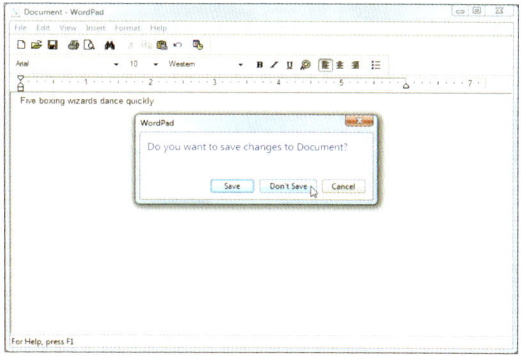

Let's Go Pro!

Understanding the Icons at the Bottom of the Welcome Screen

Depending on the computer's configuration, you will see either two or three icons at the bottom of the Welcome screen:

● Ease of Access

Click this icon to display the Ease of Access dialog box, which lets you turn accessibility features on or off. See the section "Using the Ease of Access Features" in Chapter 3 for details.

● Keyboard Layout

Windows provides many different keyboard layouts. The keyboard layout controls how Windows interprets the keys pressed on the keyboard. For example, the standard keyboard layout for the U.S. is the U.S. layout. When you press <H> with the U.S. layout applied, you get an H. When you press <H> with the United States–Dvorak layout applied, you get a D, so it's important to use the correct keyboard layout.

Often a computer has only one keyboard layout available—for example, the U.S. layout. In this case, the Welcome screen displays no keyboard icon. But if the computer has two or more keyboard layouts applied, the Welcome screen displays an icon.

Hover your mouse pointer over this icon to display a ScreenTip for the current keyboard layout.

To change the layout, click the [Keyboard Layout] icon, and then choose the layout from the menu that appears.

● Shut Down Button and Shut Down Options Menu

Click the [Shut Down] button to shut down the computer directly from the Welcome screen. To restart the computer, click the [Shut Down Options] button, and then choose [Restart] from the menu. To put the computer to sleep, click the [Shut Down Options] button, and then choose [Sleep].

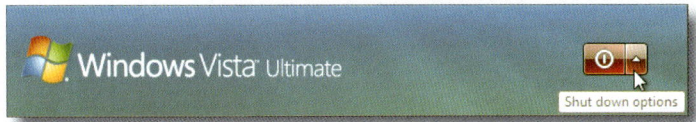

When you choose to shut down or restart the computer from the Welcome screen, Windows warns you if other users are logged on to the computer.

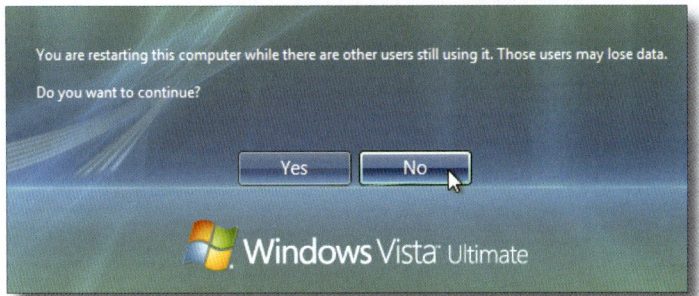

When this happens, it is usually best to click [No] so that each other user can end their session and save any unsaved data. However, sometimes you may need to shut down or restart the computer without waiting; in this case, click [Yes].

SECTION 03

Switching Users, Logging Off, and Shutting Down

When you've finished using your computer you can take any of several actions. You may be able to switch users (so that someone else can use your computer while you're still logged on); you can log off, ending your Windows session; you can also put your computer to sleep or shut it down altogether. This section shows you how to take these actions.

Switching Users

If you're using Windows Vista at home or in a small business that doesn't use a Windows server, you can switch user: change from one user account to another without closing all your programs and ending your Windows session.

User switching makes it easier for several people to share a computer. When you switch back to your user account, all the applications you left running are still running, and you can immediately resume what you were doing.

To switch users click the [Start] button, then click the [right arrow] button to the right of the Lock icon, and then choose [Switch User].

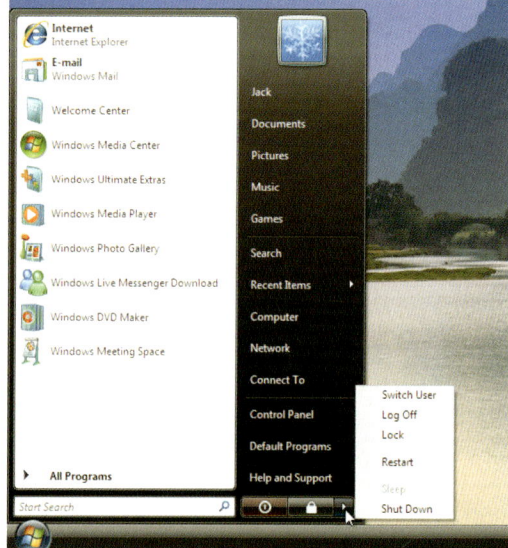

Windows displays the Welcome screen, which lists your user as "Logged On" to show that you have a user session open. This message helps avoid another user shutting down the computer without realizing that you have a user session open.

tip >>

Switching User Does Not Work on a Windows Server Network

Switching user does not work when your computer is connected to a Windows Server network, so normally you cannot use this feature with Windows Vista Business Edition. You also cannot use it with Windows Vista Ultimate Edition when your computer is connected to a Windows Server network.

24

From the Welcome screen, another user can log on as usual.

Switching users via the Switch User command is awkward, because you have to click the right arrow button next to the Lock icon. You can also get the same effect more easily by "locking" your user session, as described next.

Locking Your User Session

When you need to leave your computer, you can lock your user session so that no one else can use your computer without logging on.

To lock your user session, click the [Start] button, and then click the [Lock] icon at the bottom of the Start menu.

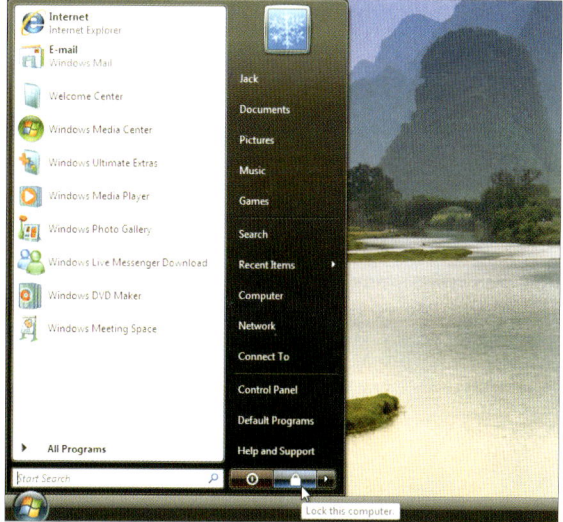

Windows displays the Locked screen, which is like the Welcome screen except that it shows your user name, the word Locked, and a password box.

You can log back in by typing your password and then pressing <Enter>, or by clicking the [right arrow] button. Any other user of this computer can log in by clicking the [Switch User] button to display the Welcome screen, and then logging in as usual.

Logging Off When You've Finished

When you've finished using Windows, you can log off. Windows then closes all the programs you have been using, thus ending your Windows session.

To log off click the [Start] button, click the [right arrow] button to the right of the Lock icon, and then choose [Log Off].

Windows closes all your programs and prompts you to save any unsaved data. Windows then displays the Welcome screen, so that you, or another user, can log back on.

Making Your Computer Sleep

When you've finished using your computer for the time being, and nobody else will be using it, you can put it to sleep.

Sleep is a power-saving mode in which the computer uses enough power to maintain the information in the computer's memory (RAM), but switches off the hard disk and display. Awakening your computer from sleep takes just a few seconds.

Use sleep when you do not want to shut your computer down, but you want to stop using it for the time being.

To put your computer to sleep, click the [Start] button, and then click the [Power] icon at the bottom of the Start menu.

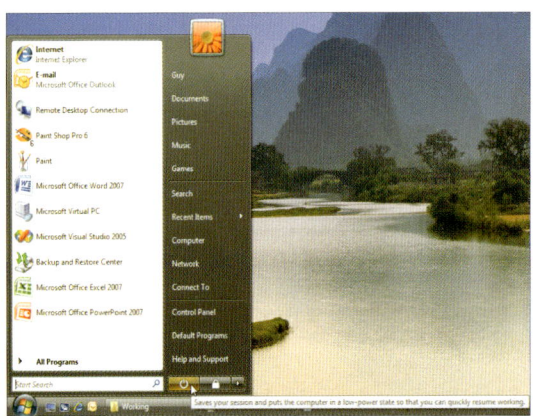

Windows puts the computer to sleep and the screen goes blank.

To awaken your computer from sleep, press either the [Power] button or any button on the keyboard. Windows displays the Locked screen. Type your password and then press <Enter> or click the [arrow] button to log on.

Restarting Your Computer

Microsoft has made Windows Vista much more stable than previous versions of Windows, and if all is well, you should not need to restart it frequently. Normally, you can leave Windows running for several days, or even weeks, putting it to sleep when it is not in use.

You may, however, need to restart Windows after installing hardware or software. You may also need to restart Windows after a problem has occurred and a Windows component has stopped responding normally.

To restart Windows click the [Start] button, click the [right arrow] button to the right of the Lock icon, and then choose [Restart].

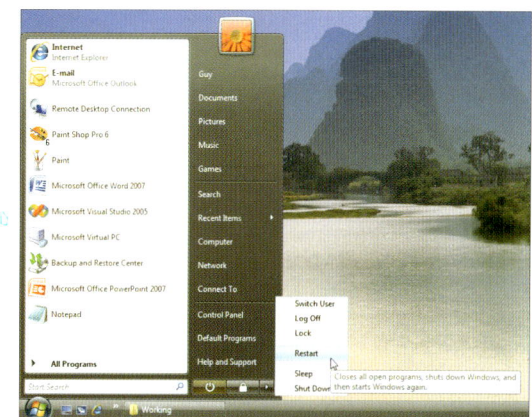

Shutting Your Computer Down

When you don't want to leave your computer running or put it to sleep, you can shut it down. To do so, click the [Start] button, click the [right arrow] button to the right of the Lock icon, and then choose [Shut Down].

When you need to restart your computer, press the [Power] button.

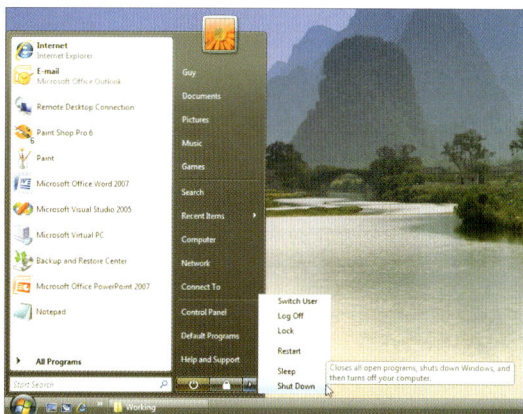

Chapter 2

Navigating the User Interface and Running Applications

In this chapter, you'll learn to navigate the Windows user interface, starting with the Start menu, the taskbar, and the other components of the desktop. After that, the chapter shows you how to run applications (also known as programs), so that you can get your work or playing done. You may already have all the applications you need installed on your computer, but it is likely that you'll need to install some applications yourself. You may also need to remove some of the applications that you do not find useful.

SECTION 01 Using the Desktop, Start Menu, and Taskbar

The Windows user interface consists of several main components, including the desktop, the Start button and menu, the taskbar, and the Sidebar. This section explains these components and shows you how to use them.

Understanding the Desktop

The desktop is the main area of the screen (everything you see in the previous illustration except for the Start button, taskbar, and notification area).

When you open an application, it appears on the desktop as a window that occupies part or all of the desktop. You can open as many windows as you need for your work or entertainment, although having many windows open can make it difficult to see what you're doing.

The Recycle Bin icon appears on the desktop by default. You can remove the Recycle Bin icon or place other icons on the desktop as needed. Chapter 4 shows you how to customize your desktop.

The desktop is a folder in Windows Explorer, the application you use for managing files and folders in Windows. (Chapter 3 shows you how to manage your files and folders with Windows Explorer.) This means that you can store files and folders on your desktop, which is useful for items for which you need instant access.

ⓐ Start Button
ⓑ Quick Launch Toolbar
ⓒ Taskbar
ⓓ Notification Area
ⓔ Sidebar
ⓕ Desktop
ⓖ Recycle Bin Icon

Using the Start Menu to Open Applications and Choose Settings

The Start menu lets you easily open applications, choose settings, and take other actions (for example, putting your computer to sleep or shutting down Windows, as you learned in Chapter 1).

Click the [Start] button to display the Start menu. You can then click one of the commands that appears directly on the Start menu, or click the [All Programs] link to display a list of all the applications on your computer. You'll learn about running applications later in this chapter.

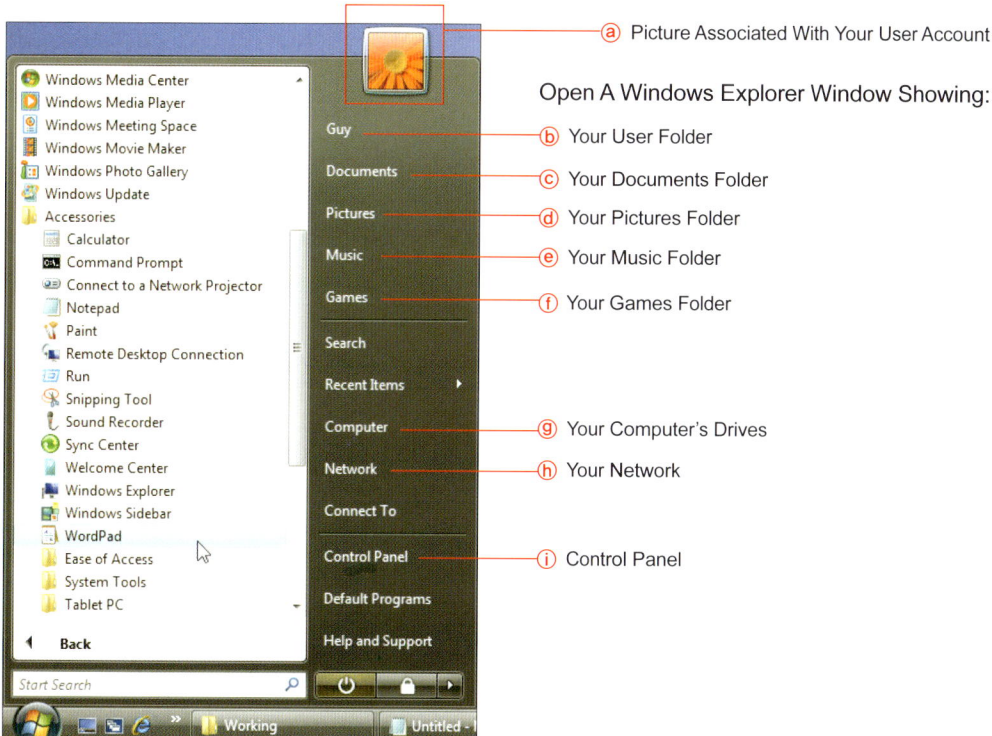

Most of the buttons on the right side of the Start menu open Windows Explorer windows to key folders within your Windows user account. For example, click the button with your user name to open a Windows Explorer window to your main user folder.

The links in the upper-right corner of the Start menu go to key folders within your Windows user account.

Using the Taskbar

The taskbar normally appears at the bottom of the screen, below the desktop. The taskbar contains a button for each open window. In the next illustration, the taskbar contains a button for the open Computer window, a button for a minimized Word document window, and a minimized Chess Titans window.

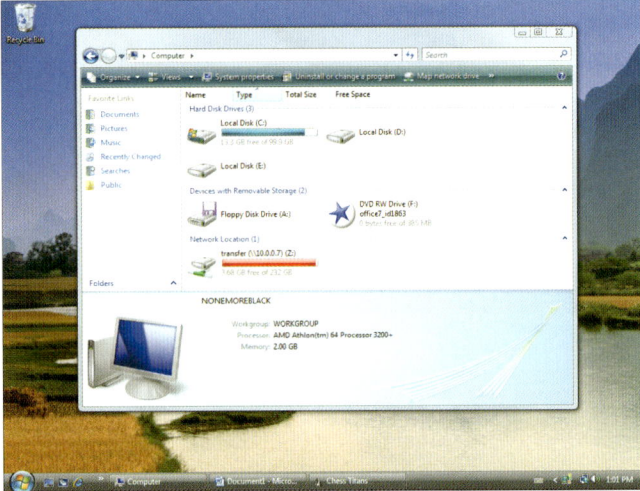

To switch to another window, click it. For example, the next illustration shows the result of clicking the button for the minimized Word document window: Windows restores it to its previous size (maximized) and brings it to the front.

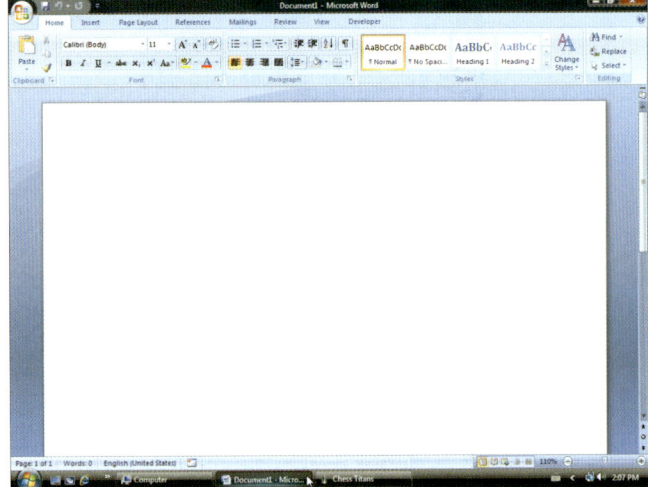

If you're using the Windows Aero user interface, you can get a preview of a window by hovering the mouse pointer over the window's taskbar button for a moment. The preview helps you select the right window.

Click the [taskbar] button for the active window (the window in which you're working), in order to minimize it and shrink it down to its taskbar button. Click the [taskbar] button for a minimized window to return it to its previous size. To close a window, right-click its [taskbar] button and then choose [Close] from the context menu.

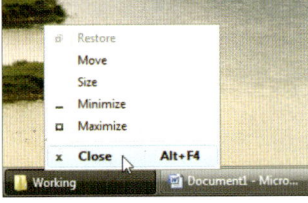

Using the Notification Area

The notification area, also called the system tray, is the part of the taskbar that appears at the opposite end from the Start button. When the taskbar is positioned along the bottom edge of the desktop, as it is by default, the notification area appears in the lower-right corner of the desktop.

The notification area contains the clock, icons for frequently used features (such as Volume Control and Networking), alerts (such as Windows Security alerts), and some applications.

To open an item click its notification-area icon. To see what an icon represents, hover the mouse pointer over it for a moment. Windows displays for a few seconds a ScreenTip: a small floating window of information.

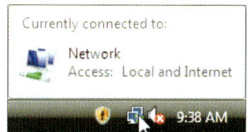

If the notification area doesn't have enough space to display the icons, Windows displays the Show Hidden Icons button. Click this button to display the remaining icons. Windows automatically hides them again after a few seconds.

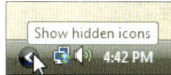

Using the Quick Launch Toolbar

Windows includes several toolbars that you can display on the desktop to give yourself instant access to applications, files, or folders that you need frequently. By default, Windows displays the Quick Launch toolbar next to the Start button, at the left end of the taskbar.

Initially, the Quick Launch toolbar contains the following icons:

■ Show Desktop
Click this icon to hide all open windows, showing the desktop. This lets you quickly reach an icon, file, or folder on the desktop.

■ Switch Between Windows
Click this icon to display a stack of open windows. To bring the window you want to the front, click it.

Once you use some major applications, such as Internet Explorer (the Web browser), Windows Media Player (a music and video player), or Outlook (the Office e-mail application), Windows adds icons for them to the Quick Launch toolbar.

If all the icons won't fit on the Quick Launch toolbar, Windows displays the >> button (ⓓ) at the toolbar's end. Click ⓓ to open a panel showing the hidden icons.

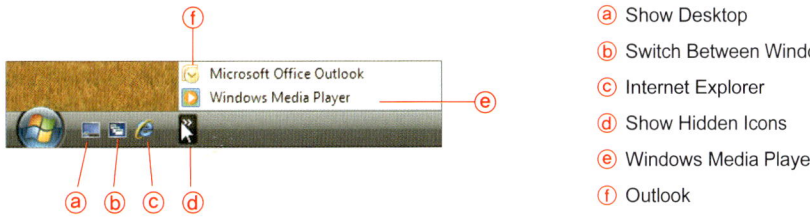

ⓐ Show Desktop
ⓑ Switch Between Windows
ⓒ Internet Explorer
ⓓ Show Hidden Icons
ⓔ Windows Media Player
ⓕ Outlook

Let's Go Pro!

Choosing Which Applications Appear on the Start Menu

To help you run the applications you need as easily as possible, Windows keeps a short list of your most used applications on the left side of the Start menu. Windows changes the list as you work, adding and promoting the applications you use more frequently, and demoting or removing those you use less frequently.

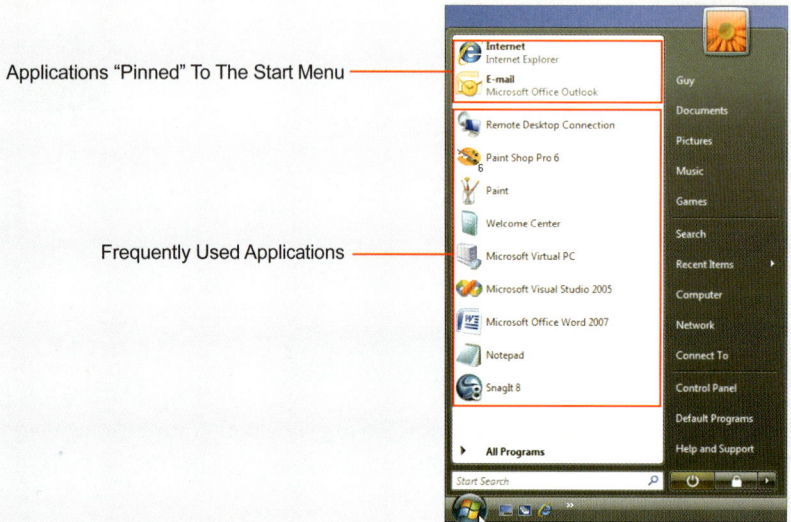

Applications "Pinned" To The Start Menu

Frequently Used Applications

To change the pinned list and frequently used list, follow these steps:

① To pin an application to the Start menu, right-click it in its current place on the Start menu, and then choose [Pin To Start Menu] from the context menu.

② To remove a pinned application, right-click it in its pinned place, and then choose [Unpin From Start Menu] from the context menu.

③ To remove a frequently used application, right-click it, and then choose [Remove From This List] from the context menu.

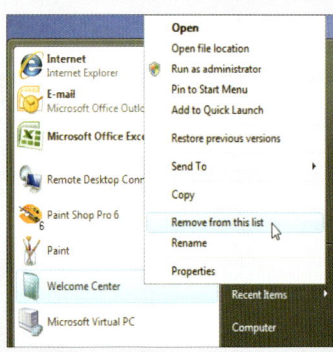

tip>>

changing the number of frequently used applications

To change the number of frequently used applications, see the section "Customizing the Start Menu" in Chapter 4.

SECTION 02 Working with Application Windows

Windows Vista normally displays each application in a separate window. To work with an application, you make its window active so that your mouse clicks and keystrokes go into that window.

Switching from One Window to Another

To work in a window, you can simply click in the window if you can see it; if you can't see the window, you can click its taskbar button instead.

Windows also provides several other ways to switch from one window to another:

■ Windows Flip 3D

If you're using the Vista Aero user interface, hold down <Windows> and press <Tab>. Windows darkens the screen and displays the open windows in a rotating stack. Holding down <Windows>, press <Tab> until the window you want comes to the front, and then release <Windows> to display the window. Alternatively, hold down <Windows> and click the window you want.

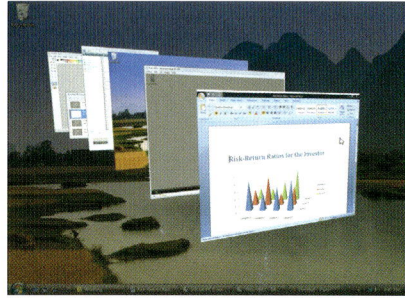

■ Windows Flip

With either Vista Aero or Vista Basic, hold down <Alt> and press <Tab>. Windows displays a window showing the open windows. Holding down <Alt>, press <Tab> to select the window you want, and then release <Alt>. Alternatively, hold down <Alt> and click the window you want.

■ Cascade the Windows

Right-click the notification area and choose [Cascade Windows] from the context menu to arrange the windows in a cascading stack, where you can see part of each window. Click the window you want.

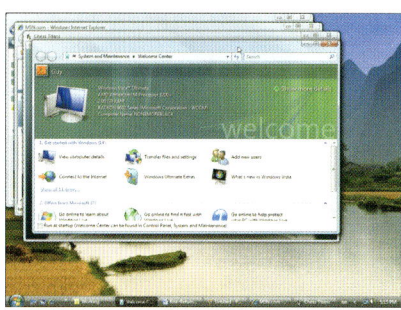

■ Stack the Windows

Right-click the notification area and choose [Show Windows Stacked] from the context menu to arrange the windows in a horizontal stack.

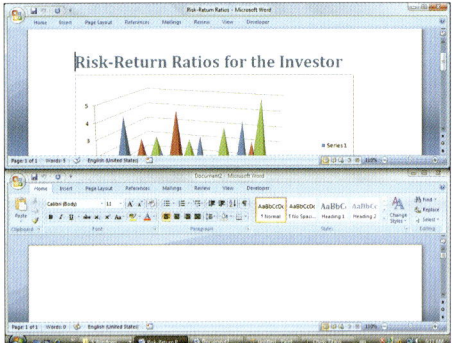

■ Show Windows Side By Side

Right-click the notification area and choose [Show Windows Side By Side] to arrange the windows side by side.

Using the Cascade, Stacked, and Side By Side Commands Note >>>

The Cascade Windows command is useful for locating the window you want when you have many windows open.

The Show Windows Side By Side command is useful when you have two windows open and want to arrange them horizontally, giving each half of the desktop space.

The Show Windows Stacked command is useful when you have two windows open and want to arrange them vertically, giving each half of the desktop space.

Maximizing, Minimizing, and Restoring Windows

An application window can have three sizes:

■ Maximized

The window takes up all the space on the desktop apart from that occupied by the taskbar. Click the Maximize button to maximize a normal window.

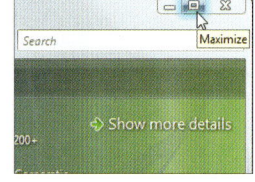

■ Minimized

The window appears only as a taskbar button. It does not take up any space on the desktop. Click the [Minimize] button to minimize a window.

■ Normal

The window takes up part of the desktop. Click the [Restore Down] button to restore a maximized window.

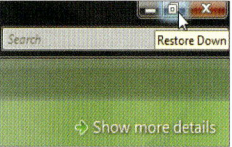

tip>>

Maximizing and Restoring a Window Quickly

To quickly maximize or restore a window, double-click its title bar.

SECTION 03 — Using or Turning Off the Sidebar

The Sidebar, a new feature in Windows Vista, is a shaded, vertical strip that appears at one edge of the desktop. The Sidebar can hold various small applications called gadgets that run all the time and display information—for example, a clock or a news feed.

Windows automatically runs the Sidebar when you log on, and places several gadgets in the Sidebar to begin with. You can change the selection of gadgets to suit your needs. If you have a small screen and much to get done, you'll probably want to turn off the Sidebar.

Changing the Gadgets in the Sidebar

To change the gadgets in the Sidebar, follow these steps:

1. Click the [Gadgets] button (the + symbol) at the top of the Sidebar. Windows displays the Gadget Gallery window, which shows all available gadgets.

2. Most gadgets are easy to recognize, but if you need more information on a gadget, click it, and then click [Show Details]. Windows displays an extra section at the bottom of the Gadget Gallery showing information about the gadget.

3. To add a gadget to the Sidebar, drag it from the Gadget Gallery to where you want it to appear on the Sidebar. If you add more gadgets than the Sidebar can display at once, click the [arrow buttons] at the top of the Sidebar to display the next column of gadgets or the previous column.

4. To remove a gadget from the Sidebar, move the mouse pointer over it so that Windows displays buttons in its upper-right corner, and then click the [Close] button (the button).

5. To choose settings for a gadget, right-click it and choose [Options] from the context menu. (You can also move the mouse pointer over the gadget and then click the [wrench] button that Windows displays.) Choose [Options] in the dialog box that appears. For example, here you can choose a different clock face, change the time zone, or display the second hand. Click [OK] when you've finished.

6. To rearrange gadgets in the Sidebar, drag a gadget to where you want it. Windows rearranges the other gadgets to make space.

7. To move a gadget out of the Sidebar and place it elsewhere on your desktop, simply drag it. To return the gadget to the Sidebar, either drag it or right-click it and choose [Attach To Sidebar] from the context menu.

Installing More Gadgets

If you like the Sidebar you'll probably want to add more gadgets to it than Windows includes. To get more gadgets follow these steps:

1. Click the [Gadgets] button (the + symbol) at the top of the Sidebar. Windows displays the Gadget Gallery window.

2. Click the [Get More Gadgets Online] link. Windows opens an Internet Explorer window to the Windows Vista Sidebar Web site.

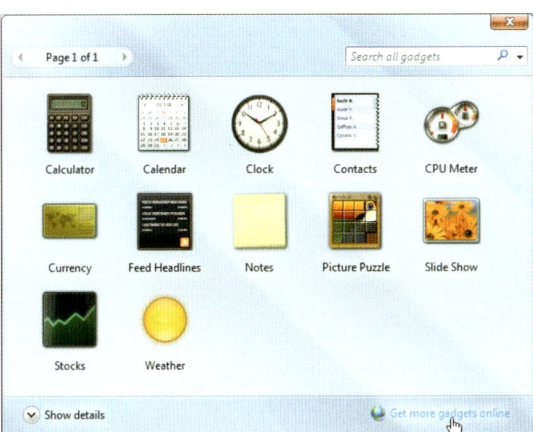

3. Explore the available gadgets and then click a [Download] link to download a gadget. Windows may display a Windows Internet Explorer dialog box warning you to "Only install applications from developers you trust."

4. If you trust the developer (from what you've read about the gadget online), click the [OK] button. Windows starts the download and displays the File Download dialog box.

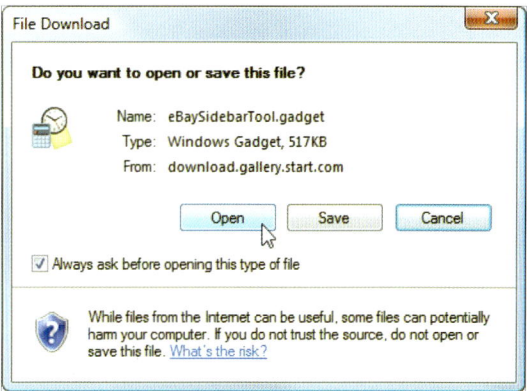

5. Click the [Open] button. Windows displays an Internet Explorer Security dialog box telling you that "A website wants to open web content using this program on the computer."

6. Verify that the Name readout shows "Windows Sidebar," and then click the [Allow] button. Windows may then display a Windows Sidebar - Security Warning dialog box to tell you that Windows cannot verify the publisher of the gadget, because the file does not have a valid digital signature.

7. If you want to proceed with the installation, click the [Install] button. Files from the Windows Vista Sidebar Web site should normally be safe to install. You can then add the gadget to the Sidebar from the Gadget Gallery.

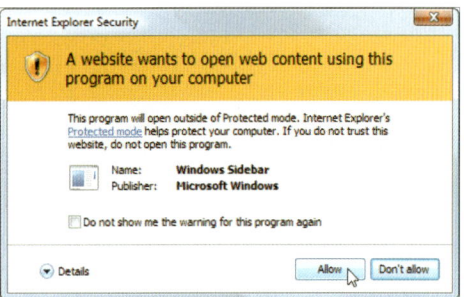

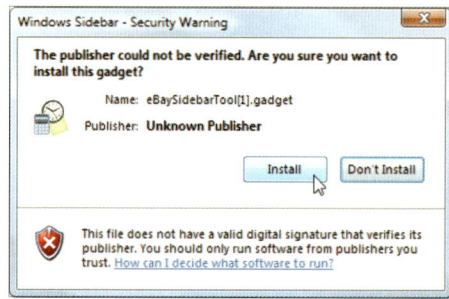

Closing the Sidebar

To close the Sidebar, right-click in the Sidebar and choose Close Sidebar from the context menu.

After you've closed the Sidebar, you need to restart it manually if you want to use it again. To restart it, click the [Start] button, click [All Programs], click [Accessories], and then click [Windows Sidebar].

Moving the Sidebar or Turning It Off

If you don't want the Sidebar to appear at the right side of your screen, or if you want to turn it off, follow these steps:

1. Right-click the [Sidebar], and then choose [Properties] from the context menu. Windows displays the Windows Sidebar Properties dialog box.

- To prevent Windows from running the Sidebar, clear the [Start Sidebar When Windows Starts] check box.

- In the Arrangement box, choose the [Right option] button or the [Left option] button in the Display Sidebar On This Side Of Screen area. If you want to keep the gadgets visible all the time, select the [Sidebar Is Always On Top Of Other Windows] check box (this is usually a bad idea). If you have multiple monitors, choose the monitor in the [Display Sidebar On Monitor] drop-down list.

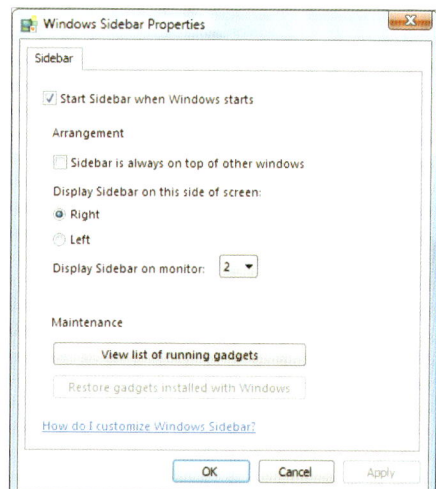

2. Click the [OK] button. Windows closes the Windows Sidebar Properties dialog box and applies your changes. The next illustration shows the Sidebar on the left side of the screen, and with the Sidebar Is Always On Top Of Other Windows setting applied.

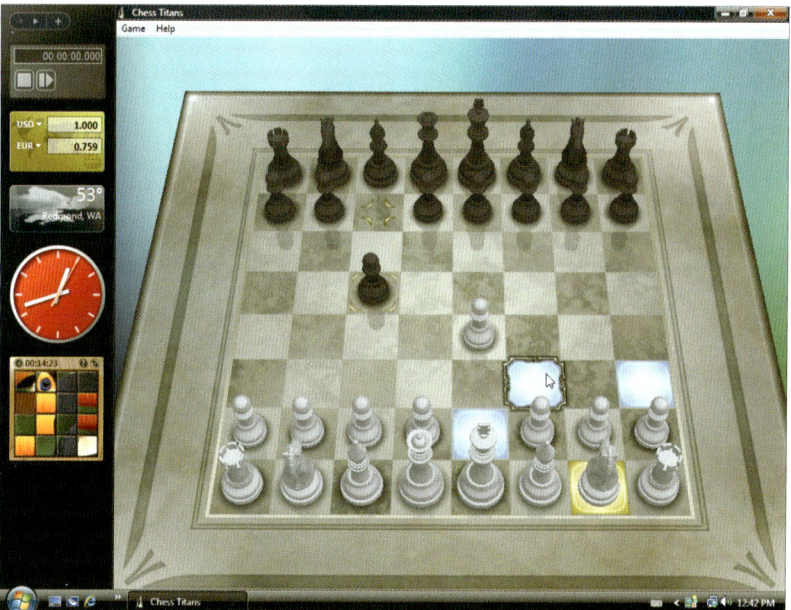

SECTION 04 — Running, Installing, and Removing Applications

To use an application, you run it or open it. You can easily run any application that is installed on your computer. If you have an Administrator user account, you can install other applications as needed.

Running an Application

The Start menu includes a link for running each application that's designed for users. To run an application, follow these steps:

1. Click the [Start] menu. Windows opens the Start menu. If the application you want to run appears directly on the Start menu, click its link. For example, in the illustration, you can click the [Microsoft Office Word 2007] link to run Word 2007.

2. If the application doesn't appear directly on the Start menu, click the All Programs link. Windows displays the [All Programs] menu. (You can also hover the mouse pointer over the All Programs link for several seconds to make Windows display the All Programs menu.)

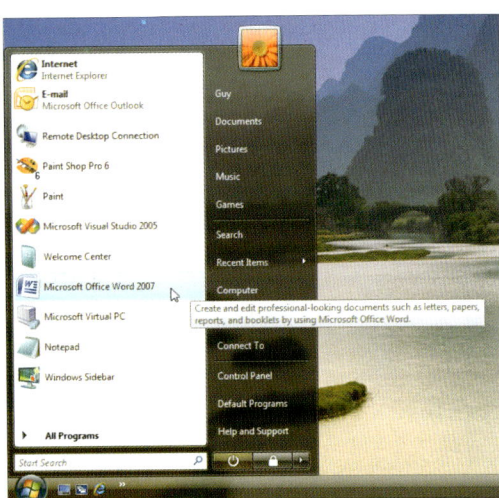

> **Understanding Why Some Applications Don't Appear on the Start Menu** Note >>>
>
> Most applications are designed for all computer users, but Windows also includes some applications that are intended for use by administrators only. To help users avoid running administrator-only applications inadvertently, the Start menu does not include links for running such applications.

3. If the application appears directly on the More Programs menu, click it. Otherwise, click its folder to open the [folder], and then click the [application].

4. The application opens. You can then maximize or restore the window as needed.

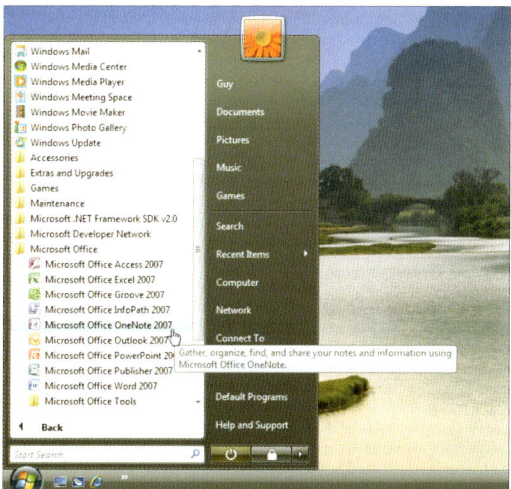

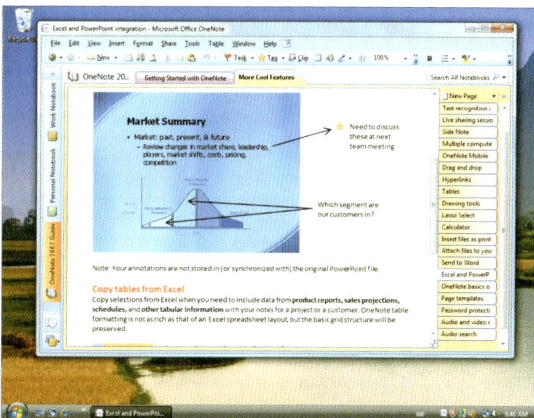

Installing an Application

If you need to use an application that isn't installed on your computer, you must install it. To install an application, follow these general steps. The precise steps vary depending on the application involved; not all applications come with the same set of installation instructions.

To install an application from a CD or DVD, follow these steps:

1. Close all the applications you're running, and then insert the CD or DVD in your computer's optical drive. Windows' AutoPlay feature normally detects the CD or DVD and displays the AutoPlay dialog box. Click the button under the [Install Or Run Program] heading—for example, click the [Run Setup.exe] button.

2. Windows' displays a User Account Control dialog box to verify that you're trying to run the application. Click the [Allow] button.

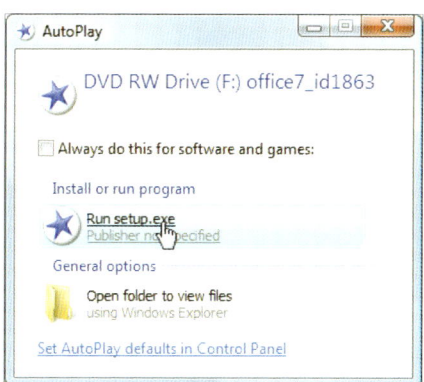

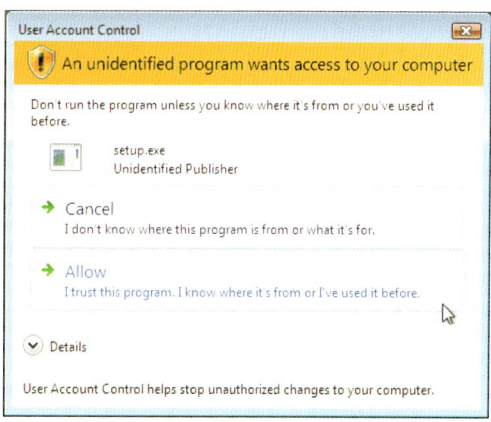

3. Windows allows the installation routine to run, and you see the first screen. Here is an example.

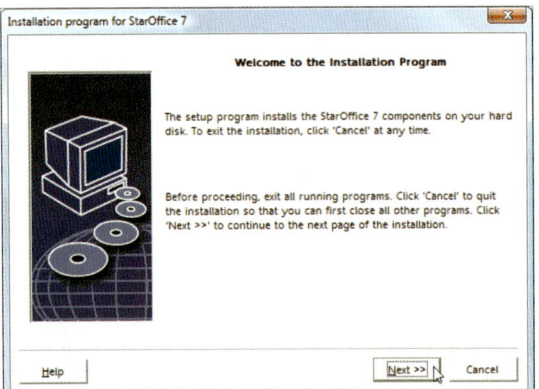

4. Click the [Next] button, and then follow through the screens of the installation routine, clicking the Next button to move from one screen to the next. The details vary, but for many applications you must accept a license agreement, as shown here.

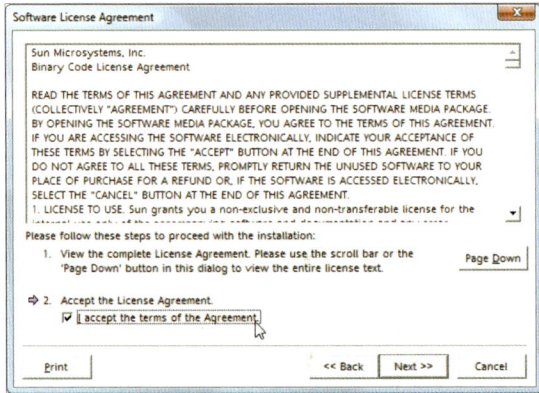

5. If the installation routine offers you a choice of different installation types, select the one you want. The StarOffice™ application shown here lets you choose among a Standard Installation, a Custom Installation, and a Minimum Installation.

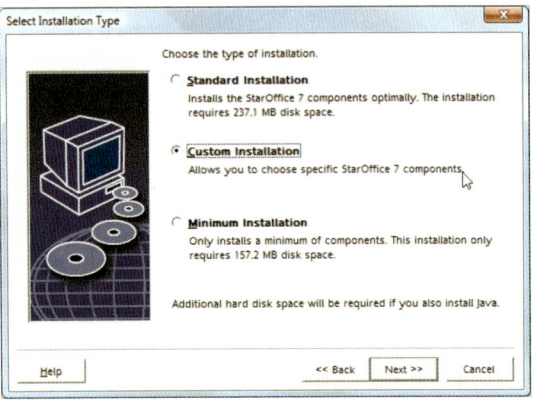

6. If you choose a Custom Installation, the installation routine lets you choose which items to install. The example installation routine uses different-colored arrows to show which components will be installed. Many installation routines use check boxes, which are easier to read: Each component with a selected check box will be installed.

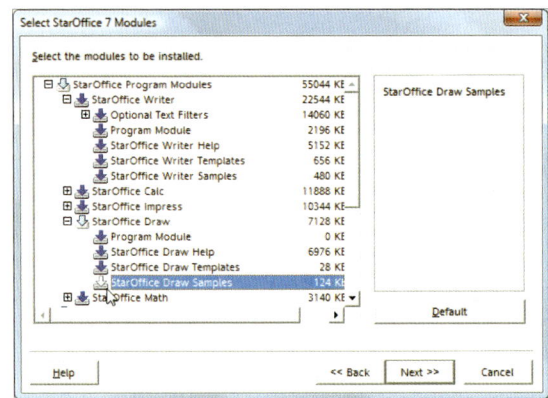

A Full or Custom Installation Is Usually Best   Note >>>

In the 1990s, when hard disks had much lower capacity than they do now, a Minimum Installation was often a good idea, as it let you keep down the amount of space the application took up. But now that hard disk capacity has risen dramatically, it's usually best to install all of an application—unless you know that you do not need some of its features.

If there's no Full Installation option, select the Custom Installation option, and then select all the components on the Custom Installation screen.

Chapter 02. Navigating the User Interface and Running Applications

7. If the installation routine prompts you to choose the folder or directory in which to install the application, you can usually safely accept the default folder. Normally, this is a folder with the application's name in the Program Files folder on your computer. If you want to use another folder, click the [Browse] button, and then use the resulting dialog box to identify the folder.

8. Once you've made all the required decisions, the installation routine installs the application. This may take several minutes. When the installation routine has finished, it usually notifies you by displaying a screen like the Installation Completed screen shown here. Click the [Complete] button.

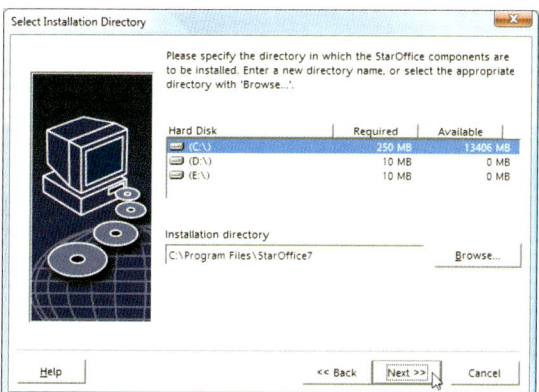

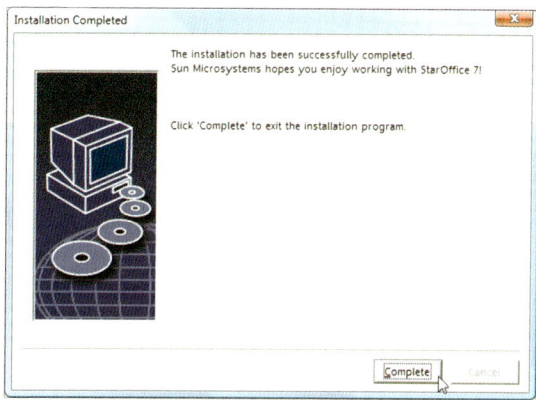

9. You can then run the application from the folder that the installation routine has created on the Start menu. Windows puts a yellow highlight over each new folder or item on the Start menu to help you find new applications.

Installing an Application Using Compatibility Settings

Some installation routines for applications designed for older versions of Windows cannot successfully install the applications on Windows Vista using standard settings. Windows Vista provides special compatibility settings for such applications.

45

■ Dealing with Known Compatibility Issues

If Windows Vista detects that an application you're installing has compatibility issues, it displays a Program Compatibility Assistant dialog box like the one shown here.

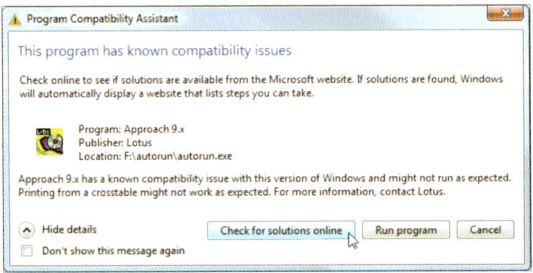

Evaluate the seriousness of the issue, and click the [Check For Solutions Online] button if you want to check for solutions to the compatibility issues. If Windows recommends solutions, follow them in order to install the application successfully. However, there is no solution for some applications, as with the application in the next illustration.

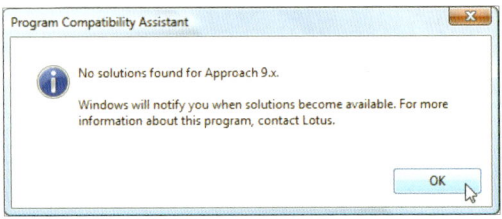

■ Using Preset Compatibility Settings

When Windows Vista detects that an installation routine appears not to have completed successfully, it displays the Program Compatibility Assistant dialog box.

Click the [Reinstall Using Recommended Settings] button, and then follow through the installation procedure.

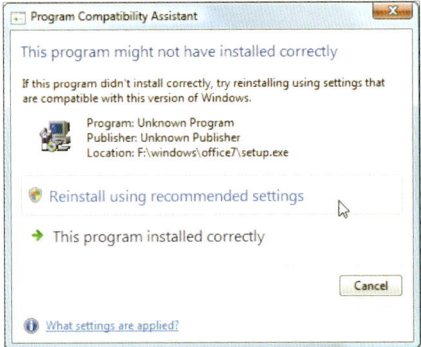

■ Choosing Custom Compatibility Settings

Sometimes you may need to choose custom compatibility settings for installing an application. Follow these steps:

1. Click the [Start] button, and then click [Default Programs]. Windows displays the Default Programs window. In the Address bar click the [Programs] link. Windows displays the Programs window.

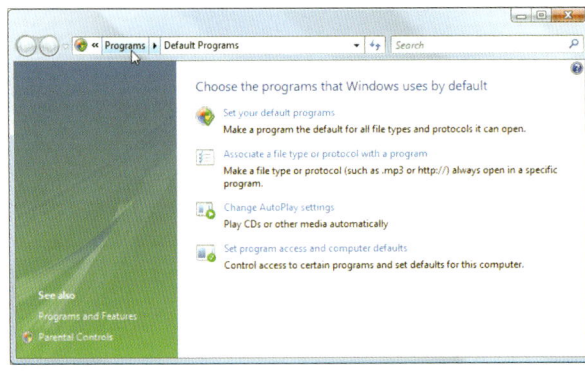

Chapter 02. Navigating the User Interface and Running Applications

2. Under the Programs And Features heading, click the [Use An Older Program With This Version Of Windows] link. Windows launches the Program Compatibility Wizard. Click the [Next] button on the wizard's welcome screen to reach the screen shown in the next illustration.

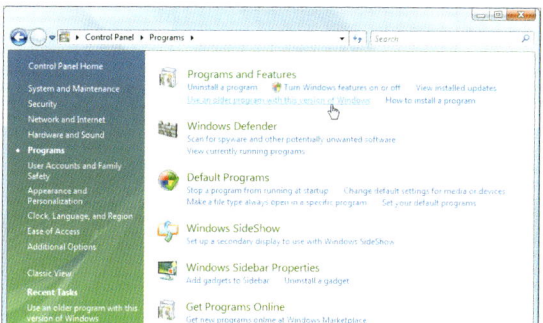

3. If you're installing from CD or DVD, as is usual, select the [I Want To Use The Program In The CD-ROM Drive] option button. Click the [Next] button. The wizard displays the Select A Compatibility Mode For The Program screen.

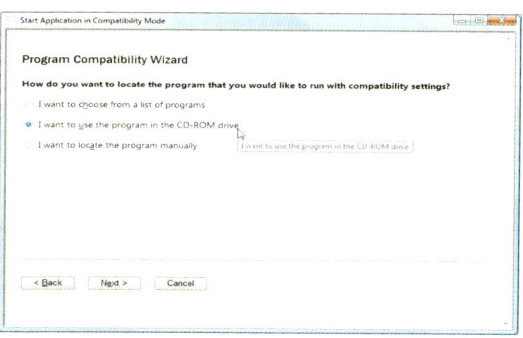

4. Select the option button for the version of Windows for which you know the application works. For example, if the application runs on Windows 98, select the [Microsoft Windows 98/Windows Me] option button. Click the [Next] button.

5. The wizard displays the Select Display Settings For The Program screen. If you know the application needs certain display settings, select the check boxes. Normally, it is better to leave these check boxes cleared until you have tried running the application on Windows Vista and found there is a display problem. Click the [Next] button.

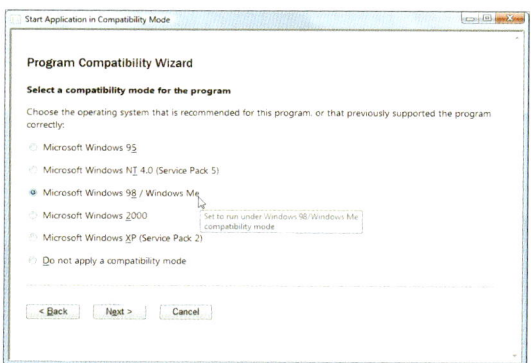

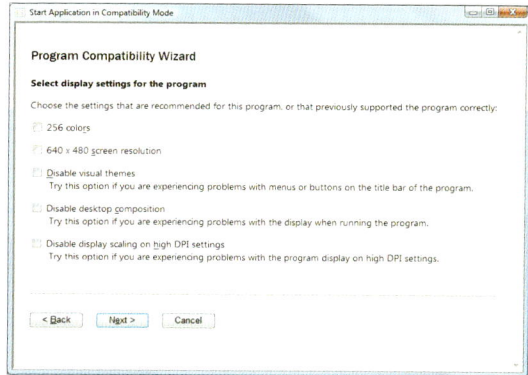

6. The wizard displays the Does The Program Require Administrator Privileges? screen. If installation has failed with a message about permissions, select the [Run This Program As An Administrator] check box. Click the [Next] button.

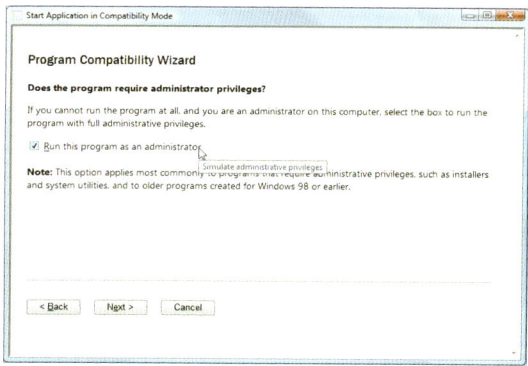

47

7. The wizard displays the Test Your Compatibility Settings screen. Click the [Next] button, and verify that the installation routine works.

8. Return to the wizard, which displays the Did The Program Work Correctly? screen. If the installation routine worked, select the [Yes, Set This Program To Always Use These Compatibility Settings] option button. Click the [Next] button, and then finish the wizard. If the installation routine did not work, select the [No, Try Different Compatibility Settings] option button, and then click the [Next] button to go back to the Select A Compatibility Mode For The Program screen (step 3) and try again.

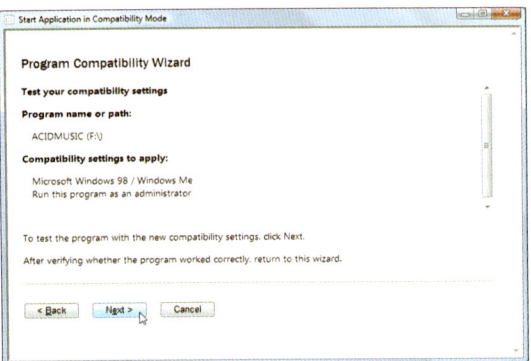

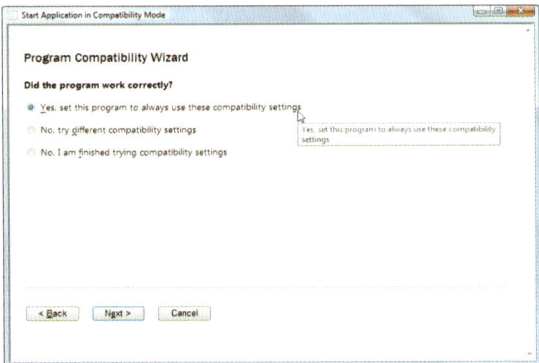

Removing an Application

If you find your computer contains applications that neither you nor other users of your computer use, you can remove them. To remove an application, follow these general steps. As with installation, some specifics of the uninstallation process depend on the application.

1. Click the [Start] button, and then click [Control Panel]. Windows displays the Control Panel window. If Control Panel shows a dot next to Classic View in the left pane, click the [Control Panel] Home link to switch to Control Panel Home view.

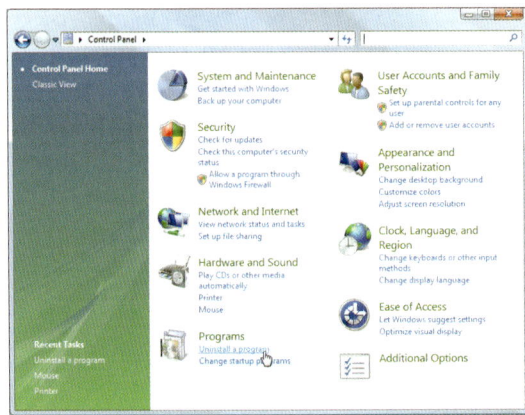

2. In Under the Programs heading, click the [Uninstall A Program] link. Windows displays in the Programs And Features window.

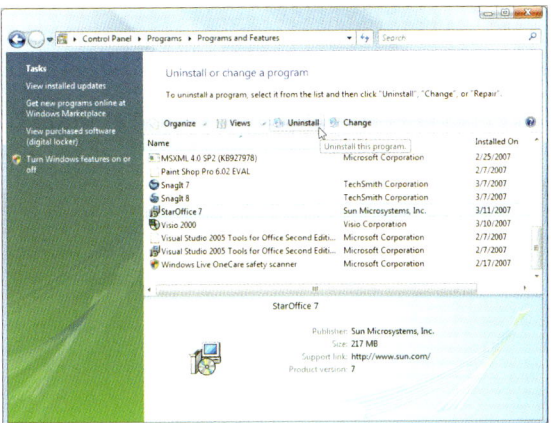

3. Click the [application you want to remove], and then click the [Uninstall] button. Go through User Account Control for the Uninstall Or Change An Application item. Windows then launches the uninstallation routine for the application, as in the illustration shown.

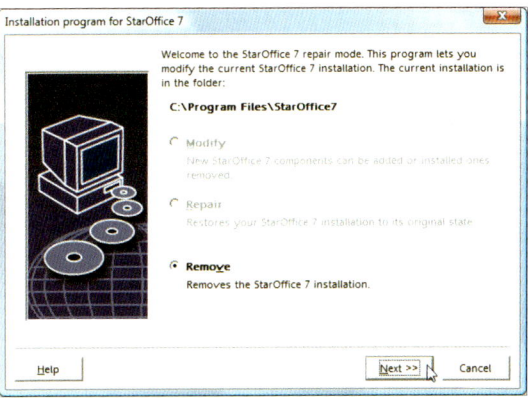

4. Verify that the Remove option or Uninstall option is selected, and then click the [Next] button. You may then need to confirm the uninstallation or decide whether to delete any files you've created in the application, as in the next illustration. Normally, you will want to keep any data files you've created, or at least review them and then delete any useless files manually.

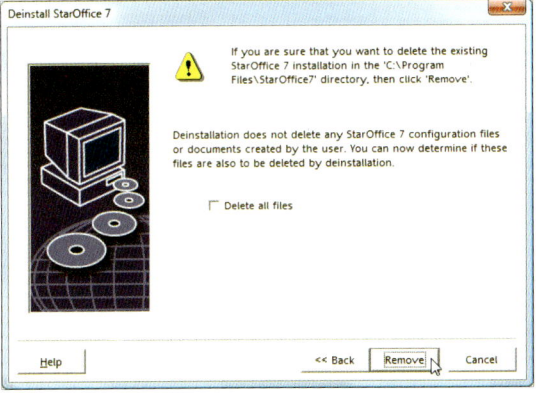

5. When it has finished, the uninstallation routine typically displays an information screen, such as the one shown in the next illustration. Click the [Complete] button or [Finish] button to close the uninstallation routine.

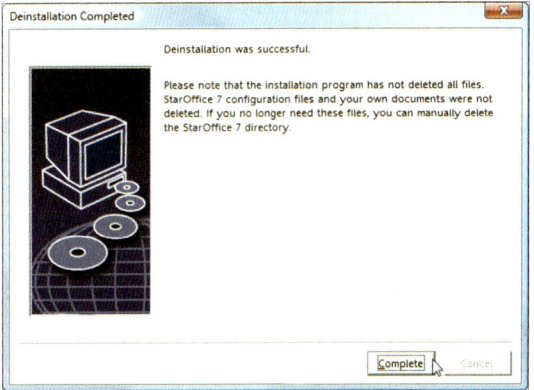

Restarting Windows After Removing an Application — Note >>>

After removing some applications, you may need to restart Windows. If so, the uninstallation routine normally prompts you to restart Windows. You can choose to restart Windows immediately, but sometimes you may need to close your other applications manually before restarting.

Let's Go Pro!

Understanding User Account Control

User Account Control is a safety mechanism designed to prevent malware (malevolent software) from being installed on your computer without your knowledge. Whenever User Account Control notices that someone (or some program) is trying to make a significant change to Windows, it displays a dialog box to make sure you're the one making the change. Examples of such changes include creating a user name, changing another password, or installing an application.

To authorize any change that User Account Control queries, you need the authority of an Administrator account. If you're logged on to Windows using an Administrator account, User Account Control lets you simply click a button to proceed. For example, in the User Account Control dialog box shown next, you can click the Continue button.

If you're logged in using a Standard account rather than an Administrator account, the User Account Control dialog box includes a password text box. Type the password for the administrator user shown (in the example, Jack is the administrator), and then click the [OK] button.

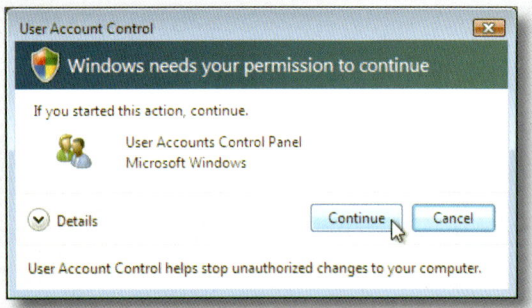

From this point on, this book does not show the User Account Control dialog boxes, but simply mentions them, telling you to "go through User Account Control" and naming the application or feature involved.

Windows marks each link or button that requires User Account Control approval with the four-colored "security" shield symbol. For example, in the Control Panel window shown next, commands such as Check Firewall Status and Turn Windows Firewall On Or Off have the shield.

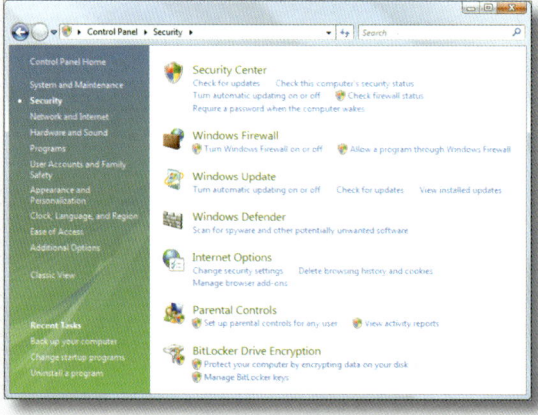

50

If you don't respond to a User Account Control dialog box within a couple of minutes, Windows closes the User Account Control dialog box and cancels the action that had been requested.

User Account Control can be annoying when you are administering a computer, but it provides important protection against malware. However, Windows does allow you to turn User Account Control off altogether if you choose, even though turning it off makes your computer more vulnerable to malware.

① Close all the applications you're using and save your work. You will need to restart Windows after making this change.

② Click the [Start] button, and then click [your picture] at the top of the Start menu. Windows displays the User Accounts window. Click the [Turn User Account Control On Or Off] link, and then go through User Account Control for the User Accounts Control Panel feature.

③ Windows displays the Turn User Account Control On Or Off Screen. Clear the Use User Account Control (UAC) To Help Protect Your Computer check box, and then click the [OK] button.

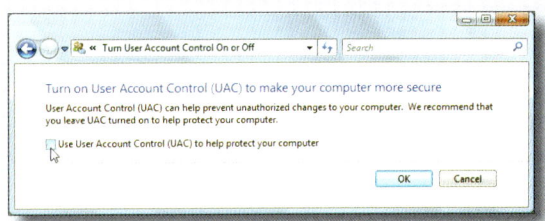

④ Windows displays the following dialog box, telling you that you must restart your computer to apply the change. Click the [Restart Now] button. Windows restarts your computer.

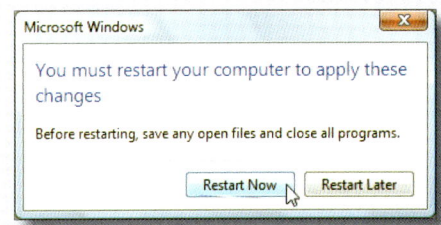

Chapter | 3

Working with Files and Folders

In this chapter, you'll learn how to work with files and folders to store information and keep it arranged so that you can find the files you need. You'll also learn how to copy and move files and folders, how to search for items you need, how to delete items, and how to create shortcuts that allow you quick access to the files and folders you need most.

For most of this chapter, you will use Windows Explorer, the file-management tool that Windows provides. To teach you how to work with Windows Explorer, this chapter shows examples using the sample files that Windows includes. Once you've learned these techniques using the sample files, you can use the techniques with your own files and folders.

SECTION 01

Using Windows Explorer

To work with files and folders in Windows, you use the Windows Explorer application, which is often referred to simply as "Explorer." First, you need to open a Windows Explorer window.

Understanding What Files and Folders Are

Your computer stores information on its hard drive or other drives (for example, network drives) in storage containers called files and folders. A file is a named storage container. Windows represents files using icons, as in the next illustration, which shows an Excel workbook file on the left, a text document file in the middle, and a picture file on the right.

Budget Estimates

List of Pictures

My Dog

For example, you might save a photo of your dog in a file named "My Dog.jpg." The part of the name after the period is called the file extension. The file extension tells Windows which type of file this is and which application to use to open it. In this case the file extension is jpg, which indicates that the file has the JPEG picture format, so Windows opens the file containing the Windows Photo Gallery application.

A *folder* is a special type of file designed to contain other files or folders. You organize your files into folders so that you can find the files you need. For example, you might save the photos of your dog in a folder named Dog Photos, as shown on the left in the next illustration. On the right is an empty folder named Vacation.

Dog Photos

Vacation

Opening a Windows Explorer Window

As with other applications, you can open Windows Explorer from the Start menu. However, because most people need to use Windows Explorer many times in each computing session, the Start menu contains not just a single item for Windows Explorer (as with most other applications) but several links to the most important folders in your user account, as shown here.

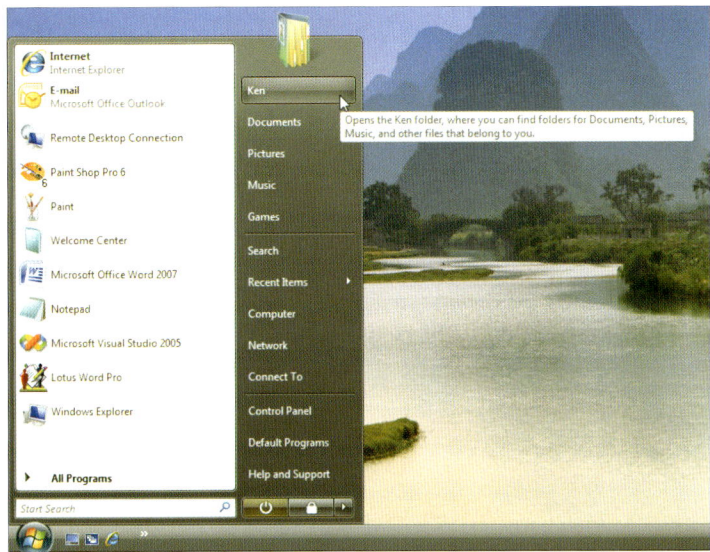

The links in the top two sections on the right side of the Start menu open Windows Explorer windows as follows:

Start Menu Link	Opens This Windows Explorer Folder
[your user name]	Your user folder, which contains your user account
Documents	Your Documents folder, in which Windows applications store files such as Word documents or Excel workbooks
Pictures	Your Pictures folder, in which Windows stores picture files by default
Music	Your Music folder, in which Windows stores music files by default
Games	Your Games folder, which contains Windows' games and other games you install
Search	A Search Results folder, which you can use to search for files
Recent Items	Displays a menu of files you've used recently, so that you can open them again
Computer	Your Computer folder, which shows the drives and devices on your computer
Network	The Network folder, which shows the computers on the network to which your computer is connected

Follow this example to start working with files and folders:

1. Click the [Start] button, and then click the link with your [user name]. Windows opens a Windows Explorer window showing your user account folder, as shown here. This folder contains folders for your music, pictures, and videos; your documents; your contacts; your downloads; your desktop; and your favorites, links, and searches. In the main part of the window, double-click the [Pictures] item.

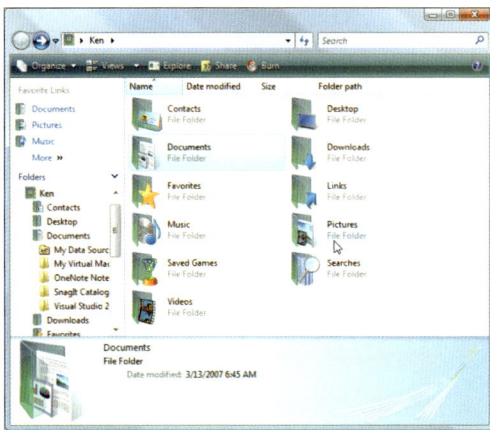

2. Windows Explorer opens your Pictures folder in the same window, as shown here. At first, your Pictures folder may contain only one item, as shown here: a link to the Sample Pictures folder. You can tell that this is a link because it has an arrow in its lower-left corner. Double-click the [link].

3. Windows Explorer opens the linked folder, the Sample Pictures folder, in the same window. Double-click the [Desert Landscape picture].

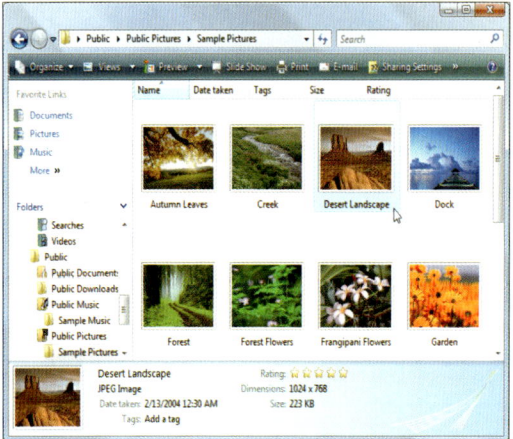

4. Windows opens the picture in the Windows Photo Gallery application. Click the [Close] button (the [X] button) at the upper-left corner of the Windows Photo Gallery window.

5. Windows Photo Gallery closes and Windows makes the Windows Explorer window active again. Click the [Back] button, which is the blue button with the left arrow in the upper-left corner of the Sample Pictures window.

6. Windows Explorer displays the Pictures folder again. Click the [Organize] button on the toolbar, and then click [Close].

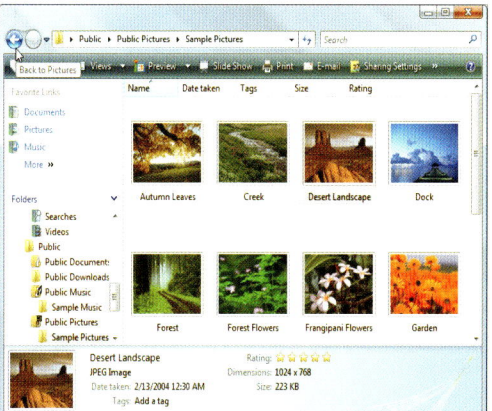

7. Explorer closes the window, returning you to the desktop.

Understanding Your User Account

When you set up Windows on your computer, you created a user account for yourself—a set of folders and settings that tells Windows how to arrange your desktop and applications, and where to store your files.

Microsoft recommends that each user of a Windows computer have his or her own separate user account. If you follow this recommendation, each user can access only his or her own files, and can change settings only for himself or herself.

Having separate user accounts helps you keep your private data away from other users. However, you can also share files and folders with other users of your computer if you want to. See Chapter 8 for details on sharing and networking.

Navigating Drives and Folders

Each Windows Explorer window consists of several different areas, as shown in the next illustration.

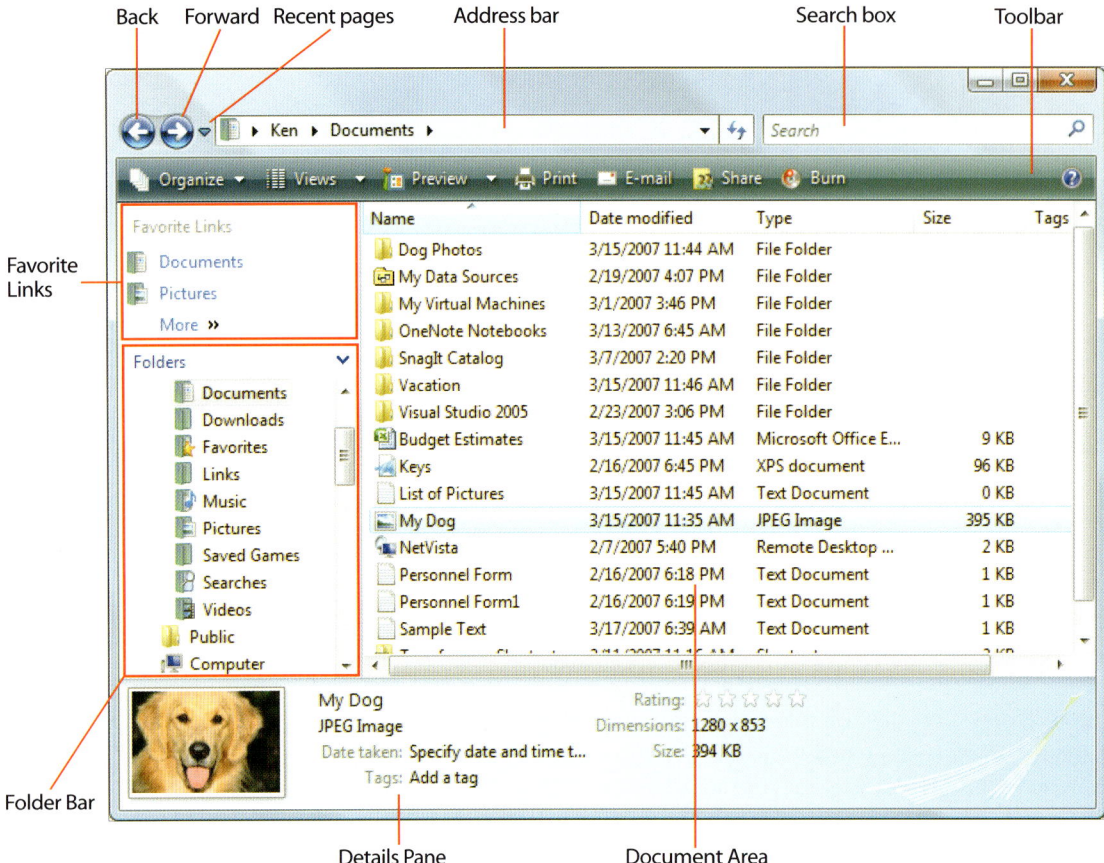

Follow these steps to learn what the areas are and how to use them.

1. Click the [Start] button, and then click [Computer]. Windows opens a Windows Explorer window showing the drives and devices on your computer. The Address bar at the top of the window shows the address of the current folder or view—in this case, Computer. The computer shown has three hard disks, a floppy disk and DVD drive, and a network drive.

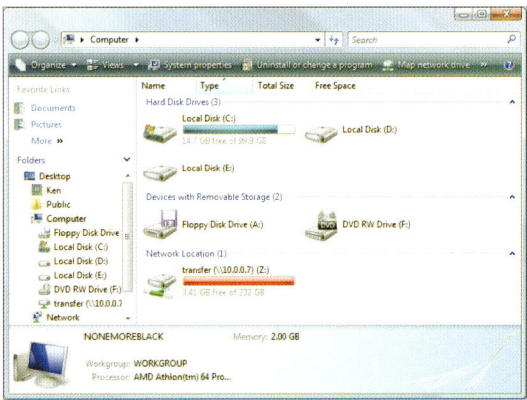

2. The Folders bar on the left side of the window shows the item that's currently selected—again, Computer—and lets you navigate to other drives and folders. The Details Pane at the bottom of the window shows information about the selected object—in this case, the computer's name (NONEMOREBLACK), workgroup, processor, and memory. Click the [Local Disk (C:)] item in the main part of the window. The Details Pane changes to show information about the hard drive: its total size, its file system, the space used, and the space free. Double-click the [Local Disk (C:)] item in the main part of the window.

3. Windows Explorer opens the C: drive in the same window and displays its folders, which include the following folders. Double-click the [Users] folder.

Folder	Contents
Program Files	Applications
Users	User accounts
Windows	System files

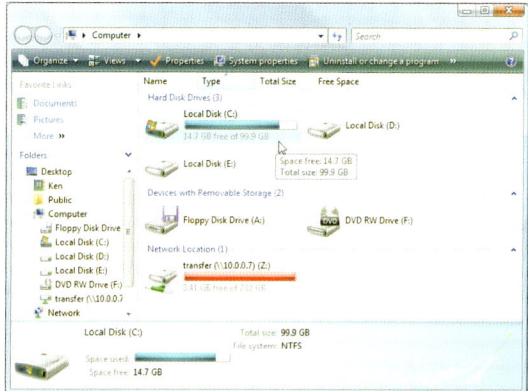

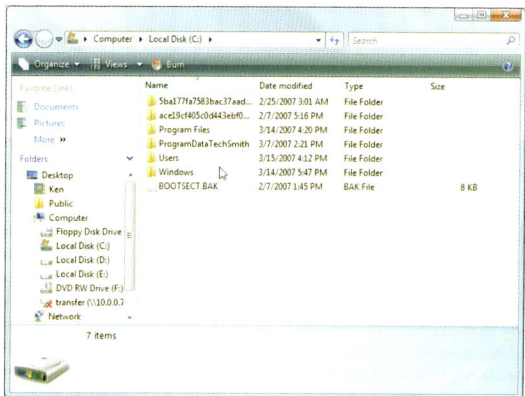

4. Windows Explorer opens the Users folder, which contains several folders, as listed here. Double-click the folder that has your user name.

Folder	Contents
Administrator	The administrator's account (on some computers only)
[User Name]	A folder for each user—in the example, a folder for Ken and a folder for Mila
Public	A folder for files shared among all users—for example, the files in the Sample Music folder

5. Windows Explorer opens the folder you double-clicked. Notice that the Address Bar shows the path to your user folder—for example, Local Disk (C:) > Users > Ken >—and that the Folders Bar shows the folder to which you have navigated. Double-click the [Pictures] item in the main part of the window.

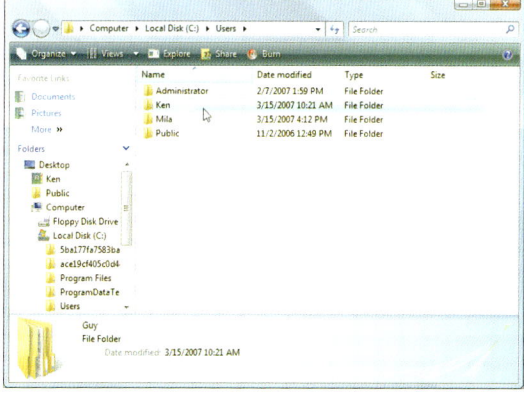

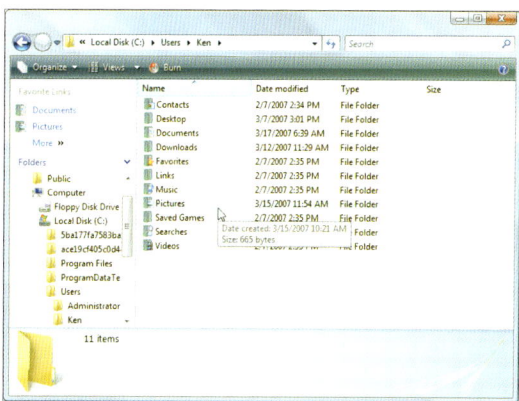

6. Windows Explorer opens the Pictures folder. This folder may contain only a shortcut to the Sample Pictures folder. In the Favorite Links area in the upper-left corner of the window, click the [Documents] link.

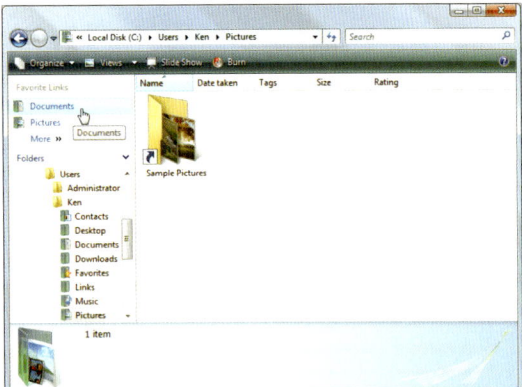

7. Windows Explorer opens the Documents folder. In the Folders Bar, click the [Pictures] item.

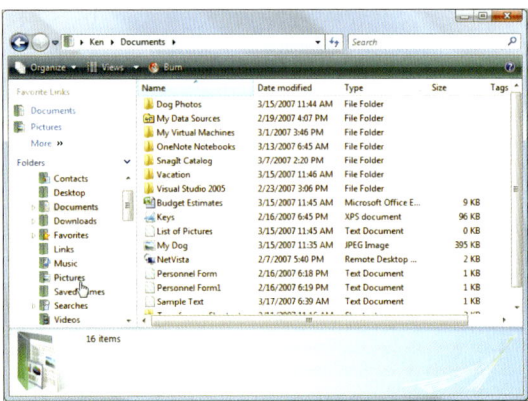

8. Windows Explorer opens the Pictures folder again. In the Address Bar, each of the arrows opens a menu of folders contained by the folder to the left of the arrow. Click the [arrow to the right of your user name], and then click the [Music] item on the menu that appears.

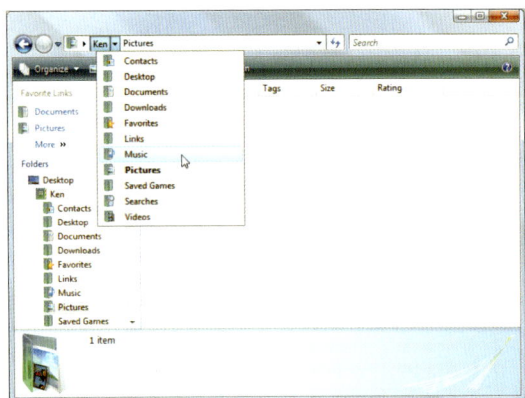

9. Windows Explorer opens the Music folder. In the Address Bar, click the [arrow to the left of your user name], and then choose [Computer] from the menu that appears.

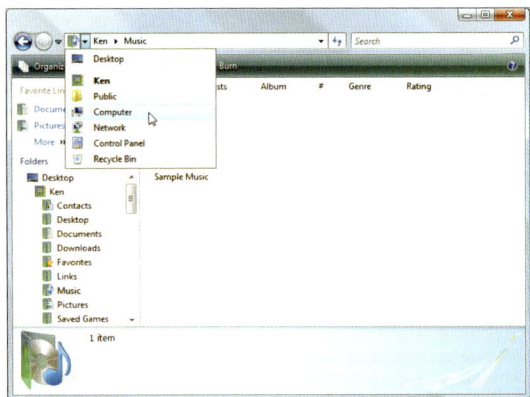

10. Windows Explorer opens the Computer folder again. Click the [Recent Pages] button, the small button with the downward arrow just to the left of the Address Bar. The menu that appears lists the folders you've used recently. Click the [Documents] folder.

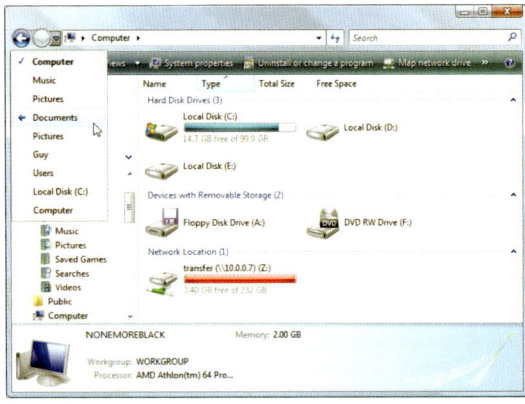

Chapter 03. Working with Files and Folders

11. Windows Explorer opens the Documents folder again. Click the [Forward] button.

12. Windows Explorer displays the next folder in the sequence of folders you opened—in this case, the Pictures folder you opened in step 8. Click the upper-left corner of the Windows Explorer window and then choose [Close] from the menu that appears. This is the control menu, which used to have an icon in earlier versions of Windows, but is hidden in Windows Vista. Windows Explorer closes the window.

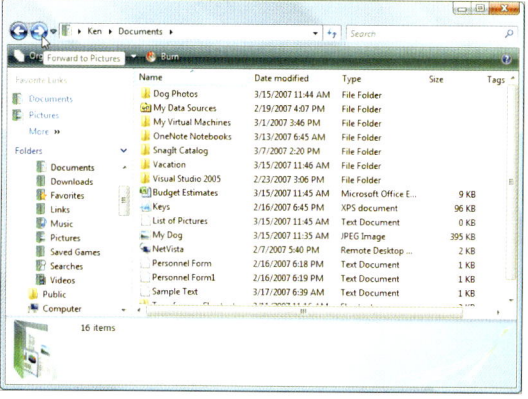

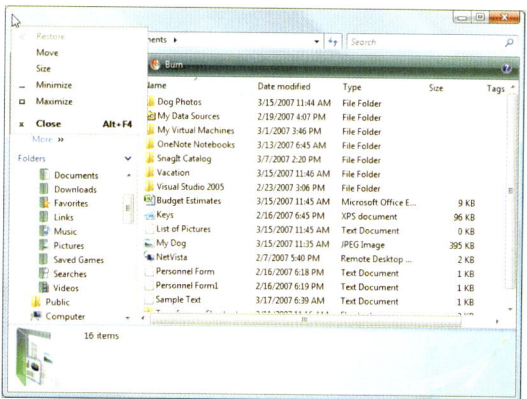

Using Views in Windows Explorer

Windows Explorer lets you view your files and folders in several different ways. Follow these steps to practice using views in Windows Explorer.

1. Click the [Start] button, and then click the [Pictures] link. Windows displays your Pictures folder. Double-click the [Sample Pictures] link. Windows displays the Sample Pictures folder. Click the [Views] button on the toolbar.

2. Windows shows the view options. Drag the slider up to Extra Large icons, and then release the mouse button.

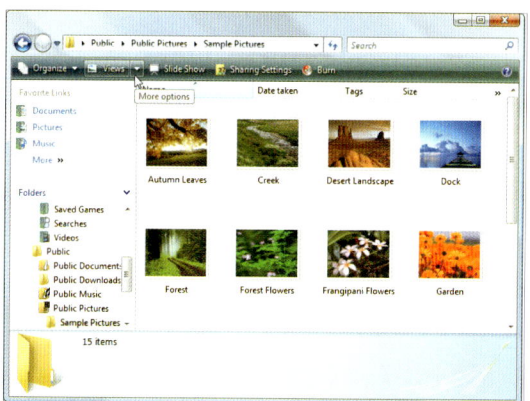

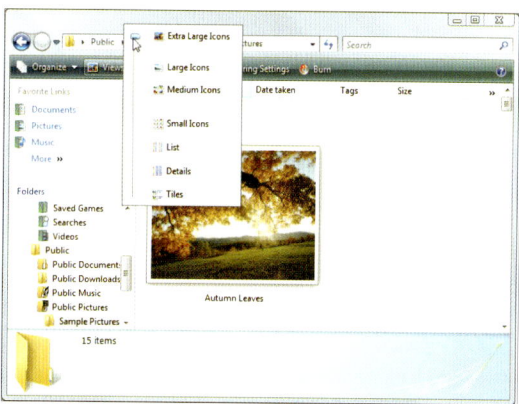

61

3. Windows Explorer displays the pictures at a larger size. Click the [Views] button again, drag the slider down to Small Icons, and then release the mouse button.

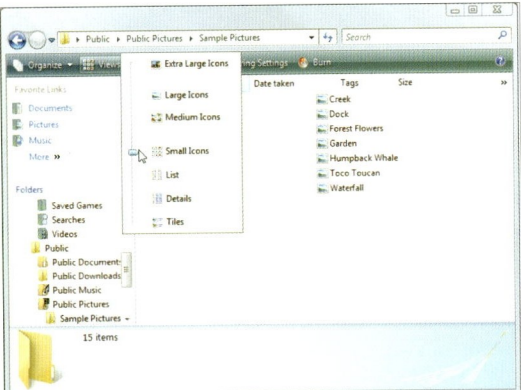

4. Windows Explorer makes the icons smaller and assigns each a generic picture rather than a preview of the actual picture. Click the [Views] button again, drag the slider down to List, and then release the mouse button.

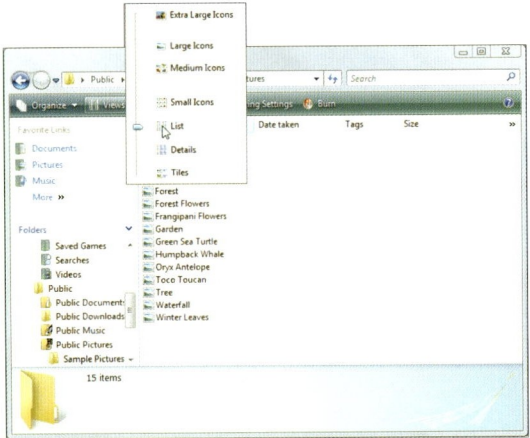

5. Windows Explorer displays a list of the files without any extra data. Click the [Views] button again, drag the slider down to Details, and then release the mouse button.

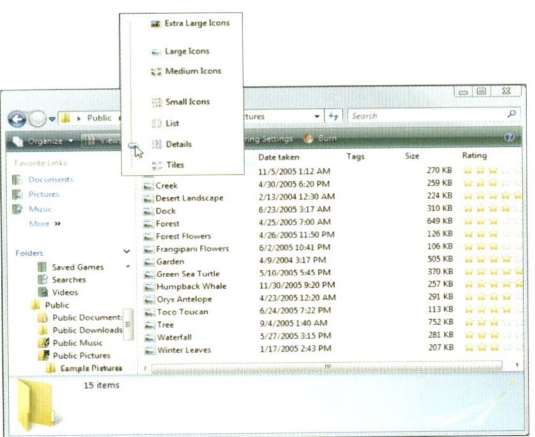

6. Click the [Views] button again, drag the slider down to Tiles, and then release the mouse button. Windows Explorer displays a "tile"—a small rectangle—for each file. Each tile consists of a small preview, the file's name, type, and size.

Understanding the Folder Changes in Windows Vista from Windows XP — Note >>>

Where Windows XP provides folders with "My" names—My Documents, My Music, My Pictures—and so on, Windows Vista provides similar folders whose names don't use "My": Documents, Music, Pictures, and so forth.

Creating Folders

Windows provides a basic folder structure for you: the Documents folder for documents, the Music folder for music files, the Picture folder for pictures, and so on. But if you create more than a few documents, you'll need to create more folders to keep your files organized.

To create a folder, follow these steps:

1. Open a Windows Explorer window to the folder in which you want to create the new folder. For this example, click the [Start] button and then click [Documents] to open a Windows Explorer window to your Documents folder. Click the [Organize] button, and then choose [New Folder] from the menu.

2. Windows creates a new folder, names it New Folder, and displays an edit box around it. Type the new name for the folder, and then press <Enter>

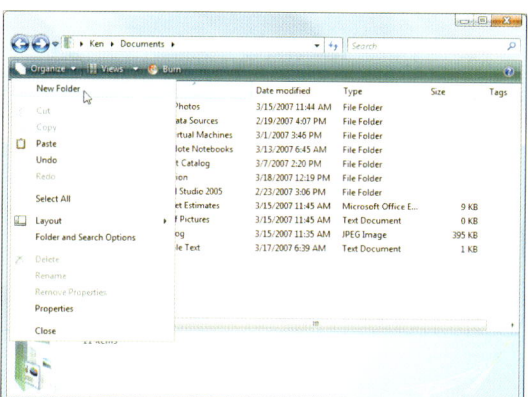

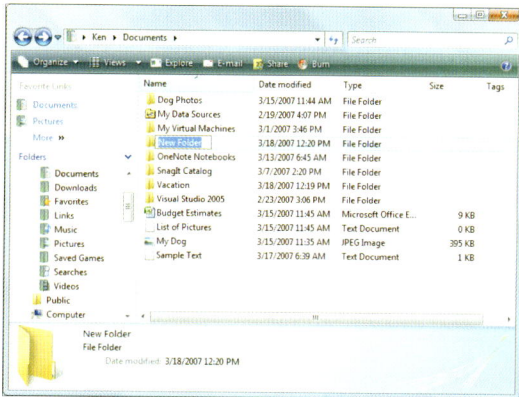

3. Windows applies the name to the folder.

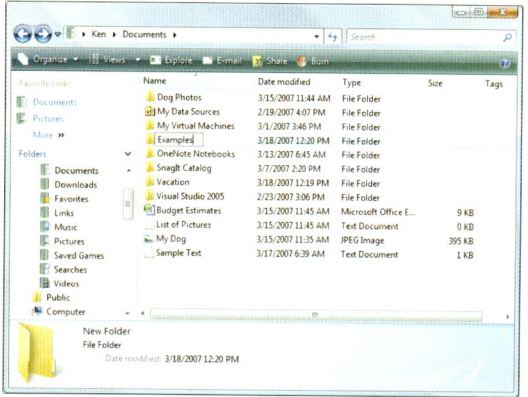

SECTION 02 Copying and Moving Files and Folders

Often, you will need to move files or folders from one folder to another. At other times you will need to copy files or folders from one folder or drive to another. For example, you may copy files from your computer's hard drive to a USB key drive so that you can carry them with you.

Windows Explorer lets you move and copy files and folders in several ways. This section teaches you the easiest and most consistent way of moving and copying files and folders. It also briefly mentions some of the other ways of moving and copying.

Copying a File or Folder

You can copy however many files or folders you need to in a single step, provided that you can select them all at once. In this example, you copy a single file. Follow these steps:

1. Open a Windows Explorer window to the folder that contains the file or folder you want to copy. For this example, click the [Start] button, click [Pictures] to open your Pictures folder, and then double-click the [Sample Pictures] shortcut.

2. Windows opens the Sample Pictures folder. Select the file or folder you want to copy. For this example, click the [Creek] picture to select it.

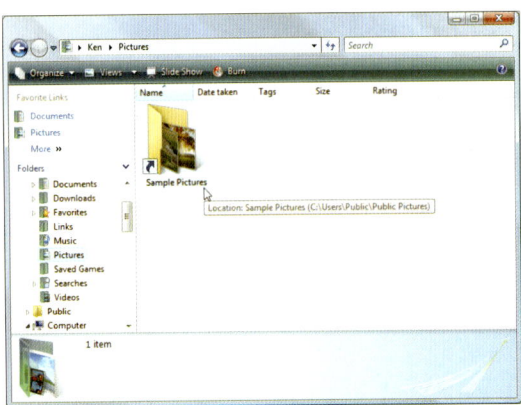

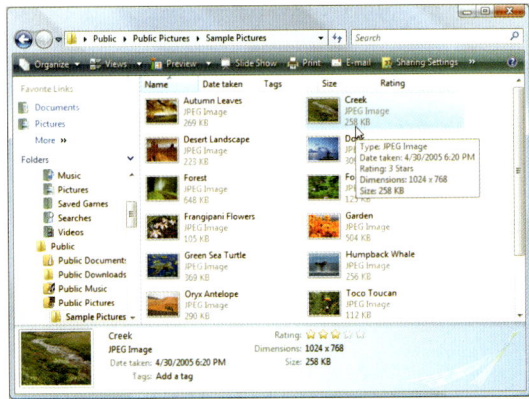

3. Press <Alt>. Windows Explorer displays the menu bar over the toolbar. Click the [Edit] menu, and then choose [Copy To Folder].

64

4. Windows Explorer displays the Copy Items dialog box.

5. In the folder tree, navigate to the folder in which you want to place the copy. For this example, click the [folder with your name] to display the folders it contains, and then click the [Pictures] folder.

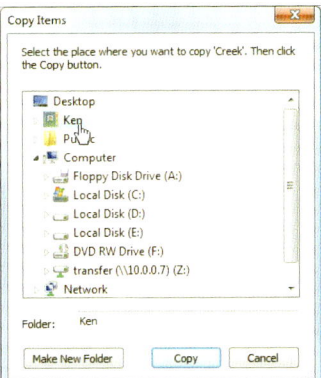

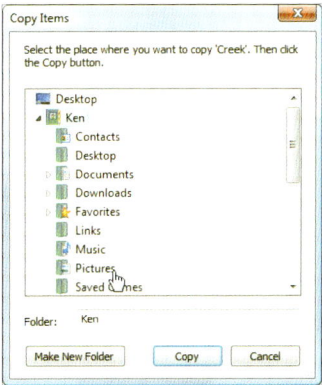

6. Click the [Copy] button. Windows Explorer closes the Copy Items dialog box and copies the file to the folder you chose.

Leave the Windows Explorer window open so that you can work through the next section.

Moving a File or Folder

Instead of copying a file or folder, you may need to move the original version of a file or folder to another drive or folder. In this example, you move the file you copied in the previous section back to the Sample Pictures folder.

1. Open a Windows Explorer window to the folder that contains the file or folder you want to move. For this example, in the Windows Explorer window you opened in the previous step, click the [Pictures] link in the Favorite Links area.

2. Windows Explorer opens your Pictures folder. Select the file or folder you want to move. For this example, click the [Creek] picture to select it.

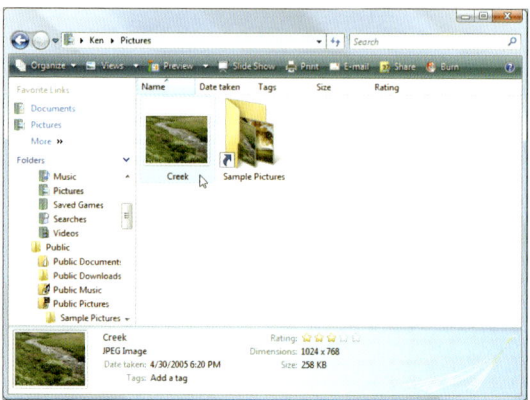

3. Press <Alt>. Windows Explorer displays the menu bar over the toolbar. Click the [Edit] menu, and then choose [Move To Folder].

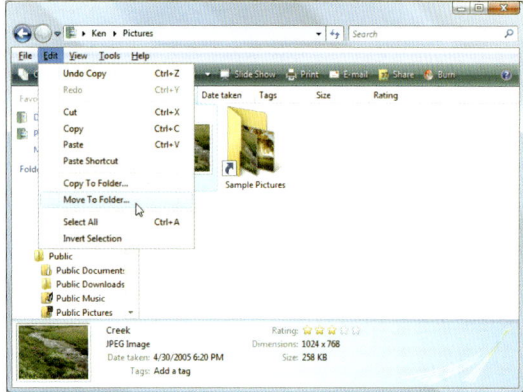

4. Windows Explorer displays the Move Items dialog box.

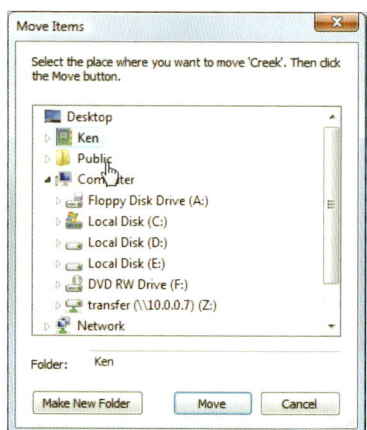

5. In the folder tree navigate to the folder in which you want to place the copy. For this example, click the [Public] folder to display the folders it contains, click the [Public Pictures] folder, and then click the [Sample Pictures] folder. Click the [Move] button.

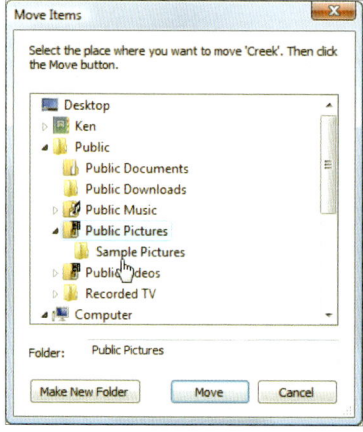

6. Windows Explorer closes the Move Items dialog box. Normally, Windows Explorer then moves the file to the folder you chose. But in this case, the destination folder already contains a file named "Creek.jpg," so Windows Explorer displays the Move File dialog box to let you decide how to resolve this problem. You can:

① Replace the existing file with the new file.

② Cancel the move (for example, so that you can rename one of the files).

③ Move the file, but rename the new file so that it does not replace the existing file.

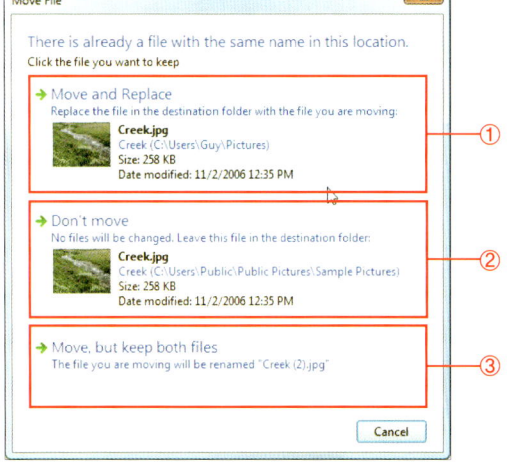

7. For this example, click the [Move And Replace] button. Windows Explorer closes the Move File dialog box and moves the file, replacing the existing file.

Using Other Methods of Copying and Moving Files or Folders

For most people, the easiest way to copy files or folders is to use the Copy To Folder command as described earlier in this chapter. Similarly, the easiest way to move files or folders is to use the Move To Folder command.

However, you may want to use some or all of the following commands for copying or moving files.

■ Copying via Copy and Paste

To copy a file or folder via copy and paste, follow these steps:

1. Select the file or folder you want to copy.
2. Click the [Organize] button, and then click [Copy] on the menu.
3. Navigate to the destination folder.
4. Click the [Organize] button, and then click [Paste] on the menu.

67

■ Moving via Cut and Paste

To move a file or folder via cut and paste, follow these steps:

1. Select the file or folder you want to move.
2. Click the [Organize] button, and then click [Cut] on the menu.
3. Navigate to the destination folder.
4. Click the [Organize] button, and then click [Paste] on the menu.

■ Copying via Drag and Drop

Windows lets you perform many actions via drag and drop, which means you click an item, drag it while continuing to hold down the mouse button, and then release the mouse button when the item is over its destination.

To copy via drag and drop, follow these steps:

1. Open a Windows Explorer window to the source folder.
2. Open another Windows Explorer window to the destination folder.
3. Arrange the two Windows Explorer windows so that you can see both.
4. Hold down <Ctrl> and drag the file or folder from the source folder to the destination folder.

■ Moving via Drag and Drop

To move via drag and drop, follow these steps:

1. Open a Windows Explorer window to the source folder.
2. Open another Windows Explorer window to the destination folder.
3. Arrange the two Windows Explorer windows so that you can see both.
4. Hold down <Shift> and drag the file or folder from the source folder to the destination folder.

You can also drag and drop without holding down <Ctrl> or <Shift>, but the effect of this action depends on whether the source folder and destination folder are on the same drive or different drives. So usually it is best to use <Ctrl> or <Shift>.

SECTION 03

Deleting Files and Folders

When you no longer need a file or folder, you can delete it—remove it from your computer. To save you from the problems caused by misjudged or accidental deletions, Windows Vista uses a two-stage deletion process for files and folders stored on your computer.

Windows Vista uses a two-stage deletion process for files and folders stored on your computer:

• When you tell Windows to delete a file or folder, Windows removes it from its current folder and places it in a special folder called the Recycle Bin.

• When you're ready to get rid of the trash, you can empty the Recycle Bin. When you do this, Windows actually disposes of the files and folders you've deleted. But until you empty the Recycle Bin, you can recover a file or folder from it.

Sending a File to the Recycle Bin

To send a file or folder to the Recycle Bin, you issue a Delete command. In this example, you send one of Windows' sample music files to the Recycle Bin; in the next example, you recover it. Follow these steps:

1. Click the [Start] button, and then click [Music]. Windows opens a Windows Explorer window showing your Music folder. Double-click the [Sample Music] shortcut.

2. Windows Explorer displays the Sample Music folder. Click the [Amanda] file, and then press <Delete>.

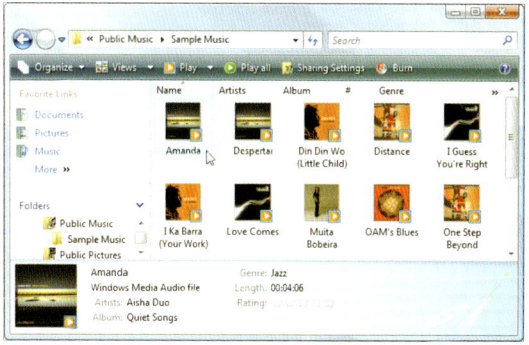

Windows Deletes Files When the Recycle Bin Is Full   Warning >>>

When the Recycle Bin becomes full, Windows automatically and without warning deletes the files that have been in it longest. For this reason, if you need to recover a file from the Recycle Bin, you should do so as soon as possible.

69

3. Windows displays the Delete File dialog box. Click the [Yes] button to confirm that you want to delete the file.

4. Windows closes the Delete File dialog box, removes the file from the Sample Music folder (as shown in the next illustration), and places the file in the Recycle Bin.

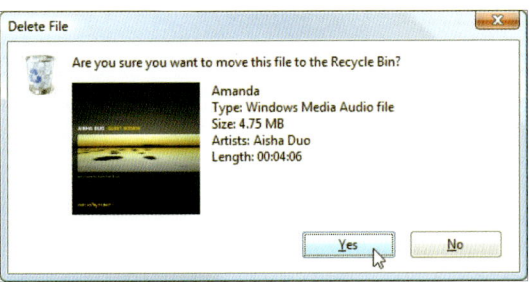

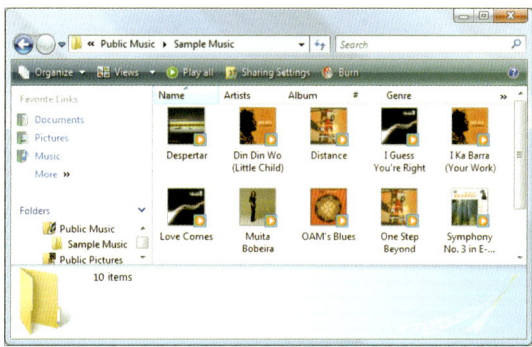

Leave the Sample Music folder open so that you can use it again in the next three sections.

Recovering a File from the Recycle Bin

If you realize that you still need a file or folder that you've placed in the Recycle Bin, recover it immediately. In this example, you restore the file that you placed in the Recycle Bin in the previous section. Follow these steps:

1. Double-click the [Recycle Bin] icon on the desktop. Windows opens a Windows Explorer window showing the contents of the Recycle Bin. Click the file you want to restore—in this case, the [Amanda] file—and then click the [Restore This Item] button on the toolbar.

2. Windows removes the file from the Recycle Bin and restores it to its previous folder—in this case, the Sample Music folder. Click the [Sample Music] folder button on the taskbar to display the Sample Music folder so that you can see the file has been restored correctly.

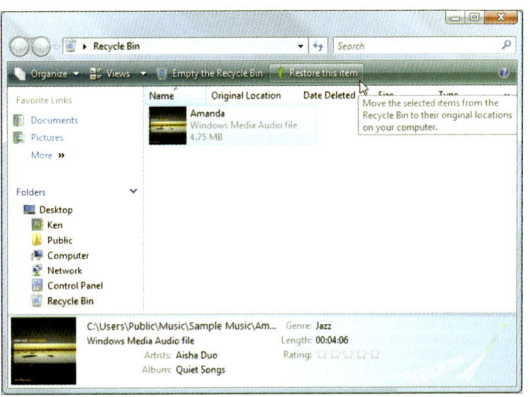

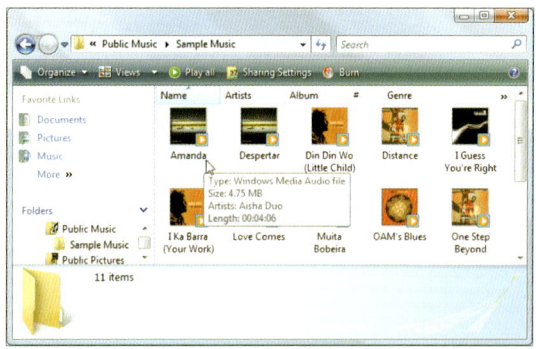

Leave the Sample Music folder open so that you can use it again in the next two sections.

Emptying the Recycle Bin

When you're ready to dispose permanently of any files you've placed in the Recycle Bin, you empty the Recycle Bin. Follow these steps to place some files in the Recycle Bin and then empty it.

1. In the Sample Music folder, click the [Amanda] file to select it.

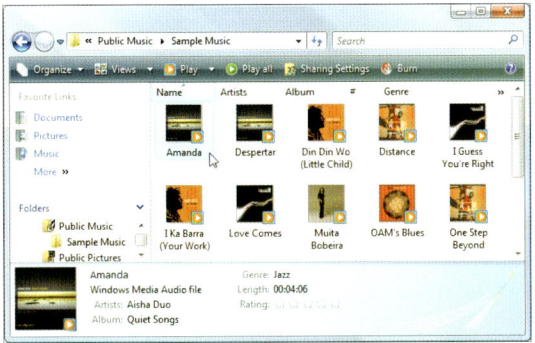

2. Hold down <Ctrl> and click the [Despertar] file and then the [Distance] file to select these files as well. (Holding down <Ctrl> adds the files you select to the existing selection).

3. Right-click any one of the selected three files, and then choose [Copy] from the context menu.

4. Windows copies the files to the clipboard. Right-click anywhere in open space in the main part of the Sample Music window, and then choose [Paste] from the context menu.

5. Windows pastes in the copied files, automatically renaming them to Amanda - Copy, Despertar - Copy, and Distance - Copy. Click the [Amanda - Copy] file to select it. Hold down <Ctrl> and click the [Despertar - Copy] file and then the [Distance - Copy] file to select these files as well. Press <Delete>.

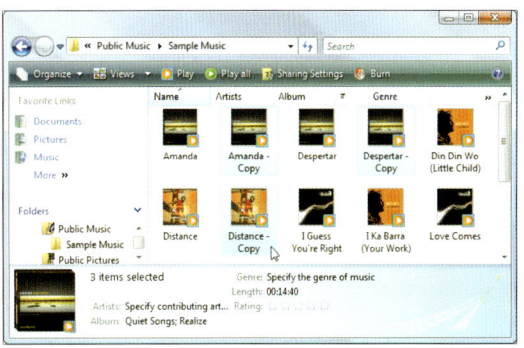

71

6. Windows displays the Delete Multiple Items dialog box. Click the [Yes] button.

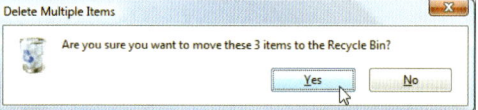

7. Windows moves the files to the Recycle Bin. Double-click the [Recycle Bin] icon on the desktop. Windows opens a Windows Explorer window showing the Recycle Bin. Click the [Empty The Recycle Bin] button on the toolbar.

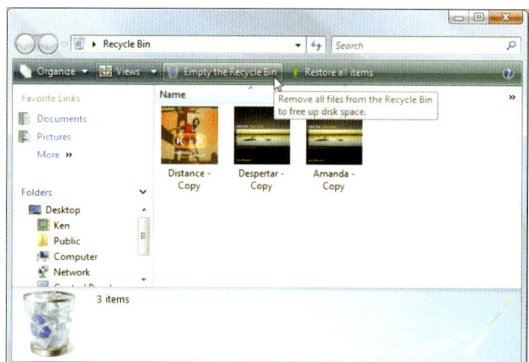

8. Windows displays the Delete Multiple Items dialog box. Click the [Yes] button.

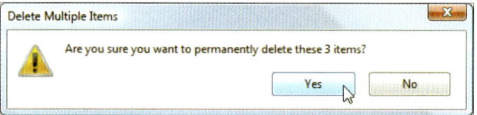

9. Windows deletes the files, leaving the Recycle Bin empty. Click the [Close] button (the ⊠ button) in the upper-right corner of the window to close the Recycle Bin window.

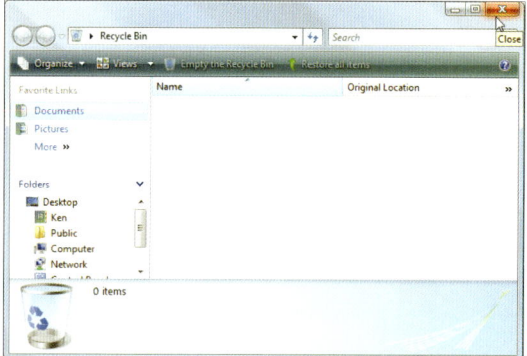

Leave the Sample Music folder open for the next section.

Deleting a File Permanently

Sometimes you may prefer not to put a file in the Recycle Bin—maybe it contains sensitive information, or is huge and you want to recover the space it occupies. In such cases you can delete a file permanently rather than put it in the Recycle Bin.

In this example, you copy a file and then delete the copy permanently. Follow these steps:

1. In the Sample Music folder, right-click the [Amanda] file, and then choose [Copy] from the context menu. Windows copies the file to the Clipboard.

2. Right-click anywhere in open space in the main part of the Sample Music window, and then choose [Paste] from the context menu. Windows pastes in the copied file, automatically renaming it to Amanda - Copy. Right-click the [Amanda - Copy] file, hold down <Shift>, and then click [Delete] on the context menu. (You can also hold down <Shift> and press <Delete>.)

3. Windows displays the Delete File dialog box, which asks if you want "to permanently delete the file." Click the [Yes] button.

4. Windows deletes the file without placing it in the Recycle Bin. You can now no longer recover this file without using specialized tools or a disk recovery service.

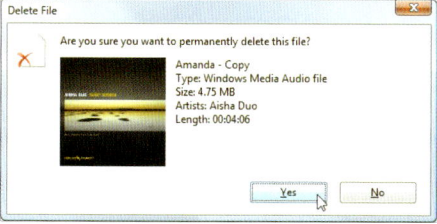

SECTION 04 — Searching for Files and Folders

If you create many files and folders, you may lose track of where some of them are. To locate particular files and folders, you can search for them. You can search either from within an existing Windows Explorer window or from a Search Results window that you open specifically for searching.

Searching from a Windows Explorer Window

Searching from a Windows Explorer window is useful when you realize that you can't find the file or folder you need. Follow these steps:

1. In the Windows Explorer window that you have opened, click in the [Search] box in the upper-right corner of the window.

2. Start typing the term for which you want to search. As you type, Windows reduces the list of files and folders displayed to show only those that match.

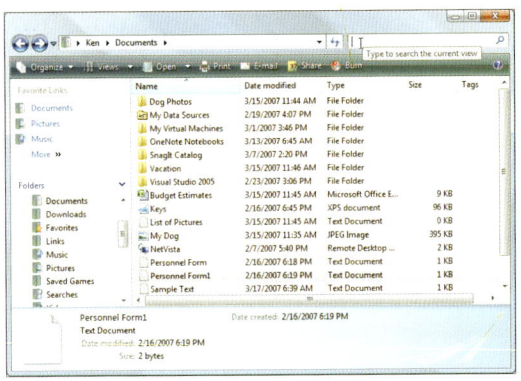

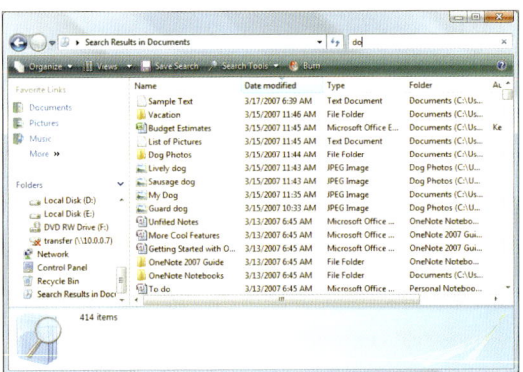

3. When you finish typing the search term, you may be able to find the file or folder easily from the search results. (If not, click the [Advanced Search] link, and then search as described in the next section.) Click an item to display it in the Details pane, or double-click an item to open it.

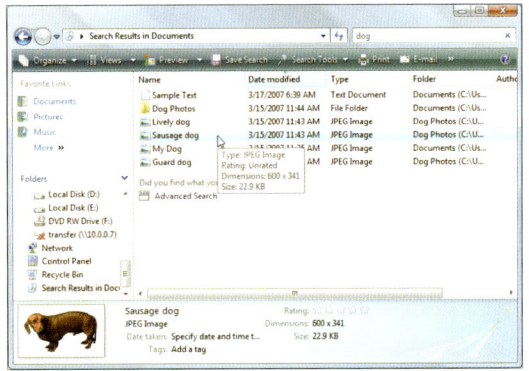

Chapter 03. Working with Files and Folders

4. To clear the search results, click the [Close] () button in the Search box.

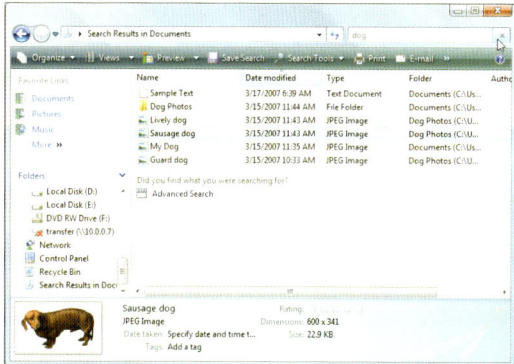

Searching from a Search Results Window

For more powerful searching, open a Search Results window. Windows then automatically searches through all the folders it has indexed for searching. In this example, you search for the Desert Landscape picture file. Follow these steps:

1. Click the [Start] button, and then click [Search]. Windows opens a Search Results window and places the insertion point in the Search box. Start typing your search term in the Search box.

2. As you type, Windows searches through your indexed folders and returns matching results. If you're searching for a particular type of file, click the E-mail, Document, Picture, Music, or Other button on the toolbar. For this example, try clicking the [Picture] button

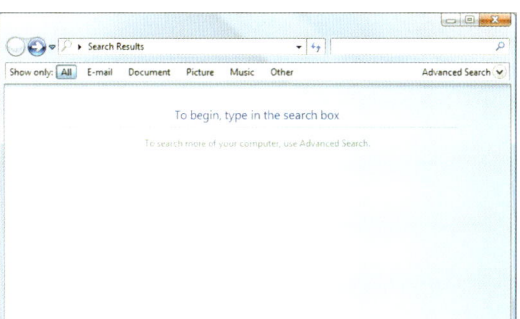

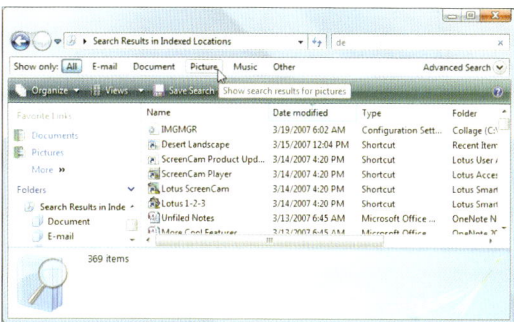

3. Windows narrows down the search to matching results.

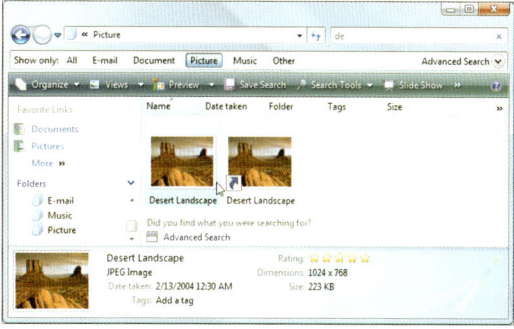

75

4. Click a result to select the file or folder, or double-click the result to open the file or folder. To open the folder that contains the file or folder, right-click, and then choose [Open File Location] from the context menu.

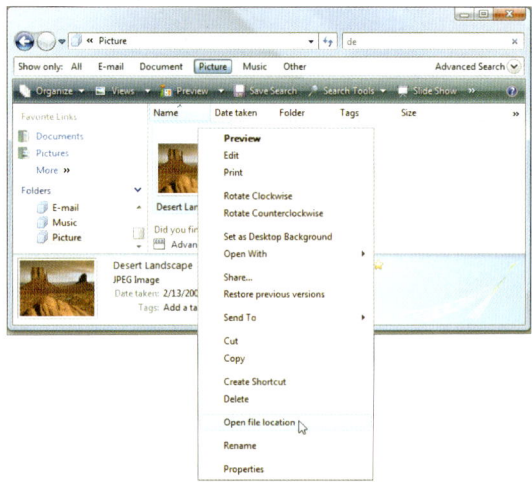

Performing an Advanced Search

If a simple search does not find the desired file or folder, you can perform an advanced search. In this example, you search to find the largest files and folders on your computer.

1. Click the [Start] button, and then click [Search]. Windows opens a Search Results window and places the insertion point in the Search box. Click the [Advanced Search] button.

2. Windows displays the Advanced Search controls. To tell Windows which types of files or folders to find, click one of the buttons on the toolbar. For this example, make sure the [All] button is selected.

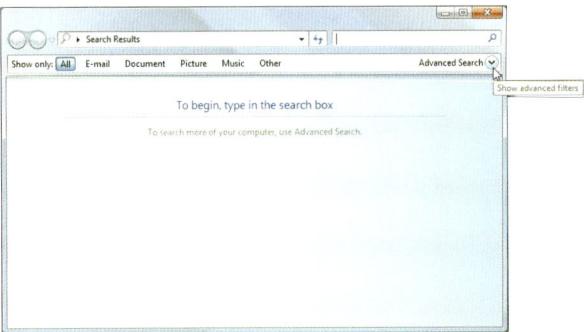
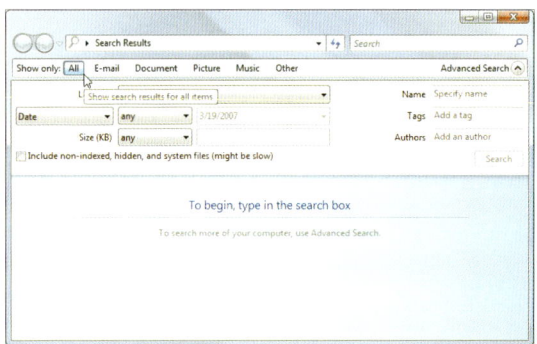

Displaying the Advanced Search Controls   Note>>>

You can also display the Advanced Search controls by clicking the Advanced Search link after performing a search as described in the previous section.

Chapter 03. Working with Files and Folders

3. In the Location drop-down list, select the location to search (see Table). For this example, choose [Local Hard Drives].

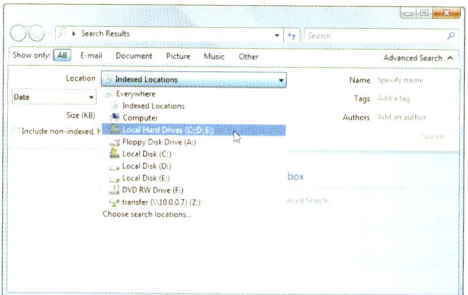

Location	Makes Windows Search
Everywhere	All folders on all your computer's drives, including network drives. This may be slow.
Indexed Locations	Only the folders that Windows indexes. This gives fast searches of the folders you normally use.
Computer	All drives on your computer.
Local Hard Drives	All the hard drives on your computer. This is good for wide ranging searches.
[a particular disk drive]	The disk drive you chose—either a local hard disk, a floppy or removable disk, or a network drive.
Choose Search Locations	Allows you to select a particular folder. Use this option when you know the folder you need to search.

4. Use the Date, Size, Name, Tags, and Authors controls to specify the details of the files you want to find. For this example, click the [Size] drop-down list, choose [Is Greater Than], and then type 40000 in the text box to find files larger than approximately 40MB. Click the [Search] button.

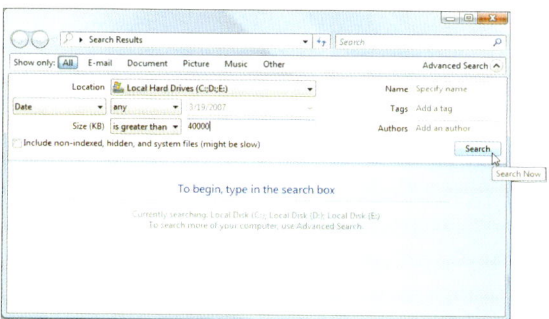

5. Windows searches for files and folders matching your criteria, and displays a list of matches.

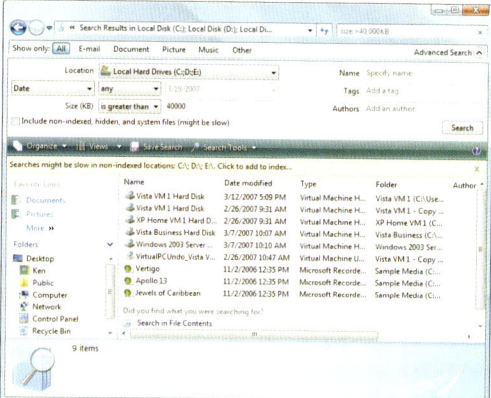

Searching for Non Indexed, Hidden, and System Files   Note>>>

If you need to search for all the files on your computer, select the [Include Non-Indexed], [Hidden], [And System Files] check box. The resulting search may be slow, but it will catch all the files that match your search criteria, not just those that Windows has indexed from your folders and shared folders.

Hidden files are files Windows hides to help you avoid changing them. *System files* are files that Windows requires to run itself and applications.

6. To see how big a file is, click it in the list, and then look at the Details pane. Alternatively, hover the mouse pointer over it, and then read the ScreenTip. Click the [Close] ( ) button in the upper-right corner. Windows Explorer closes the Search Results window.

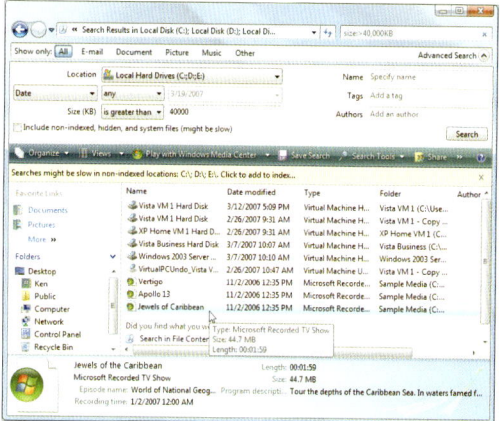

SECTION 05 Creating and Using Zipped Folders

When you need to store files as compactly as possible, you can put them in a zipped folder.
A zipped folder, also called a zip file, is a folder whose contents are compressed so that they take up as little space as possible. Zipped folders are especially useful for sending files via e-mail or cramming contents onto a USB key or other limited-capacity medium.
In this example you create a zipped folder containing the sample pictures that Windows includes. You then open the folder, extract its contents, and then delete the folder.

Creating a Zipped Folder

To create a zipped folder follow these steps:

1. Open a Windows Explorer window to the folder that contains the file or folder you want to put in the zipped folder. For this example, click the [Start] button, click [Pictures] to open your Pictures folder, and then double-click the [Sample Pictures] shortcut to open the Sample Pictures folder. Click the [Organize] button on the toolbar, and then choose [Select All].

2. Windows Explorer selects all the files in the folder. Right-click [any of the selected files], highlight the [Send To] item on the context menu, and then click the [Compressed (Zipped) Folder] item on the submenu.

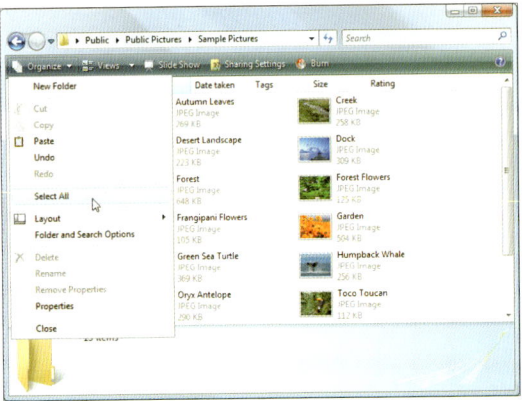
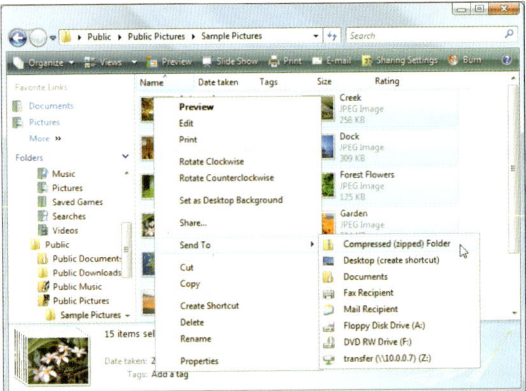

3. Windows Explorer creates the zipped folder and names it after the first file's name, but then displays an edit box around the name so that you can change it.

4. Type the new name for the zipped folder and then press <Enter>. Windows Explorer applies the name. If necessary, you can now copy or move the zipped folder to another folder.

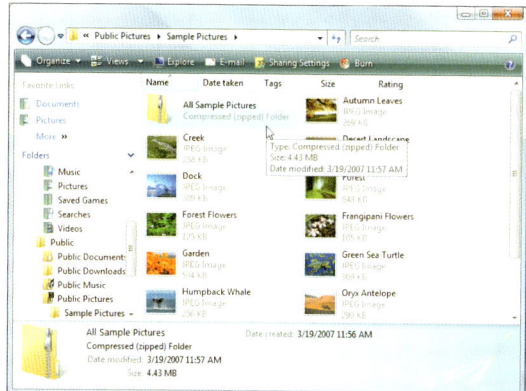

Leave the Windows Explorer window open so that you can extract the files in the next section.

Opening a Zipped Folder

To use the files contained in a zipped folder, you extract the files to another folder. Follow these steps to extract the files from the zipped folder you created in the previous section.

1. In the Windows Explorer window, right-click the [zipped folder you created], and then choose [Extract All] from the context menu.

2. Windows launches the Extract Compressed (Zipped) Folders Wizard, which displays the Select A Destination And Extract Files screen. This screen suggests extracting the files to a folder that has the same name as the zipped folder (but not the extension). If you want to use a different folder, click the [Browse] button, use the [Select A Destination] dialog box to select the folder, and then click the [OK] button. Otherwise, make sure the [Show Extracted Files When Complete] check box is selected, and then click the [Extract] button.

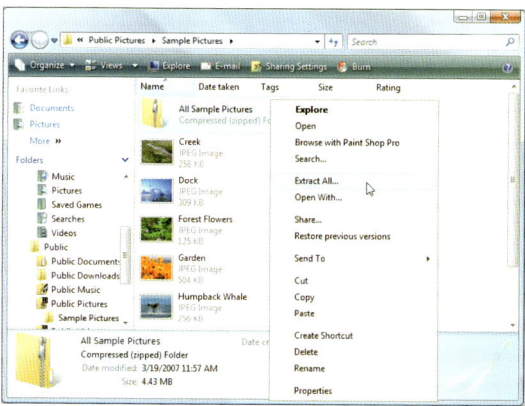
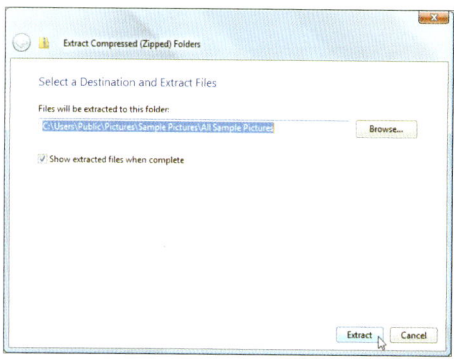

3. Windows Explorer extracts the files and then displays a window showing the extracted files. You can now work with the extracted files as with any other files.

4. However, you may want to delete the zipped folder if you no longer need it. For this example, delete both the zipped folder and the extracted files. Click the [Close] button (the button) to close the All Sample Pictures window. Windows Explorer displays the Sample Pictures window again. Click the [All Sample Pictures folder] and the [All Sample Pictures zipped folder], and then hold down <Shift> and press <Delete>.

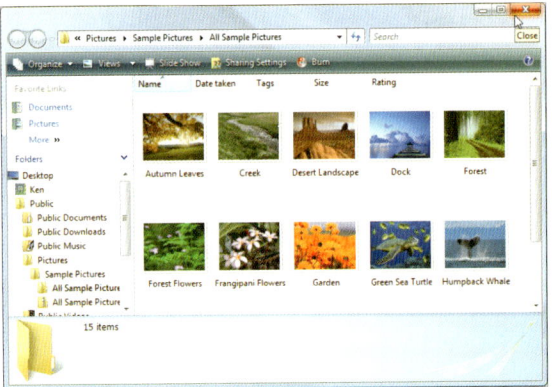

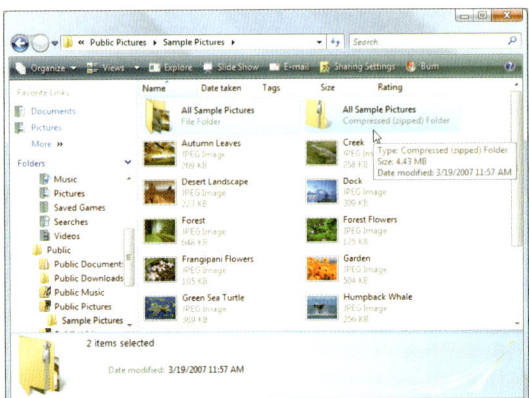

5. Windows displays the Delete Multiple Items dialog box. Click the [Yes] button.

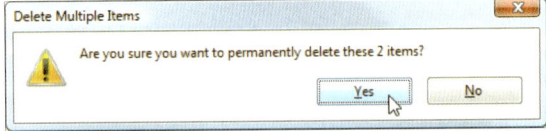

Let's Go Pro!

Using Shortcuts to Access Files or Folders Quickly

A shortcut is a means of accessing a file or folder quickly. A shortcut is a small file that acts as a pointer to the file or folder you want to access. By placing shortcuts on your desktop or in another easily accessed location, you can quickly open files or folders even if they're buried deep in your computer's file system.

You can create shortcuts to applications or to data files. In this example, you create a shortcut on your desktop to open one of the sample videos included with Windows.

To create a shortcut, follow these steps:

① Open a Windows Explorer window to the folder that contains the file or folder for which you want to create the shortcut. For this example, click the [Start] button, click your [user name], double-click the [Videos] folder in your user folder, and then double-click the [Sample Videos] shortcut to open the Sample Videos folder.

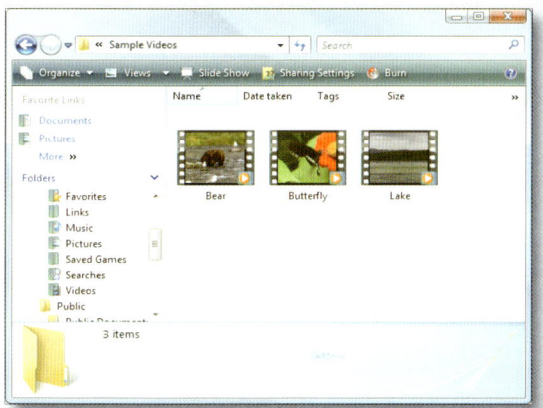

② Open a Windows Explorer window to the folder in which you want to create the shortcut. For this example, you'll use the desktop, so you don't need to open a window. Right-drag the [Bear] file from the Sample Videos window to the desktop, as shown here.

③ When you release the right mouse button, Windows displays a shortcut menu. Click the [Create Shortcuts Here] item on the menu.

④ Windows creates a shortcut named with the file's name and "Shortcut." So the shortcut in the example is named Bear - Shortcut. You can double-click the shortcut to open the file to which it refers.

81

Chapter | 4

Customizing Windows to Suit Your Needs

In this chapter you'll learn how to customize Windows to suit your needs. Windows offers many customizable settings, which can make a huge difference to your computer's behavior. Windows also includes several ease of use features, which you'll learn about at the end of the chapter.

This chapter also shows you to create user accounts so that each user of your computer can have his or her own user account, how to create a password reset disk, and how to use that password reset disk to recover from a forgotten password.

SECTION 01

Setting Up Your Screen and Desktop

In this section, you'll first choose a suitable screen resolution for your monitor so that it's easy to view. You will then set up your desktop to look the way you want by changing the desktop background and the icons that appear on it.

Choosing the Best Screen Resolution

To make Windows as easy to view as possible, you must set the correct screen resolution. The resolution is measured in pixels or picture elements, which are the dots that make up the screen. The first measurement is horizontal and the second vertical, so the 1024 X 768 resolution has 1024 pixels across the screen and 768 from top to bottom.

Setting the Correct Resolution for an LCD Screen — Note >>>

For an LCD screen, such as the screen on a laptop, you must normally use a specific resolution that matches the pixel count of the screen. The manufacturer usually states the resolution on its sales literature.

For a CRT monitor, you can usually set various resolutions. None will be as sharp as the resolution of an LCD screen, but each resolution is usable.

To set the screen resolution, follow these steps:

1. Right-click open space on the desktop, and then choose [Personalize] from the context menu. Windows opens the Personalization window. Click the [Display Settings] link near the bottom of the window.

2. Windows opens the Display Settings dialog box. If two or more monitor icons appear in the preview box, click the monitor whose resolution you want to change. Drag the Resolution slider left to decrease the resolution or right to increase it.

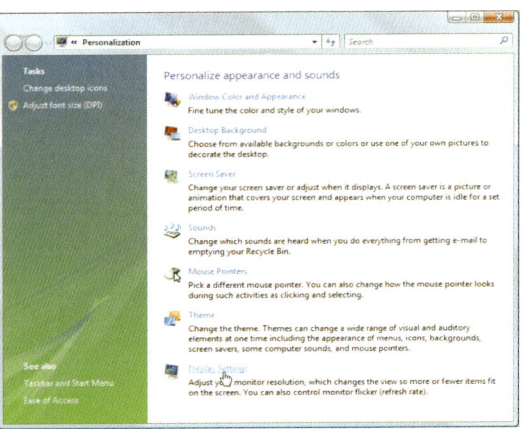

84

3. In the Colors drop-down list, select [Highest (32 Bit)], unless Windows changes the setting to Medium (16 Bit) automatically. Click the [Apply] button.

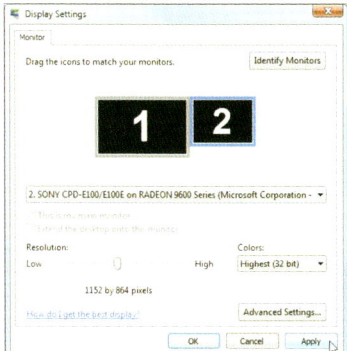

4. Windows applies the new resolution and shows the following Display Settings dialog box to verify that the setting works. If the picture looks acceptable, click the [Yes] button. If the picture is not good, either click the [No] button, or wait for the countdown timer to reach zero, at which point Windows restores the previous resolution.

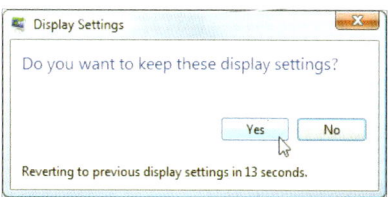

5. If the picture on a CRT monitor flickers, click the [Advanced Settings] button.

6. Windows displays the Properties dialog box for the monitor and graphics card. Click the [Monitor] tab.

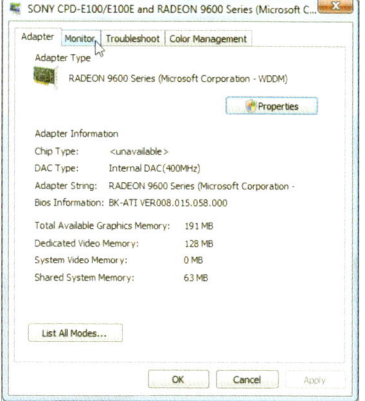

7. Windows displays the contents of the Monitor tab. In the Screen Refresh Rate drop-down list, select the highest available refresh frequently. Generally, 70 Hertz (70 cycles per second) is fast enough to eliminate flicker on medium-size CRTs and 85 Hertz is fast enough to eliminate flicker on large CRTs. Click the [Apply] button.

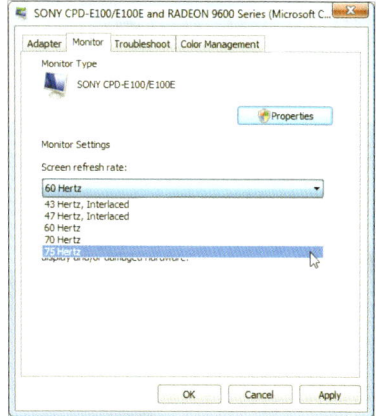

8. Windows applies the new refresh rate and shows the following Display Settings dialog box to verify the setting works. If the picture looks satisfactory, click the [Yes] button. If the picture is not good enough, either click the [No] button or wait for the countdown timer to reach zero, at which point Windows restores the previous resolution.

9. Click the [OK] button. Windows closes the Properties dialog box for the monitor and graphics card. Click the [OK] button to close the Display Settings dialog box.

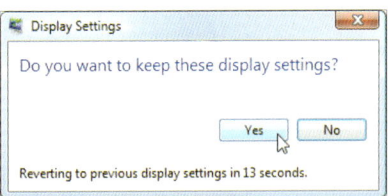

Choosing a Desktop Background

The desktop background is the picture or color that appears on your desktop. Any window you open appears in front of the desktop background.

To change the desktop background, follow these steps:

1. Right-click open space on the desktop, and then choose [Personalize] from the context menu. Windows opens the Personalization window. Click the [Desktop Background] link.

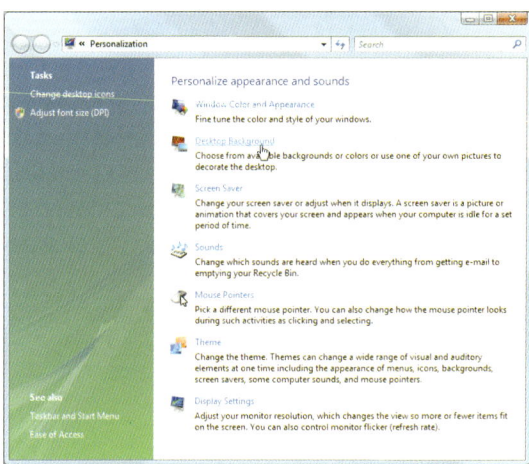

2. Windows displays the Desktop Background window. Click the [Picture Location] drop-down list, and then click the [category of pictures] you want (see Table). Windows Wallpapers is usually the best place to start, as these pictures are designed for use as backgrounds.

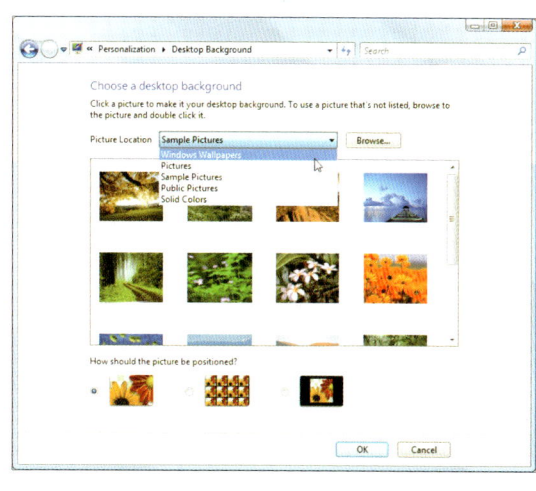

Picture Category	Explanation
Windows Wallpapers	Desktop background pictures included with Windows.
Pictures	Pictures you've placed in your Pictures folder—for example, your own photos. You can also click the Browse button to find a picture in another folder.
Sample Pictures	Pictures in the Sample Pictures folder included with Windows.
Public Pictures	Pictures you and others have placed in the Public Pictures folder on this computer—for example, shared photos.
Solid Colors	Solid colors you can use as backgrounds.

3. In the list box click the [picture] you want to use.

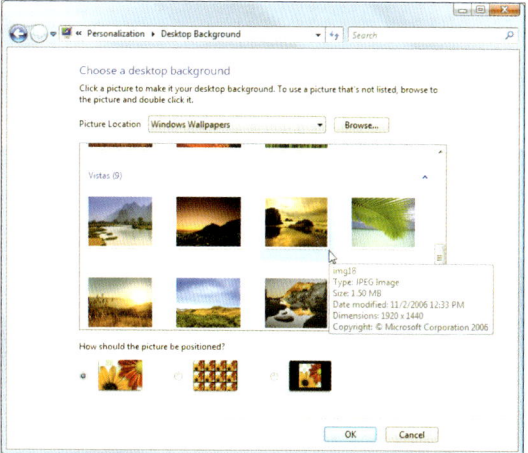

4. Windows applies it to the desktop as a preview, but you may be able to see only part of it. At the bottom of the Desktop Background window, choose one of the three option buttons for positioning the picture:

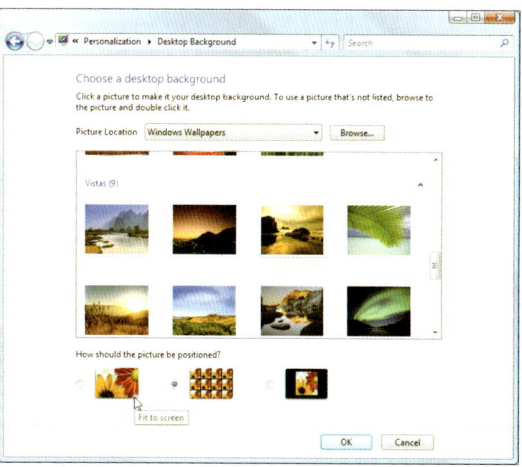

Setting	What it Does
Fit To Screen	Stretches or shrinks the picture to fit the screen
Tile	Arranges multiple copies of the picture to fill the screen. If the picture is bigger than the screen, you see only the amount of the picture that fits.
Center	Places the picture in the center of the screen with blank space around it.

5. Click the [OK] button. Windows applies the picture and closes the Desktop Background window, returning you to the Personalization window. Click the [Close] button (the [X] button). Windows closes the Personalization window.

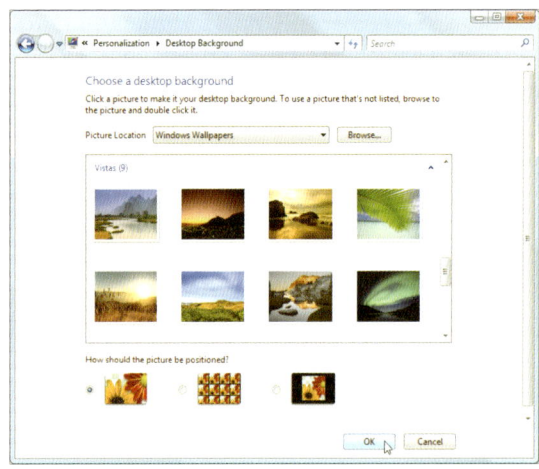

Choosing Which Items Appear on the Desktop

Windows usually shows the Recycle Bin icon on the desktop so that you can easily access the Recycle Bin, but your computer manufacturer may also have added other icons to your desktop. You can choose additional icons if you want, or remove—or hide—the existing icons.

To choose which items appear on the desktop, follow these steps:

1. Right-click open space on the desktop, and then choose [Personalize] from the context menu. Windows opens the Personalization window. In the Tasks area in the left pane, click the [Change Desktop Icons] link.

2. Windows opens the Desktop Icon Settings dialog box. Select the check box for each icon you want to display. Clear the check box for each icon you want to hide. The User's Files check box controls whether an icon with your user account name appears on the desktop.

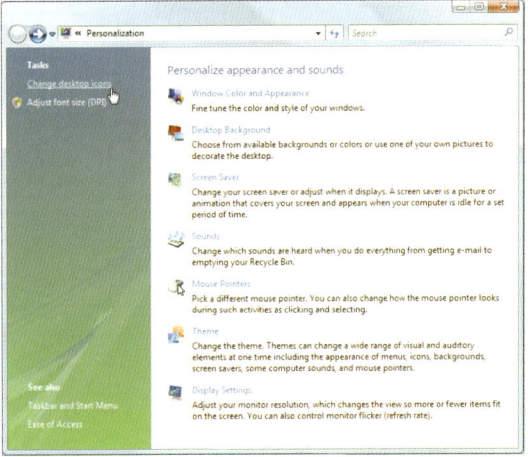

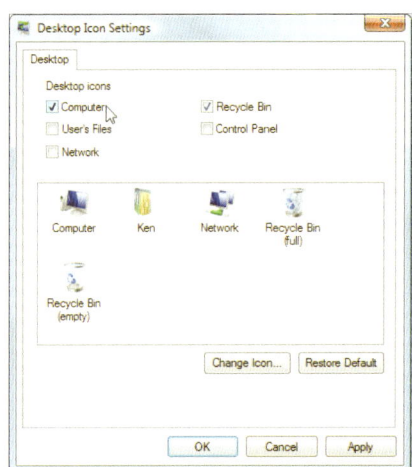

3. If you want to change the icon used for one of the items, select the item in the main box and then click the [Change Icon] button.

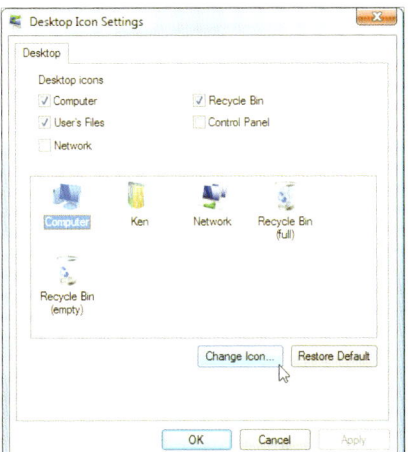

4. Windows opens the Change Icon dialog box. Click the [icon you want], and then click the [OK] button.

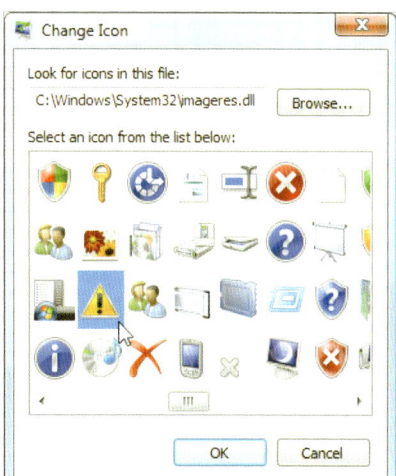

5. Windows closes the Change Icon dialog box. The Desktop Icon Settings dialog box now shows the icon you chose. Change any other icons you want by using the same method. When finished, click the [OK] button.

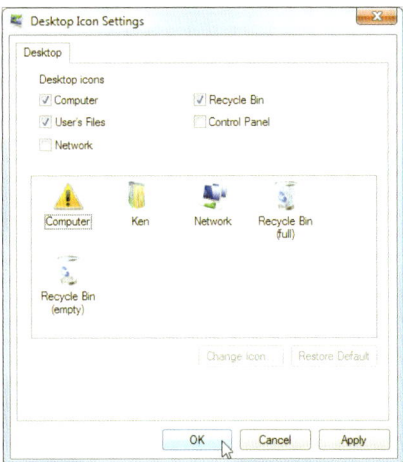

6. Windows closes the Desktop Icon Settings dialog box, and the icons you chose appear on the desktop. Click the [Close] button (the button). Windows closes the Personalization window.

Let's Go Pro!

Changing the Theme

Windows Vista includes suites of settings called themes that let you apply a different look and feel to Windows all at once. A theme can include the desktop background, sounds, custom icons, mouse pointers, and more.

Most people are better off choosing individual settings for themselves (as described in the rest of this chapter), rather than using a theme that someone else has designed. But you may come across a theme you want to try—for example, you may find a theme on the Internet, or someone may send you a theme.

To apply a theme, follow these steps:

① Save the theme to a file. For example, you could create a Themes folder in your user account folder.

② Open a Windows Explorer window to the folder in which you saved the theme, and then double-click the [theme file]. Windows Vista opens the Theme Settings dialog box and displays the theme in the Sample area.

③ Click the [OK] button. Windows closes the Theme Settings dialog box and applies the theme to your computer. Windows should now look different, and you may hear different sounds when you take certain actions—for example, when you log on or log off.

Double-clicking a theme file like this is the easy way of applying a new theme. To change the theme the normal way, follow these steps:

① Right-click open space on the desktop, and then choose [Personalize] from the context menu. Windows opens the Personalization window.

② Click the [Theme] link near the bottom of the window. Windows opens the Theme Settings dialog box.

③ In the Theme drop-down list, select the [theme] you want to apply.

④ Click the [Apply] button. Windows applies the theme.

⑤ Verify that you've chosen the theme you want. If not, change it. When satisfied, click the [OK] button. Windows closes the Theme Settings dialog box.

SECTION 02

Customizing the Taskbar, Notification Area, and Toolbars

After customizing the desktop, decide whether you want to customize the taskbar by changing its size or position, or by altering its appearance and behavior. You can also control which icons appear in the notification area and which toolbars Windows displays.

Resizing and Repositioning the Taskbar

By default Windows displays the taskbar at the bottom of the desktop and makes it one row deep. You can move it to a different side of the desktop, increase its depth, or make it hide itself.

To resize and reposition the taskbar follow these steps:

1. Right-click the taskbar anywhere no button appears, or right-click the notification area, and then click [Lock The Taskbar] to remove the check mark next to it.

2. The taskbar displays dotted divisions between its different areas. Move the mouse pointer over the border between the taskbar and the desktop so that the pointer changes into a two-headed arrow. Click and drag the border to adjust the width of the taskbar.

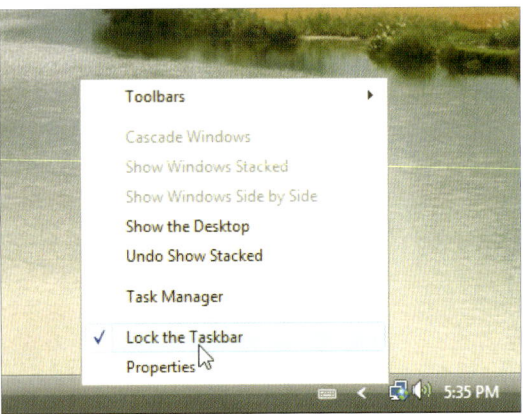

92

3. To adjust the size of one of the parts of the taskbar (for example, the notification area or the Quick Access Toolbar), move the mouse pointer over a dotted division so that the pointer changes into a two-headed arrow. Click and drag the division.

4. To move the taskbar to a different side of the desktop, click blank space in it and drag to the side of the screen you want. The next illustration shows the taskbar at the top of the desktop.

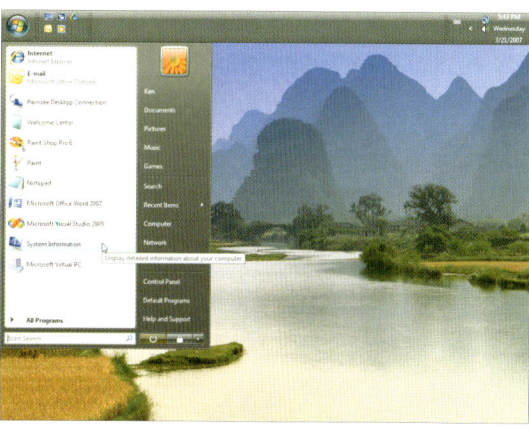

5. Once you've finished resizing and repositioning the taskbar, lock it again. Right-click the taskbar anywhere no button appears, or right-click the notification area, and then click [Lock The Taskbar] to place the check mark next to it. The taskbar removes the dotted divisions.

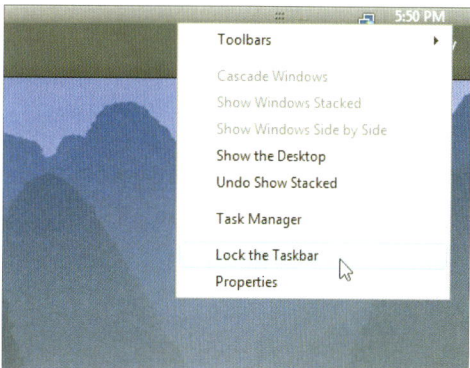

Changing the Taskbar's Appearance and Behavior

To change the taskbar's appearance and behavior, follow these steps:

1. Right-click the taskbar anywhere no button appears, or right-click the notification area, and then choose [Properties] from the context menu.

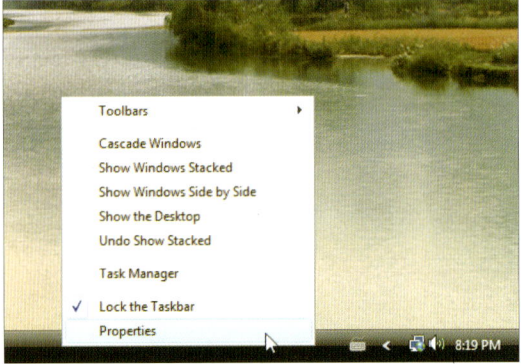

2. Windows opens the Taskbar and Start Menu Properties dialog box with the taskbar tab at the front. Select or clear the appropriate settings check boxes (see table).

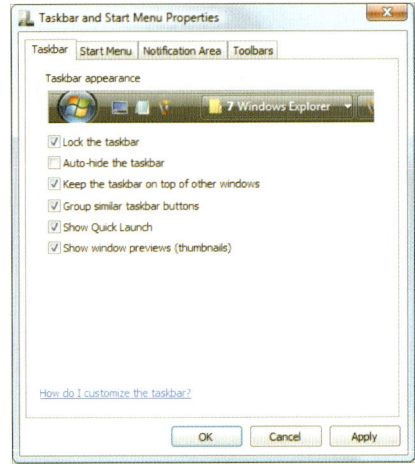

Setting	What it Controls
Lock The Taskbar	Whether or not the taskbar is locked. Normally, it's easiest to lock and unlock the taskbar by right clicking it and choosing [Lock The Taskbar] from the context menu.
Auto Hide The Taskbar	Whether the taskbar automatically hides itself, thus providing more desktop space. To display the taskbar, move the mouse pointer to the edge of the desktop where the taskbar is hiding.
Keep The Taskbar On Top Of Other Windows	Whether the taskbar appears on top of other windows (as it does by default), or whether other windows can appear on top of it.
Group Similar Taskbar Buttons	Whether Windows displays a single button for each group of related taskbar buttons when the taskbar becomes crowded—for example, one button for four Windows Explorer windows instead of four separate buttons. You click the group button to display a menu of the individual buttons.
Show Quick Launch	Whether the Quick Launch toolbar appears on the taskbar, as it does by default.
Show Window Previews (Thumbnails)	Whether Windows displays a thumbnail preview when you hover the mouse pointer over a taskbar button (Windows Aero only).

3. Click the [OK] button. Windows closes the Taskbar And Start Menu Properties dialog box and configures the taskbar as you specified.

Customizing the Notification Area Icons

The notification area at the end of the taskbar is a handy place to have frequently used icons, but so many applications put icons there that the notification area tends to get crowded. To impose order on the chaos, you can customize the icons that appear in the notification area. Follow these steps:

1. Right-click the time readout in the notification area, and then click [Properties] on the context menu. Windows opens the Taskbar And Start Menu Properties dialog box with the Notification Area tab at the front. In the Icons group box, make sure the Hide Inactive Icons check box is selected. Then click the [Customize] button.

2. Windows opens the Customize Notification Icons dialog box. For each icon, click the [Behavior] column, and then choose [Hide When Inactive], [Hide], or [Show] in the drop-down list.

3. When you've finished, click the [OK] button. Windows closes the Customize Notification Icons dialog box and returns you to the Taskbar And Start Menu Properties dialog box.

4. In the System Icons group box, select or clear the [Clock] check box, the [Volume] check box, the [Network] check box, and the [Power] check box as appropriate. The Power check box is available only for laptops. When you've finished, click the [OK] button. Windows closes the Taskbar And Start Menu Properties dialog box and displays the icons you chose in the notification area.

Displaying Desktop Toolbars

As you've seen earlier in this book, Windows Vista automatically includes the Quick Access Toolbar on the desktop for you, to give you a way of quickly launching applications. Windows also includes several other toolbars you can display on the desktop as needed. The table explains the main desktop toolbars; your installation of Windows Vista may include others.

Toolbar	Explanation
Address	Puts an Address box on the taskbar. You can type a URL to display that Web site in your default browser. You can also open a Windows Explorer window.
Windows Media Player	Puts a miniaturized version of Windows Media Player on the taskbar. See Chapter 7.
Links	Puts a Links button on the taskbar from which you can access your Internet Explorer links.
Tablet PC Input Panel	Puts a button on the taskbar that you can click to launch the Tablet PC Input Panel (for using a stylus with Windows).
Desktop	Puts a desktop toolbar on the taskbar. You can click this toolbar to access the icons on your desktop. Usually it's easier to use the icons on the desktop itself.
Quick Launch	Displays the Quick Launch toolbar, which contains icons for frequently used applications. The Quick Launch toolbar is displayed by default.
Language Bar	Displays the Language Bar, which lets you switch among different input languages.
New Toolbar	Lets you create a new toolbar from an existing folder. This can be useful if you find yourself frequently opening the same folder.

To display or hide a desktop toolbar, right-click the time readout in the notification area, highlight Toolbars on the context menu, and then click the [toolbar] you want to display or hide.

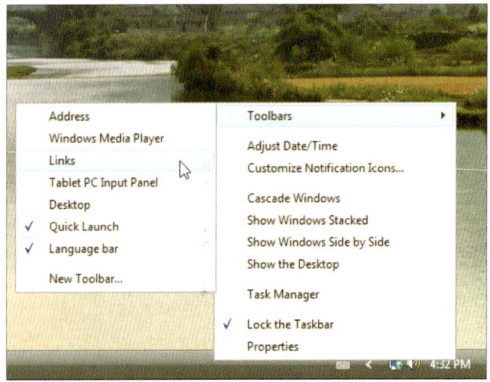

96

SECTION 03

Changing Sounds, Appearance, and the Start Menu

Your next step in customizing Windows is to choose a sound scheme that appeals to you. You may also want to change the user interface that Windows uses from Vista Aero to Vista Basic, or simply change the color and appearance of windows. You can also customize the Start menu so that it contains the items you need.

Changing the Sounds That Windows Plays

As long as your computer has a sound card and speakers or headphones, Windows gives you a lot of feedback via sound. For example, when you log on, Windows plays a sound. And when you do something that Windows considers a bad idea, it plays a warning sound.

To change the sounds that Windows plays follow these steps:

1. Right-click open space on the desktop, and then choose [Personalize] from the context menu. Windows opens the Personalization window. Click the [Sounds] link.

2. Windows opens the Sound dialog box with the Sounds tab foremost. In the Program list box, select the [item] for which you want to change the associated sound.

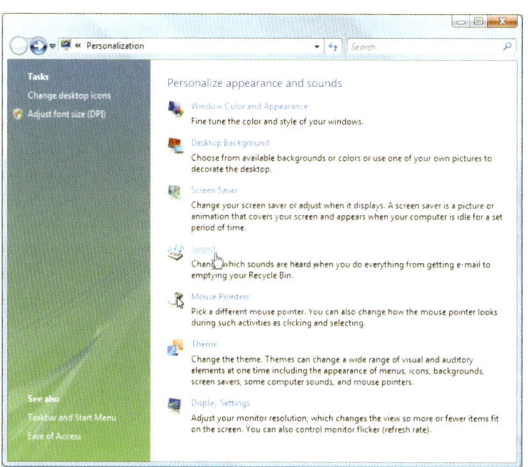

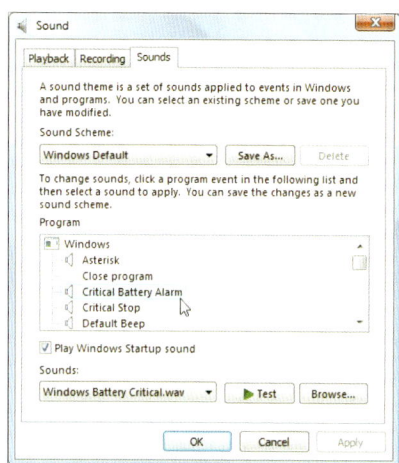

97

3. Click the [Sounds] drop-down list, and then select the [sound] you want from the list. To select a sound file that doesn't appear in the list, click the [Browse] button, use the Browse For Sound dialog box to select the [file], and then click the [Open] button. To test the selected sound, click the [Test] button.

4. Once you've changed all the sounds you want to change, you can save the sound scheme. Click the [Save As] button, type the name in the Save Scheme As dialog box, and then click the [OK] button.

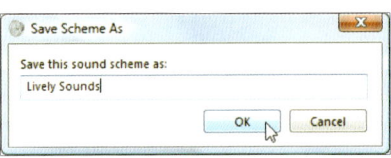

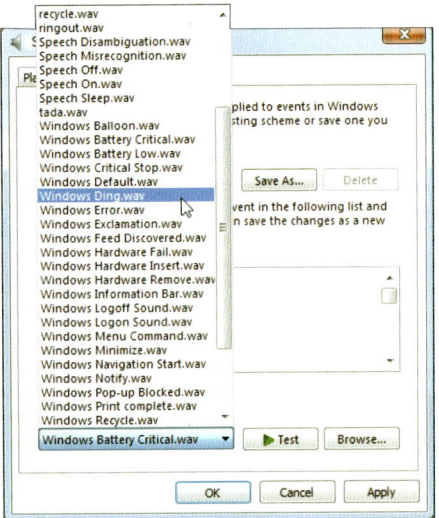

5. After saving a scheme you can reapply it from the Sound Scheme drop-down list. When you've finished changing sounds, click the [OK] button. Windows closes the Sound dialog box and uses the sounds you've chosen.

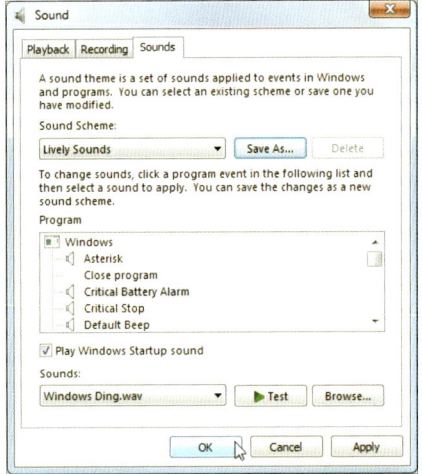

Changing from Vista Aero to Vista Basic

All versions of Windows Vista, except Home Basic, include the Vista Aero graphical interface, which is shown in most of the screens in this book. Home Basic uses the Vista Basic user interface instead, which has fewer visual effects.

If your computer's graphics card is not powerful enough to run Vista Aero, Windows automatically uses Vista Basic. You can also use Vista Basic instead of Vista Aero if you prefer a cleaner look with less eye candy.

To change from Vista Aero to Vista Basic, or vice versa, follow these steps:

1. Right-click open space on the desktop, and then choose [Personalize] from the context menu. Windows opens the Personalization window. Click the [Window Color And Appearance] link at the top of the window.

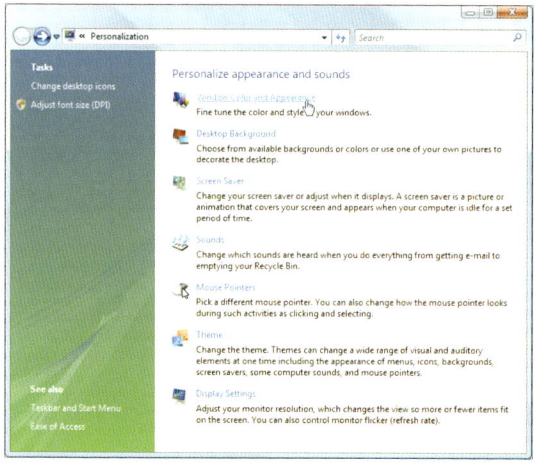

2. If you're currently using Vista Aero, Windows opens the Windows Color And Appearance window. Click the [Open Classic Appearance Properties For More Color Options] link. If you're currently using Vista Basic, Windows opens the Appearance Settings dialog box; go to step 3.

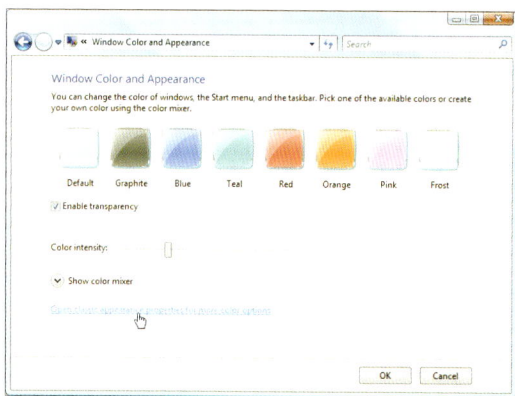

3. Windows opens the Appearance Settings dialog box. In the Color Scheme list box, select the [Windows Aero] or the [Windows Vista Basic] scheme. See the "Understanding the Other Color Schemes" sidebar for information on the other choices in this list box.

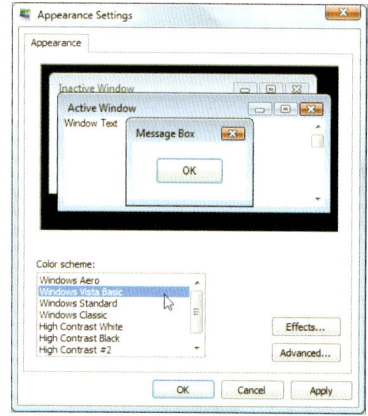

4. Click the [OK] button.

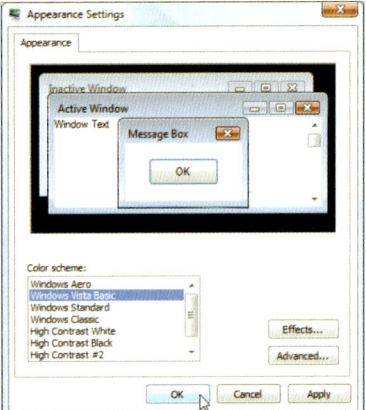

5. Windows closes the Appearance Settings dialog box and applies the color scheme you chose. The following illustration shows the Personalization window with the Windows Vista Basic color scheme applied. You can see the differences in the window borders and icons.

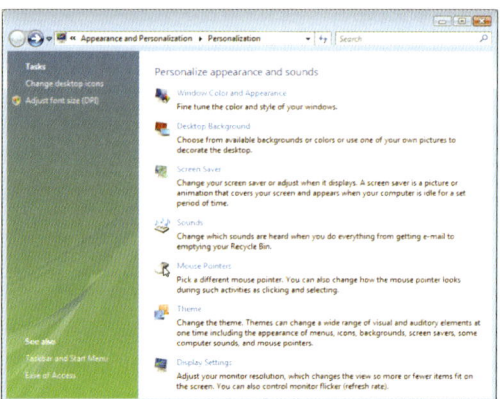

Understanding the Other Color Schemes   Note >>>

Apart from Windows Aero and Windows Vista Basic, the Appearance Settings dialog box offers several other color schemes.

Windows Standard
Applies the look of Windows 2000, with square corners on the windows.

Windows Classic
Applies the look of older versions of windows, also with square corners.

High Contrast White
Applies a high-contrast look with a white theme.

High Contrast Black
Applies a high-contrast look with a black theme.

High Contrast #2
Applies a high-contrast look with bright colors.

High Contrast #1
Applies a high-contrast look with other bright colors.

The High Contrast schemes are helpful if you need to use your computer in difficult lighting conditions—for example, in sunlight.

Changing the Window Color and Appearance

Whether you use Vista Aero or Vista Basic, you can also change the color and appearance of windows. To change the look of windows, follow these steps:

1. Right-click open space on the desktop, and then choose [Personalize] from the context menu. Windows opens the Personalization window. Click the [Window Color And Appearance] link at the top of the window.

2. If you're using Vista Aero, Windows opens the Windows Color And Appearance window, as shown next. If you're using Vista Basic, Windows opens the Appearance Settings dialog box; go to step 9. At the top of the window, click the [color] you want to apply to windows. Windows applies the color as a preview.

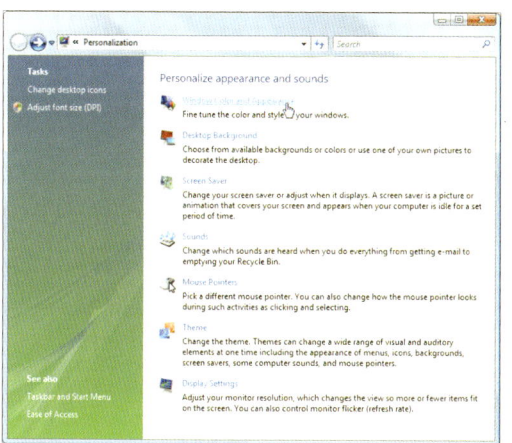
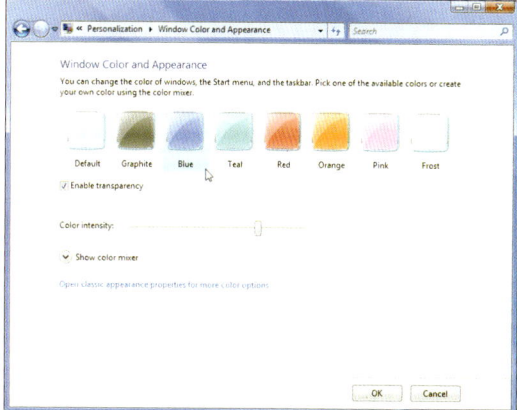

3. If you want the desktop background, or other windows, to show through the foreground window's title bar and frame, select the [Enable Transparency] check box. In the next illustration, which has transparency enabled, notice how the desktop background and the notepad window show through the title bar and frame of the Window Color And Appearance window.

4. To increase the color intensity, drag the Color Intensity slider to the right. To decrease it, drag the slider to the left.

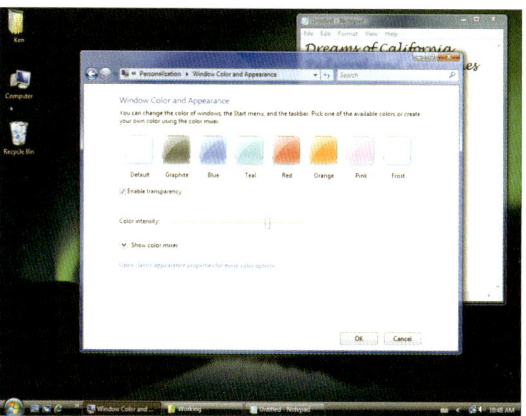
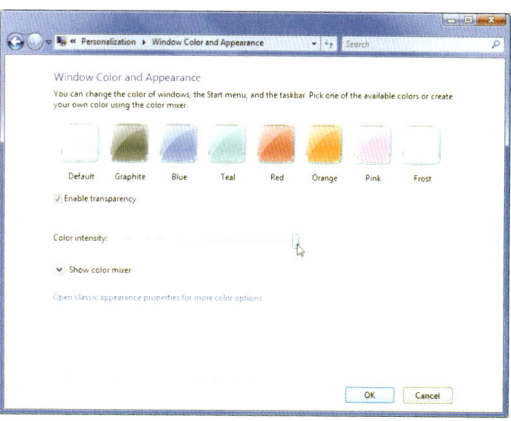

5. If you want to change the colors, click the [Show Color Mixer] button, and then drag the Hue slider, Saturation slider, and Brightness slider to produce the color you want. When you've finished, click the [Hide Color Mixer] button to hide the color mixer again.

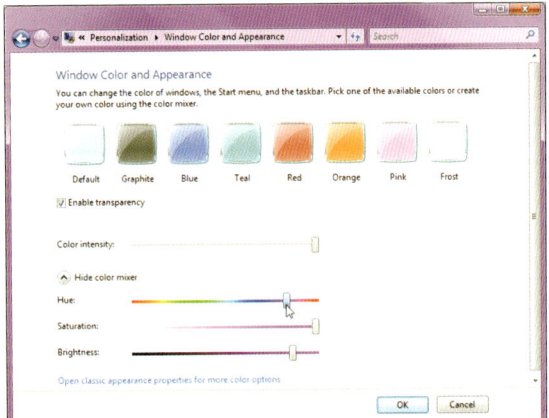

6. To make further changes, click the [Open Classic Appearance Properties For More Color Options] link.

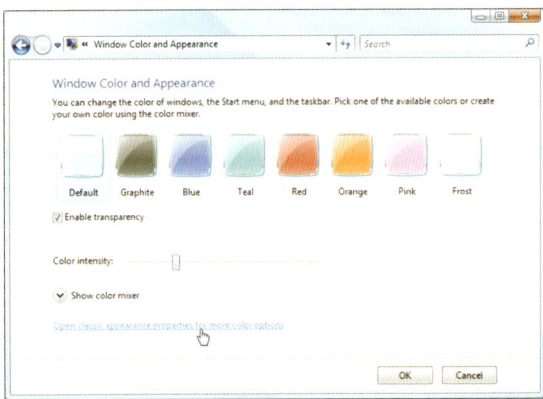

7. Windows opens the Appearance Settings dialog box. Click the [Effects] button.

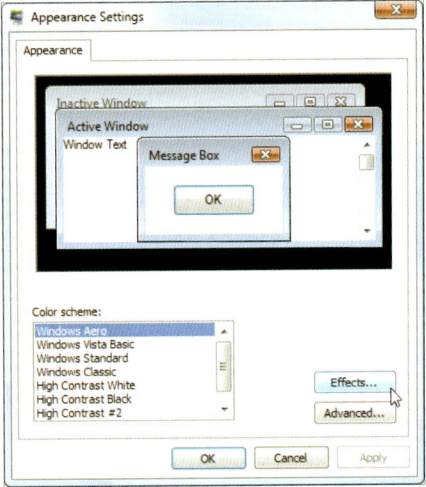

8. Windows opens the Effects dialog box, in which you can choose the following settings. Click the [OK] button when finished.

① **Font Smoothing**—If you want to smooth fonts, select the [Use The Following Method To Smooth Edges Of Screen Fonts] check box. Click the drop-down list, and select [ClearType] if your computer has an LCD screen or [Standard] if it has a CRT.

② **Shadows Under Menus**—Select the [Show Shadows Under Menus] check box if you want Windows to display these shadows..

③ **Window Contents**—Select the [Show Windows Contents While Dragging] check box if you want to see the contents of a window while you drag it around your screen. Clear this check box if you're content with seeing only the window frame while you drag it.

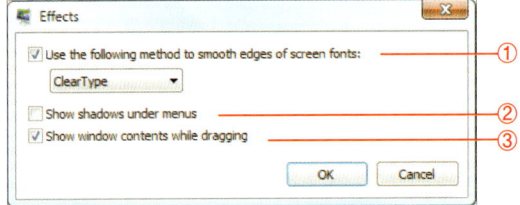

9. In the Appearance Settings dialog box, click the [Advanced] button. Windows displays the Advanced Appearance dialog box. In the preview area at the top, click the [item] you want to change—for example, the title bar of the window named Active Window. Alternatively, select the item from the Item drop-down list.

10. You can then use the controls at the bottom of the dialog box to change the item's appearance. For example, you might change the font color, as shown next.

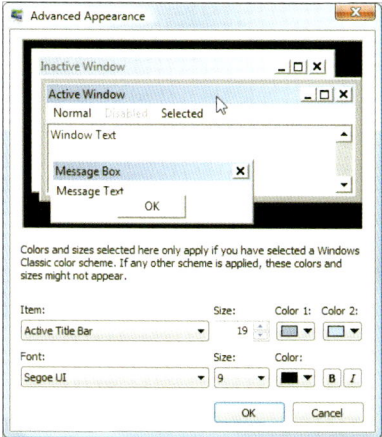

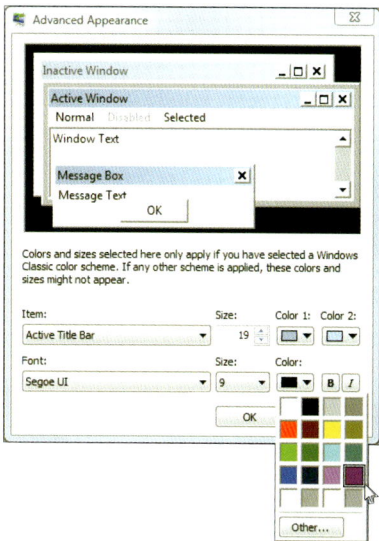

11. When you've finished changing the appearance of windows, click the [OK] button to close the Advanced Appearance dialog box, and then click the [OK] button to close the Appearance Settings dialog box. You can make substantial changes to the way Windows looks—although your choices may not appeal to other people.

103

Changing the Screen Saver and Power Settings

After your computer has been left unused for a number of minutes, Windows can automatically run a screen saver, power off the monitor or hard drive, or take other power-saving actions. To configure these settings, follow these steps:

1. Right-click open space on the desktop, and then choose [Personalize] from the context menu. Windows opens the Personalization window. Click the [Screen Saver] link.

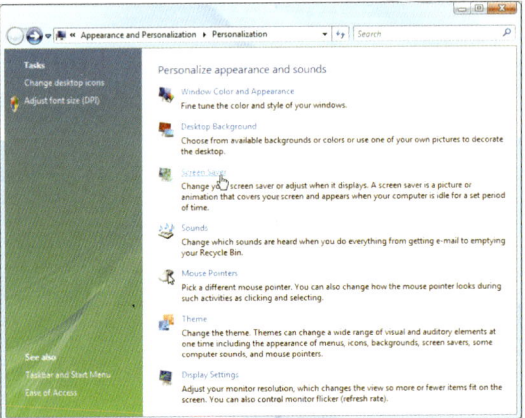

2. Windows opens the Screen Saver Settings dialog box. Click the [Screen Saver] button and then select the screen saver you want from the drop-down list.

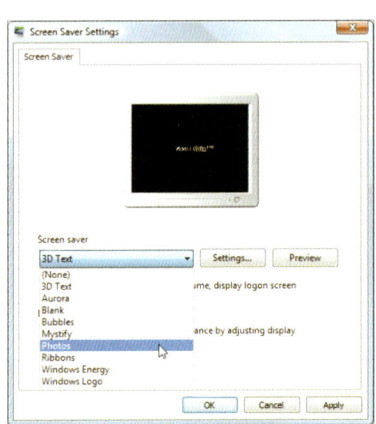

3. After a few seconds the preview screen displays a sample of the screen save. You can get a full-screen preview by clicking the [Preview] button; click anywhere to cancel the preview. For some screen savers you can configure options by clicking the [Settings] button and working in the resulting dialog box. In the Wait box, set the number of minutes Windows should wait before starting the screen saver.

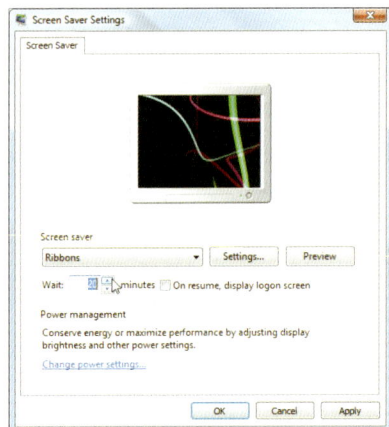

4. In the Power Management box, click the [Change Power Settings] link.

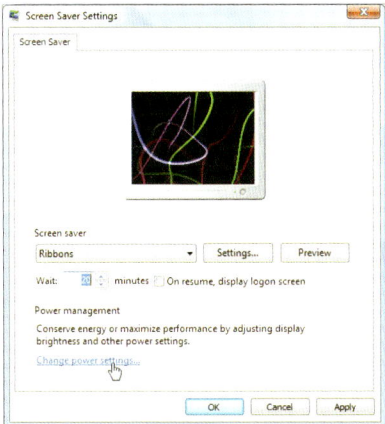

5. Windows opens the Power Options window. In the Preferred Plans area, click the [option] button for the power plan you want: Balanced (which balances energy savings with performance), Power Saver, or High Performance.

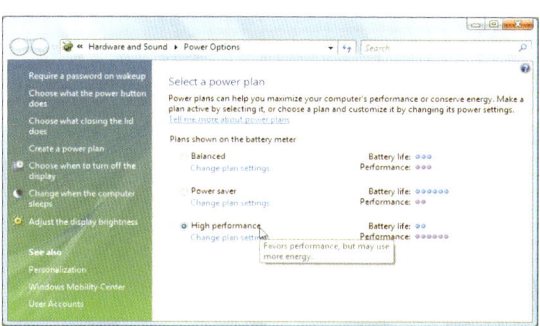

tip>>

Make Windows Display the Logon Screen for Security

If you want Windows to display the logon screen when someone interrupts the screen saver, select the [On Resume, Display Logon Screen] check box. This setting is good for security.

6. Click the [Change Plan Settings] link below the plan name.

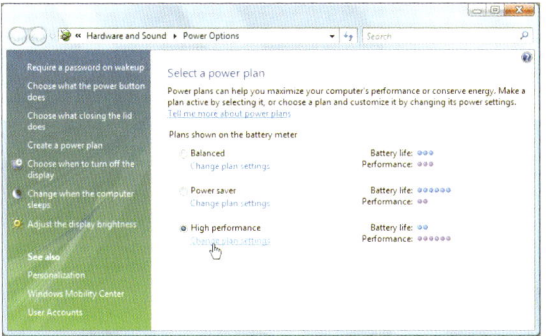

7. Windows displays the Edit Plan Settings window. Choose a suitable length of time in the Turn Off The Display drop-down list and the Put The Computer To Sleep drop-down list. For a laptop computer, you can choose settings both for when it is running on its battery and when it is plugged in. For a laptop computer you can also adjust the display brightness.

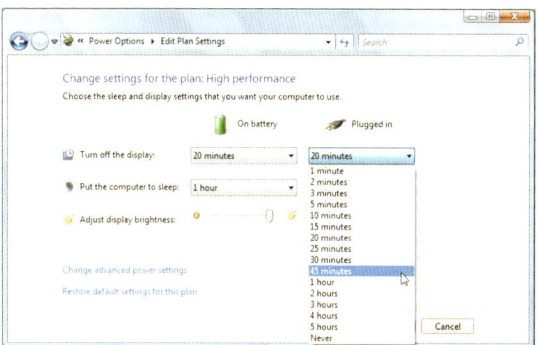

tip>>

Laptops Have More Power Settings

The screens shown in this section are for a laptop computer. A desktop computer does not have the Choose What Closing The Lid Does link, the Adjust The Display Brightness link, or the Windows Mobility Center link in the left pane of the Power Options window.

8. Click the [Save Changes] button. Windows saves the changes and closes the Edit Plan Settings window, returning you to the Power Options window. Click the [Close] button (the button) in the upper-right corner to close the window.

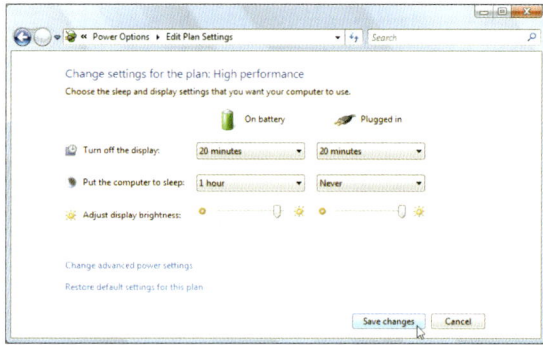

Choosing Advanced Power Settings

Note >>>

For most computers, you'll need to set only the power settings described in the main text of the book. But Windows also provides advanced power settings that you may want to set when you need to get the best possible performance out of your computer, or the longest possible battery life out of your laptop.

To reach these power settings, click the [Change Advanced Power Settings] link in the Edit Plan Settings window for your power plan. Windows opens the Power Options dialog box. You can then expand one of the categories and work with the settings inside it. For example, click the [+] sign next to Processor Power Management to display its contents, and then click the [+] sign next to Minimum Processor State. You can then set the minimum processor state for the computer.

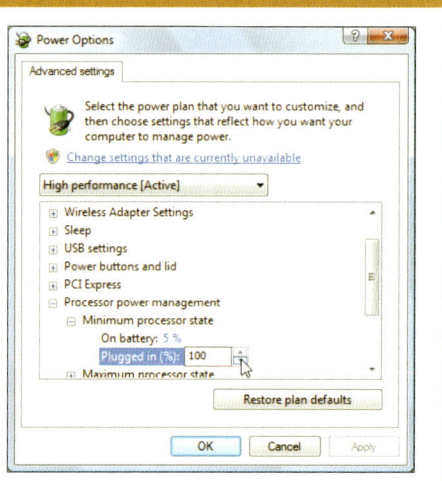

Changing Your User Picture

Windows automatically assigns a picture to each user account you create, apart from the first account, for which it lets you choose a picture. To change the picture for your user account follow these steps:

1. Click the [Start] button, and then click [your picture] at the top of the Start menu. Windows opens a User Accounts window. Click the [Change Your Picture] link.

2. Windows opens the Change Your Picture window. In the list box click [the picture you want]. To find another picture, click the [Browse For More Pictures] link, use the resulting Open dialog box to select the picture, and then click the [Open] button. Once you've chosen the picture, click the [Change Picture] button.

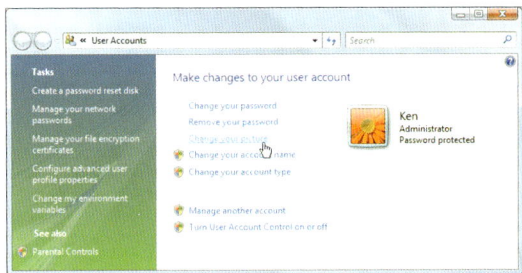

3. Windows applies the picture to your user account and returns you to the User Accounts window, which shows your new picture. Click the [Close] button (the button).

107

Customizing the Start Menu

The Start menu is vital for launching applications and opening Windows Explorer windows, and Windows lets you customize the Start menu so that it contains the items you need.

To customize the Start menu follow these steps:

1. Right-click the [Start] button, and then click [Properties] on the context menu. Windows opens the Taskbar And Start Menu Properties dialog box with the Start Menu page at the front. In the Privacy area, select the [Store And Display A List Of Recently Opened Files] check box and the [Store And Display A List Of Recently Open Programs] check box if you find this behavior helpful. If you see it as a security threat, clear these check boxes. Then click the upper [Customize] button.

2. Windows displays the Customize Start Menu dialog box. In the main list box choose which items to display on the Start menu and how to display them. For example, you can choose to display the Computer item as a link that opens a Computer window, as a menu that lets you browse folders from the Start menu, or not at all. If you mess up, you can click the [Use Default Settings] button to restore the original settings.

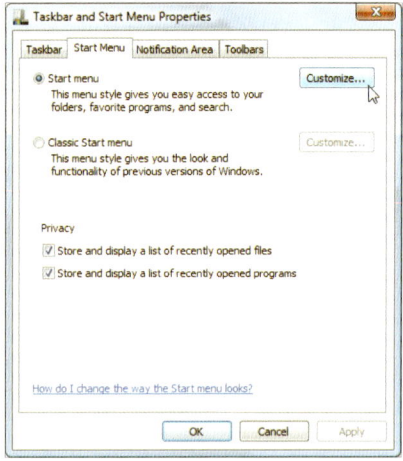

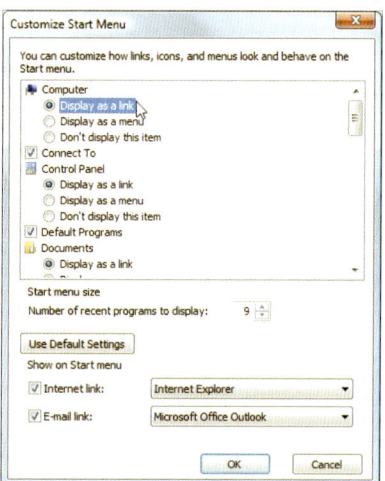

3. In the Start Menu Size area, increase or decrease the Number Of Recent Programs To Display setting. Having more applications on the Start menu can be helpful if you run many applications and have a large monitor.

4. In the Show On Start Menu area, choose whether to have an Internet Link and an E-mail Link and, if so, which applications they should run. Then click the [OK] button to close each dialog box.

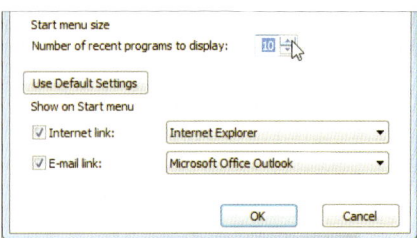

SECTION 04

Managing User Accounts and Passwords

It's best to create a separate user account for each person who uses the computer. Each person can then keep their files and settings separate from those of other users. You should apply a password to each account to prevent unauthorized access.

Creating a User Account

To create a user account, follow these steps:

1. Click the [Start] button, and then click [your picture] at the top of the Start menu. Windows opens a User Accounts window. Click the [Manage Another Account] link, and then go through User Account Control for the User Accounts Control Panel feature.

2. Windows opens the Manage Accounts window. Click the [Create A New Account] link.

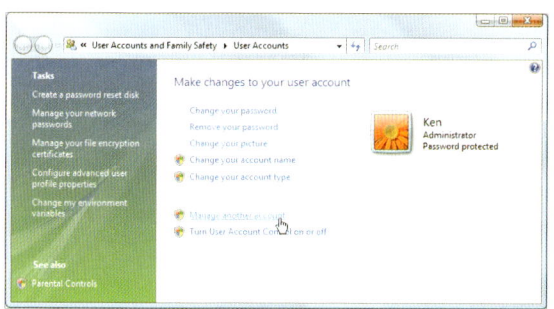

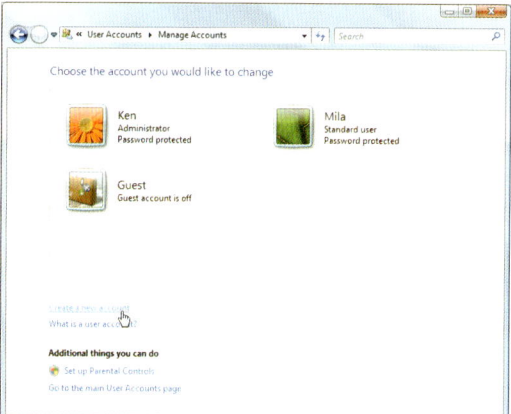

3. Windows opens the Create New Account window. Type the name for the user in the Name box at the top of the window. Select the [Standard User] option button or the [Administrator] option button as appropriate. (See the sidebar "Understanding the Differences Between Standard Users and Administrators" for details on the differences.) Then click the [Create Account] button.

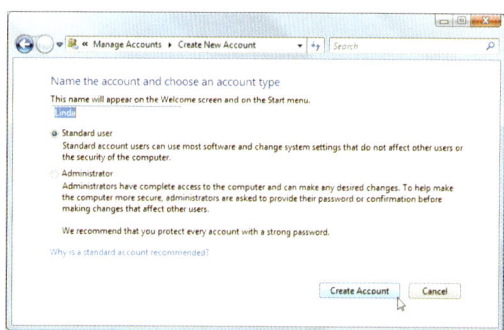

4. Windows creates the account and returns you to the Manage Accounts window, which now lists the account. To apply a password to the account, click the [account name].

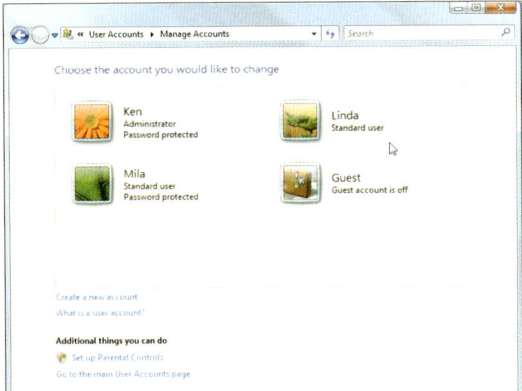

5. Windows opens the Change An Account window for the user account. Click the [Create A Password] link.

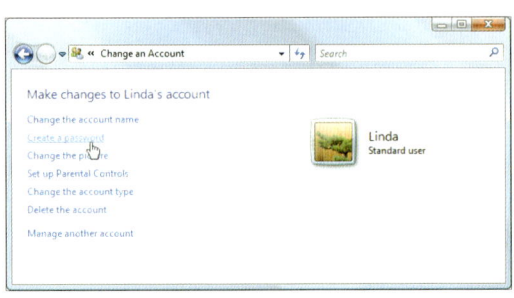

6. Windows opens the Create Password window. Type the password in the two boxes, and type a password hint if you consider it a good idea. (Normally, a password hint is not a good idea.) Then click the [Create Password] button.

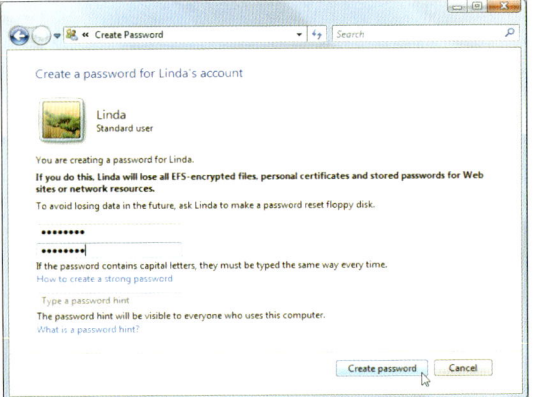

7. Windows creates the password and returns you to the Change An Account window, which now shows that the account is password protected. Click the [Close] button (the ![x] button). Windows closes the window.

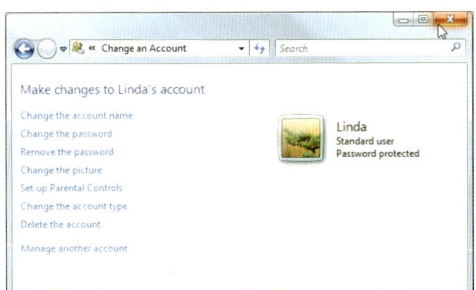

8. After the user logs in to the account, he or she should change the password so that you do not know the account's password. To change the password the user should click the [Start] button, click their [user picture], and then click the [Change Your Password] link in the User Accounts window.

> ### Understanding the Differences Between Standard Users and Administrators — Note >>>
>
> Windows Vista has three types of users for stand-alone computers: Administrator, Standard User, and Guest.
> Administrators can make systemwide changes to the computer, such as installing hardware or applications, and can go through User Account Control for any feature. Each computer must have at least one Administrator user, so Windows creates the first account (which you make while setting up Windows) as an Administrator.
> A Standard User can make changes to his or her own account but cannot make systemwide changes.
> The Guest account can make very few changes. Windows creates the Guest account automatically on setup, but leaves it turned off. You can turn it on when you need to allow a guest to use the computer.

Deleting a User Account

If you no longer need a user account, you can delete it. Follow these steps:

1. Click the [Start] button, and then click [your picture] at the top of the Start menu. Windows opens a User Accounts window. Click the [Manage Another Account] link, and then go through [User Account Control] for the User Accounts Control Panel feature.

2. Windows opens the Manage Accounts window. Click the [account you want to delete].

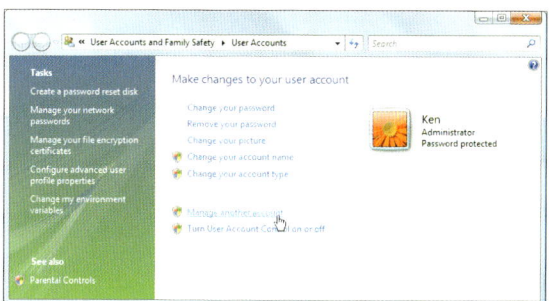

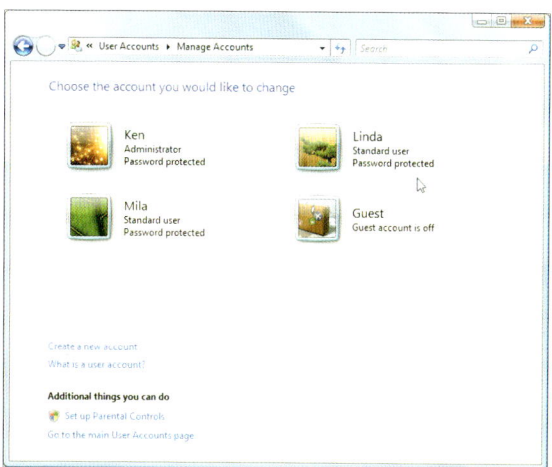

3. Windows opens the Change An Account window. Click the [Delete The Account] link.

4. Windows opens the Delete Account window, which gives you the option of keeping or deleting a user's files. If you want to keep the files, click the [Keep Files] button. If you want to delete the files, click the [Delete Files] button, as shown here.

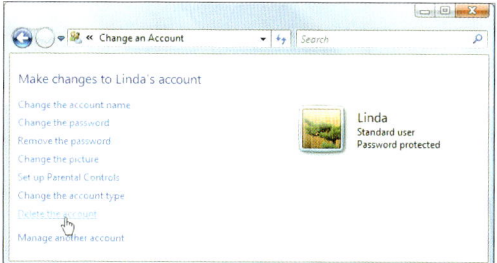

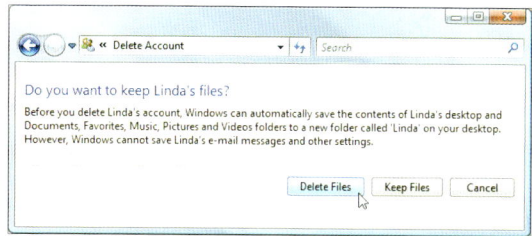

5. Windows opens the Confirm Deletion window. Click the [Delete Account] button. Windows deletes the user account and returns you to the Manage Accounts window. Click the [Close] button (the ⊠ button).

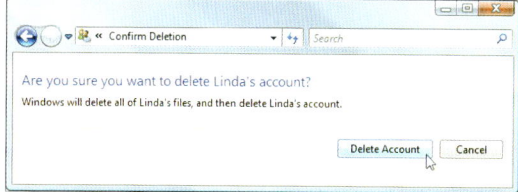

Creating a Password Reset Disk

Creating a strong password (as described earlier in this chapter) helps protect your user account—but if you forget that password you will not be able to log on. To give yourself a way around this problem, create a password reset disk, a floppy disk or USB drive containing a tool for resetting your password.

To create a password reset disk, insert a floppy disk or USB drive in your computer, and then follow these steps:

1. Click the [Start] button, and then click [your picture] at the top of the Start menu. Windows opens a User Accounts window. In the Tasks pane on the left, click the [Create A Password Reset Disk] link.

2. Windows launches the Forgotten Password Wizard. Click the [Next] button to reach the Create A Password Reset Disk screen. In the I Want To Create A Password Key Disk In The Following Drive drop-down list, choose the [drive you want] to use. (The wizard may already have selected the correct drive.) Click the [Next] button.

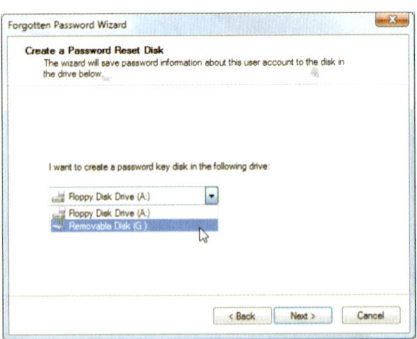

3. The wizard displays the Current User Account Password screen. Type your current password, and then click the [Next] button.

4. The wizard creates the password reset disk. Click the [Next] button. The wizard displays its final screen. Click the [Finish] button, remove the disk, and then store it safely.

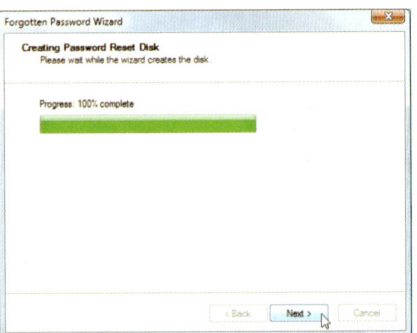

tip »

Creating Strong Passwords

To create a strong password, use at least six characters that include both uppercase and lowercase letters, one or more symbols, and one or more numbers. Never use a real word and never create a password hint.

Resetting a Password

After you've created a password reset disk, as described in the previous section, you can reset your password if you forget it. Follow these steps:

1. When your logon fails with the message "The User Name Or Password Is Incorrect," click the [OK] button.

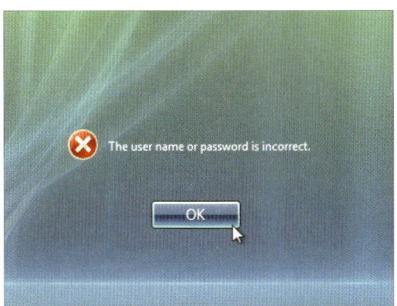

2. Windows displays the logon screen again, but this time with the Reset Password link. Click the [Reset Password] link.

3. Windows launches the Password Reset Wizard, which displays its first screen. Click the [Next] button to move along to the Insert The Password Reset Disk screen. Insert your password reset disk. In The Password Key Disk Is In The Following Drive drop-down list, select the [correct drive]. (The wizard may already have selected the drive.) Click the [Next] button.

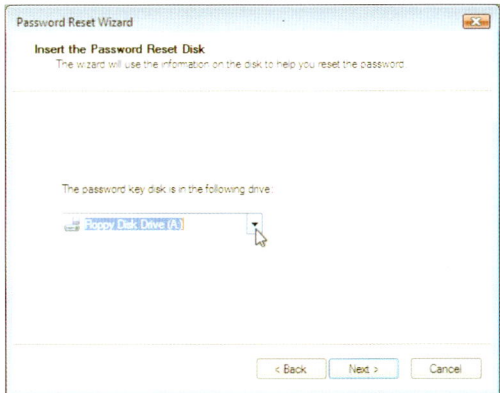

4. The wizard displays the Reset The User Account Password screen. Type a new password in the Type A New Password box and the Type The Password Again To Confirm box. You can also type a new password hint, but this is never a good idea. Click the [Next] button.

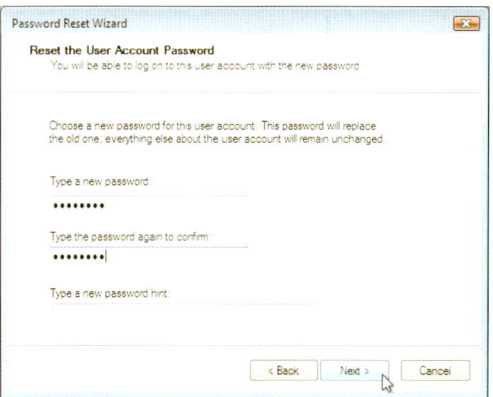

5. The wizard displays the Completing The Password Reset Wizard screen. Click the [Finish] button. Remove your password reset disk (you don't need to update it) and store it somewhere safe. Type your new password in the password box on the logon screen, and then press <Enter> or click the [arrow button].

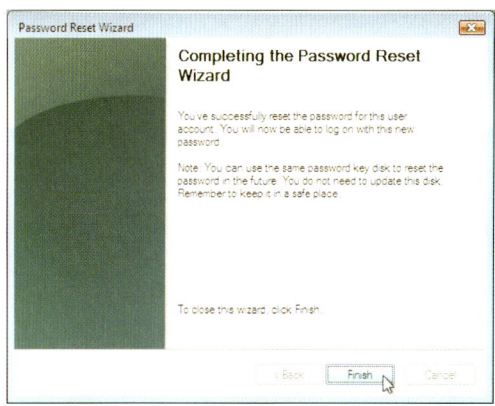

SECTION 05 — Using Parental Controls and Activity Reports

If your children use your computer, you may want to apply parental controls that restrict what they can do and allow you to monitor their actions. You can apply parental controls only to Standard User accounts. After applying parental controls, you can view activity reports to see which programs your children have used, which Web sites they have visited, and so on.

Applying Parental Controls

To apply parental controls, follow these steps:

1. Click the [Start] button, and then click [your picture] at the top of the Start menu. Windows opens a User Accounts window. In the See Also area of the Tasks pane on the left, click the [Parental Controls] link, and then go through User Account Control for the Parental Controls feature.

2. Windows opens the Parental Controls window. Click the [name of the user] for whom you want to apply parental controls.

3. Windows opens the User Controls window, which summarizes the restrictions applied to the user. Select the [On, Enforce Current Settings] option button in the Parental Controls area. If you want to monitor the user's activities, select the [On, Collect Information About Computer Usage] option button. Then click the [Windows Vista Web Filter] link.

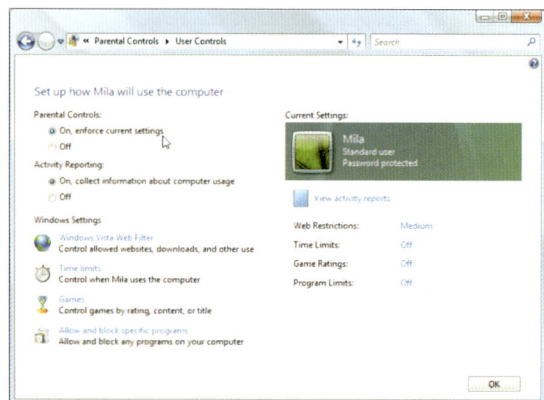

4. Windows opens the Web Restrictions window. If you want to allow or block particular Web sites, select the [Block Some Websites Or Content] option button, and then click the [Edit The Allow And Block List] link.

5. Windows opens the Allow Block Webpages window. Create the list of allowed and blocked Web sites by typing each address in the Website Address box in turn and then clicking the [Allow] button or [Block] button, as appropriate. You can also import a list of allowed and blocked sites if someone has given you a file containing such a list. Click the [OK] button.

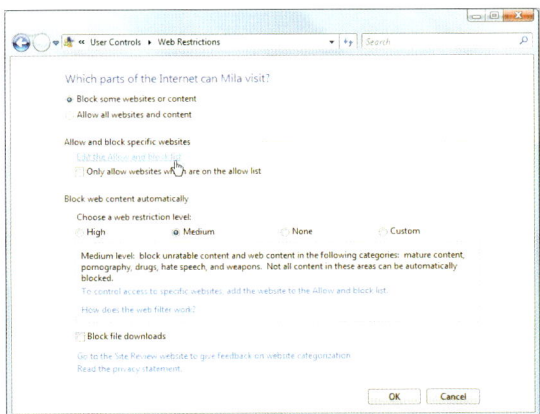

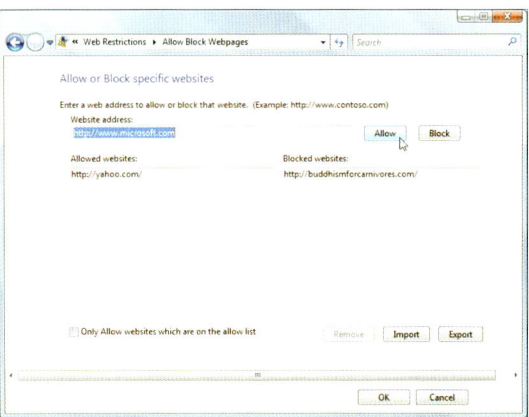

6. Windows closes the Allow Block Webpages window and returns you to the Web Restrictions window. If you want the user to be able to access only those Web sites you placed on the Allow list, select the [Only Allow Websites Which Are On The Allow List] check box. Otherwise, you can block Web content automatically based on Windows' built-in criteria by clicking the [High] option button, [Medium] option button, [None] option button, or [Custom] option button. If you choose the Custom option button, select the check box for each content category you want to block, as shown here.

7. If you want to prevent the user from downloading files from Web sites, select the [Block File Downloads] check box. This is a good security measure, but many users will find it excessively restrictive. Click the [OK] button.

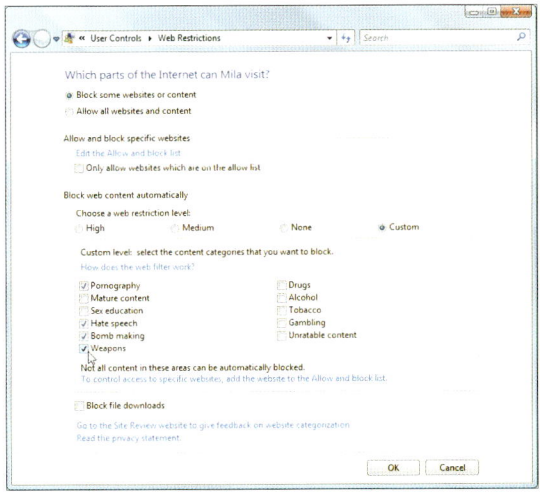

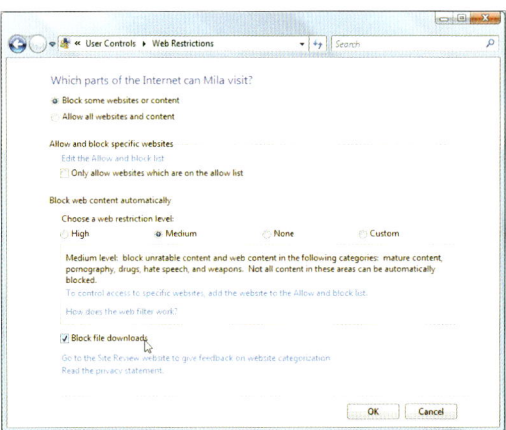

8. Windows closes the Web Restrictions window and returns you to the User Controls window, which shows that Web restrictions are applied. Click the [Time Limits] link.

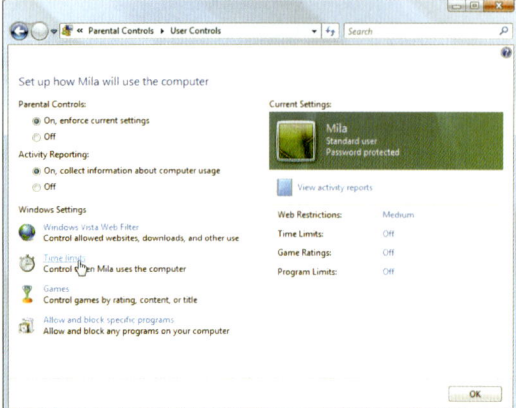

9. Windows displays the Time Restrictions window. Click or drag through the hours you want to block, turning them blue and leaving the allowed hours white. Click the [OK] button.

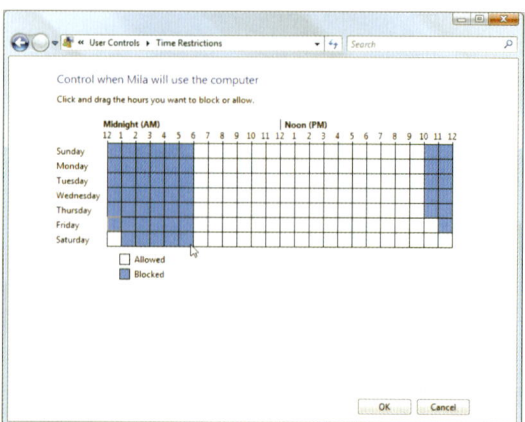

10. Windows closes the Time Restrictions window and returns you to the User Controls window, which shows that time restrictions are applied. Click the [Games] link.

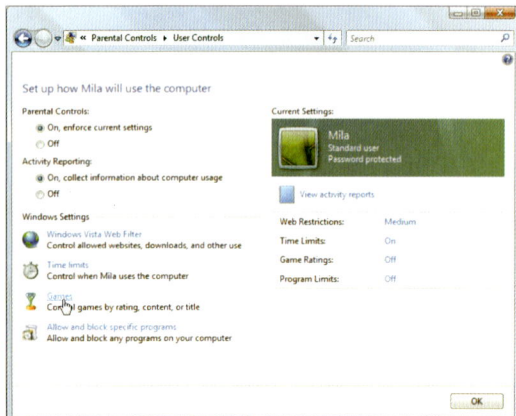

11. Windows displays the Game Controls window. If you want to block all games, select the [No] option button at the top of the window, and then go to step 16. To permit some games, select the [Yes] option button, and then click the [Set Game Ratings] link.

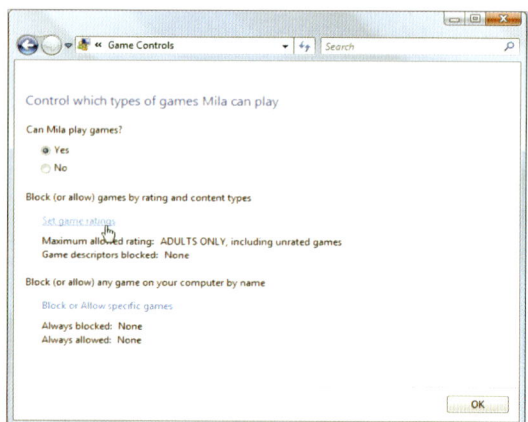

12. Windows displays the Game Restrictions window. In the If A Game Has No Rating area, select the [Allow Games With No Rating] option button or the [Block Games With No Rating] option button as appropriate. In the rest of the window, choose the option button for the allowable ratings—Early Childhood, Everyone, Everyone 10+, Teen, Mature, or Adults Only—and then select the check box for each type of content you want to block (for example, Drug Reference or Real Gambling). Click the [OK] button.

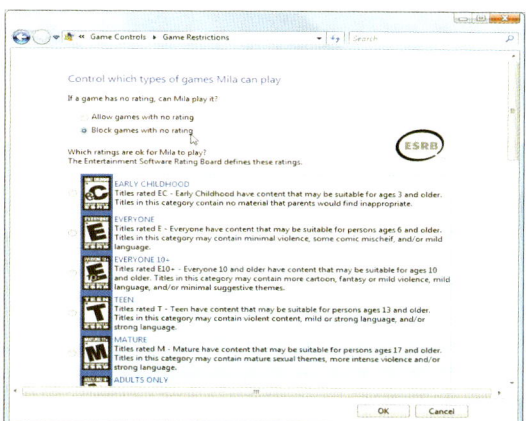

13. Windows closes the Game Restrictions window and returns you to the Game Controls window. If you want to allow or block particular games, click the [Block Or Allow Specific Games] link.

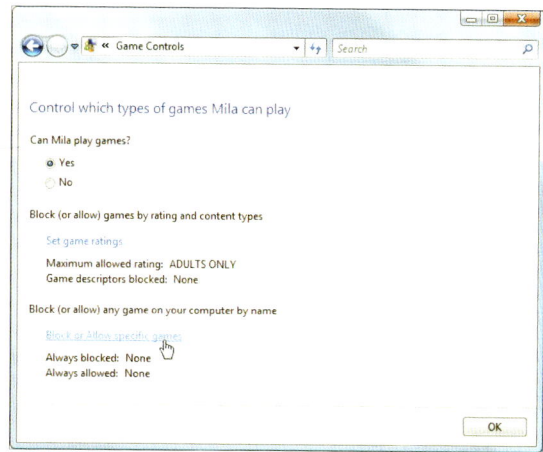

14. Windows opens the Game Overrides window, which lists the games currently installed on your computer. For each game select the [User Rating Setting] option button (to have the user rating control whether the user can play the game), the [Always Allow] option button, or the [Always Block] option button. When you've finished click the [OK] button. Windows closes the Game Overrides window, returning you to the Game Controls window. Click the [OK] button.

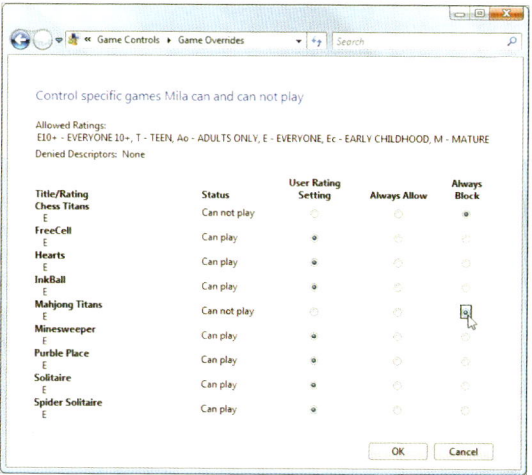

15. Windows closes the Game Controls window and returns you to the User Controls window, which shows a summary of the game restrictions. To control whether a user may or may not use certain applications, click the [Allow And Block Specific Programs] link.

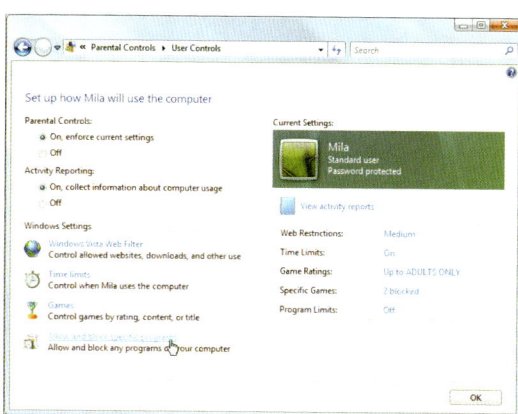

16. Windows opens the Application Restrictions window. At the top of the window, select the [User Can Use Only The Programs I Allow] check box. In the list box, select the check box for each application the user may use. Click the [OK] button.

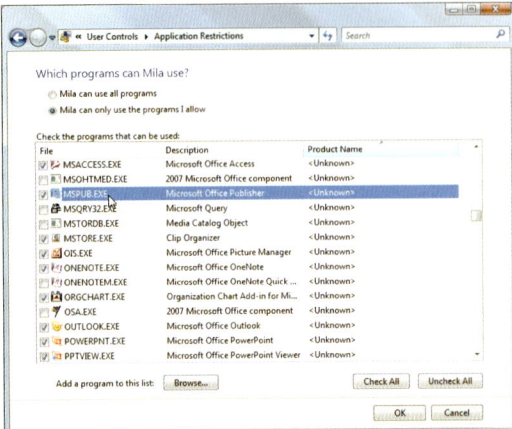

17. Windows closes the Application Restrictions window and returns you to the User Controls window, which shows a summary of the application restrictions. Click the [OK] button.

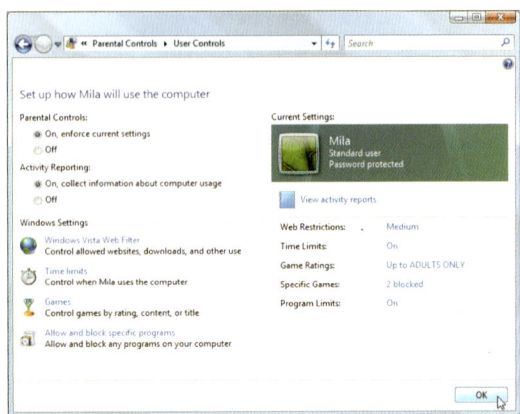

18. Windows closes the User Controls window, returning you to the Parental Controls window. If you chose to monitor the user's activity, click the [Family Safety Options] link in the left pane. Windows opens the Family Safety Options window.

19. Select the [frequency of reminders]—Weekly, Every Day, or Never—and then click the [OK] button. Windows closes the Family Safety Options window and returns you to the Parental Controls window. Click the [Close] button (the ![X] button).

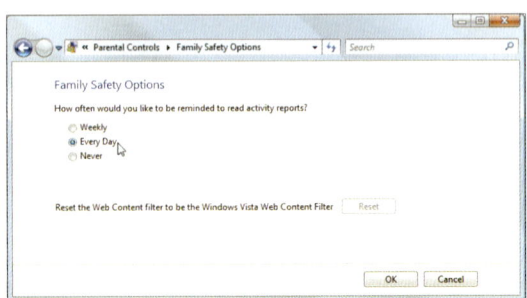

Getting Activity Reports for a User

To get activity reports for a user to whose account you've applied parental controls and activity logging, follow these steps:

1. Click the [Start] button, and then click [your picture] at the top of the Start menu. Windows opens a User Accounts window. In the See Also area of the Tasks pane on the left, click the [Parental Controls] link, and then go through User Account Control for the Parental Controls feature.

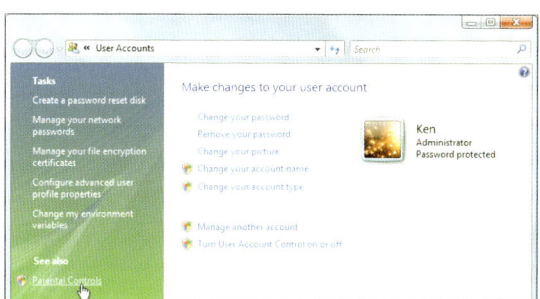

2. Windows opens the Parental Controls window. Click the [icon for the user's account].

3. Windows opens the User Controls window for the user. Click the [View Activity Reports] link.

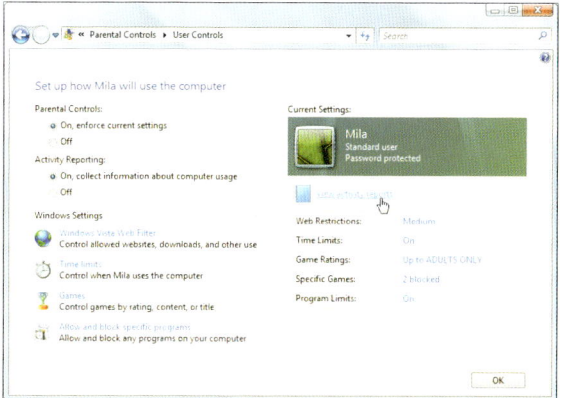

4. Windows opens the Activity Viewer window for the user. Expand the category of item you want to review, and then click the subcategory to see the items it contains. For example, you can click the [Web Browsing] category and then click the [Web sites Blocked] subcategory to see information on which blocked Web sites the user tried to view. Click the [Close] button (the [X] button) when you've finished reviewing the user's activities.

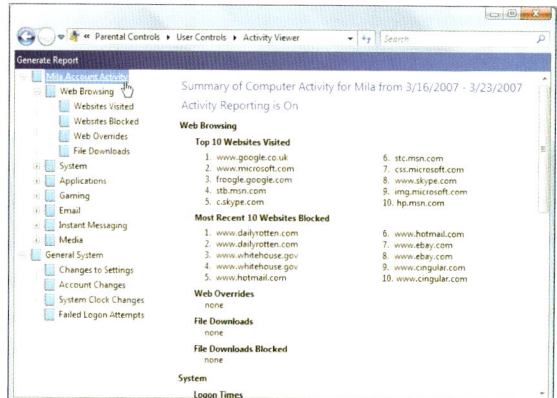

Working with Parental Controls On — Note >>>

When you apply parental controls to a user's account, discuss the matter with the user so that they understand why you've applied the controls, what the controls do, and what you'll see in the activity reports if you're monitoring the user's actions.

When parental controls are on, a Parental Controls icon appears in the notification area, as shown here. The user can double-click the icon to display the details of the parental controls, but they cannot change them.

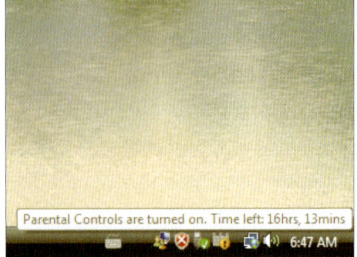

The user also sees information about parental controls whenever they run into a blocked action—for example, when they try to run an application that's not permitted, as shown here.

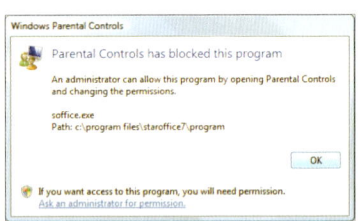

The user also learns quickly about any Web restrictions you've applied, as shown here.

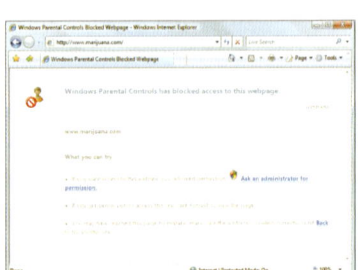

Let's Go Pro!

Setting Up Ease of Access Features

Windows offers several features for making computers easier to use for those with vision problems, hearing difficulties, or physical disabilities. For example, you can use the Magnifier feature to make the screen easier to read, turn on visual cues in place of audio prompts, or use speech recognition to control your computer and create and edit documents.

Windows includes a wizard to help you choose which ease of access features to implement. To run the wizard, follow these steps:

① Click the [Start] button, and then click [Control Panel]. Windows opens a Control Panel window. If the window is in Classic view, click the [Control Panel Home] link at the top of the left pane. Under the Ease Of Access heading, click the [Let Windows Suggest Settings] link.

② Windows launches the Get Recommendations To Make Your Computer Easier To Use Wizard, which walks you through five steps to identify the features that may help you.

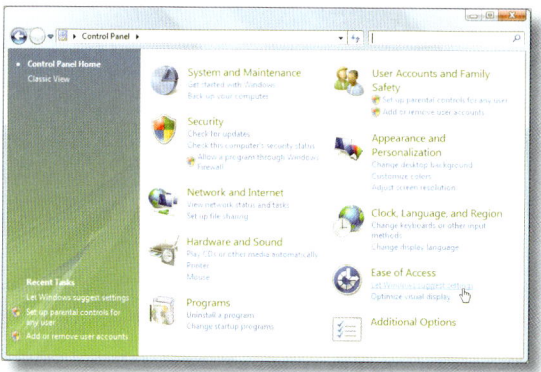

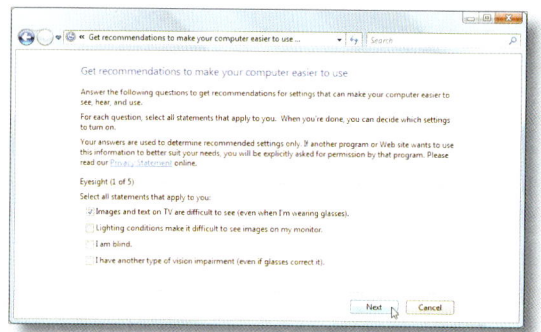

③ At the end of the five steps the wizard presents a screen of Recommended Settings, where you can choose which features to use. Select the check box for each feature you want to use, and then click the [Apply] button.

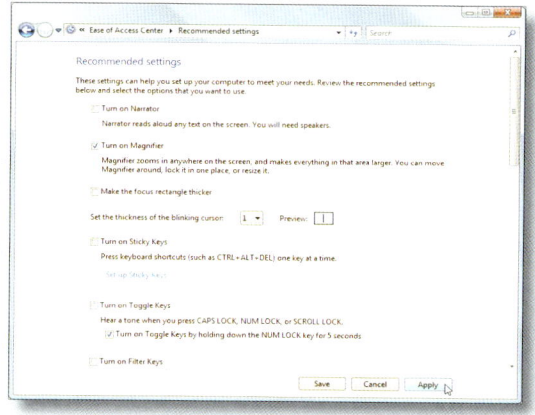

④ When you're satisfied with your choices, click the [Save] button. Windows closes the wizard and applies the settings you chose.

Chapter 5

Connecting to the Internet and Using Internet Explorer

Over the past few years, the Internet has become a vital part of everyday computing. It provides a worldwide communications network, allowing you to browse a huge variety of Web sites; communicate via e mail, telephony, videoconferencing, or instant messaging; and even publish your own information instantly and at minimal cost.

This chapter shows you how to connect to the Internet, using either a broadband connection (such as a cable connection or a digital telephone line) or a modem. It then shows you how to use Internet Explorer to browse the Web and locate information.

SECTION 01

Setting Up an Internet Connection

Before you can use the Internet, you must connect to it. The usual ways of connecting are via a broadband connection or a dial-up modem connection. This section shows you how to set up such connections. If you already have a working Internet connection, skip this section.

Getting an Internet Account

The first step in setting up an Internet connection is to get an account with an Internet service provider (ISP) for the type of Internet service you need. The ISP will provide you with the information you need to connect, such as the following:

- Your user name and password for the Internet account
- Your e-mail address and password
- The addresses of the e-mail servers and their type (POP3, IMAP, or HTTP)
- The ISP's phone number (for a dial-up connection only)

Setting Up a Broadband Connection

The steps for setting up a broadband connection depend on the technology. The following general steps normally apply.

1. Order the broadband connection from the ISP. For example, order cable broadband from your cable television company, or order DSL broadband from a telephony provider.

2. The ISP may supply, and even install, the connection equipment you need. If not, read the ISP's guidelines and recommendations, and then buy suitable equipment. For example, buy an ADSL modem/router for a DSL connection.

3. Install the connection equipment. For example, connect the cable modem/router to your cable connection, or connect the ADSL modem/router to your telephone line and install any ADSL splitter that is required.

4. Connect your computer or network to the modem/router, and then perform any necessary configuration. For example, for most types of connection, you must configure the modem/router with network address information. You may also need to configure the computers that will connect to the Internet via the modem/router.

Setting Up a Modem Connection

There are two parts to setting up a modem connection. First, you must install the modem in your computer if it is not already installed. Second, you must create a dial-up networking connection that connects to the Internet via the modem.

■ Installing a Modem

If you need to install a modem, follow these steps:

1. Connect the modem to your computer using the appropriate method described in the following list. Connect the phone line to the modem. If the modem has a power switch, turn it on.

Modem Type	How to Connect the Modem
USB	Plug the modem's cable into a USB socket on the computer.
PC Card	Insert the PC Card modem into a PC Card slot on your laptop.
Serial port	Connect the modem's cable to a serial port on your computer. Plug the modem's power supply into a power socket.
PCI card	Shut down your computer and disconnect all cables. Open the case and install the modem card in an empty PCI card slot. Close the case, reconnect all the cables, and then start your computer.

2. If Windows displays a pop-up message in the notification area saying that it has found new hardware, allow it to install the software. If your modem included a software disc, you may need to provide that disc.

If Windows doesn't notice that you've plugged in a modem, follow these steps:

1. Click the [Start] button, and then click [Control Panel]. Windows opens a Control Panel window. If the window is in Classic view, with a dot appearing next to Classic View in the left panel, click the [Control Panel Home] link to switch to Control Panel Home view. Click the [Hardware And Sound] link.

2. Windows opens a Hardware And Sound window. Click the [Phone And Modem Options] link.

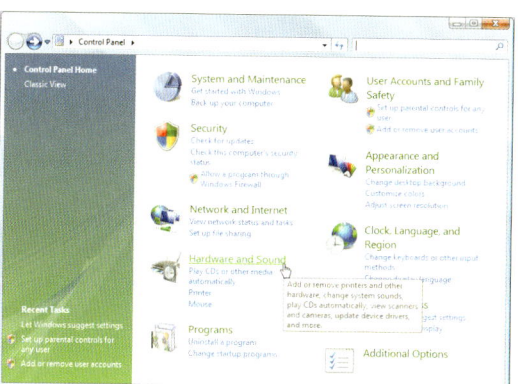

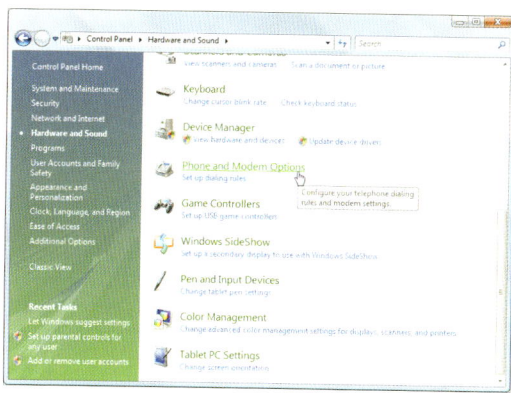

3. Windows may display the Location Information dialog box. (This dialog box appears the first time you set up a modem on Windows.) In the What Country/Region Are You In Now? drop-down list, select your [country] or [region]. Type your area code in the What Area Code (Or City Code) Are You In Now? box. Specify other dialing options, such as the carrier code or a number you must dial to reach an outside line, as needed. Then click the [OK] button.

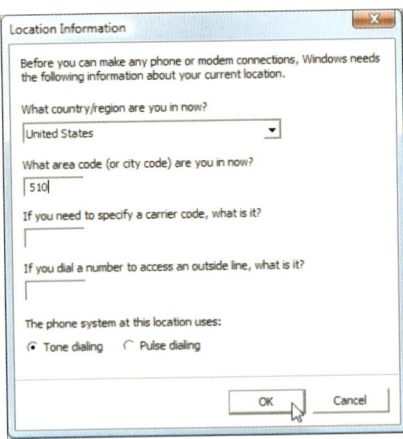

4. Windows closes the Location dialog box and displays the Phone And Modem Options dialog box. Click the [Modems] tab if it's not already displayed, and then click the [Add] button and go through User Account Control for the [Add Modems] feature.

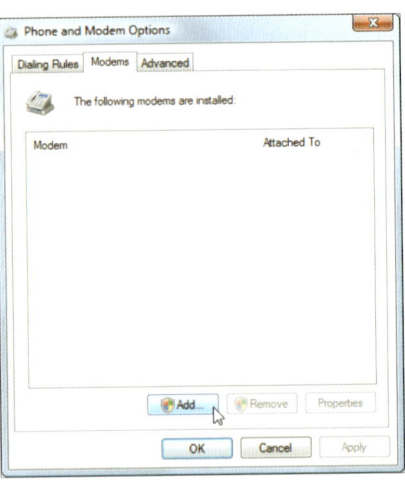

5. Windows launches the Add Hardware Wizard, which displays the Install New Modem screen. Click the [Next] button.

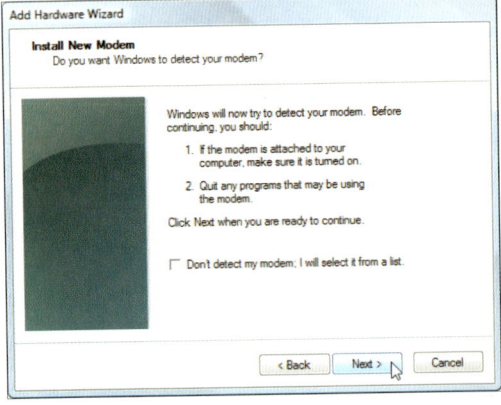

6. The wizard searches for the modem. You will probably see a pop-up message in the notification area as the wizard installs software for the modem. The wizard then displays a screen to tell you that your modem has been set up successfully. Click the [Finish] button.

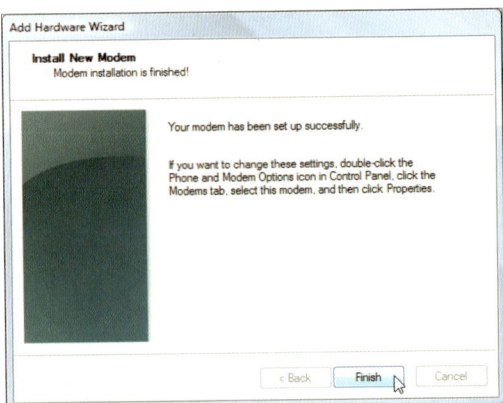

7. The modem then appears on the Modems tab in the Phone And Modem Options dialog box. Click the [OK] button. Windows closes the Phone And Modem Options dialog box.

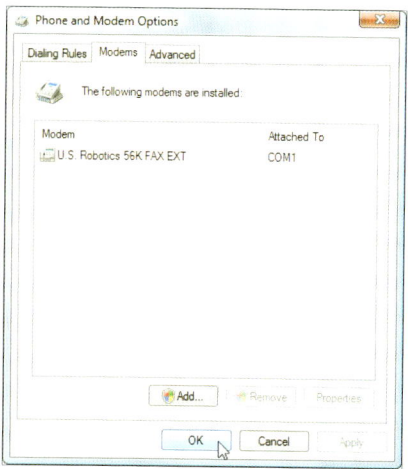

■ Setting Up a Dial-Up Connection

Once you've installed your modem you can create a dial-up connection that uses the modem to connect to the Internet. Follow these steps:

1. Click the [Start] button, right-click the [Network] item, and then click [Properties] on the context menu.

2. Windows opens a Network And Sharing Center window. In the Tasks pane on the left, click the [Set Up A Connection Or Network] link.

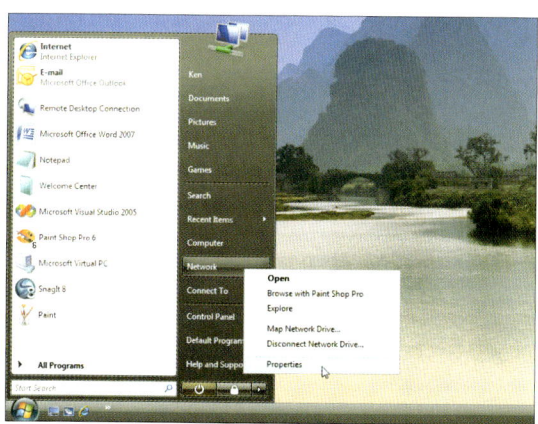

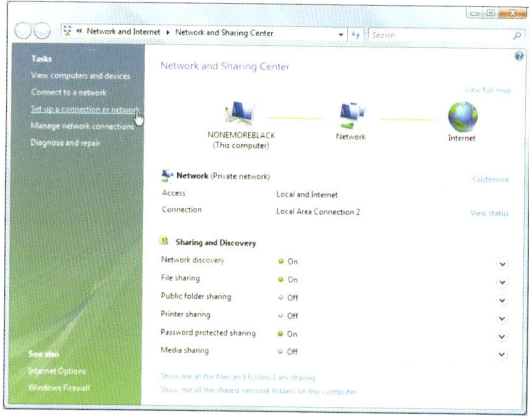

3. Windows launches the Set Up A Connection Or Network Wizard, which displays the Choose A Connection Option screen. In the list box, click the [Set Up A Dial-Up Connection] item, and then click the [Next] button.

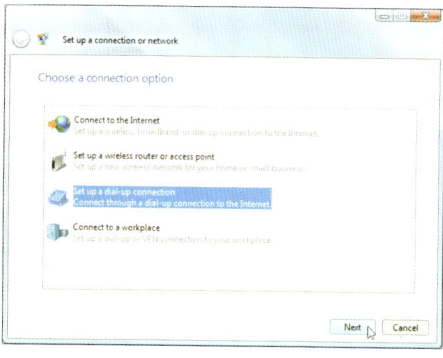

127

4. Windows launches the Set Up A Dial-Up Connection Wizard. Type your ISP's phone number, your user name, and password. You can select the [Show Characters] check box if you want to see the characters you type for the password, rather than the dots that Windows displays for security reasons. Select the [Remember This Password] check box if you want Windows to store the password (this is convenient). Type the connection name in the Connection Name text box, or accept the default name (Dial-up Connection). If you want other users of the computer to be able to use the connection, select the [Allow Other People To Use This Connection] check box, and then go through User Account Control for the Network Connections feature. Click the [Connect] button.

5. The wizard dials your Internet connection, signs on using the name and password you provided, and then tests the Internet connection.

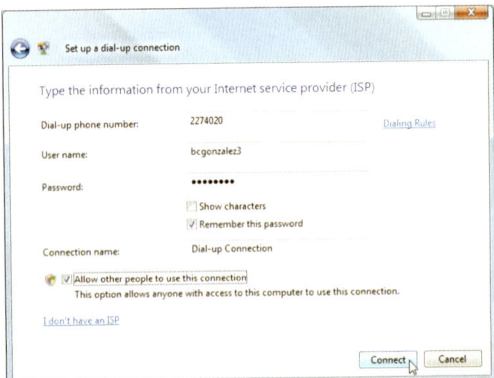

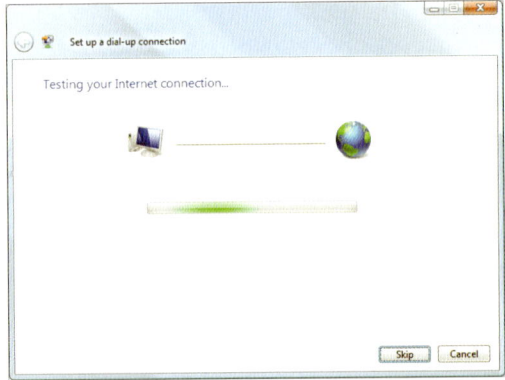

6. When the wizard has finished testing, it displays the You Are Connected To The Internet screen. Click the [Close] button.

7. The wizard closes and launches the Set Network Location Wizard. Because the Internet is a public network, click the [Public Location] button.

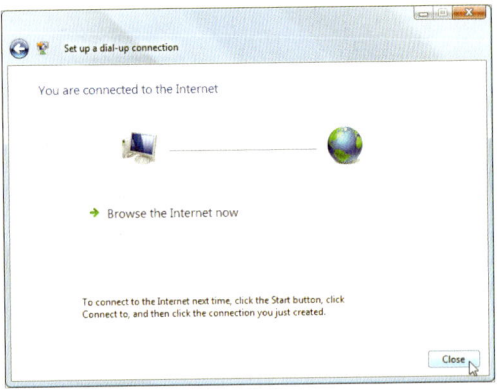

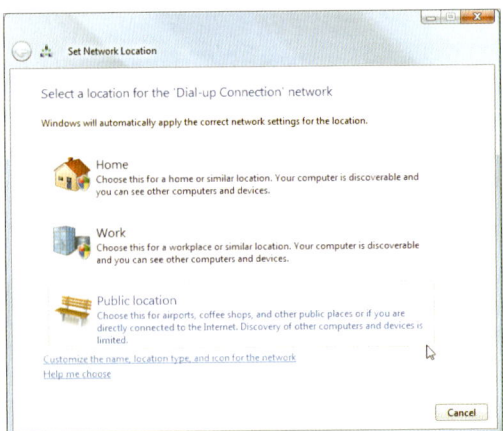

8. The wizard sets the network location and then displays the Successfully Set Network Settings screen. Click the [Close] button. The wizard closes.

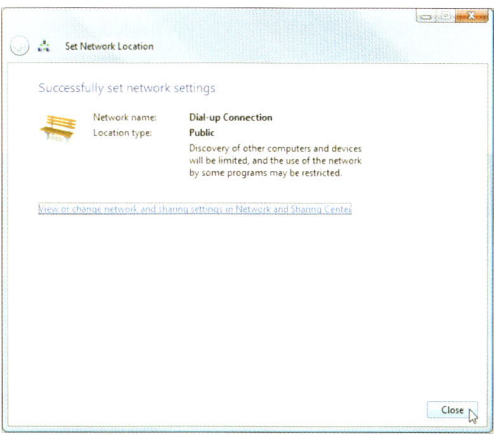

Your computer is now connected to the Internet, and you can browse the Internet using Internet Explorer, as described later in this chapter. See the next section for instructions on disconnecting from the Internet when you've finished using it.

> **Understanding What Network Locations Are** Note >>>
>
> The first time your computer connects to a new network, Windows runs the Set Network Location Wizard, which prompts you for the network type: Home, Work, or Public Location.
>
> When connecting to the Internet via dial-up, always choose the Public Location network type. This makes Windows apply protective network settings that help shield your computer from malefactors. By contrast, when you connect to a home network, you should tell Windows the network is the Home network type, which applies less restrictive settings that allow you to share files, printers, and other resources with other computers on the network.

■ Disconnecting a Dial-up Connection

To disconnect a dial-up connection, follow these steps:

1. Click the [network icon] in the notification area (the icon that shows two overlapping monitors and a colored globe). Windows displays a panel, as shown here, showing your computer's current network connections. Click the [Connect Or Disconnect] link.

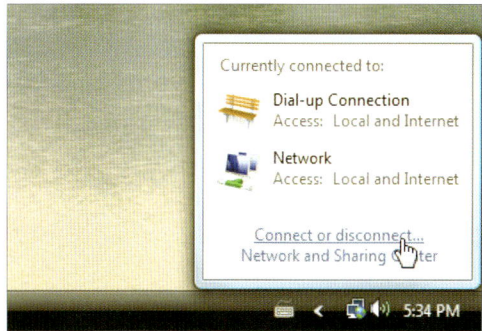

129

2. Windows launches the Connect To A Network Wizard, which displays the Disconnect Or Connect To Another Network screen. Click the [name of your dial-up connection] (it may be selected already), and then click the [Disconnect] button.

3. The wizard disconnects your dial-up connection and then displays the Successfully Disconnected screen. Click the [Close] button. The Connect To A Network Wizard closes.

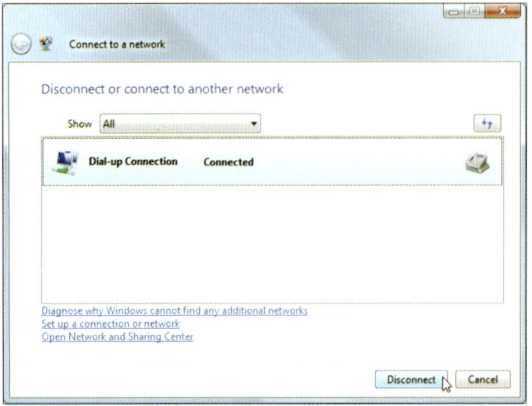

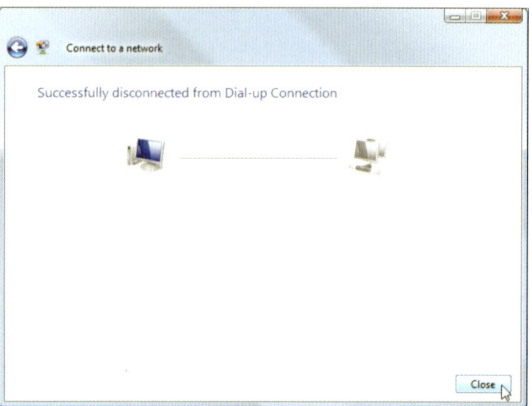

Connecting to the Internet Again

Earlier in this chapter, you connected to the Internet via a dial-up connection as part of the process for setting up that dial-up connection. Once you've set up the connection you can connect to the Internet more simply. Follow these steps:

1. Click the [Start] button, and then click [Connect To]. Windows launches the Connect To A Network Wizard. In the list of network connections, click your dial-up connection. (If you have many connections, you can choose [Dial-Up And VPN] in the Show drop-down list to show only dial-up connections.) Click the [Connect] button.

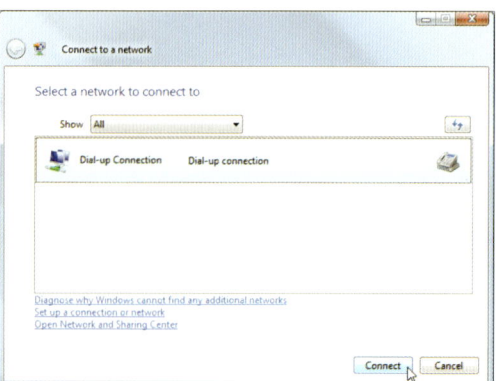

2. If you haven't yet saved the connection's user name and password, Windows displays the Connect Dial-Up Connection dialog box. If you want to save the user name and password, select the [Save This User Name And Password For The Following Users] check box, and then select the [Me Only option] button or the [Anyone Who Uses This Computer option] button, as appropriate. If you select the Anyone Who Uses This Computer option button, you must go through User Account Control for the Network Connections feature. When you're ready, click the [Dial] button.

3. Windows dials the connection and signs you in. You can then browse the Web with Internet Explorer, send e-mail, or perform other Internet activities.

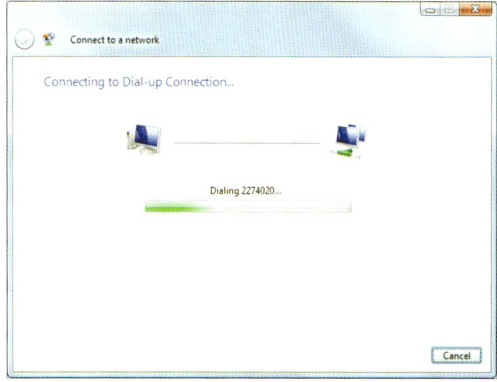

SECTION 02

Browsing with Internet Explorer

The World Wide Web, or simply the Web for short, consists of many million Web sites, each of which contains various Web pages. Each Web page is identified by a unique uniform resource locator, or URL. For example, the URL for the front page of the Microsoft Web site is http://www.microsoft.com. (The "http://" part indicates that the URL uses HTTP, the HyperText Transport Protocol, to transfer the information.)

Internet Explorer

To view Web pages, you use a Web browser. Most installations of Windows Vista include the Internet Explorer Web browser, which is made by Microsoft, so this book assumes that you are using Internet Explorer.

However, the manufacturer of your computer may have installed a different Web browser. If so, you have the option of using that Web browser or of installing Internet Explorer yourself. If you prefer to use Internet Explorer, you can download it from the Microsoft Web site (http://www.microsoft.com).

Launching Internet Explorer

Windows Vista's Start menu includes a link for launching your Web browser—the Internet link in the upper-left corner of the Start menu. Normally, this link runs Internet Explorer, so you can launch Internet Explorer by choosing [Start] [Internet]. If this link is set to run another application you can change it to run Internet Explorer. See the section "Customizing the Start Menu" in Chapter 4.

132

Opening Web pages in Internet Explorer

When you launch Internet Explorer, it displays your home page—the Web page that Internet Explorer is set to use first. At first, this page may be Internet Explorer's default home page (MSN.com) or a home page that your computer's manufacturer has set. For example, you may see the MSN.com home page, as shown in the next illustration. You can change your home page to any Web page you choose; see the section "Changing Your Home Page," later in this chapter, for instructions.

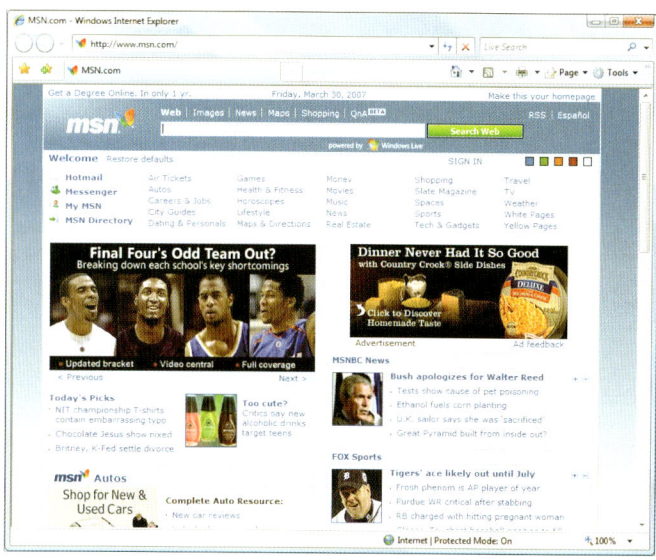

To open Web pages in Internet Explorer, follow these steps:

1. Web pages often contain links (formally called *hyperlinks*) to other Web pages. Links usually appear in a different color than other text on a page so that you can easily identify them. When you position the mouse pointer over a link, Internet Explorer changes the pointer to a hand and underlines the link text.

2. To open a Web page that's linked to the Web page you're currently viewing, click the [link]. Internet Explorer opens the Web page in the same window

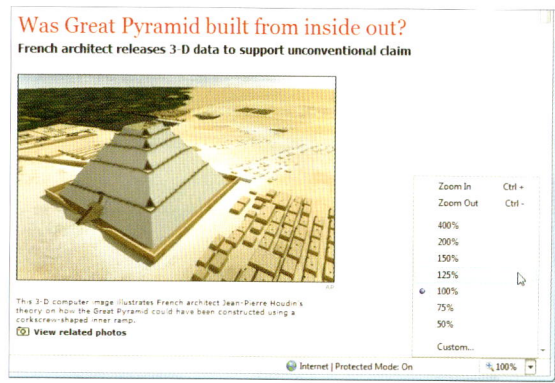

Understanding Why Some Links Open in a New Window Note >>>

Instead of creating a link that opens in the same browser window, a Web designer can create a link that opens in another window—usually, so that the window showing the designer's own site stays open even when you navigate to another site. For this reason, Internet Explorer will sometimes open a link in a new window rather than in the same window.

3. If you find the Web page is too small or too large to read comfortably, click the [Zoom] button in the lower-right corner, and then choose a different zoom percentage from the Zoom menu.

4. To navigate to a Web page that's not linked to the current Web page, click the [Address] box, type the URL of the Web page you want to access, and then press <Enter> or click the [Go] button. You can omit the "http://" at the beginning of the URL: Internet Explorer automatically adds this for you when you press <Enter> or click the [Go] button.

To open multiple Web pages at once, you can browse using tabs, as described next.

Browsing with Tabs

Often you will want to open more than one Web page at a time—for example, when you're searching for information or comparing products. Internet Explorer lets you open multiple tabs within the same window, with each tab showing a separate Web page.

To practice browsing with tabs, follow these steps:

1. Open [Internet Explorer] if it's not already open, and navigate to a page that contains links. This example uses the Yahoo! page, http://www.yahoo.com. Right-click the [link you want to open], and then choose [Open In New Tab] from the context menu.

Chapter 05. Connecting to the Internet and Using Internet Explorer

2. Internet Explorer adds another tab and opens the Web page in it, but does not display the tab yet. Click the [tab] to display it. When you hover the mouse pointer over the tab, Internet Explorer displays a ScreenTip showing the Web page's title and URL.

3. To open a new tab without following a link, click the [New Tab] button at the right end of the tab bar or press <Ctrl>+<T>.

4. Internet Explorer adds a new tab, displays an informational message about tabs in it, and places the focus in the Address box so that you can type the URL you want. Type the URL, and then press <Enter> or click the [Go] button.

5. Internet Explorer opens the Web page in the tab. To change from one tab to another, click the [tab you want to see]. If the tab titles are too short to let you identify a tab's contents, click the [Tab List] drop-down button, and then choose the [tab] from the drop-down list.

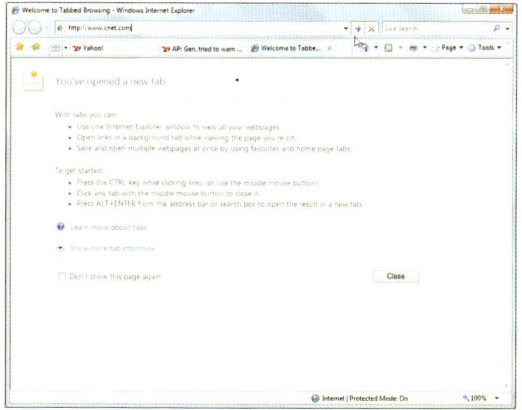

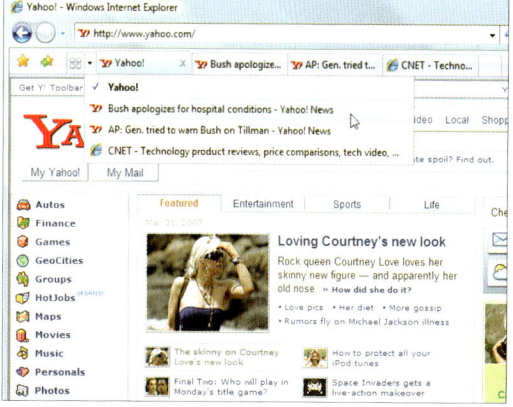

6. To get a graphical overview of all the open tabs, click the [Quick Tabs] button or press <Ctrl>+<Q>.

135

7. Internet Explorer displays a thumbnail picture of each tab. Click the [thumbnail] for the tab you want to display. You can also click a [Close] button (the [x] button) on a thumbnail to close that tab, or right-click to produce a context menu of actions, such as refreshing the tab or refreshing all tabs.

8. To close a tab, click its [Close] button (the [x] button) if it is displayed. If not, right-click the [tab], and then choose [Close] from the context menu. You can also choose [Close Other Tabs] from the context menu if you want to leave open only the tab you clicked.

9. To close the Internet Explorer window including all the tabs it contains, click the [Close] button (the [x] button) in the upper-right corner of the Internet Explorer window. In the Internet Explorer dialog box that appears, click the [Close Tabs] button.

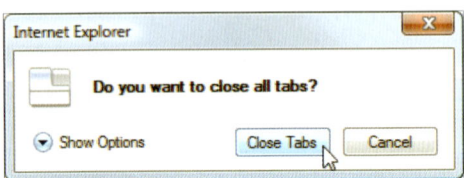

10. If you want to use the same set of tabs again the next time you run Internet Explorer, you can instead click the [Show Options] button, select the [Open These The Next Time I Use Internet Explorer] check box, and then click the [Close Tabs] button.

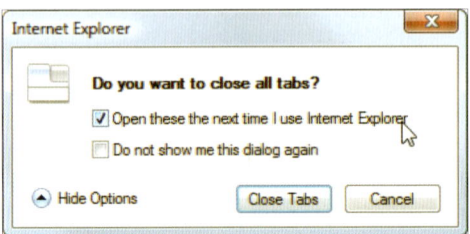

Browsing with Multiple Windows   Note >>>

Instead of opening multiple tabs within the same Internet Explorer window, you can open another window. To do so, right-click the [link you want to open], and then choose [Open In New Window] from the context menu. Opening another window is useful when you need to look at two Web pages at the same time, rather than switching from one page to another.

SECTION 03

Searching, Using Favorites, and Navigating

The Web contains so much information that it can often be difficult to find what you need. Unless you've read or received the exact URL you need, your best bet is usually to search for information using a search engine. Once you've found information, you can save it as a favorite, or simply navigate back to it from another Web page.

Searching for Information

To search using a search engine follow these steps:

1. Internet Explorer comes equipped with the Windows Live Search engine, which Microsoft owns. To search using Windows Live Search, click in the [Search] box in the upper-right corner of the Internet Explorer window. Type the search terms you want to use, and then press <Enter>.

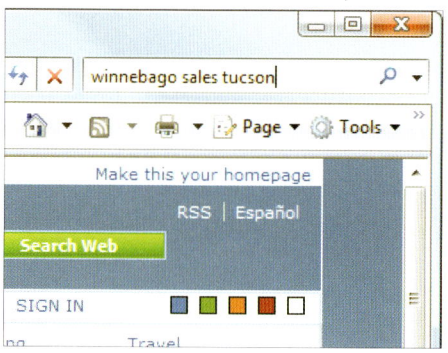

2. Internet Explorer searches using Windows Live Search, and then returns a page of results. Click a search result to open the Web page.

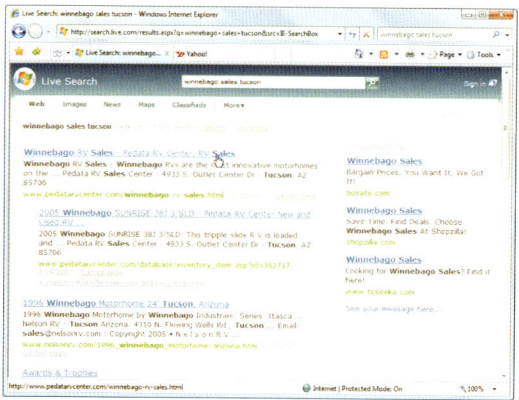

137

Changing Your Search Engine

Microsoft is working hard to make Windows Live Search effective and popular, but many people prefer to use other search engines. For example, you might choose to use the Google search engine (http://www.google.com) instead, as in the following example.

If you want to use another search engine once in a while, you can simply open its Web page and search. But if you want to use another search engine regularly, you can configure Internet Explorer to use that search engine instead of Windows Live Search.

To change your search engine, follow these steps:

1. In Internet Explorer, click the [drop-down] button to the right of the Search box, and then choose [Change Search Defaults] from the drop-down menu.

2. Internet Explorer displays the Change Search Defaults dialog box. Click the [Find More Providers] link.

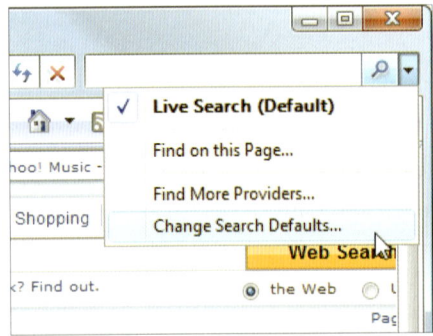

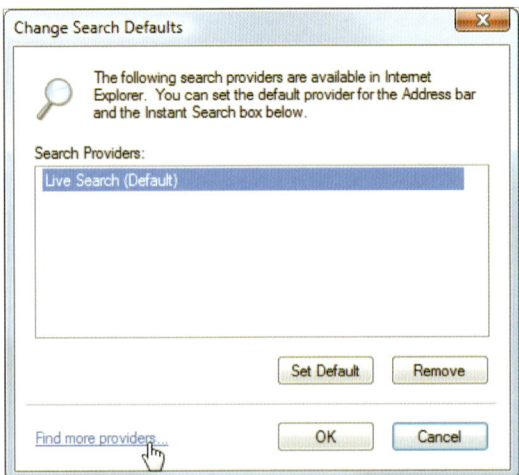

3. Internet Explorer opens a new window showing the Add Search Providers To Internet Explorer 7 page. Click the [link] for the search engine you want to use. For example, click the [Google] link, as shown here.

4. Internet Explorer displays the Add Search Provider dialog box. Select the [Make This My Default Search Provider] check box, and then click the [Add Provider] button.

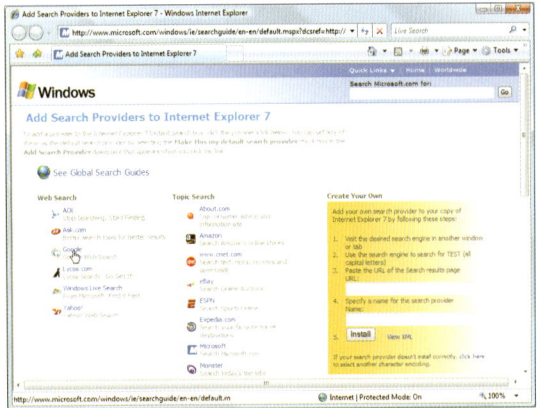

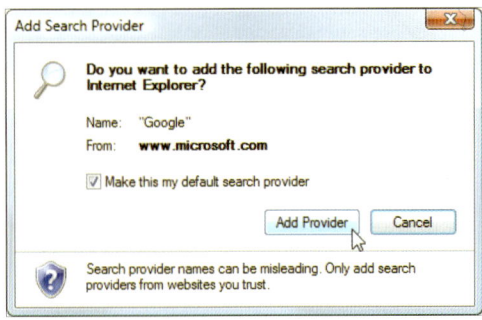

Chapter 05. Connecting to the Internet and Using Internet Explorer

5. Internet Explorer closes the Add Search Provider dialog box and adds the search engine. Click the [Close] button (the [X] button) on the Add Search Providers To Internet Explorer 7 window, in order to return to the original window. The search engine you chose now appears in the Search box. To search, type your search terms in the Search box, and then press <Enter>.

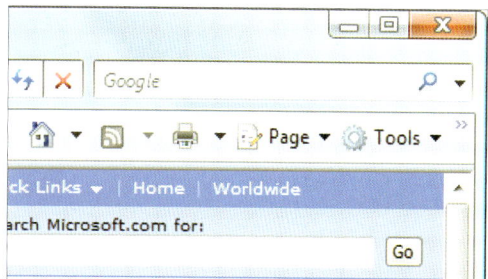

Understanding Google's Cookie

Warning >>>

If you choose to use Google as your search engine, here's something you should know. Google places a tracking file called a cookie on your computer. Many Web sites do this in order to help them keep track of your activities or to keep you logged in. But because Google's cookie lasts for several years, it has the potential to collect a vast amount of information about your searches. If you prefer not to have such information collected, use a Google scraper such as Scroogle (http://www.scroogle.org) to search Google without allowing it to use its cookie on your computer.

Changing Your Home Page

Internet Explorer displays your home page every time you launch the application, so you'll probably want to choose a Web page that interests you. You can have either a single home page or a set of home pages that Internet Explorer loads on different tabs. Having multiple home pages is often convenient, but Internet Explorer may take a while to load if you have a slow Internet connection.

To change your home page, follow these steps:

1. In Internet Explorer, go to the Web page you want to make your home page. For example, type the address in the Address bar, and then press <Enter>. Click the [Home] drop-down button on the toolbar, and then choose [Add Or Change Home Page] from the drop-down menu.

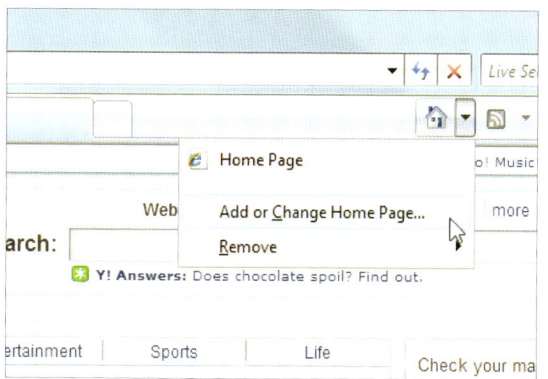

2. Internet Explorer displays the Add Or Change Home Page dialog box. Select the [Use This Webpage As Your Only Home Page] option button if you want just one home page. If you want to add this Web page to your home page tabs, select the [Add This Webpage To Your Home Page Tabs] option button, as shown here. Click the [Yes] button.

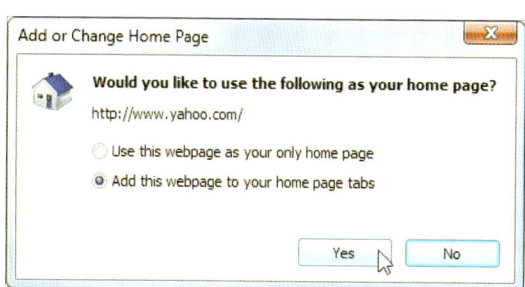

139

3. If you chose to have multiple home pages, you can remove a home page from the tab set by clicking the [Home] drop-down button, highlighting [Remove], and then clicking [the page you want to remove].

Keeping a List of Favorites

As you browse the Web, you will probably find Web sites that you will want to visit again. To access such sites easily in the future you can create *favorites* for them. Other Web browsers call favorites "bookmarks," so you may be familiar with that term instead.

■ Creating a Favorite

To create a favorite, follow these steps:

1. Navigate to the Web page for which you want to create the favorite. Click the [Add To Favorites] button on the toolbar, and then choose [Add To Favorites] from the drop-down menu.

2. Internet Explorer displays the Add A Favorite dialog box. If necessary, change the name in the Name text box. For example, you might type a more descriptive name.

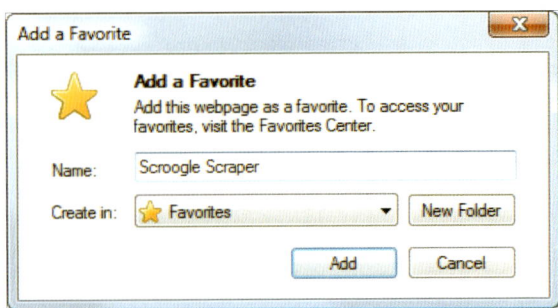

Chapter 05. Connecting to the Internet and Using Internet Explorer

3. To change the folder in which Internet Explorer stores the favorite, click the [Create In] drop-down list, and then choose the folder from the list. To add a new folder to the list, click the [New Folder] button, type the name for the folder in the Create A Folder dialog box, and then click the [Create] button. Click the [Add] button. Internet Explorer closes the Add A Favorite dialog box and adds the site to your favorites list.

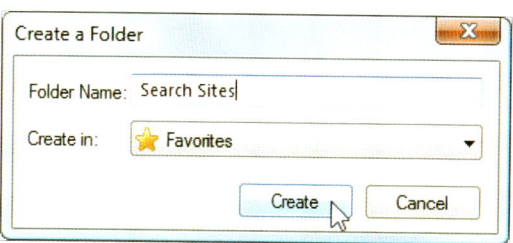

■ Going to a Favorite

To go to a favorite, follow these steps:

1. Click the [Favorites Center] button at the left end of the toolbar. Internet Explorer displays the Favorites Center pane.

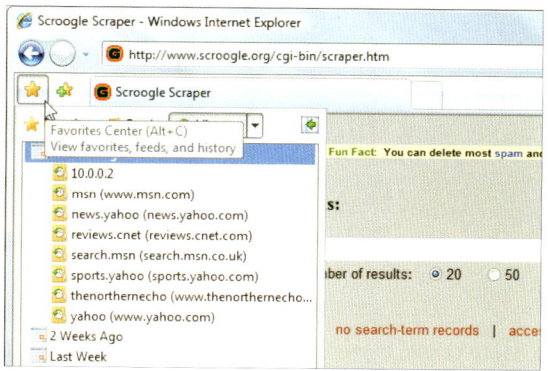

2. At first, the Favorites Center may display your browsing history—the Web sites and Web pages you have visited within the last few days and weeks. In this case, click the [Favorites] button to display your list of favorites.

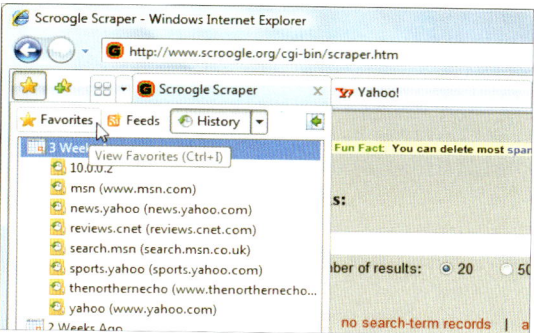

3. If you can see the favorite you want, click it to open it. If not, click the [folder] that contains the favorite, and then click the [favorite] to open it.

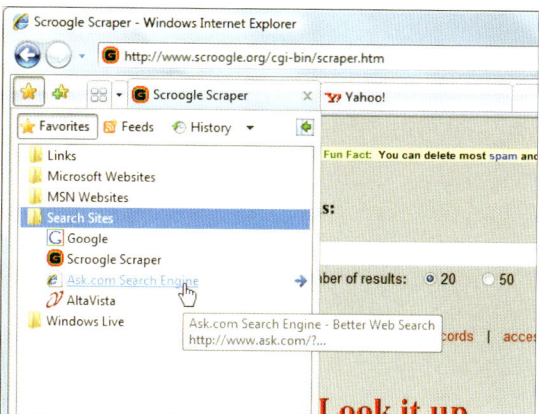

4. Once you click the favorite, Internet Explorer hides the Favorites Center again. If you want to keep the Favorites Center pane displayed as you browse so that you can move from favorite to favorite more quickly, click the [Pin The Favorites Center] button in the upper-right corner of the pane. When you want the Favorites Center to hide itself again automatically, click the [Close] button (the ▭✕▭ button) on the Favorites Center to "unpin" the Favorites Center.

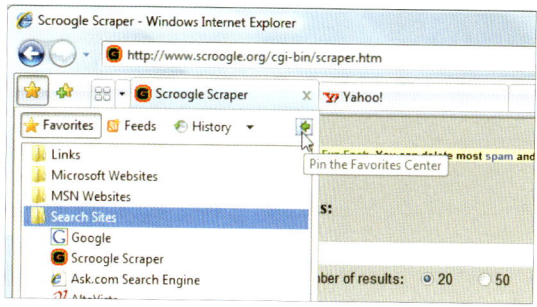

141

Navigating Back, Forward, and with History

As you browse the Web, you may want to move back to a Web page you visited earlier in your browsing session. Assuming you've been browsing so far in this chapter and have visited several Web pages, follow these steps to practice navigating:

1. Click the [Back] button to move back by one page.

2. To move forward by one page, click the [Forward] button. This button works only after you've clicked the Back button one or more times—otherwise there's no Web page to which you can move forward.

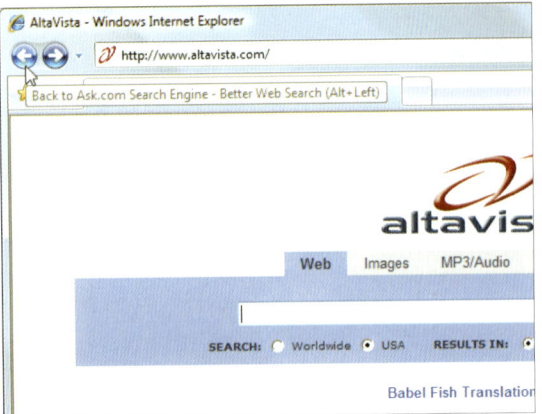

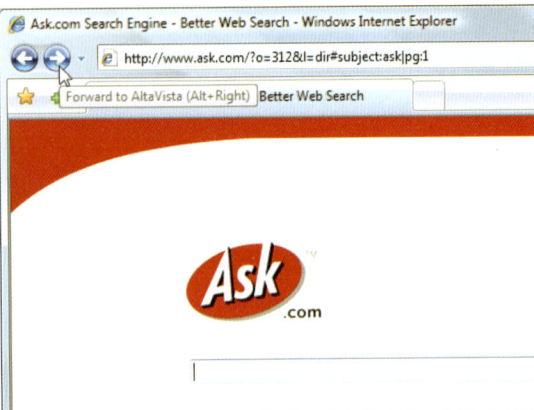

3. To return to a Web page you've visited recently, click the [Recent Pages] button, and then choose the page from the drop-down list.

4. To return to a Web page you've visited in the last few days or weeks, use the History feature. Click the [Favorites Center] button at the left end of the toolbar. Internet Explorer displays the Favorites Center pane.

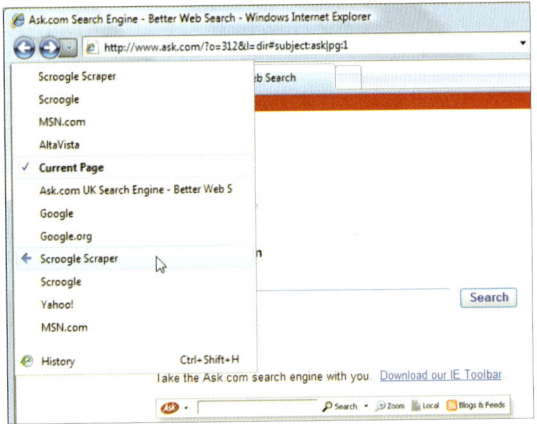

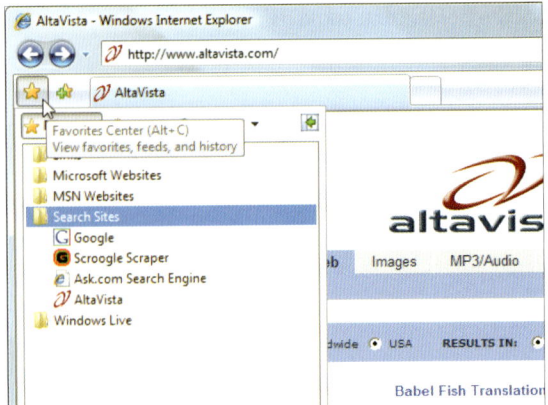

5. If the Favorites Center doesn't display your history at first, click the [History] button.

6. If necessary, choose a different view by clicking the [History] drop-down button and then clicking an [item on the drop-down list]: By Date, By Site, By Most Visited, or By Order Visited Today. You can also search your history by clicking the [Search] item and then specifying a search term.

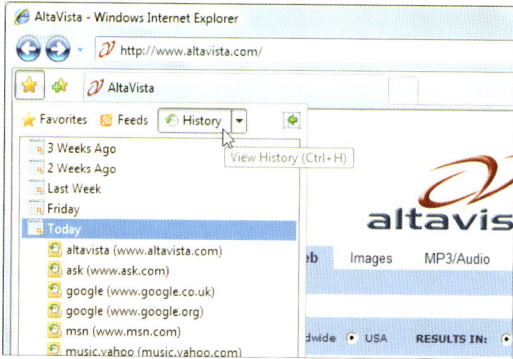

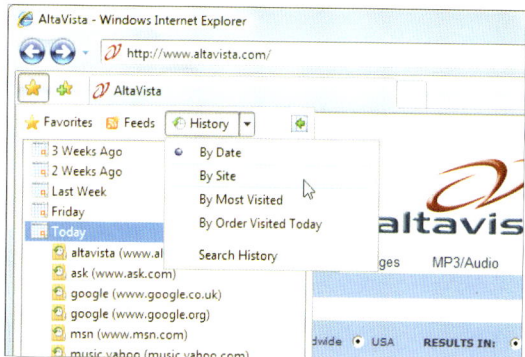

7. Click the folder you want to open, and then click the site, as shown in the next illustration.

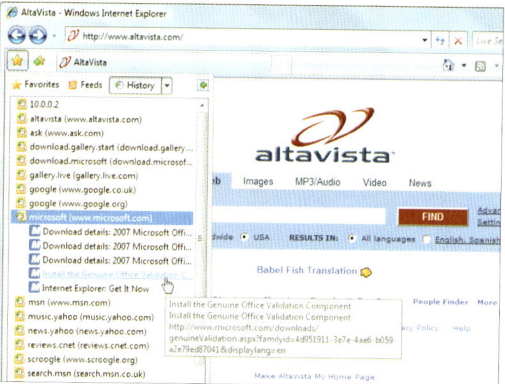

Understanding How Navigation Works with Tabs   Note >>>

Internet Explorer maintains a separate navigation stream for each tab that you have opened in a window. This behavior allows you to retrace your path for each tab, which is most helpful when you pursue complex paths in your browsing. However, it also means that when you have opened a Web page in a new tab, Internet Explorer offers you no Web page to which you can return, because you have started a new browsing path.

Closing Internet Explorer

Web browsing is such an important aspect of modern computing that you may choose to keep Internet Explorer open most of the time you are using Windows.

When you are ready to close Internet Explorer, click the [Close] button (the ❌ button). If Internet Explorer displays a dialog box asking if you're sure you want to close all the tabs, click the [Close Tabs] button.

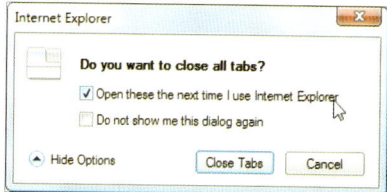

143

Chapter 6

Making the Most of E-mail and Instant Messaging

E mail—electronic mail—has rapidly become an essential form of communication for many people who have an Internet connection. Windows Vista includes Windows Mail, an e mail program. Instant messaging—which includes text based chat, audio, and even video—has also become extremely popular now that so many people are online. You can download Microsoft's Windows Live Messenger program for instant messaging.

SECTION 01

Setting Up Windows Mail and Sending Messages

Before you can send e mail with Windows Mail, you must set up an e mail account. This e mail account can be either one that your ISP provides with your Internet account or one that you get from a third party e mail provider.

Understanding the Two Types of E-mail

There are two main types of e-mail:

Computer-based: This type uses an e-mail application based on your computer, such as Windows Mail. Once you've received messages, they're stored in mailboxes on your computer.

Web-based: This type uses a Web browser to access mail stored on a Web-based service. Web-based e-mail services include Microsoft's Hotmail service and Google's Gmail.

> **Choosing Which E mail Application to Use** — Note >>>
>
> Normally, you will use a single e-mail application to access all your e-mail. (By contrast, you might use different graphics applications to create different types of graphics.) If your computer has another e-mail application installed as well as Windows Mail, you will need to choose between them.
>
> For example, if Microsoft Office is installed on your computer, Office's e-mail and desktop information management application, Microsoft Outlook, may be installed. Outlook is much more powerful than Windows Mail, so in this case, you would usually do better using Outlook rather than Windows Mail.

Setting Up an E-mail Account

To set up an e-mail account using Windows Mail, follow these steps:

1. Click the [Start] button, and then click [E-mail] at the top of the Start menu. If this item is set to run another e-mail application (such as Microsoft Outlook), but you're not using that application, you can change this item back to running Windows Mail. See the section "Customizing the Start Menu" in Chapter 4 for instructions.

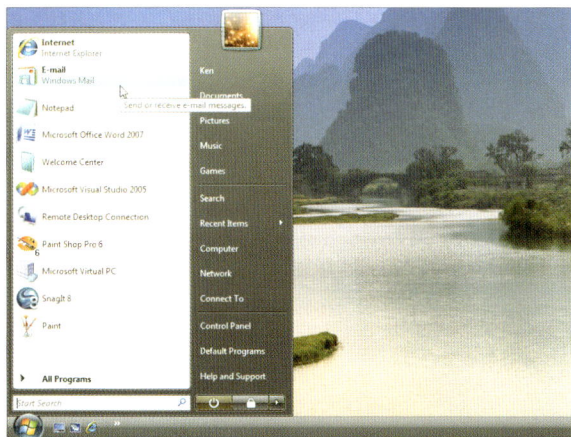

2. Windows Mail starts. If this is the first time you have run Windows Mail, it automatically launches a wizard for setting up an e-mail account. The wizard displays the Your Name screen. In the Display Name text box, type your name as you want it to appear on your messages. (For example, you might use a diminutive or nickname instead of your full first name.) Click the [Next] button.

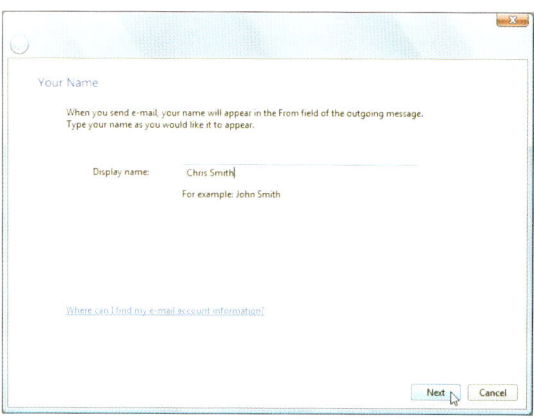

3. The wizard displays the Internet E-mail Address screen. Type your e-mail address in the E-mail Address text box and then click the [Next] button.

4. The wizard displays the Set Up E-mail Servers screen. In the Incoming E-mail Servers drop-down list, select the [server type] your ISP has told you: POP3 or IMAP. The list contains an HTTP item as well, but Windows Mail does not support HTTP mail (Windows Mail's predecessor, Outlook Express, did support HTTP mail). Type the server addresses in the two text boxes. If you have to provide a password for the outgoing mail server, select the [Outgoing Server Requires Authentication] check box. Click the [Next] button.

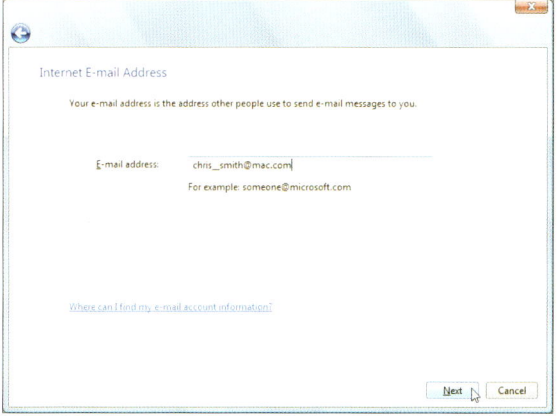

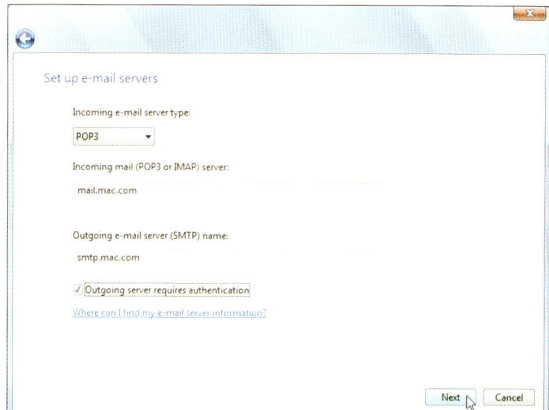

5. The wizard displays the Internet Mail Logon screen. If necessary, change the name in the E-mail Username text box (the wizard enters the first part of the e-mail address automatically for you). Type your password in the Password text box, and then select the [Remember Password] check box if you want to store the password for convenience. Click the [Next] button.

6. The wizard displays its final screen. Usually, you'll want to download any e-mail messages that are waiting for you. But if you don't want to download your e-mail messages from this e-mail account now, select the [Do Not Download My E-mail At This Time] check box. Click the [Finish] button. The wizard closes. If you chose to download your e-mail, Windows Mail checks the account for mail.

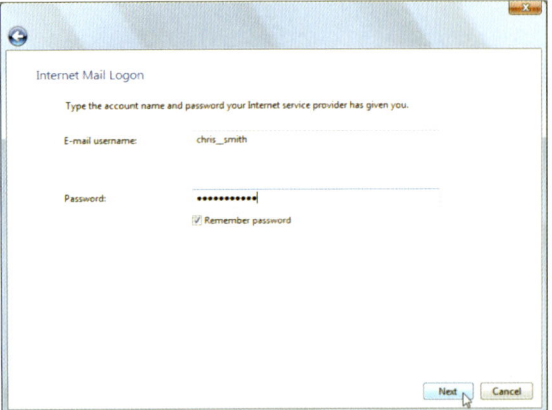
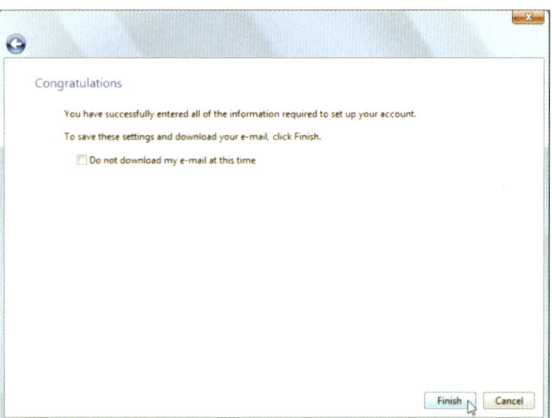

Reading Your E-mail

Windows Mail automatically creates a welcome message for you, so even if you have received no other e-mail messages yet, you will find one message in your Inbox.

To read your e-mail, follow these steps:

1. In Windows Mail, check for e-mail by clicking the [Send/Receive] button on the toolbar.

2. If Windows Mail displays a Windows Security dialog box prompting you for your password, type the password and then click the [OK] button.

3. Windows Mail contacts your mail servers, sends any outgoing messages, and downloads any incoming messages to your Inbox. Click a message in the list to display its contents in the Preview pane.

4. If you want to open a message in a separate window, double-click it in the message list. Opening separate windows is useful when you need to compare two or more e-mail messages. From a message window you can take regular actions on the message, such as replying to it or deleting it, or simply click the [Close] button (the ⊠ button) to close the message window.

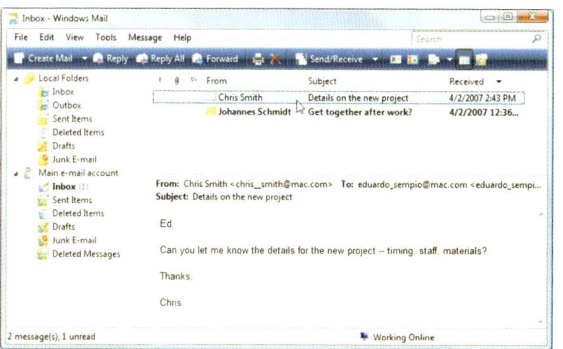

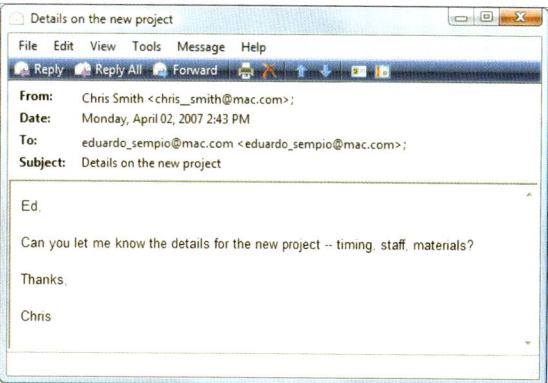

How the Inbox and Preview Pane Display Messages   Note >>>

Unread messages appear listed in bold type in the Inbox, while messages you've read appear in regular type. When you click an unread message to display its contents in the Preview pane, Windows Mail marks the message as read after a few seconds.

The bar across the top of the Preview pane displays brief details on the message: the sender's e-mail address, the recipient's e-mail address (which is useful if you use Windows Mail to check several e-mail accounts), and the subject line.

5. When you're done with a message, you can delete it or store it in a different folder. To delete the message, click [it] in the message list, and then click the [Delete] button on the toolbar or press <Delete>.

6. To store a message in a folder, click the [message] in the message list and drag it to the folder in the left pane.

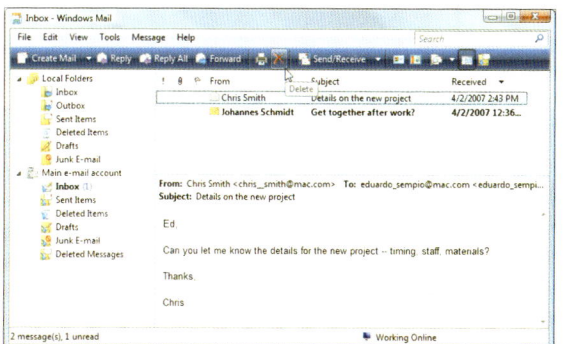

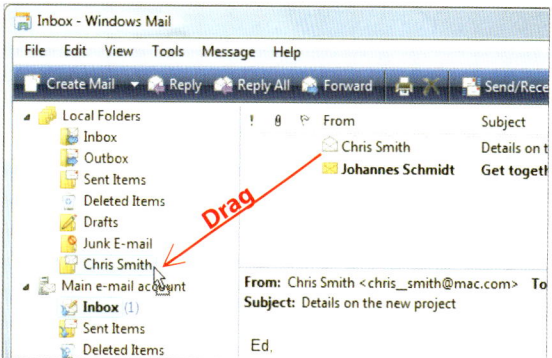

149

7. To create a new folder, choose [File] [Folders] [New]. Windows Mail displays the Create Folder dialog box. Type the folder name, click the [folder] in which you want to create it, and then click the [OK] button. You can then store messages in that folder.

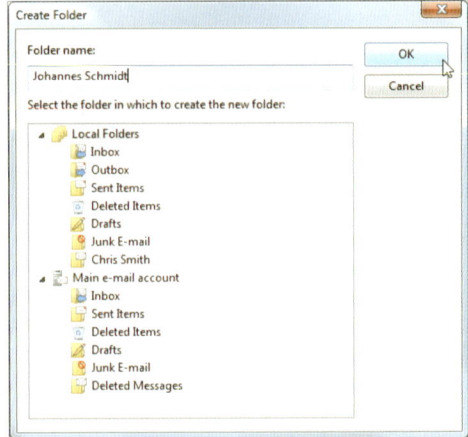

Creating a New Message

To create a new message, follow these steps:

1. Click the [Create Mail] button on the toolbar if you want to create a plain message. Windows Mail opens a new message in its own window. Type the recipient's e-mail address in the To box. To use more than one address, put a semicolon (;) between each address. To add recipients of "carbon copy" versions of the message, click to the [Cc] box, and then add the names.

2. If a recipient is in your Windows Contact list, click the [To] button or the [Cc] button to open the Select Recipients dialog box. Click the [recipient's name] in the list box, and then click the [To] button or the [Cc] button to add the name to the list. You can also add "blind carbon copy" recipients by using the [Bcc] button. These recipients receive the message without their name or address being visible to other recipients. Click the [OK] button when you've finished selecting recipients.

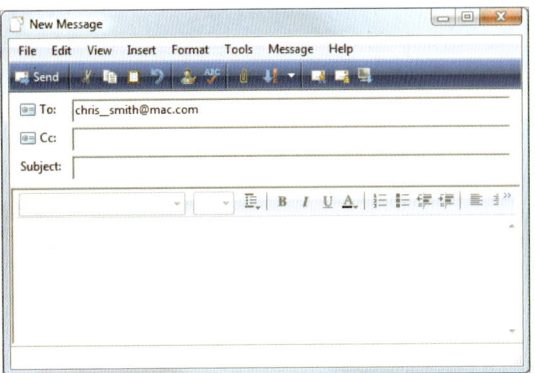
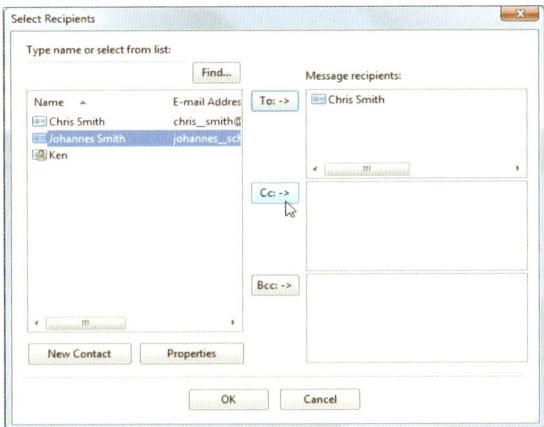

> **Creating a New Message Using Stationery** Note >>>
>
> If you want to create a message using decorative stationery, click the [Create Mail] drop-down button, and then choose the [stationery] from the drop-down list. The example uses a plain message rather than stationery.

3. Type the subject for the message in the Subject box. To encourage the recipient to read the message, make it descriptive, concise, and helpful. Then type the message in the main text box. If you wish, you can apply formatting by using the buttons on the toolbar above the main text box. You may also want to spell-check the message by clicking the Spelling button on the main toolbar. When you've completed the message, click the [Send] button.

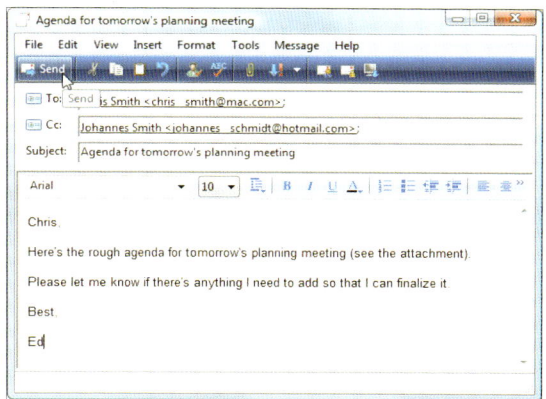

> ### Sending Messages   Note >>>
> If you have a broadband Internet connection that's always connected (see Chapter 5 for a discussion of broadband), Windows Mail normally sends mail immediately when you click the Send button in the message window. If you have an on/off Internet connection, or if Windows Mail is configured not to send mail immediately, Windows Mail queues your message for sending. To send the mail, click the [Send/Receive] button on the toolbar of the main Windows Mail window. Windows Mail establishes an Internet connection if necessary, and then sends the queued messages.

Replying to Messages or Forwarding Them

Instead of creating new messages from scratch, you'll often want to reply to messages you've received, and possibly forward such messages to other people.

To reply to a message, follow these steps:

1. Select the [message] in the message list, and then click the [Reply] button on the toolbar. You can also click the [Reply] button on the toolbar of a separate window in which you've opened the message.

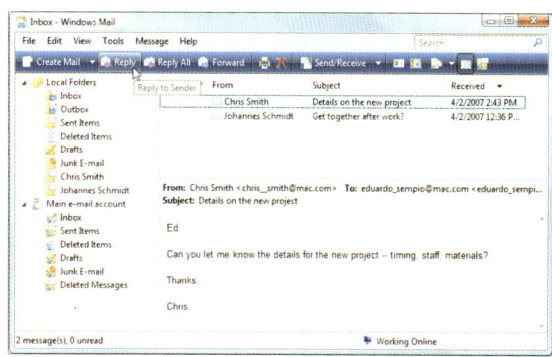

> ### Replying to All Recipients of a Message   Caution >>>
> If the message was sent to multiple recipients, you can reply to all of them by clicking the [Reply All] button instead. Use this option with caution—often you do not need to include all recipients on a reply, although doing so can sometimes be helpful. Windows creates a reply to the sender and all other recipients. You can then remove individual recipients manually, or add other recipients as needed.

2. Windows Mail creates a reply to the sender. Windows Mail adds Re: to the beginning of the subject line to show that the message is a reply. Add any other recipients for the message, and then compose your message.

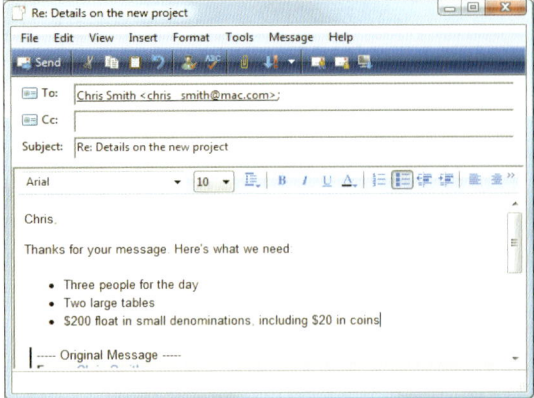

3. When the message is ready, click the [Send] button.

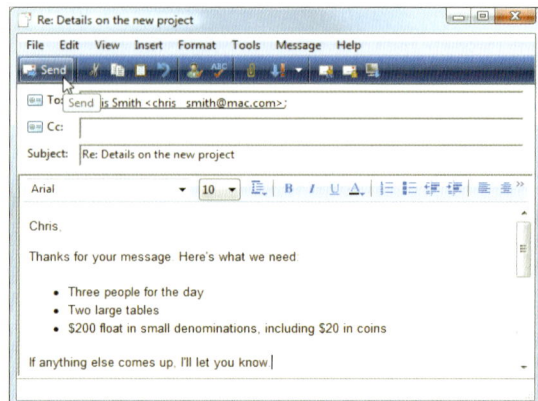

To forward a message to someone else, follow these steps:

1. Select the [message] in the message list, and then click the [Forward] button on the toolbar. You can also click the [Forward] button on the toolbar of a separate window in which you've opened the message, as shown here.

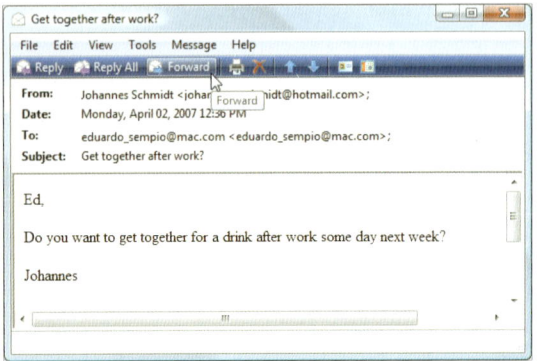

2. Windows Mail creates a new message based on the original message, marking the original message with greater-than characters (>) to indicate that it is forwarded rather than new. Windows Mail adds FW: to the beginning of the subject line (and to the title bar) to show that the message has been forwarded. Enter the recipient's address in the To box. Add any other recipients or carbon copy recipients you want to receive the e-mail.

3. Type the message, and then click the [Send] button.

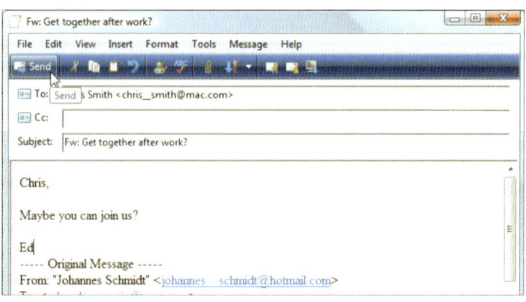

SECTION 02

Using Signatures and Attachments

E mail is not only a great means of communication, but you can also use it to transfer files, provided that they are not too big (most ISPs' mail servers block attachments larger than several megabytes). To complete your messages quickly, you can make Windows Mail automatically add predefined text to the ends of your messages—for example, to add your name, address, and contact information.

Attaching a File to a Message

To attach a file to a message you're sending, follow these steps:

1. Click the [Attach File To Message] button on the toolbar of the message window. Alternatively, open the [Insert] menu, and then click [File Attachment].

2. Windows Mail displays the Open dialog box. Select the [file] or [files] you want to attach, and then click the [Open] button. Windows Mail closes the Open dialog box and adds an Attach box below the Subject box in the message window showing the files you've attached. You can then send the message as usual.

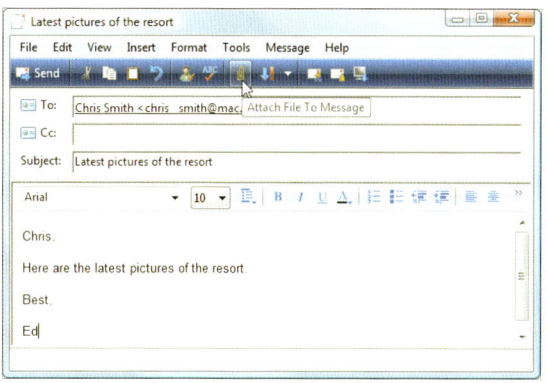

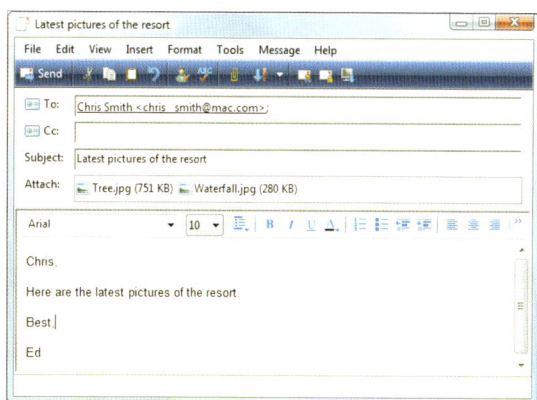

153

Receiving an Attached File

When someone sends an attachment to you, that message appears in your Inbox with a paperclip icon two columns to the left of the From column. To save the attachment or attachments, follow these steps:

1. Click the [message] in the message list, click the [paperclip] icon on the bar across the Preview pane, and then choose [Save Attachments].

2. Windows Mail displays the Save Attachments dialog box. In the Attachments To Be Saved list box, select the [attachment] or [attachments] you want to save. Choose the [destination folder] in the Save To list box, and then click the [Save] button. Windows Mail closes the Save Attachments dialog box and saves the attachments.

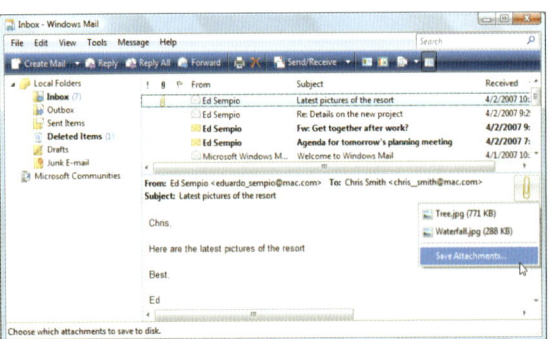
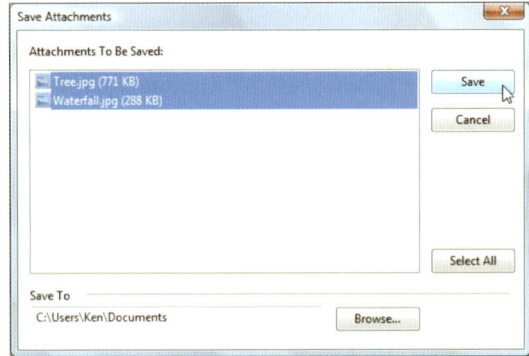

Adding a Signature to Your Messages

In e-mail, a signature is standard text that you can insert easily at the end of a message. You can create as many signatures as you want, and then either insert one manually in any message, or set Windows Mail to add a default signature to messages automatically.

To create and use a signature, follow these steps:

1. In the main Windows Mail window, choose [Tools] [Options]. Windows Mail displays the Options dialog box. Click the [Signatures] tab, and then click the [New] button.

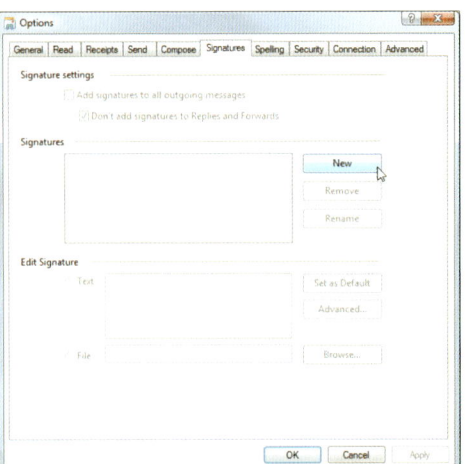

2. Windows Mail adds a new signature to the Signatures box. Type the text for the signature in the Edit Signature box.

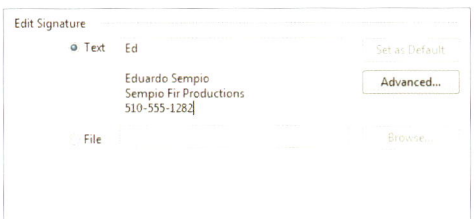

3. In the Signatures box, click the [signature], and then click the [Rename] button. Windows Mail displays an edit box around the name Signature #1. Type a descriptive name for the signature, and then press <Enter>.

> tip>>
> **Adding an Existing Signature from a File**
> If you have a ready-made signature stored in a file, load it by selecting the [File option] button, clicking the [Browse] button, selecting the [file] in the resulting Open dialog box, and then clicking the [Open] button.

4. Create other signatures as needed. If you create more than one, set your [default signature] by clicking it in the Signatures box, and then clicking the [Set As Default] button.

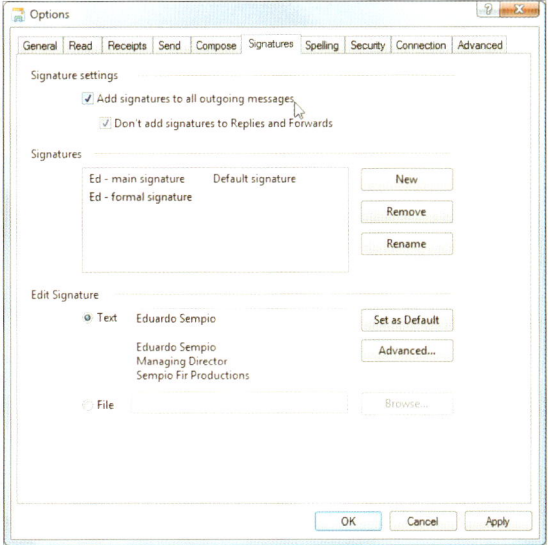

5. If you want Windows Mail to add your signature automatically to outgoing messages, select the [Add Signatures To All Outgoing Messages] check box. Select the [Don't Add Signatures To Replies And Forwards] check box unless you want replies and forwarded messages to have your signature (normally, such messages do not need a signature). When you've finished creating signatures, click the [OK] button to close the Options dialog box.

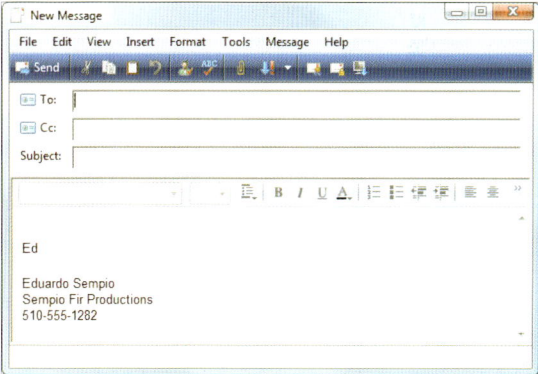

155

6. If you chose to sign messages automatically, Windows Mail inserts your default signature when you start a new message, as shown here.

7. If you chose not to sign messages automatically, insert a signature when needed by clicking the [Insert] menu, highlighting [Signature], and then choosing the signature you want, as shown here.

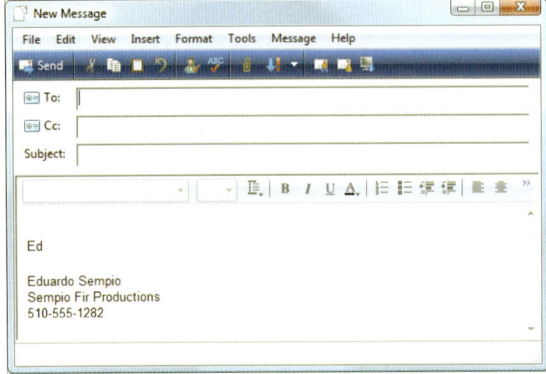

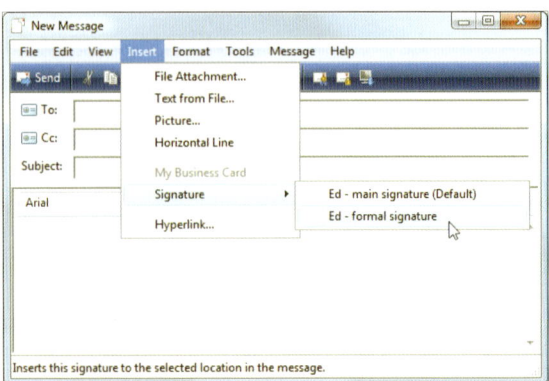

Communicating via Web Based E mail   Note >>>

Standard e-mail is great when you use a single computer and you want to have all your messages on it. You can write messages when your computer is not connected to the Internet, then connect and send them.

The alternative to standard e-mail is Web-based e-mail, e-mail implemented through a Web site and which you access using a Web browser. Web-based e-mail is especially convenient when you need to be able to check your e-mail from any computer. For example, many people check their Web-based e-mail from work as well as from home.

To use Web-based e-mail, use a Web browser such as Internet Explorer to sign up for a Web-based e-mail service. Various such services are available, including Google's Gmail (http://www.gmail.com), Microsoft's Hotmail (http://www.hotmail.com), and Yahoo's Yahoo! Mail (http://www.yahoo.com).

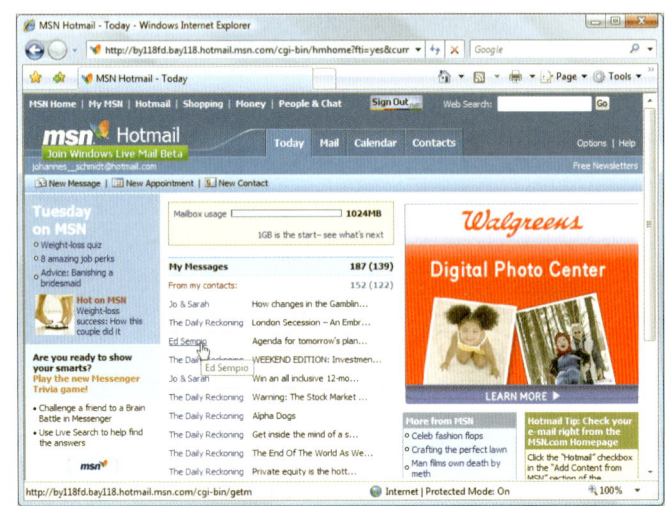

Web-based e-mail services have easy-to-use interfaces. The next illustration shows the Inbox in a Hotmail account. To open a message, you simply click its hyperlink.

SECTION 03

Getting and Setting Up Windows Live Messenger

E mail is great for communicating with other people at your convenience and theirs. You can write and send a message whenever it suits you, and they normally will receive the message the next time they check their e mail. But when you need to communicate with other people in real time, instant messaging is a better choice. This section shows you how to download and install the Windows Live Messenger program that Microsoft provides for free.

Downloading and Installing Windows Live Messenger

To download and install Windows Live Messenger, follow these steps:

1. Open [Internet Explorer] and go to [http://www.microsoft.com/downloads]. In the Search box at the top of the Download Center area, type **windows live messenger**, and then click the [Go] button.

2. Internet Explorer displays a Search Results page. Click the [Windows Live Messenger] link.

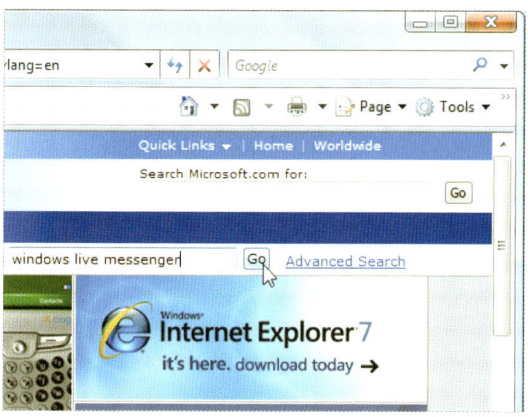

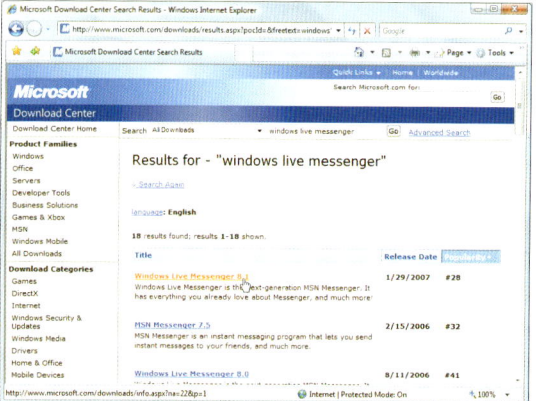

3. Internet Explorer displays the Download Details page for Windows Live Messenger. Click the [Download] button.

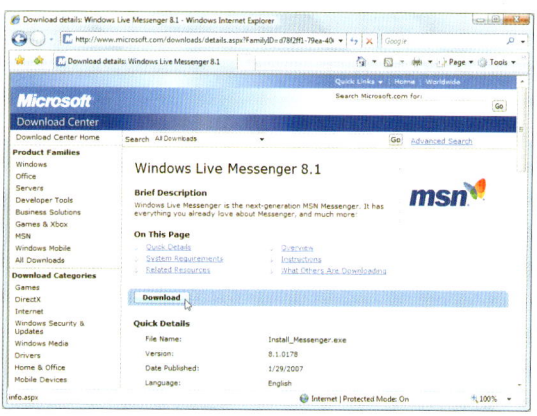

4. Internet Explorer displays a File Download – Security Warning dialog box. Click the [Run] button.

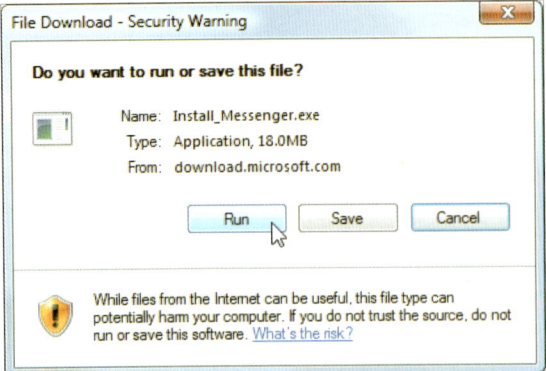

5. Internet Explorer downloads the file.

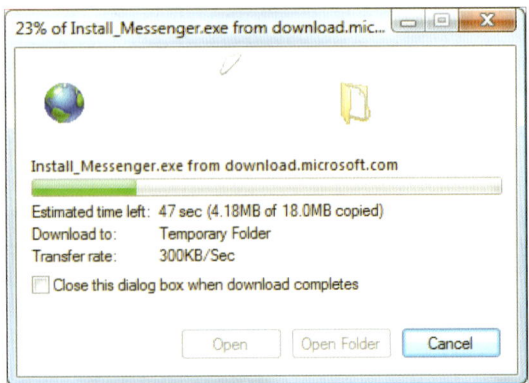

6. When the download is complete, Internet Explorer displays an Internet Explorer - Security Warning dialog box. Verify that the program name shown is Windows Live Messenger and that the publisher is Microsoft Corporation, and then click the [Run] button.

7. Internet Explorer launches the Windows Live Messenger Setup Wizard. Click the [Next] button.

8. The wizard displays the Terms Of Use And Privacy Statement screen. Read the Microsoft Service Agreement for Windows Live Messenger in the dialog box. You should also read the Microsoft Online Privacy Statement by opening an Internet Explorer window to the URL shown on the Terms Of Use And Privacy Statement screen. If you can accept the terms, select the [I Accept The Terms Of Use And Privacy Statement option] button, and then click the [Next] button. (If you can't accept the terms, you must cancel the installation.)

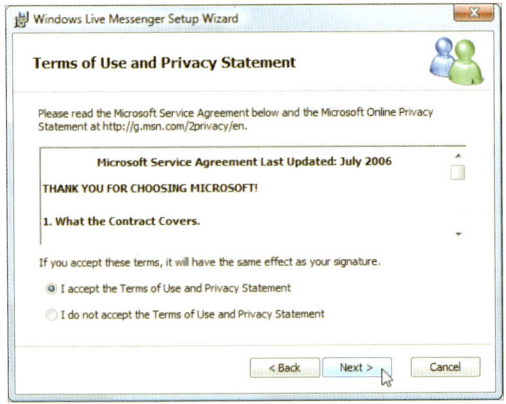

Chapter 06. Making the Most of E-mail and Instant Messaging

9. The wizard displays the Choose Additional Features And Settings screen. Clear the check box for each additional feature you do not want to install. (The wizard selects all the check boxes by default.) Click the [Next] button, and then go through User Account Control for the Windows Live Messenger feature.

10. The wizard installs Windows Live Messenger and the features you chose, and then displays the Windows Live Messenger Has Been Installed screen. Click the [Close] button. The wizard closes.

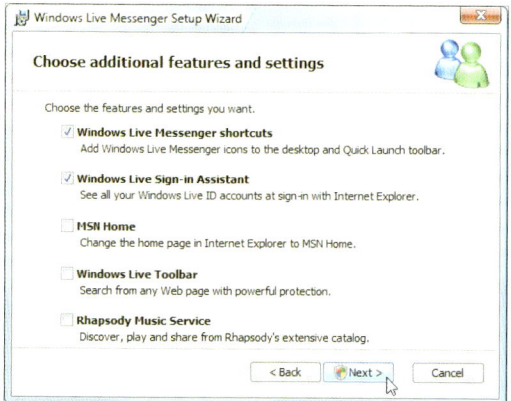

> **Deciding Which Additional Features Are Useful** Note >>>
>
> Many people find the Windows Live Messenger Shortcuts feature and the Windows Live Sign-In Assistant feature useful. You probably do not want to change your Internet Explorer home page to MSN Home, install the Windows Live Toolbar, or install the Rhapsody Music Service.
> If you choose to install these features, setup occurs after the wizard finishes. For example, if you chose the Windows Live Sign-In Assistant feature, you must go through User Account Control for the Windows Live Login Browser Helper Object. When installation has completed, Windows Live Messenger starts.

Launching Windows Live Messenger and Signing In

Once you've installed Windows Live Messenger, you can launch it and sign in, creating a Windows Live ID along the way if necessary. Follow these steps:

1. If you let Windows Live Messenger place an icon on your desktop or the Quick Launch toolbar, click that [icon]. Otherwise, click the [Start] button, click [All Programs], and then click [Windows Live Messenger]. (Or, if you just installed Windows Live Messenger and it launched automatically, skip this step.)

159

2. The main Windows Live Messenger window opens. If you have a Windows Live ID, skip ahead to step 4. Otherwise, click the [Sign Up For A Windows Live ID] link near the bottom of the window.

3. Windows opens an Internet Explorer window to the Windows Live Web site. Click the [Sign Up] link, and then follow through the process of creating the account, providing the required information, and reading and accepting the Windows Live Service Agreement and Privacy Statement. When you've created the Windows Live ID, return to the Messenger window.

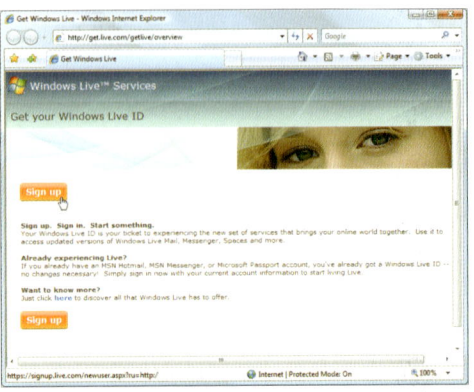

4. Type your Windows Live ID user name and password. Click the [Sign In] button.

Understanding What Windows Live ID is   Note >>>

Like most instant-messaging services, Windows Live Messenger requires you to sign in with a user name and password. This identification is called a *Windows Live* ID, which is the latest name for the electronic ID formerly known as Microsoft Password and Microsoft .NET Password. This is the same ID that you use for a Microsoft Hotmail account—so if you already have Hotmail, you're ready to use Windows Live Messenger. If not, you can sign up for a Windows Live ID when you start using Messenger.

5. Messenger signs you in to the instant messaging service and then displays a Welcome window, which contains an informational message. Click the [Close] button (the ❌ button) if you want to close the Welcome window.

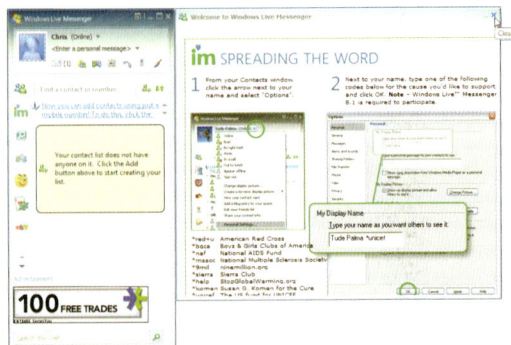

> **Deciding Whether to Save Your Password and Sign In Automatically**   Note >>>
>
> Select the [Remember Me] check box if you want Messenger to remember your user name; select the [Remember My Password] check box if you want Messenger to store your password as well. These settings are useful when you're using Messenger on your own computer, but you should never use them on public computers. Select the [Sign Me In Automatically] check box if you want Messenger to sign you in the moment you log on to Windows.

Closing the Messenger Window, Signing Out, and Signing In

You've only just started Messenger, but it's time to learn how to close it, because Messenger behaves differently from most other Windows programs. This is because when you close the main Messenger window, Messenger keeps running so that you can still receive instant messages from your contacts. However, you can also sign out of the Messenger service, or even exit Messenger entirely.

To practice signing out, closing Messenger, and restarting Messenger, follow these steps:

1. Click the [Close] button (the [X] button). Messenger closes its main window and reduces itself to an icon in the notification area, but keeps running. To restore Messenger, either double-click the [Messenger] icon (the green figure) or right-click it, and then choose [Open Messenger] from the context menu.

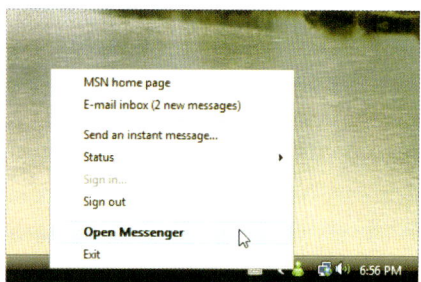

2. To sign out from the Messenger service, click the [Show Menu] button, highlight [File], and then choose [Sign Out]. Messenger signs you out of the service. You can then click the [Close] button (the [X] button) to close the Messenger window. Again, Messenger keeps running as an icon in the notification area, but you are no longer signed in. If you want to close Messenger, right-click the [icon], and then choose [Exit] from the context menu.

3. To sign back in again, right-click the [Messenger] icon in the notification area, and then choose [Sign In] from the context menu. In the Messenger window, click the [Sign In] button if Messenger isn't set to sign you in automatically.

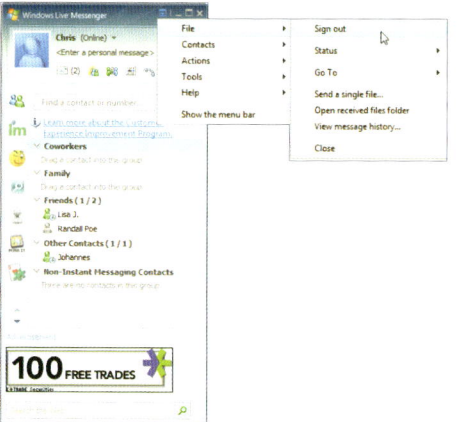

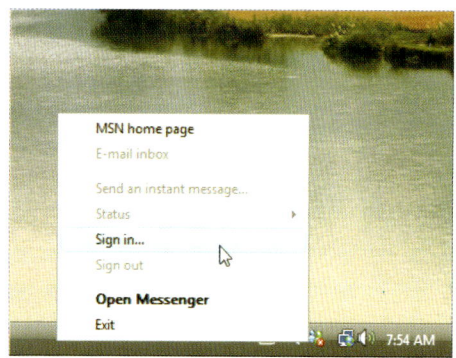

SECTION 04

Communicating via Windows Live Messenger

Before you can start sending and receiving instant messages, you must have the names and instant messaging addresses of the people with whom you want to communicate. Messenger calls these people your contacts, so your first task is to add contacts to your list.

Adding Contacts

To add a contact, follow these steps:

1. Click the [Add A Contact] button. Messenger displays the Windows Live Contacts-Add A Contact dialog box. Type the contact's address in the Instant Messaging Address text box, and type a message in the Personal Invitation text box. Type a short name for the contact in the Nickname text box, and then choose a group—Family, Friends, or Coworkers—in the Group drop-down list. Click the [Add Contact] button.

2. Messenger closes the dialog box and adds the contact to the list in the window.

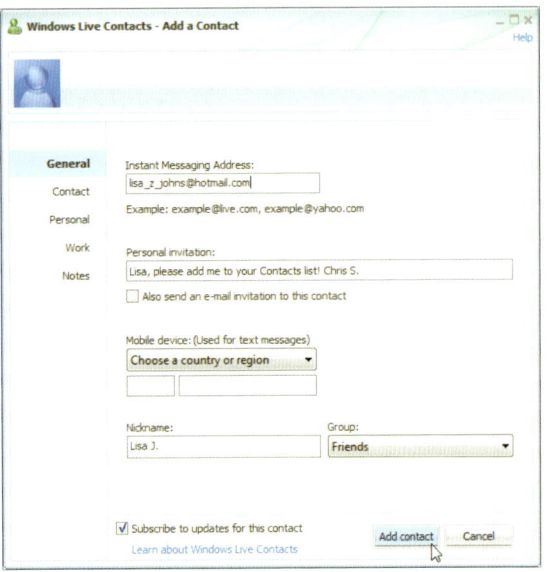

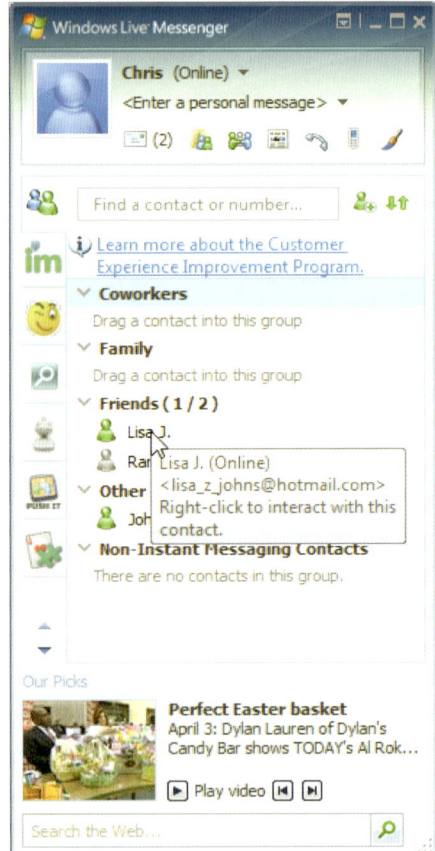

162

Adding a Contact When Someone Sends You a Message — Note >>>

You can also add a contact when someone sends you a message. If the sender isn't a contact, Messenger includes a link at the top of the Conversation window that you can click to add the sender to your contact list, as shown here.

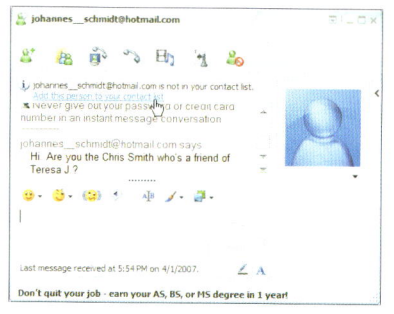

Chatting with a Contact

Once you've added your contacts to Messenger, you can easily chat with them. Follow these steps:

1. Double-click the [contact] in the main Messenger window. Messenger opens a Conversation window for the contact. Type a message in the lower text box, and then press <Enter> or click the [Send] button.

2. Messenger sends the message to your contact who sees a pop-up window containing your message (or the first part of it). If your contact replies, the reply appears in the top box in the Conversation window. You can then continue the conversation.

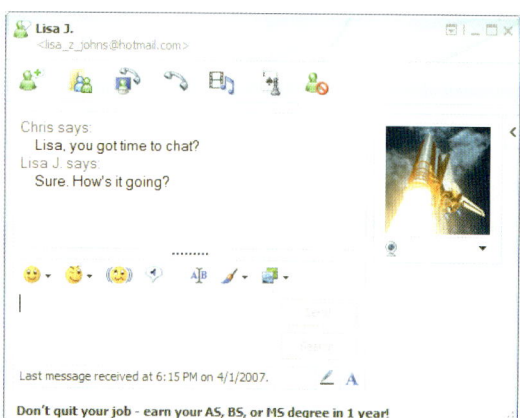

Continuing Your Last Conversation with a Contact — Note >>>

When you open a Conversation window for a contact with whom you've chatted before, Messenger automatically loads your last conversation so that you can continue it, if you want to. If you prefer to start a new conversation each time, click your user name in the main Messenger window and choose [Options]. In the Options dialog box, click the [Messages] category in the left pane, clear the [Show My Last Conversation In New Conversation Windows] check box, and then click the [OK] button.

3. To include an emoticon (an icon conveying an emotion or idea), click the [Emoticon] button above the message box, and then choose the emoticon from the panel that appears. You can also send a wink (an animation) by clicking the [second button] and selecting the wink from the panel that appears. You can also send a nudge by clicking the [third button]; this makes the Messenger window bounce to gain the recipient's attention.

4. To add another person to the conversation click the [Invite Someone To This Conversation] button.

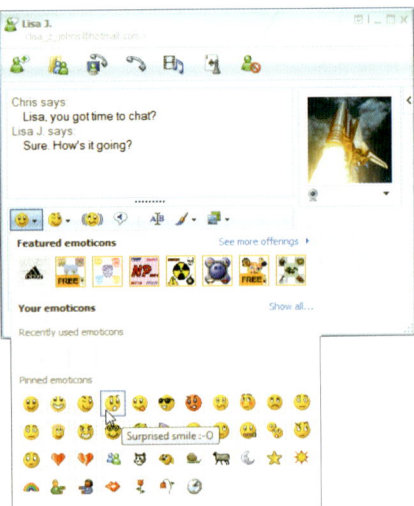

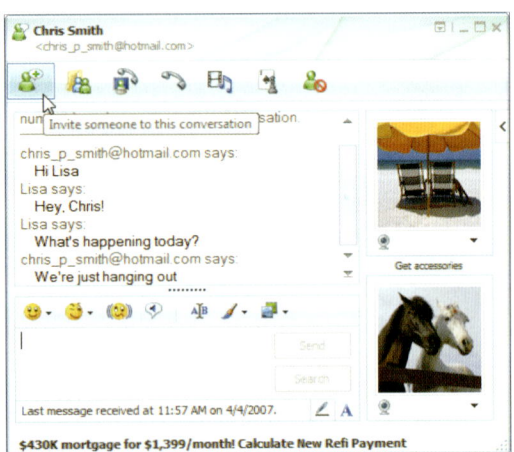

5. Windows Live Messenger displays the Windows Live Contacts-Select Contacts dialog box. Click each [contact] you want to add, selecting the contact's check box, and then click the [OK] button.

6. Windows Live Messenger closes the dialog box and adds the contact or contacts to the conversation. All participants in the conversation can then chat. When you've finished chatting, click the [Close] button (the ⊠ button). The first time you close a Conversation window, Messenger opens the dialog box shown here, asking if you want to save your text conversations. Select the [Yes, Save My Messages On This Computer option] button if you want to save them; otherwise, select the [No, Do Not Save My Messages On This Computer option] button. Click the [OK] button. Messenger closes the dialog box.

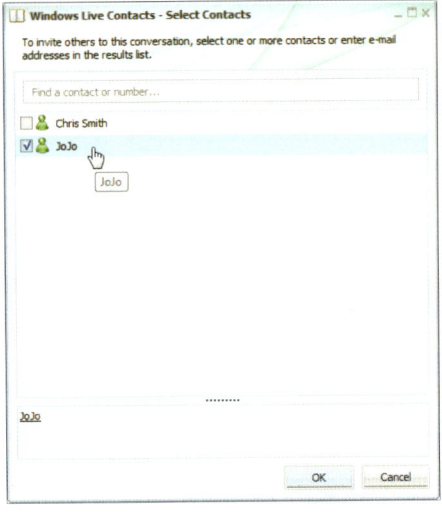

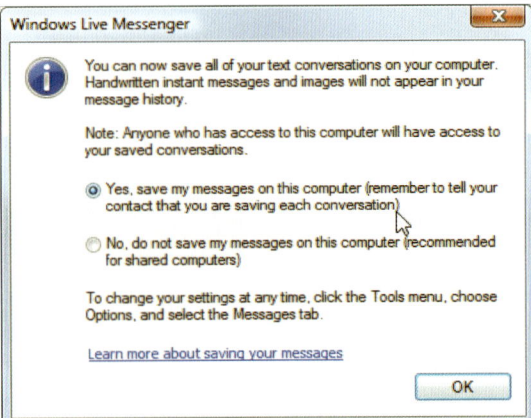

Let's Go Pro!

Set Up Audio and Video

If you want to make audio or video calls with Messenger, you must configure Messenger to use your audio and video equipment. Connect the equipment (if it is not already connected) and then follow these steps:

① Click the [Show Menu] button, highlight [Tools], and then choose [Audio And Video Setup] from the menu. Windows Live Messenger launches the Audio And Video Setup Wizard, which displays its first screen. Click the [Next] button.

② The wizard displays the Speaker Setup screen. In the [Select The Speakers Or Headset You Would Like To Use] drop-down list, select the speakers or headset. Select the [Click Here If You Are Using Headphones] check box if you are using headphones. Click the [Play Sound] button to play a test sound, and then drag the Speaker Volume slider to a suitable level. Click the [Next] button.

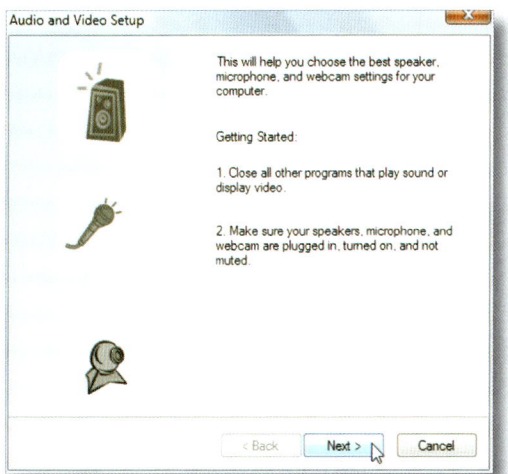

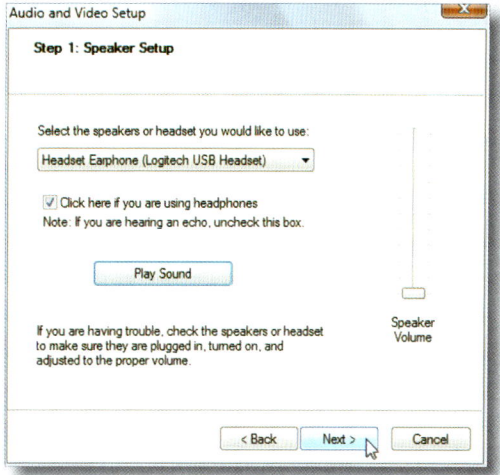

③ The wizard displays the Microphone Setup screen. In the [Select The Microphone You Would Like To Use] drop-down list, select the [microphone], and then drag the Microphone Volume slider to a volume that makes the indicator bar go into the yellow area as you speak. Click the [Next] button.

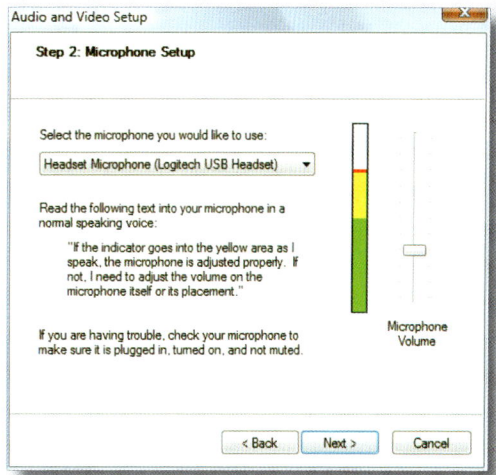

④ The wizard displays the Webcam Setup screen. In the [Select The Webcam You Would Like To Use] drop-down list, select the [Webcam]. Your picture appears in the preview box. Click the [Options] button.

⑤ The wizard displays the Properties dialog box for the camera. Choose [options] for the Webcam. The options available depend on the Webcam's capabilities, but may include picture improvements (such as adjusting hue, saturation, and contrast), zooming in, or applying effects and frames (as in the example shown). Move the Properties dialog box so that you can see the preview box in the Audio And Video Setup Wizard, and choose [settings] you like. When you've finished, click the [OK] button to return to the wizard.

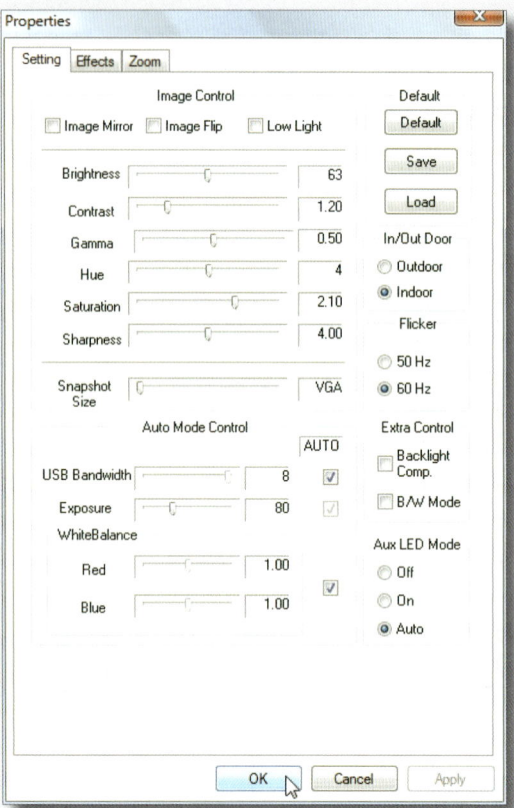

⑥ Click the [Finish] button. The wizard closes and applies your settings.

● Making Audio and Video Calls

Chatting via text can be fun, especially if you have lively or witty friends. But if you have audio and video hardware available, and you have a broadband Internet connection, you can make audio calls or audio-and-video calls as well.

To make an audio or video call follow these steps:

① Right-click the [contact] in the Messenger window, and then choose [Call] [Call Computer] to start an audio call or [Video] [Start A Video Call] to start a video call. This example uses a video call.

② Windows Mail opens a Conversation window and calls the contact. When the contact replies, you hear the contact's voice and (if you're making a video call) see the contact's video in the main window. Chat via audio or via text. When the conversation ends, click the [Close] button (the [X] button) to close the Conversation window.

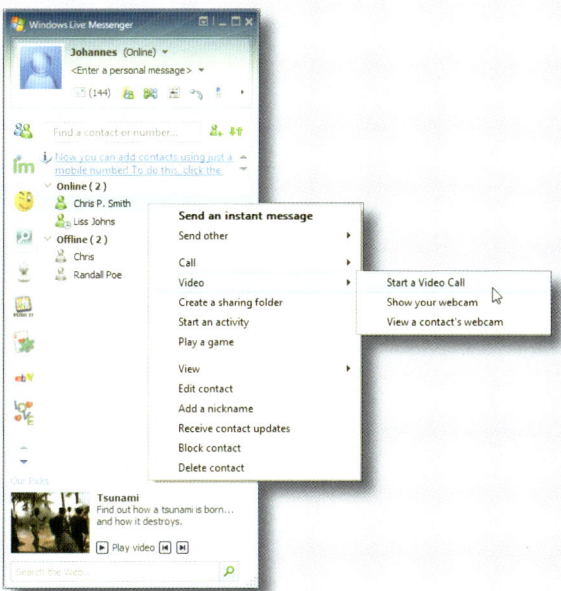

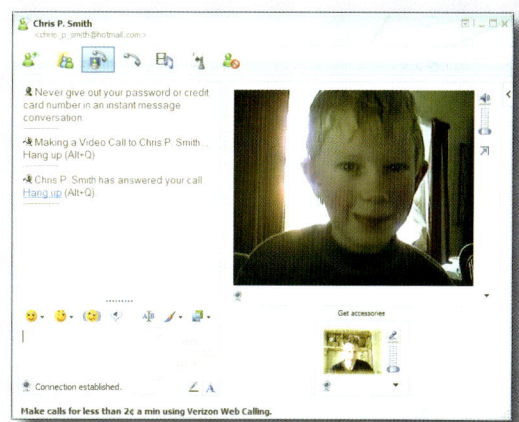

Adding Audio or Video to an Existing Chat — Note >>>

If you've already started a text-based chat, you can add audio by clicking the [Call A Contact] button on the toolbar. You can add both audio and video by clicking the [Start Or Stop A Video Call] button on the toolbar. When you go to add audio or video, your contact can choose whether to accept or decline the call.

Chapter 7

Enjoying Music, Video, DVD, and TV

As you've seen earlier in this book, Windows Vista can run pretty much any business application you need. But Windows Vista also comes fully equipped for enjoying music, videos, and DVDs. All versions of Windows Vista include the powerful Windows Media Player program, which can handle these media. Windows Vista Home Premium and Ultimate Editions also include Windows Media Center, which lets you watch, record, and play back TV as well.

SECTION 01

Starting Windows Media Player and Creating Your Library

This section shows you how to get started with Windows Media Player by setting up Windows Media Player, using its different play modes, and adding files to your media library.

Setting Up Windows Media Player

The first time you run Windows Media Player, you have to set it up. Follow these steps:

1. Click the [Start] button, click [All Programs], and then click [Windows Media Player]. The Welcome To Windows Media Player screen appears. Select the [Express Settings option] button, and then click the [Finish] button.

2. Windows Media Player applies the recommended settings, and then opens the program. Windows Media Player automatically searches your computer's hard disk for music files and video files. It shows the files it has found—for example, sample music files in the Sample Music folder inside the Public Music folder, which is shared among all users of the computer.

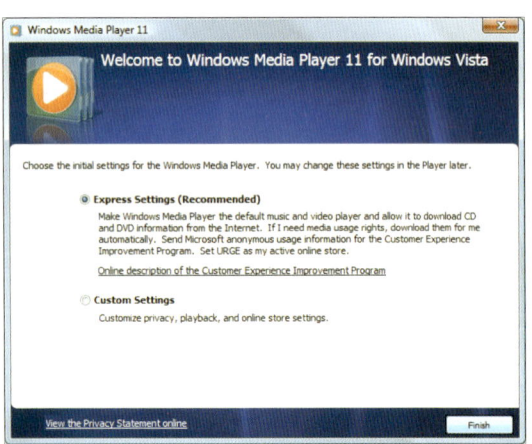

Using Windows Media Player's Modes

Windows Media Player can appear not only as a normal window but also in several different modes that you may find useful at different times. To switch among modes, follow these steps:

1. Windows Media Player at first appears in a normal window—one that is not maximized or minimized, and that has standard window borders. Click the [Switch To Compact Mode] button.

2. Windows Media Player switches to Compact mode, in which the title bar readout rotates among the artist, composer, CD title, and song title. Click the [Return To Full Mode] button.

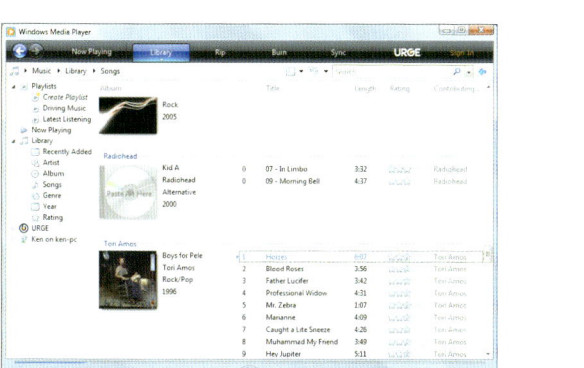

3. Windows Media Player returns to Full mode. Press <Alt> to display the menus, click [View], and then click [Skin Chooser].

4. Windows Media Player switches to Skin mode. Browse the skins, select the one you want to apply, and then click the [Apply Skin] button.

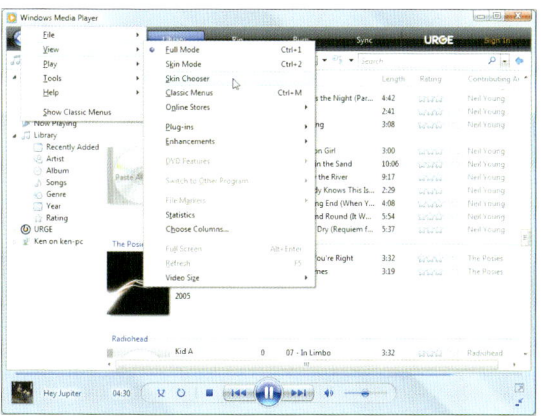

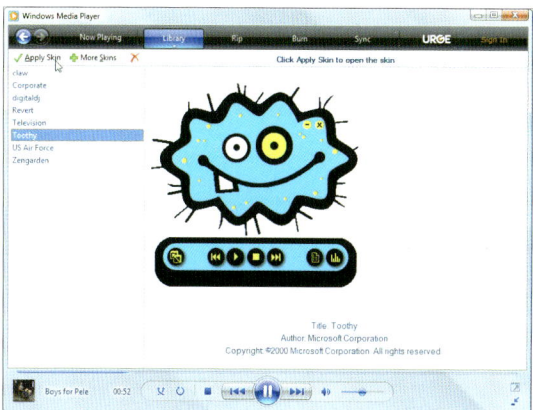

Getting More Skins   Note >>>

Depending on your computer manufacturer's choices, there may only be a few skins here. To get more, click the [More Skins] button. Windows Media Player opens an Internet Explorer window to the Microsoft Web site, where you can download many different skins.

171

5. Windows Media Player applies the skin, making the program look completely different. When you're ready to return to Full mode, click the [Return To Full Mode] button, which can appear anywhere on the skin. Alternatively, right-click, and then choose [Return To Full Mode].

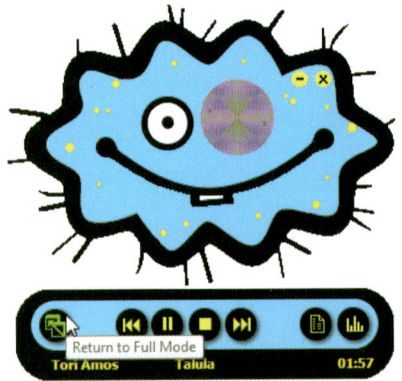

6. Windows Media Player switches back to Full mode. Click the [Minimize] button.

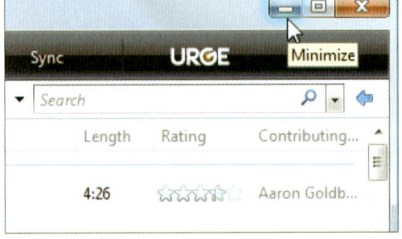

7. Windows Media Player shows a dialog box asking if you want the Windows Media Player toolbar on your taskbar. Click the [Yes] button.

8. Windows Media Player appears as a toolbar on the taskbar. Move the mouse over the toolbar to display a pop-up window of information about the current song. When you are ready to return to Full mode, click the [Restore] button.

Creating Your Media Library

If Windows Media Player finds some music files on your computer, you can double-click a file to play it. But what you'll often need to do is add other music files or video files to your music library. You can add existing files (as described here), create new files by copying from CD (as described in "Ripping CDs with Windows Media Player"), or purchase music online (as described in "Purchasing Music Online").

To add files on your computer, follow these steps:

1. Click the [Library] tab on the toolbar, and then click [Add To Library].

2. Windows Media Player shows the Add To Library dialog box. To add files only from your own folders, select the [My Personal Folders] option button. To add files from all available folders, select the [My Folders And Those Of Others That I Can Access] option button.

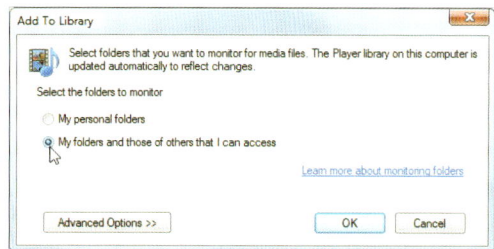

3. To add specific folders click the [Advanced Options] button.

4. Windows Media Player expands the Add To Library dialog box, showing the list of monitored folders. Click the [Add] button, use the [Add Folder] dialog box to select the folder, and then click the [OK] button to add the folder to the list. When you have finished adding folders, click the [OK] button.

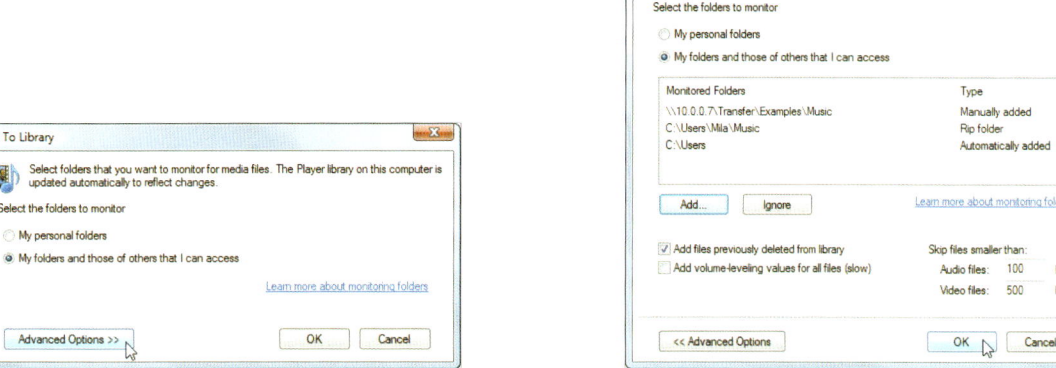

173

5. Windows Media Player shows the Add To Library By Searching Computer dialog box while it finds media files and adds them to the library. Click the [Close] button when you want to close the dialog box. The search continues in the background until it is complete.

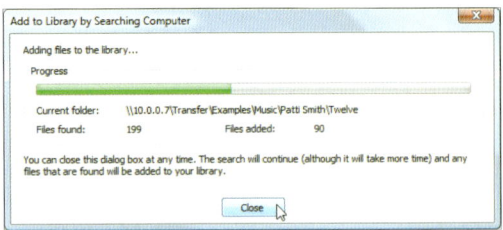

6. Windows Media Player shows its Library page, which now includes the files you have added.

Adding Further Files Quickly and Easily — Note >>>

Once you've told Windows Media Player which folders to monitor, you can add files to your media library by placing them in one of those folders. The next time Windows Media Player checks the monitored folders, it finds the files and adds them to your media library automatically.

Ripping CDs with Windows Media Player

To add songs to your media library by ripping (copying) them from a CD follow these steps:

1. Insert the CD in your computer's optical drive. If the AutoPlay dialog box appears, see the sidebar "Setting Windows to Rip Songs from CD Automatically." If Windows automatically starts ripping the CD, simply wait. If not, click the [Rip] tab to display its contents, and then click the [Start Rip] button.

2. Windows Media Player starts ripping the CD.

Chapter 07. Enjoying Music, Video, DVD, and TV

3. Click the [Rip] drop-down button (the down-arrow below the word "Rip"), and then click [Eject CD After Ripping], placing a check mark next to this item on the menu. When Windows Media Player finishes ripping the songs, it ejects the CD. (You can also eject the CD manually.)

Setting Windows to Rip Songs from CD Automatically   Note >>>

When Windows detects the CD you've inserted in the optical drive, it may open the AutoPlay dialog box. From here, if you want, you can set Windows to rip songs automatically when you insert a CD. To do so, select the [Always Do This For Audio CDs] check box, and then click the [Rip Music From CD] button, as shown here.

If you want to rip only this CD, but not other audio CDs, clear the [Always Do This For Audio CDs] check box, and then click the [Rip Music From CD] button.

Purchasing Music Online

Windows Media Player makes it easy to purchase music online. If you use the Express setup option, as recommended earlier in this chapter, Windows Media Player sets itself up to use the URGE online music service, but you must download URGE software before you can use the service. You can also set Windows Media Player to use other online music services, such as Napster or eMusic.

Windows Vista A·c·c·e·l·e·r·a·t·e·d

■ Downloading the URGE Software

Downloading the URGE Software

1. Click the [URGE] drop-down button (the down-arrow below the URGE logo), and then click [URGE] on the menu. Windows Media Player shows the Download Online Store Software screen.

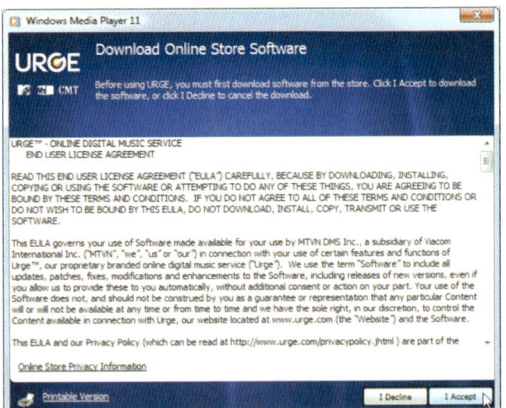

2. Read the license agreement, and then click the [I Accept] button if you want to proceed. Wait while Windows Media Player downloads the software.

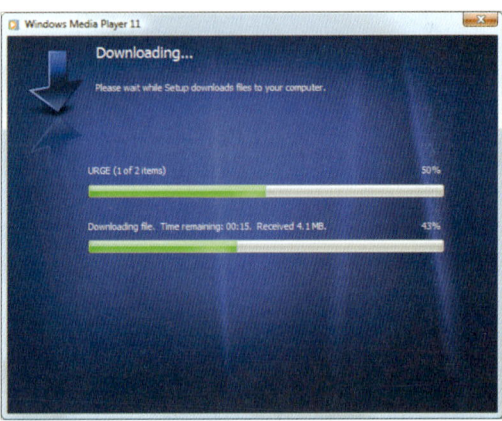

3. The Microsoft Windows Media Configuration Utility - Security Warning dialog box appears. Verify that the name shown is URGE and the publisher is MTV Networks. If so, click the [Run] button, and then go through [User Account Control] for the [UrgeSetup] program.

4. Windows Media Player installs URGE, and then displays an URGE dialog box prompting you to close Windows Media Player. Close [Windows Media Player], and then click the [OK] button. The installation completes.

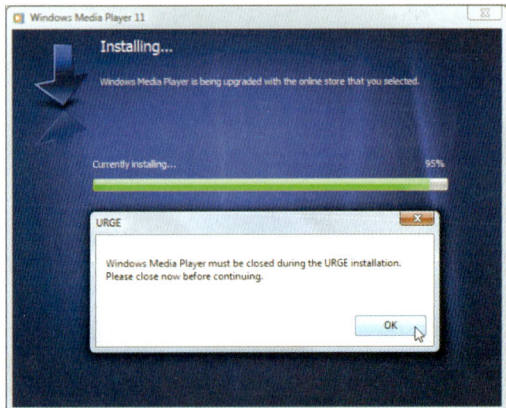

■ Creating an Account and Buying Music from URGE

Once you've installed URGE, you can create an account and buy music. Follow these steps:

1. Click the [Start] button, click [All Programs], and then click [Windows Media Player] to restart Windows Media Player. Click the [URGE] button to access URGE.

2. If the URGE screen includes a [Try It Free] button, as shown here, this is usually the best place to start. If not, click the [URGE drop-down] button, click [URGE], and then click [Create An Account] to start setting up an URGE account.

3. From the URGE main screen, click [links] or search to find the music you want. When you want to buy a song, click the [Buy] button.

Windows Media Player Cannot Play All Music Formats   Warning>>>

When buying music online, make sure you buy it in a file format that Windows Media Player can play. All files sold by music services that you can access through Windows Media Player should be fine for Windows Media Player, but Windows Media Player cannot play (for example) files in the AAC file format used by Apple's iTunes Music Store.

Let's Go Pro!

Changing Your Ripping Settings

The bit rate specifies the amount of data that a file uses to represent each second of music. For example, the 128 Kbps bit rate uses 128 kilobits of data to represent each second of music.

Generally speaking, the higher the bit rate, the higher the audio quality, although the quality also depends on the encoding format used. And always, the higher the bit rate, the larger the resulting file.

By default, Windows Media Player rips CDs to Windows Media Audio format at the 128 Kbps bit rate. This produces good quality music files suitable for playing via your computer or listening to on portable devices that can use the Windows Media Audio format.

However, you may want to use another of the six formats to which Windows Media Player can rip music. For example, you may prefer to use the MP3 format so that you can listen to songs on devices, such as iPods, that cannot use Windows Media Audio. The following table explains the formats briefly.

Format Name	Bit Rates Available (Kbps)	Advantages	Disadvantages
Windows Media Audio	48, 64, 96, 128, 160, 192	Gives high audio quality with compact file size. Plays on many devices.	Does not play on some devices (such as iPods) or software (such as iTunes).
Windows Media Audio Pro	32, 48, 64, 96, 128, 160, 192	Gives high audio quality with more compact file size than WMA.	Plays on relatively few devices and software.
Windows Media Audio (Variable Bit Rate)	40–355 (varies depending on the quality chosen)	Gives high audio quality with compact file size, saving more data for more complex audio.	Plays on fewer devices and software than Windows Media Audio.
Windows Media Audio Lossless	470–940 (adjusted automatically)	Gives full audio quality with some compression.	Files are modestly compressed and are large.
MP3	128, 192, 256, 320	Gives full audio quality at acceptable file sizes. Plays on all devices and software.	Requires a larger file size than Windows Media Audio to give similar audio quality.
WAV (Lossless)	Not applicable	Gives full audio quality. Plays on all software.	Files are uncompressed and therefore huge.

To change the ripping format and bit rate follow these steps:

① Click the [Rip] drop-down button (the down-arrow below the word "Rip"), click [Format] to open the submenu, and then click the [format you want].

② Click the [Rip] drop-down button again, click [Bit Rate] to open the submenu, and then click the [bit rate you want].

SECTION 02

Playing Music

You can play music either by simply navigating to the CD or song you want to play (as described first) or by creating custom playlists (as described after that). You will probably want to use both methods in order to enjoy your music to the full.

Playing Music

To play music, follow these steps:

1. Click the [Library] button on the toolbar. Windows Media Player shows the Library page. In the [Primary Views] list, double-click the [view you want to use]: Recently Added, Artist, Album, Songs, Genre, Year, or Rating. Alternatively, click the [view] in the Library section of the list in the navigation pane on the left.

2. If you want to change the view, click the [View Options] drop-down button, and then choose [Icon], [Tile], or [Details]. Icon shows a picture with the item's name. Tile shows a picture with the name and brief details. Details shows more extensive information.

3. Double-click the [item] whose contents you want to see.

4. Double-click the [song] you want to play.

179

5. Windows Media Player starts playing the song. Click the [Now Playing] tab if you want to watch visualizations (entertaining graphics) while the music plays.

6. Windows Media Player shows the Now Playing screen and starts displaying visualizations. You can drag the Volume slide to change the volume.

7. To change the sound of the music, click the [Now Playing] drop-down button, click [Enhancements], and then click [Graphic Equalizer].

8. To apply a preset equalization, click the [drop-down] button, and then choose the [equalization] from the list. The drop-down button shows the current equalization.

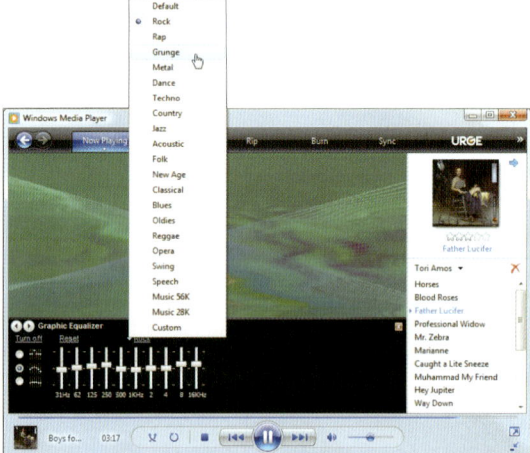

9. Windows Media Player applies the equalization. If you want to adjust the sound further, click the appropriate [option] button on the left for controlling the graphic equalizer sliders: Move Independently (the top option button), Move In A Loose Group (middle), or Move In A Tight Group (bottom).

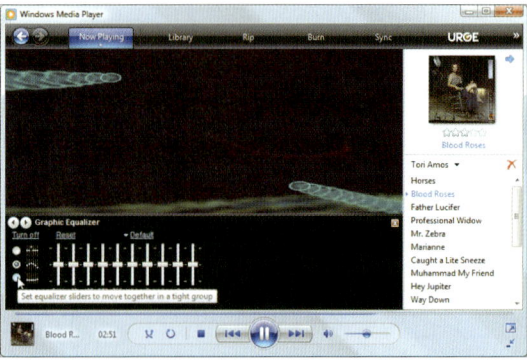

Chapter 07. Enjoying Music, Video, DVD, and TV

10. Drag one or more sliders to change the sound to how you want it. The leftmost slider controls the lowest frequencies (bass) and the rightmost slider the highest frequencies (treble). Click the [Reset] link if you want to reset the graphic equalizer.

11. Click the [Close] button (the button) to close the Graphic Equalizer pane.

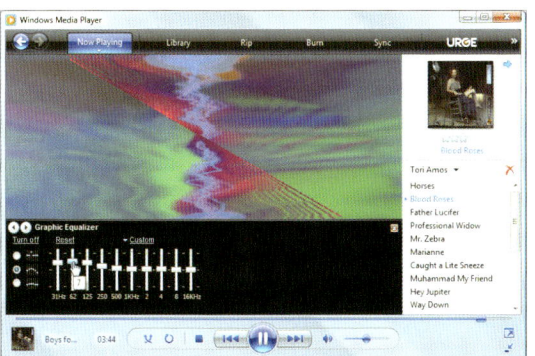
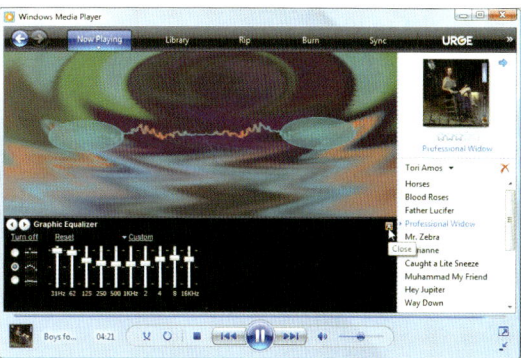

Creating and Using Playlists

Playing a single song, or playing a CD's songs in order, is easy, but you may prefer to play songs from different artists and CDs in an order you choose. To do so, you create a playlist.

■ Creating a Playlist

Follow these steps:

1. Click the [Library] button on the toolbar. If the Playlists item in the navigation pane is collapsed, double-click [Playlists] to expand it. Then click the [Create Playlist] item.

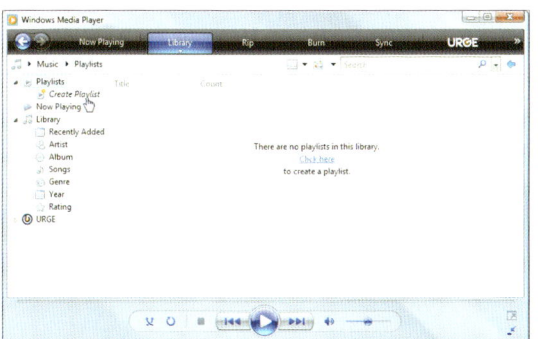

2. Windows Media Player creates a playlist, provisionally titles it New Playlist, and shows a box around the name.

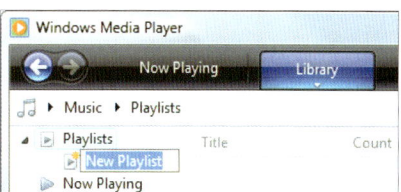

181

3. Type the name you want to give the playlist, and then press <Enter>.

4. Windows Media Player gives the playlist the name you typed, and then shows the List pane on the right. In the navigation pane, click your [preferred view for navigating] your media library (for example, click [Artist]).

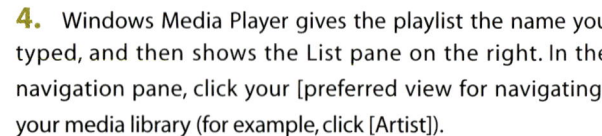

5. Navigate to a song you want to add to the playlist, and then drag it to the List pane. Repeat the procedure for other songs you want to add. Alternatively, drag entire CDs, artists, or even existing playlists.

6. To change the order of the songs in the playlist, drag one or more songs up or down. Click to select [one song]; <Shift>-click to select from the current selection to the song you click; or <Ctrl>-click to select songs one by one.

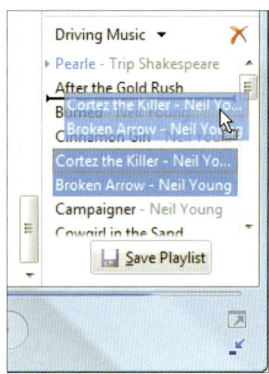

7. If you want to sort the playlist, click the [drop-down arrow] on its name in the [List] pane, click [Sort], and then click the [type of sort]—for example, [By Title]. You can also shuffle the playlist into random order by clicking [Shuffle List Now].

8. When you have finished creating the playlist, click the [Save Playlist] button.

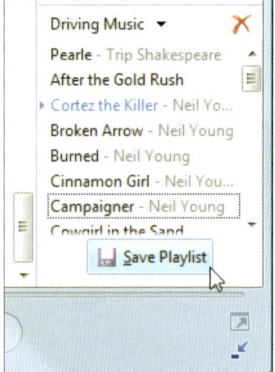

Chapter 07. Enjoying Music, Video, DVD, and TV

■ Playing a Playlist

To play a playlist, follow these steps:

1. Click the [Library] button on the toolbar to display the Library page. Double-click the [Playlists] item in the navigation pane if the playlists are collapsed, and then double-click the [playlist you want to play].

2. Windows Media Player starts playing the playlist at the first song. To see visualizations, click the [Now Playing] button.

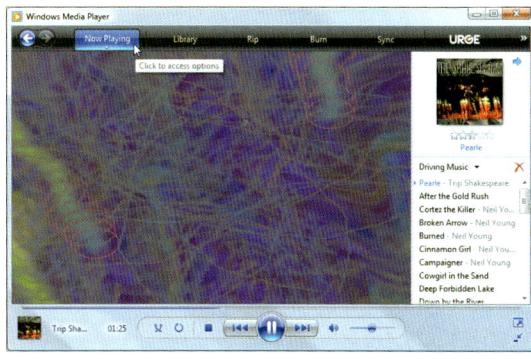

183

SECTION 03

Burning CDs and Sharing Music

As well as playing music, Windows Media Player lets you burn audio CDs that you can play in any CD player. You can also share your media library with other Windows Media Player users across a network.

Burning Audio CDs

Windows Media Player lets you burn an audio CD either from an existing playlist or from a new playlist you create. For example, after creating a playlist, you can burn a CD so that you can listen to it using a CD player or in your car. Or, you can create a custom playlist for a CD.

To burn an audio CD, follow these steps:

1. Click the [Burn] button. Windows Media Player shows the Burn List pane on the right side.

2. If you want to start from a playlist, drag that playlist from the navigation pane to the Burn List pane. Otherwise, create a new playlist from scratch in the Burn List pane by dragging songs to it.

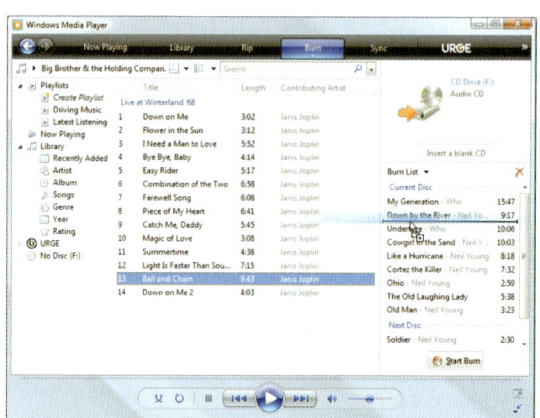

3. Windows Media Player shows Current Disc at the beginning of the playlist to indicate which songs will be on the first CD and Next Disc to indicate where the next disc will start. If you want to make sure all songs fit on one disc, delete any extra songs by [selecting them], right-clicking, and then clicking [Remove From List].

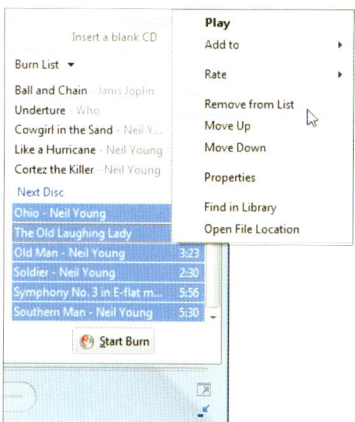

4. Insert a blank CD in your computer's optical drive. If the AutoPlay dialog box appears, click the [Burn An Audio CD Using Windows Media Player] button.

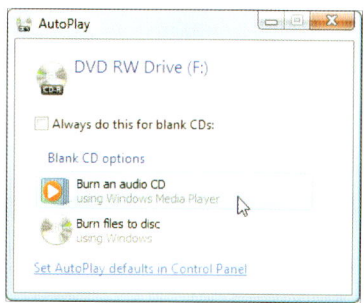

5. Windows Media Player displays details of the CD. Look at the readouts of the amount of music that can fit on the CD and the amount of space remaining once you burn this playlist. Add or remove songs as needed, and then click the [Start Burn] button.

6. Wait while Windows Media Player burns the CD.

7. When Windows Media Player has finished burning the CD, it ejects it. Remove the CD and label it using a CD marker pen. If you want to create another CD with the same contents, insert another blank CD and click the [Start Burn] button. Otherwise, click the [Burn List] button and either click [Clear List] (to dispose of the playlist) or click [Save Playlist As] (if you want to keep the list).

Sharing Music with Other People

Windows Media Player allows you to share the music on your computer with other people on the same network. You can also listen to the music that other people are sharing.

■ Setting Up Sharing the Easy Way

To set up sharing the easy way, follow these steps:

1. When Windows Media Player detects another computer nearby that is sharing music, it displays a pop-up message in the notification area. Click the [pop-up].

2. Windows Media Player shows the Windows Media Player Library Sharing dialog box, which lists the computer that has been found. To share your media with this computer, click the [Allow] button.

■ Setting Up Sharing Manually

To set up sharing at other times, follow these steps:

1. Click the [Library drop-down] button on the toolbar, and then click [Media Sharing]. Windows Media Player opens the Media Sharing dialog box. Verify that the information readout shows that your network is a private network.

2. Select the [Find Media That Others Are Sharing] check box if you want to find shared media. If you want to share your own media, select the [Share My Media] check box. Click the [OK] button, and then go through User Account Control for the Windows Media Player Configuration feature if necessary.

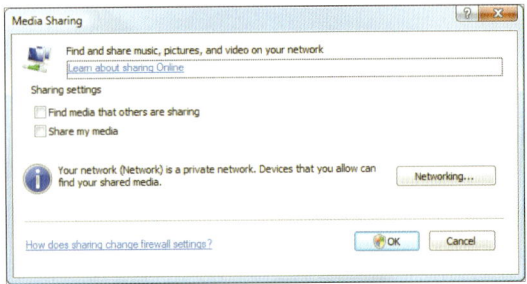

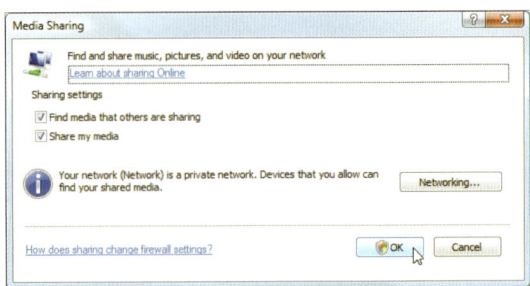

3. Windows Media Player expands the Media Sharing dialog box. If you want to share with other users of your PC, click the [Other Users Of This PC] icon, and then click the [Allow] button.

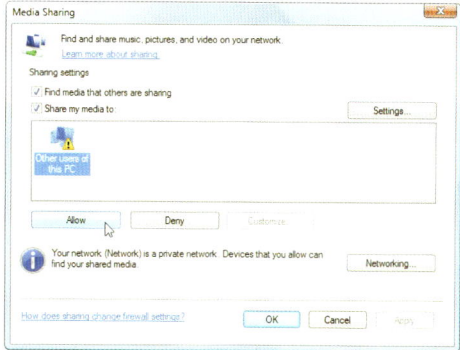

4. Windows Media Player applies a green circle with a check mark to the Other Users Of This PC icon. To allow users of another computer to share your files, click [that computer's name], click the [Allow] button, and then go through User Account Control for the Windows Media Player Configuration feature if necessary.

5. When you have finished choosing sharing settings, click the [OK] button to close the Media Sharing dialog box.

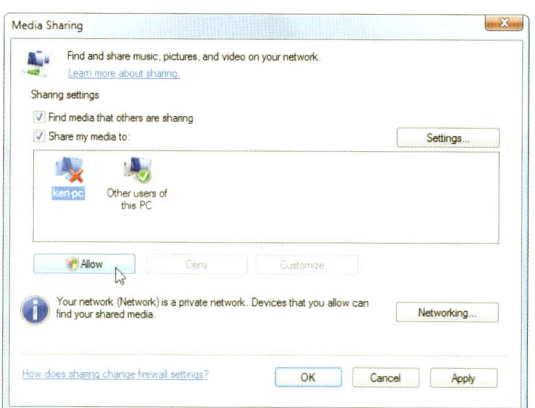

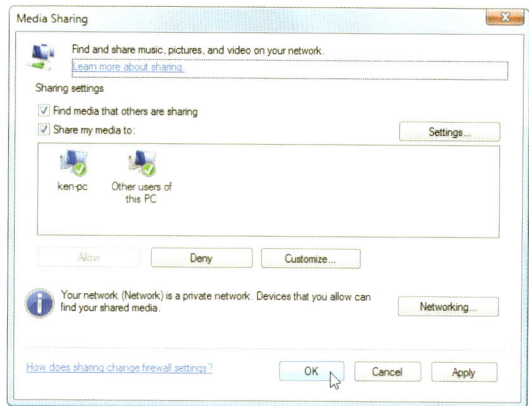

Playing Music Another Computer Is Sharing

To play music that another computer is sharing, follow these steps:

1. Click the [Library] button on the toolbar. Windows Media Player displays the Library page. In the navigation pane, double-click the [entry for the sharing computer].

2. Click the [view that you want to see]. For example, click [Artist] to see the songs listed by artist, and then double-click the [album] to display its contents.

3. Double-click the [song] you want to play.

SECTION 04

Playing Videos and DVDs

If your computer includes a DVD player (as most modern computers do), you can use Windows Media Player to play back DVDs.

Playing DVDs

To play a DVD, follow these steps:

1. Insert the DVD in your computer's DVD drive. Windows Media Player starts playing the DVD automatically.

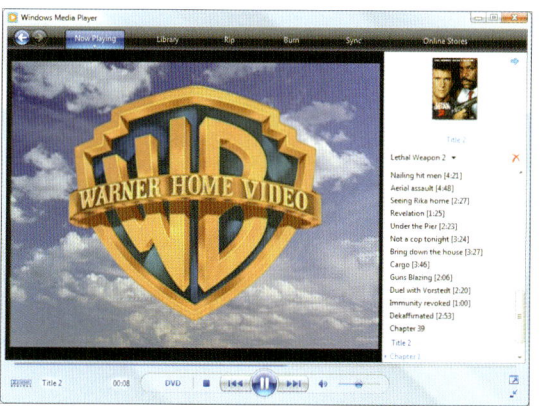

2. Use the play controls to play the movie, or use the List Pane on the right to navigate from scene to scene.

3. To close the List Pane, click the [blue arrow button] in its upper-right corner.

189

Playing Videos

To play a video, follow these steps:

1. Click the [Library drop-down] button, and then click [Video].

2. Windows Media Player displays the All Video list in your media library. Windows Vista normally includes several sample video files, so you will have some videos even if you haven't added any. Double-click the [video you want to play].

3. Windows Media Player shows the Now Playing tab and starts playing the video. Use the controls at the bottom of the window to control playback.

tip>>
Creating Video Playlists
You can create video playlists using the same techniques you learned for creating audio playlists. You can also mix videos and songs in the same playlist, so you see the video content when a video is playing and visualizations when a song is playing.

SECTION 05

Getting Started with Windows Media Center

If you have Windows Vista Home Premium or Windows Vista Ultimate Edition, Windows Vista includes Windows Media Center, the TV style media program.

Playing Performing Essential Setup Steps

Windows Media Center is very easy to use, no matter whether you use your mouse, your keyboard, or a remote control.

The most complex part of using Windows Media Center is setting it up to use your TV antenna or set-top box. To access the setup screens, follow these steps:

> **How Is Windows Media Center Different from Windows Media Player?** Note >>>
>
> Windows Media Center overlaps with Windows Media Player in several areas: Both can play music, show videos, and play back DVDs. Windows Media Center's has two main differences:
>
> **You can watch TV—and record it**
>
> Provided that your computer has a compatible TV card and is connected to an antenna or set-top box, Windows Media Center lets you watch TV, record TV, and play back recorded TV. Windows Media Player does not have these capabilities.
>
> **"Ten-foot interface"**
>
> You can navigate Windows Media Center using either your mouse or a remote control. This allows you to make Windows Media Center the focus of home entertainment, even if you use a large computer screen, instead of displaying Windows Media Center's output on a TV.

1. Click the [Start] button, click [All Programs], and then click [Windows Media Center]. Windows Media Center opens and shows its starting screen. Click the [down arrow], or press <↓> on the keyboard, to access the Tasks item in the vertical list of task categories.

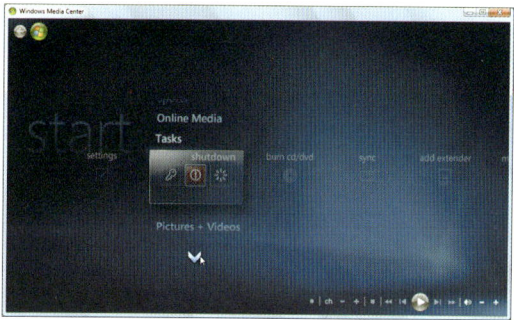

191

2. In the horizontal list of items within the Tasks category, click the [Settings] item.

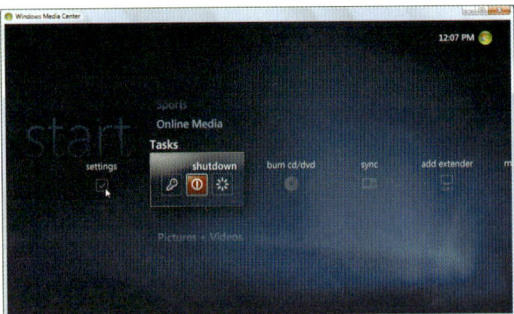

3. The Settings screen appears. Click the [TV] item.

4. The TV screen appears. Click the [Set Up TV Signal] button.

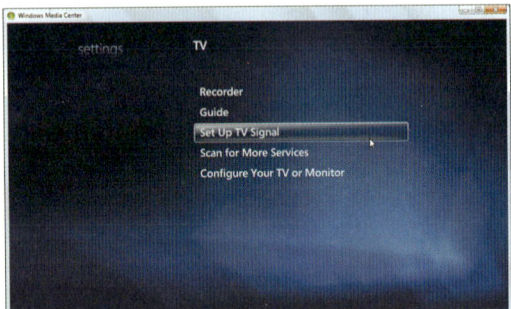

5. The Set Up Your TV Signal Wizard starts. Click the [Next] button, and then follow through the steps of the wizard. The steps vary depending on the type of TV signal you're using—for example, an antenna or a set-top box.

Chapter 07. Enjoying Music, Video, DVD, and TV

Watching TV

To watch TV using Windows Media Center, follow these steps:

1. On the Windows Media Center starting screen, click the [TV + Movies] category in the vertical list, and then click the [Live TV] item in the horizontal list.

2. Windows Media Center displays the first channel. Use the channel buttons at the bottom of the screen to navigate to the channel you want to watch.

Recording a TV Show

To record a TV show using Windows Media Center, follow these steps:

1. Click the [TV + Movies] category in the vertical list, and then click the [Recorded TV] item in the horizontal list.

2. Click the [Add Recording] button.

193

3. Windows Media Center shows the Add Recording screen. Click the button for the way you want to create the recording—from the Guide (as in this example), by searching, by specifying the channel and time, or by using a keyword. Follow the steps on the resulting screen to choose the show.

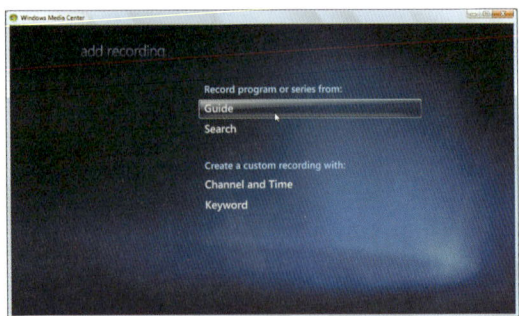

Playing Back Recorded TV Shows

To play back a recorded TV show using Windows Media Center, follow these steps:

1. Click the [TV + Movies] category in the vertical list, and then click the [Recorded TV] item in the horizontal list.

2. Windows Media Center shows a list of the recorded shows. Click the [show you want to watch].

Watching a DVD

To watch a DVD in Windows Media Center, follow these steps:

1. Insert the DVD in your computer's optical drive. If Windows opens an AutoPlay dialog box, select the [Always Do This For DVD Movies] check box if you want always to use Windows Media Center, and then click the [Play DVD Movie Using Windows Media Center] link.

2. If Windows does not open an AutoPlay dialog box, and Windows Media Center does not start playing the DVD automatically, click the [TV + Movies] category in the vertical list, and then click the [Play DVD] item in the horizontal list.

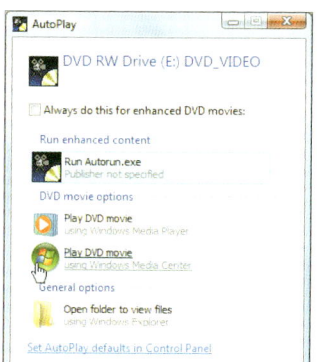

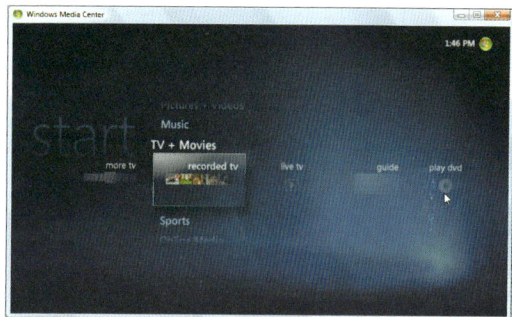

3. Use the play controls to control playback.

Chapter 8

Networking Your Computers and Sharing Files

As you've seen earlier in this book, connecting your computer to the Internet lets you browse the Web, send e mail to anyone with an Internet e mail account, and share files. Closer to home, you may want to connect your computer to a local area network so that you can share files with your family, friends, or coworkers.
This chapter shows you how to choose a suitable network type, build the network, connect your computers to the network, and share files across the network.

SECTION 01 — Creating a Wired Network

This section shows you how to create a wired network. You will need to buy suitable equipment, and then connect it together.

If you already have a wired network, see "Connecting Your Computer to a Wired Network" at the end of this section for instructions on connecting your computer to it.

Buying Equipment for a Wired Network

For a wired network, you need a network switch, network cables, and a network adapter in each computer, as in the first diagram on page 201.

■ Buying a Network Switch

The *network switch*, or simply *switch*, is the junction box into which you connect the network cables to create the network. When buying a network switch, it is wise to consider these three main features, along with price and aesthetics:

- **Speed:** If possible, buy Gigabit Ethernet, which is the fastest technology (up to 1 gigabit per second—1Gbps). Fast Ethernet is the next choice (100 megabits per second—100Mbps). Regular Ethernet (10Mbps) is too slow for modern networks unless you have old equipment that you must reuse.

- **Ports:** The switch needs one port, or connector, for each cable that you will connect: one for each computer, one for each printer or network storage device, and maybe one for your broadband Internet connection. Switches typically come with 4, 8, 16, or 24 ports. Buy a switch with the next greater number of ports than you currently need, so that you can add computers to the network as your needs grow.

- **Other features:** Some switches include features such as a print server (letting you print via the network), a DSL modem or cable modem, or USB connectors for adding network storage. Choose according to your needs.

■ Buying Network Cables

For modern networks, buy Category 5e (enhanced) or Category 6 network cables. You can either buy precut cables, which come in various lengths and a choice of colors; or buy a reel of cable, connectors, and a crimping tool, and create cables of exactly the lengths you require.

■ Buying Network Adapters

Most recent computers include a network adapter, so you will probably not need to add one. On the computer, look for a socket that resembles an oversize phone socket.

If you do need to add a network adapter to your computer, there are two main considerations to keep in mind:

- **Connection type:** You can connect a network adapter via a PCI slot (for a desktop computer), via a PC Card slot (for a laptop computer), or via a USB connector (for either). USB is easy, but it typically means that the network adapter will be projecting from the computer—so PCI is usually best for a desktop and PC Card for a laptop. (A PC Card projects a short way from the laptop, but usually not enough to cause problems.)

- **Speed:** Choose network adapters to match the speed of the network switch. For example, if you chose a Gigabit Ethernet switch, buy Gigabit Ethernet network adapters.

Setting Up a Wired Network

To set up a wired network, follow these general steps. The specifics will vary depending on the equipment you have purchased.

1. Position the switch at the logical center of the network—wherever you will be able to connect it to your Internet connection (assuming you have one) and run the cables to the computer. Connect the switch's power supply.

2. Install a wired network adapter in each computer that does not already have one:

   - **PCI card:** Shut down Windows. Unplug all cables, open the computer's case, and locate an empty PCI slot. Insert the card, secure it with a screw, and close the case. Reconnect the cables, and then start Windows.
   - **USB adapter**: Connect the adapter to one of the computer's USB connectors while Windows is running.
   - **PC Card**: Insert the card in the PC Card slot while Windows is running.

   When Windows discovers the network card it attempts to locate and load the driver software for it. You may need to provide software on a disc that came with the network card.

3. Connect one end of a network cable to a port on the switch, and then connect the other end to the port on the computer. If the switch and the computer are in the same room, this step should be easy. If they are in different rooms, you will have to run the cable from one room to the other.

4. Connect your Internet connection. Depending on the type of Internet connection, you may have to configure it using a computer.

5. Connect any other devices—for example, you may have a printer or a network disk that you can share by connecting it

Connecting Your Computer to a Wired Network

Once you've connected your computer's network port to a port on the switch, you may not need to perform any further configuration. Windows automatically tries to detect suitable network settings and apply them to your computer so that it can access the network and (if the network is connected to the Internet) the Internet.

The mechanism that Windows uses to determine network settings is called Dynamic Host Configuration Protocol (DHCP). DHCP runs by default on many routers and Internet-sharing devices; if you set up a home network or small business network, you may be using DHCP unless you choose to switch it off.

Sometimes, however, you may need to change the network configuration to get the computer connected satisfactorily. See the section "Specifying an IP Address Manually," later in this chapter, for details.

Let's Go Pro!

Choosing a Network Technology

If you use your computer in a networked situation such as a company or a college dorm, you need do little more than plug into the network.

But if you want to create a network at home, you'll need to choose a networking technology, buy the equipment, and put it together. This isn't difficult, but it takes a little while and involves several decisions.

For home or small office users, there are two main networking technologies: wired networks and wireless networks. Your first task is to decide which to use.

● When to Choose a Wired Network

In a wired network each computer connects to the network via a cable. Typically, each cable connects to a central device called a switch, as in the next diagram, which shows a small wired network such as might suit a home or small office.

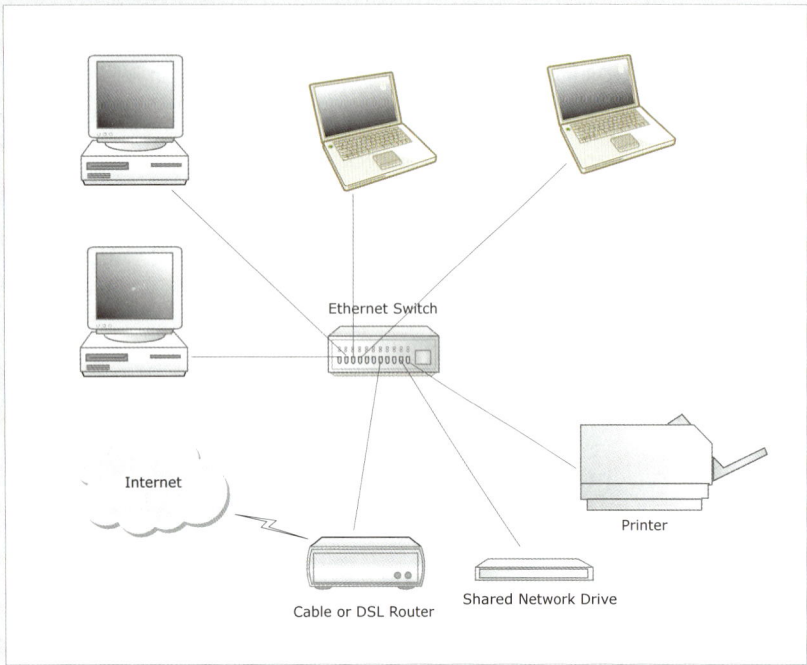

Choose a wired network in these circumstances:

- You can easily connect the computers using cables—even if the computers are in different rooms.

- You are concerned about security—you are worried, for example, that your neighbors might try to access a wireless network.

- You need the fastest possible network speeds—possibly because you regularly transfer vast files from one computer to another.

200

When to Choose a Wireless Network

In a wireless network, each computer connects to the network via radio waves. Typically, a wireless network is built around one or more wireless access points, devices to which the computers connect. The next diagram shows a small network such as you might use in a home or small office.

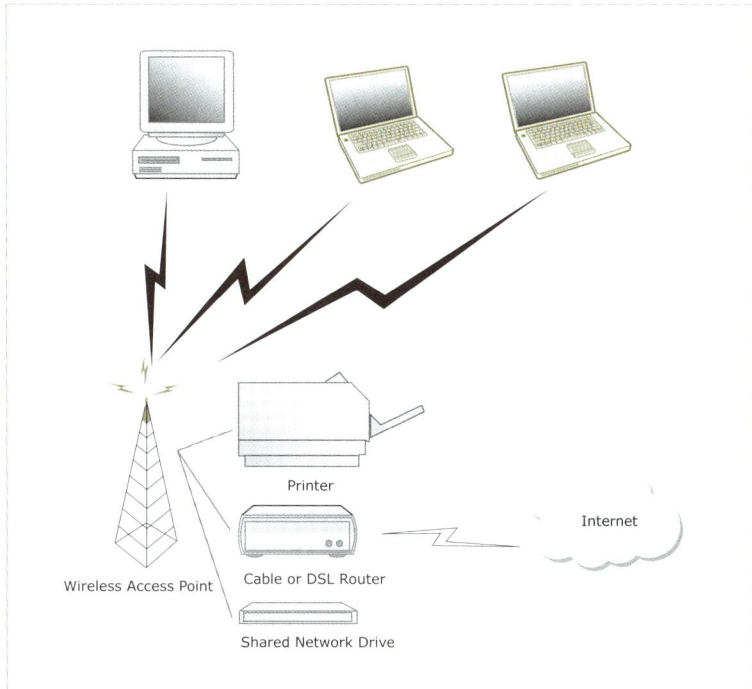

Choose a wireless network in these circumstances:

- It is awkward to run cables among the computers—maybe because you're renting an apartment.

- You need to be able to move one or more computers freely—for instance, you have a laptop computer.

- You need only adequate network speed, not the fastest network speed available.

When to Choose a Combined Network

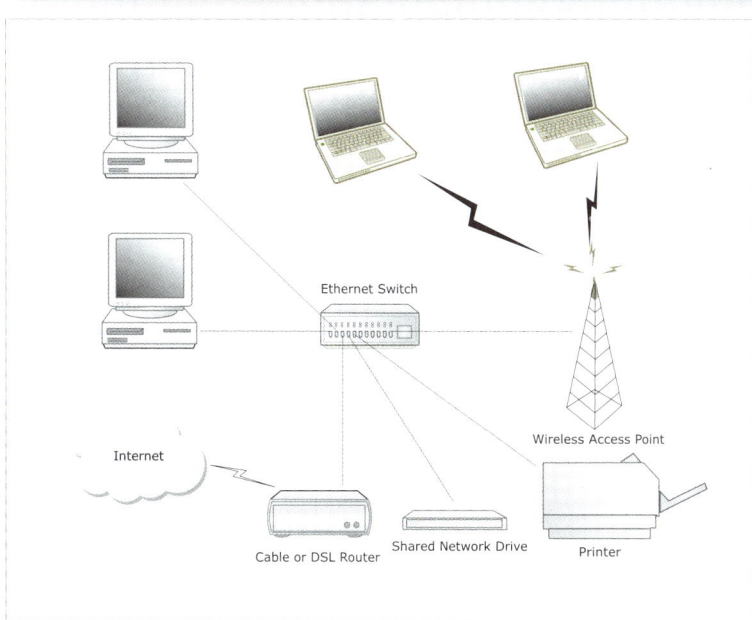

You can also create networks that include a wired part and a wireless part, as illustrated in the following diagram. In such a network the computers that do not need to move (for example, desktops) are typically connected via cables, while computers that do need to move (for example, laptops) are connected wirelessly.

SECTION 02 Creating a Wireless Network

This section shows you how to create a wireless network. You will need to buy suitable equipment and then configure it to work together. While setting up the network, you will typically configure your computer to connect to it at the same time, so that once the network is ready, the computer will be ready too.

If you already have a wireless network, see the next section for instructions on connecting your computer to it.

Buying Equipment for a Wireless Network

For a wireless network, you need a wireless network adapter for each computer, and a wireless access point to which the computers connect.

Your first decision when buying equipment for a wireless network is to decide which wireless network standard to use. At this writing, there are three main contenders: 802.11g, 802.11b, and the unratified 802.11n. 802.11g is the best choice, as it provides the fastest speed with reliable interoperation.

Standard Number	Standard Name	Maximum Speed	How to Connect the Modem
802.11n	802.11n	270Mbps	This new standard is under development and is expected to be ratified in 2009. Until then, pre-802.11n equipment from different vendors may not interoperate reliably.
802.11g	Wireless G	54Mbps	The latest established standard. 802.11g equipment typically also includes 802.11b capability
802.11b	WiFi	11Mbps	The most widespread standard, still used in many public networks (such as Internet cafes and hotspots).
802.11a	(none)	54Mbps	A fast standard that's not widely used. 802.11a is not compatible with 802.11b or 802.11g, although some equipment is 802.11a/b/g capable.

■ Buying a Wireless Access Point

The wireless access point connects the wireless computers in the network, but it can also connect wired devices as well. This means that when choosing a wireless access point, you must bear in mind several criteria:

- **Network standard:** Choose 802.11g or one of the other networking standards.

- **Internet access:** In most small networks, you will need to provide Internet access via the wireless access point. This means either connecting your Internet access device (for example, a DSL router or cable router) to your wireless access point, or buying a wireless access point with a built-in router of the appropriate type.

- **Wired connectivity:** If you will need to connect computers via a wired network, look for a wireless access point that includes enough wired ports for the wired computers.

- **Extra features:** If you need to connect a printer or shared drive to the access point, make sure it supports these devices.

> **Buying an Access Point and Network Adapters Together** — Note >>>
>
> Many manufacturers of wireless network equipment sell wireless network packages that consist of a wireless access point and one or more wireless network adapters. If you need both items, these packages are a good buy, as you not only get a better deal, but you ensure that the access point and adapters will work effectively together.
>
> This is especially important if you choose to buy equipment built to the as-yet-unratified 802.11n standard: If you buy "pre-802.11n" equipment from different vendors, it may interoperate only at 802.11g speeds—or even more slowly.

■ Buying Wireless Network Adapters

If you have a laptop computer, you may not need to buy a wireless network adapter, as most recently built laptops include a wireless network adapter. Typically, such an adapter is capable of 802.11g and either one or two earlier standards: 802.11b or 802.11a.

If your laptop computer does not have a wireless network adapter, you can add one via a PC Card or a USB slot. A PC Card is usually the best choice. Some laptop computers include a socket for an internal mini-PCI wireless network adapter, but these adapters are proprietary and tend to be more expensive.

Few desktop computers include a built-in wireless network adapter, although you may be able to specify a wireless network adapter as a build option when you order a custom-built computer. However, as just noted, you can easily add a wireless network adapter to a desktop computer via a USB port or by inserting a PCI card.

A USB adapter connected via a cable is usually the best choice, as this arrangement allows you to place the adapter (and aim the antenna) to get the best reception. However, if the signal is strong, an antenna located at the back of the computer may be adequate.

> **Creating an Ad Hoc Wireless Network** — Note >>>
>
> You can also create a wireless network that does not use an access point. Such a network is called an ad-hoc wireless network. Ad-hoc wireless networks are useful when you need to create a network quickly for temporary use—for example, when you meet some colleagues and need to collaborate on a project. But for consistent use, a wireless network that uses a wireless access point is much better. This type of network is called an infrastructure wireless network.

Setting Up a Wireless Network

To set up a wireless network, you must locate the wireless access point, power it on, and then configure it and the computers. This section explains the general steps you should follow. The specifics will vary depending on the equipment you have purchased.

■ Locating the Wireless Access Point

First, decide where to locate the wireless access point. Position it so that:

• You can connect it to a power supply.

• You can connect it to your router or Internet connection if you will share the connection via the wireless network.

• You can connect it via cables to any wired computers in the network, or to a switch in the wired network.

• The areas in which you will use the wireless computers are within range of the access point.

■ Create the Wireless Network Configuration

If your wireless access point supports configuration via a USB flash drive, follow these steps to configure it (if not, follow the instructions that come with the access point).

1. Connect the wireless access point to its power supply. If you have a wired network, you can connect the wireless access point to the network. (You might do this if you're creating a combined wired-and-wireless network.) Click the [Start] button, right-click [Network], and then click [Properties].

2. Windows opens the Network And Sharing Center window. Click the [Set Up A Connection Or Network] link in the left panel.

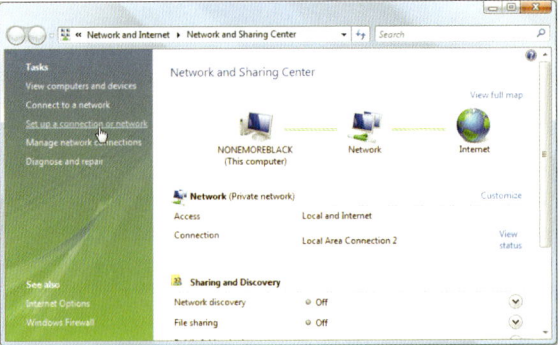

3. Windows opens the Set Up A Connection Or Network Wizard. Click the [Set Up A Wireless Router Or Access Point] item, and then click the [Next] button. On the [Set Up A Home Or Small Business Network] screen, click the [Next] button also, and then go through User Account Control for the Wireless Network Settings feature.

4. The wizard shows the Detecting Network Hardware And Settings screen. Wait while the wizard tries to find the access point.

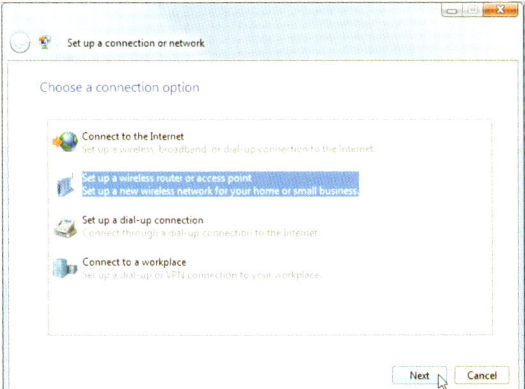

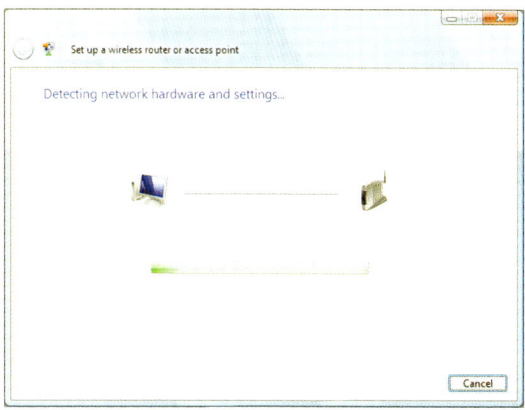

5. If the wizard cannot find your access point (as is most likely), it shows the Windows Did Not Detect Any Wireless Network Hardware screen. Click the [Create Wireless Network Settings And Save To USB Flash Drive] button.

6. The wizard shows the Give Your Network A Name screen. Type a name for the network of up to thirty-two letters and numbers, and then click the [Next] button.

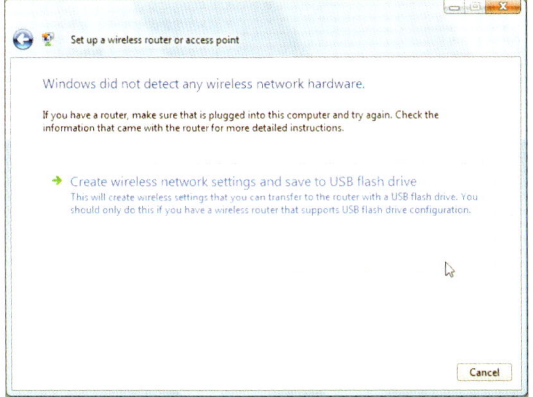

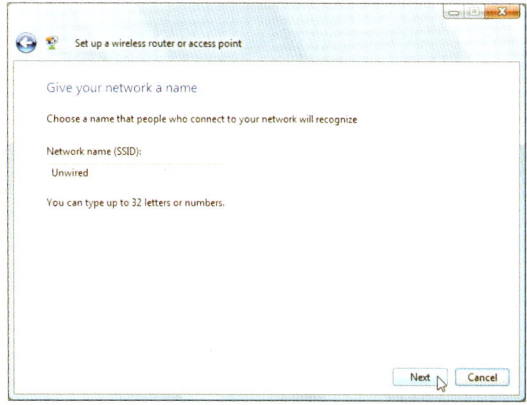

7. The wizard shows the Help Make Your Network More Secure With A Passphrase Screen. You can accept the suggested passphrase (which is hard to guess) or type a passphrase of your own. Select the [Display Characters] check box to see the characters you type. Click the [Next] button.

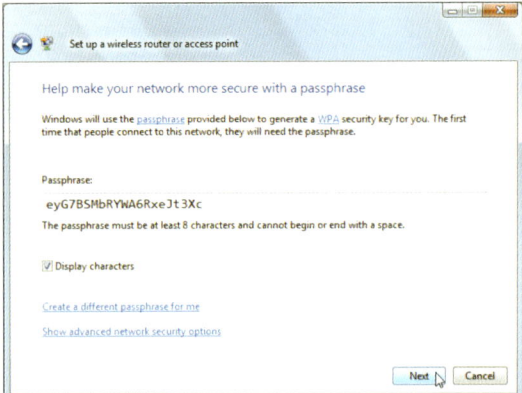

8. The wizard shows the Choose File And Printer Sharing Options screen. Choose the [Do Not Allow File And Printer Sharing option] button, the [Allow Sharing With Anyone With A User Account And Password For This Computer] option button, or the [Allow Sharing With Anyone On The Same Network As This Computer] option button. Click the [Next] button.

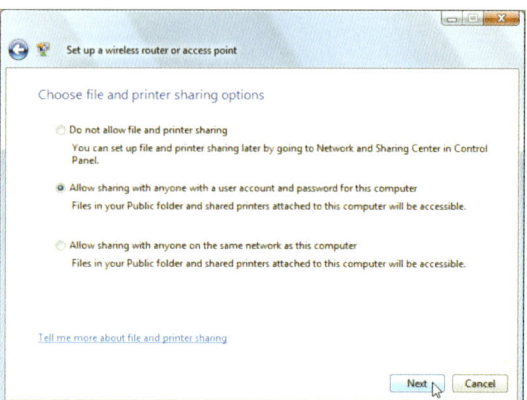

9. The wizard shows the Insert The USB Flash Drive Into This Computer screen. Insert the drive, verify that the wizard selects the drive letter in the [Save Settings To] drop-down list, and then click the [Next] button.

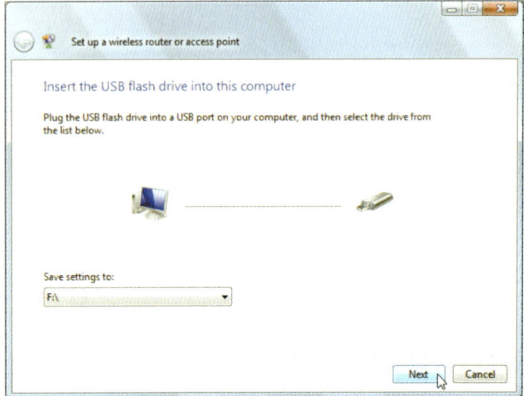

10. The wizard writes the network data to the drive, and then shows the To Add A Device Or Computer, Follow These Instructions screen. Note the instructions, and then click the [Close] button.

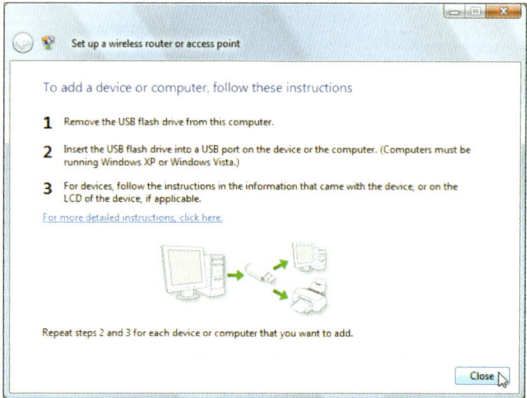

11. Click the [Safely Remove Hardware] icon in the notification area, and then click the [Safely Remove USB Mass Storage Device] item for the USB drive.

12. Windows displays the Safe To Remove Hardware dialog box. Click the [OK] button, and then remove the USB drive.

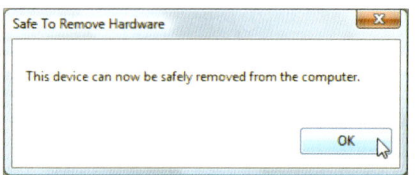

Configuring a Wireless Access Point Manually   Note >>>

If the Set Up A Connection Or Network Wizard displays the Windows Detected Network Hardware But Cannot Configure It Automatically screen (shown next), you can choose between configuring the access point manually or using a USB flash drive.

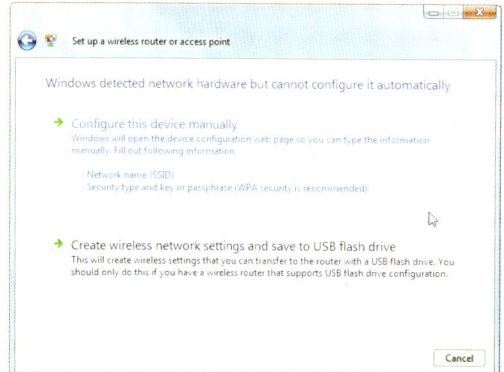

If your access point supports USB configuration, this is usually the easiest option. Click the [Create Wireless Network Settings And Save To USB Flash Drive] button, and then follow steps 9 through 12 in the previous list. If not, click the [Configure This Device Manually] button.

Windows displays a Connect To dialog box for the access point. Type your user name and password, select the [Remember My Password] check box if you want Windows to store the password, and then click the [OK] button.

Once you have logged on to the access point, use its configuration screens to set it up. The configuration screens vary depending on the device.

207

Applying the Wireless Network Configuration to the Access Point

To apply the wireless network configuration you've created to the access point, plug the USB flash drive into the wireless access point's USB connector. Wait thirty seconds for the access point to read the flash drive and apply the configuration, and then disconnect the flash drive.

Applying the Wireless Network Configuration to a Computer

To apply the wireless network configuration to a computer, follow these steps:

1. Plug the USB flash drive into the computer. Windows opens the AutoPlay dialog box. Click the [Wireless Network Setup Wizard] button.

2. The wizard prompts you to add the computer to the wireless network. If you want all users of your computer to be able to use the network, click the [Save This Network For All Users Of This Computer] option button, click the [OK] button, and then go through [User Account Control for the Manage Wireless Networks feature. Otherwise, click the [Save This Network For Me Only option] button, and then click the [OK] button.

3. The wizard adds the computer to the wireless network and displays an information dialog box. Click the [OK] button.

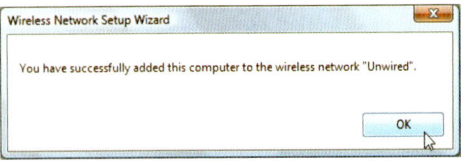

4. Click the [Safely Remove Hardware] icon in the notification area, and then click the [Safely Remove USB Mass Storage Device] item for the USB drive.

5. Windows displays the Safe To Remove Hardware dialog box. Click the [OK] button, and then remove the USB drive.

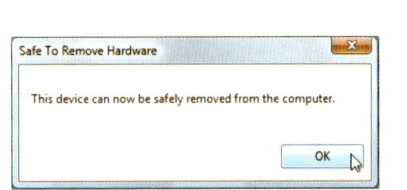

Chapter 08. Networking Your Computers and Sharing Files

Connecting Your Computer to the Wireless Network

Once you have applied the wireless network configuration to your computer and the access point, you can make your computer join the network by bringing it within range of the wireless access point.

If your computer does not join the network automatically, follow these steps:

1. Click the [Start] button, and then click [Connect To].

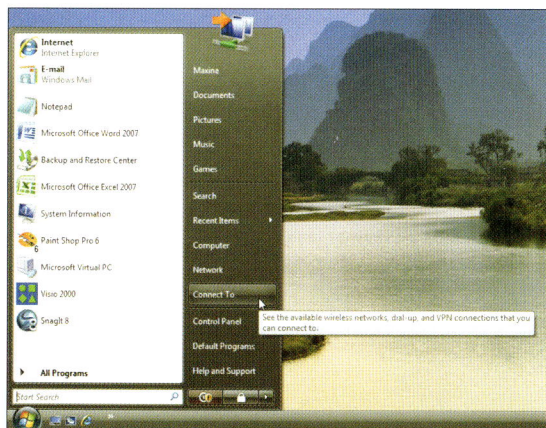

2. Windows launches the Connect To A Network Wizard, which shows the available networks. Click the [network you want], and then click the [Connect] button.

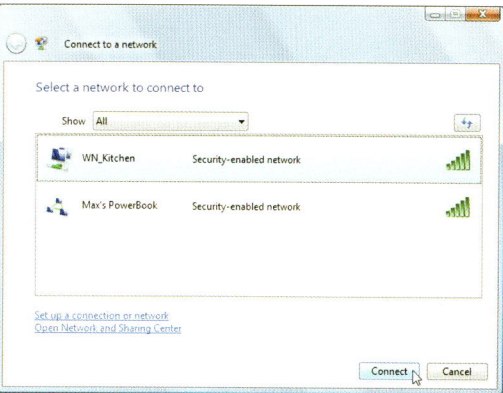

3. The wizard connects your computer to the network and then displays the Successfully Connected screen. Click the [Close] button.

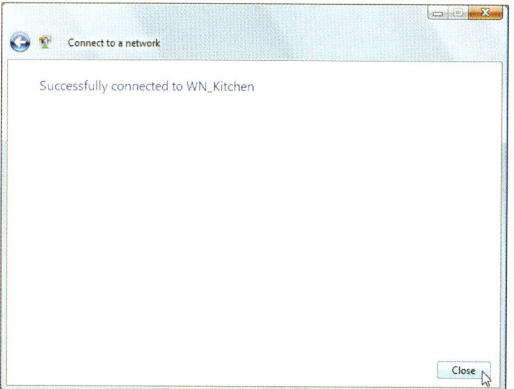

Connecting Your Computer to a Wireless Network Manually

If you have used a USB flash drive to set up a wireless network, you can add your computer to the network by using the USB flash drive as described in "Applying the Wireless Network Configuration to a Computer," discussed earlier in this chapter.

If your wireless access point does not support USB flash drive configuration, you can connect your computer to a wireless network manually. Follow the steps on the next page.

209

1. Click the [Start] button, and then click [Connect To].

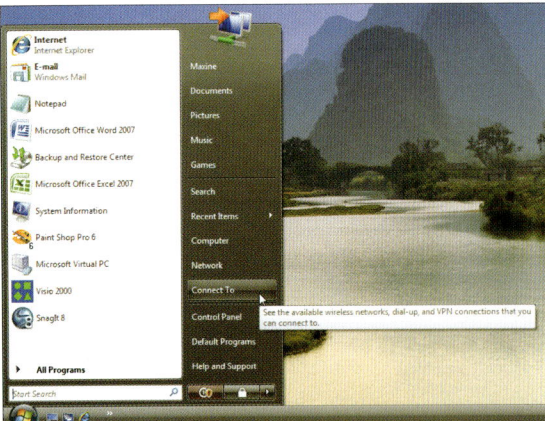

2. Windows launches the Connect To A Network Wizard, which shows the available networks. You can hover the mouse pointer over a network to see more details. Click the [network you want], and then click the [Connect] button.

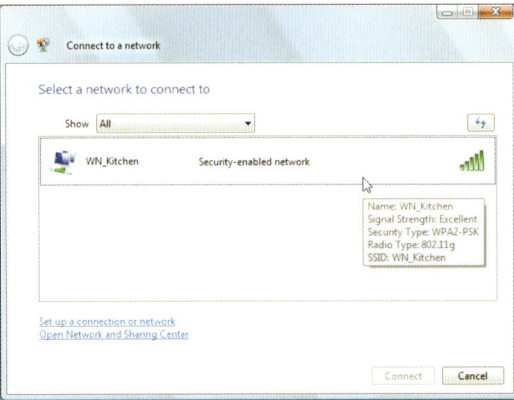

3. If the wireless network uses security, the wizard shows the Type The Network Security Key Or Passphrase screen. Select the [Display Characters] check box so you can see what you're typing, type the passphrase, and then click the [Connect] button.

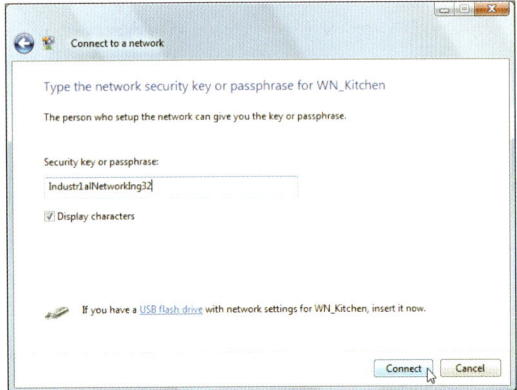

4. The wizard connects to the network and then shows the Successfully Connected screen. Select the [Save This Network] check box if you want to use this network again (as you normally will). Select the [Start This Connection Automatically] check box if you want Windows to connect automatically to this network (this too is usually helpful). Click the [Close] button.

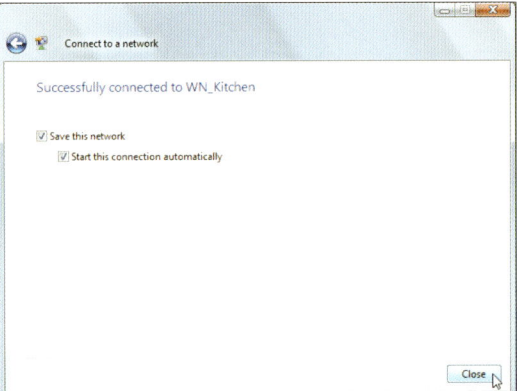

5. Windows launches the Set Network Location Wizard, which prompts you to select a location for the network you've joined. Click the [Home] button if it's a home network, the [Work] button if it's a work network, or the [Public Location] botton if it is any other type. For home or work, go through User Account Control for the Network And Sharing Center feature.

6. The wizard shows the Successfully Set Network Settings screen. Click the [Close] button.

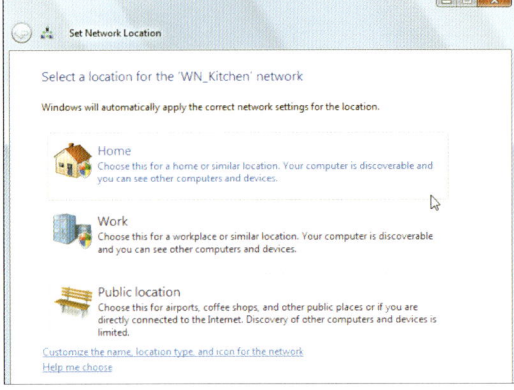

Managing the Wireless Networks Your Computer Uses

Under normal circumstances, a computer will connect only to one wired network; if it's a laptop that you move between home and work, it will connect only to one wired network at a time. But if your computer connects to wireless networks, it may need to connect to many of them.

To manage the wireless networks, follow these steps:

1. Click the [Start button], right-click [Network], and then click [Properties].

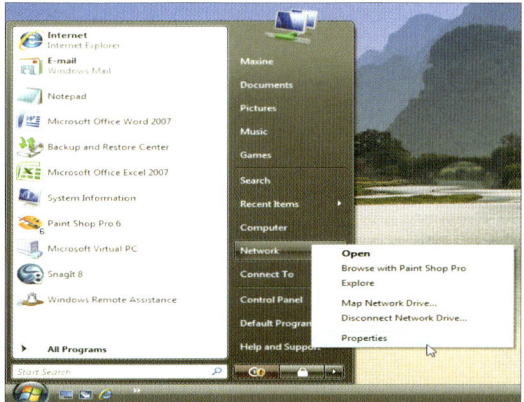

2. Windows opens the Network And Sharing Center window. Click the [Manage Wireless Networks] link in the left panel.

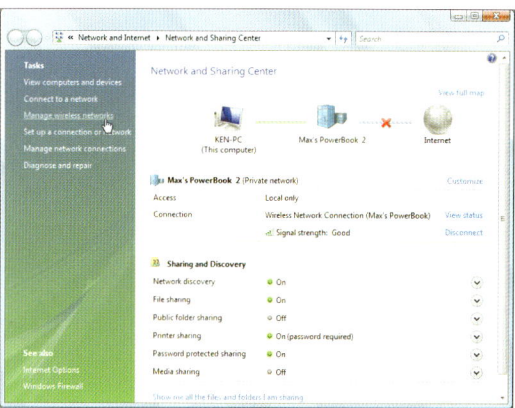

3. Windows opens the Manage Wireless Networks window. Arrange the networks into the order in which you want Windows to connect to them by clicking a network and then clicking the [Move Up] button or the [Move Down] button.

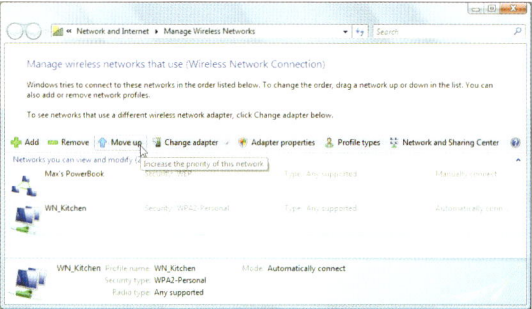

4. If you no longer need any network, remove it. Click the network in the list and then click the [Remove] button. In the Manage Wireless Networks - Warning dialog box, click the [OK] button.

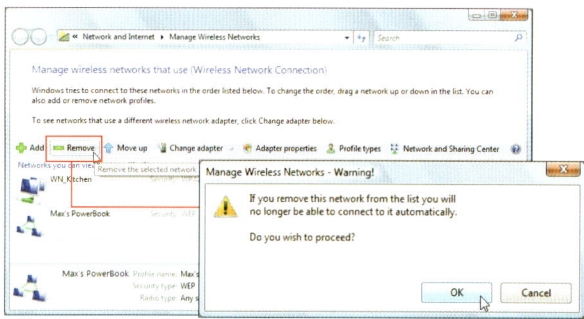

5. When you've finished managing wireless networks, click the [Close] button (the ⊠ button).

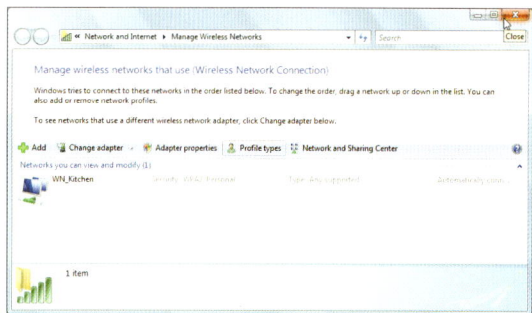

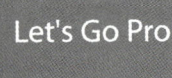

Let's Go Pro!

Connecting Your Computer to a Closed Wireless Network Manually

For security, an administrator can configure a wireless network so that it does not broadcast its name (or SSID, service set identifier). The resulting network is said to be closed.

Because Windows cannot detect the closed network, you cannot connect to it as described in the previous section. Instead, you must provide the network's name. Follow these steps:

① Click the [Start] button, and then click [Connect To]. Windows launches the Connect To A Network Wizard, which shows that Windows cannot find any networks. Click the [Set Up A Connection Or Network] link.

② The wizard shows the Choose A Connection Option screen. Click the [Manually Connect To A Wireless Network] item, and then click the [Next] button.

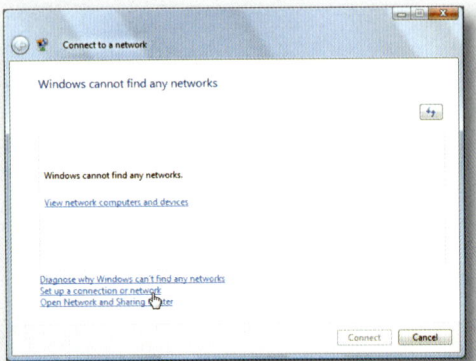

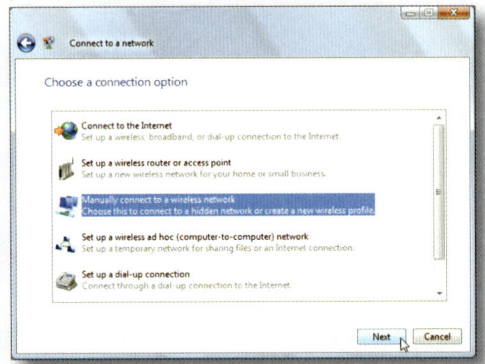

③ If your computer has two or more network adapters the wizard shows the Choose A Wireless Adapter screen. Select your [wireless network adapter], and then click the [Next] button.

④ The wizard shows the Enter Information For The Wireless Network You Want To Add. Type the network name and password, and choose the security type and encryption type. Select the [Start This Connection Automatically] check box if you want Windows to connect automatically (this is usually helpful). If the network is closed, select the [Connect Even If The Network Is Not Broadcasting] check box. Click the [Next] button.

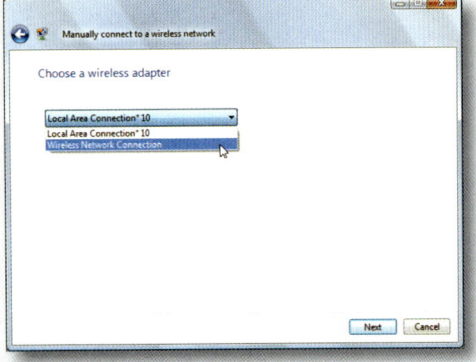

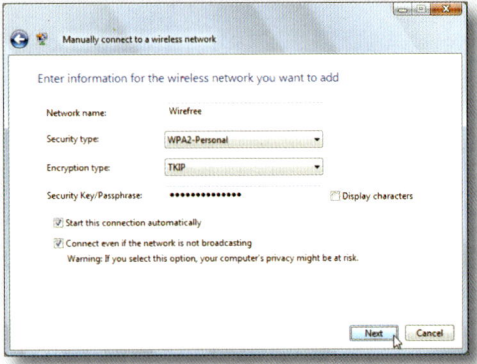

⑤ The wizard adds the network and shows the Successfully Added Network screen. Click the [Connect To] button.

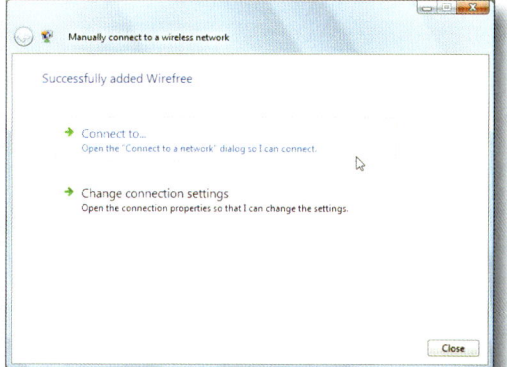

⑥ The wizard connects to the network and shows the Disconnect Or Connect To Another Network screen. Verify that the network is connected, and then click the [Cancel] button to close the wizard.

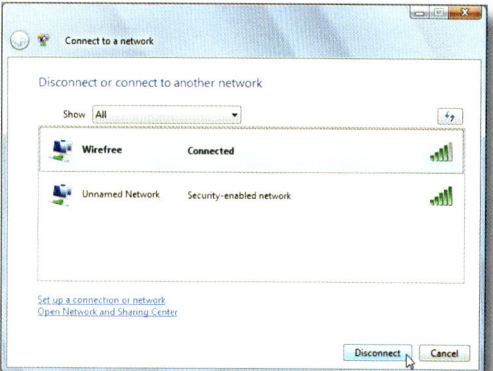

● Disconnecting from a Wireless Network

To disconnect your computer from a wireless network, follow these steps:

① Click the [Start] button, and then click [Connect To].

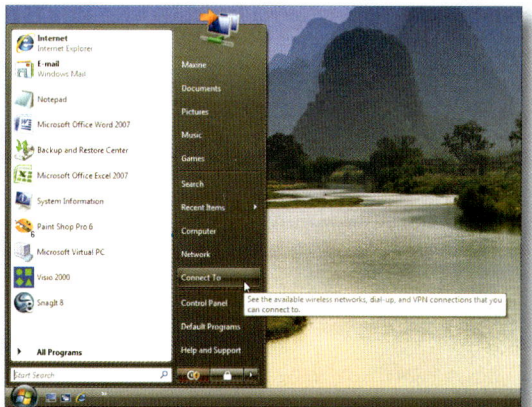

② Windows launches the Connect To A Network Wizard, which shows the network or networks to which your computer is currently connected. Click the [network], and then click the [Disconnect] button.

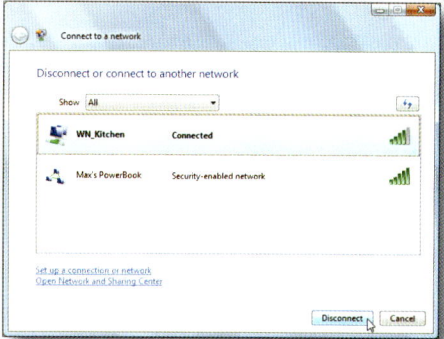

③ If the wizard shows the Are You Sure You Want To Disconnect? screen, warning that you will need to restart the computer before Windows can reconnect to this network automatically, click the [Disconnect] button.

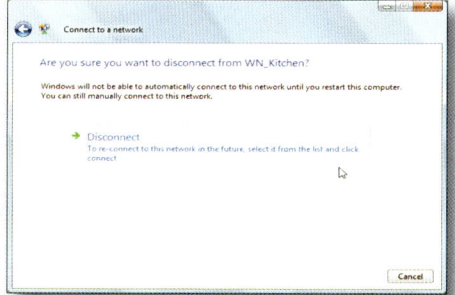

④ The wizard disconnects the computer from the network and then shows the Disconnected screen. Click the [Close] button. (Alternatively, if you need to connect to another network, click the [Connect To Another Network] button).

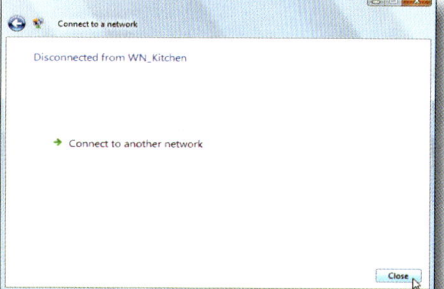

213

SECTION 03

Specifying an IP Address Manually

In some circumstances, you may need to specify an Internet Protocol (IP) address manually for your computer. To do so, you must find out the IP address and other settings required, and then apply them to the network connection your computer uses to connect to the Internet.

If your network uses Dynamic Host Configuration Protocol (DHCP) on a router or Internet device to allocate network addresses, Windows automatically configures network settings for each computer when the computer connects to the network. In this case, you probably will not need to change network settings.

However, in some cases you may need to specify an IP address manually—for instance, if your network does not use DHCP to allocate IP addresses. You will need the following information:

- **IP address:** Get this from your equipment or from an administrator.

- **Subnet mask:** For an IPv4 address, this controls how the IP address is interpreted. For an IPv6 address, you need the subnet prefix length rather than the subnet mask.

- **Default gateway**: For an IPv4 network only. This tells the computer how to connect to the Internet.

- **DNS server addresses:** Get these from your ISP.

To specify an IP address, follow these steps:

1. Click the [Start]button, right-click [Network], and then click [Properties].

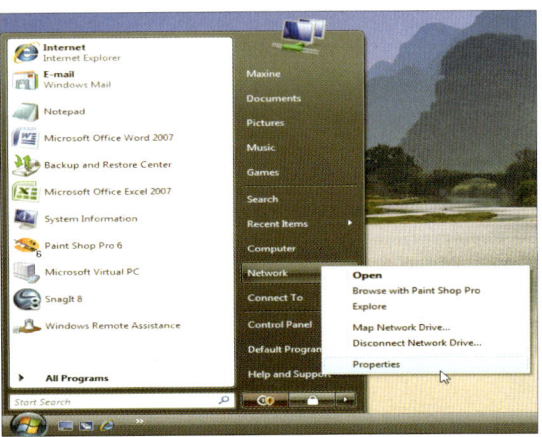

2. Windows opens the Network And Sharing Center window. Click the [Manage Network Connections] link in the left pane.

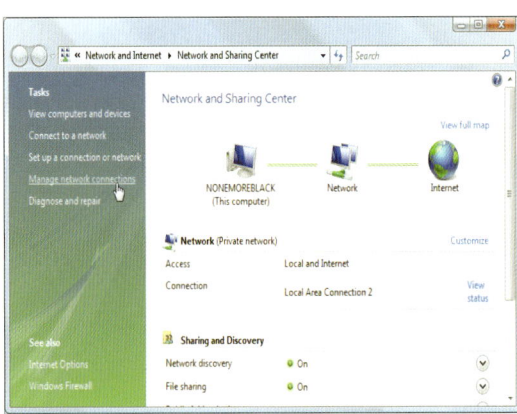

214

3. Windows opens a Network Connections window showing your computer's network connections. The computer here has one dial-up connection and two LAN connections, one of which is operational. Right-click the [connection you want to configure], choose [Properties], and then go through User Account Control for the Network Connections feature.

4. Windows opens the Properties dialog box for the connection. Click the [Internet Protocol Version 4 (TCP/IPv4)] item if your network uses IPv4; click the [Internet Protocol Version 6 (TCP/IPv6)] item if your network uses IPv6. Then click the [Properties] button.

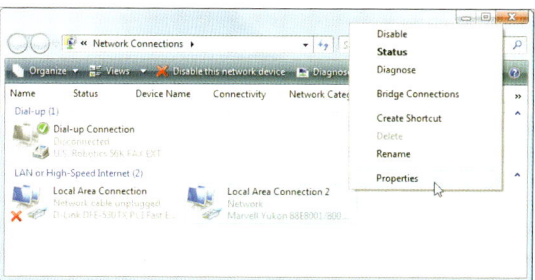

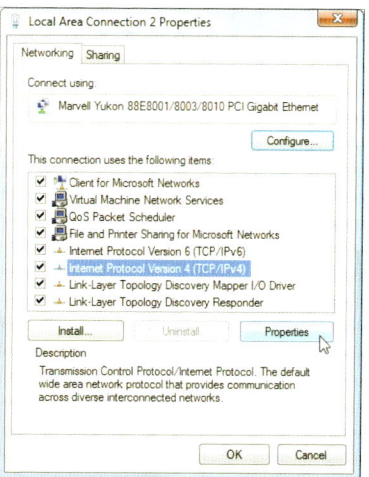

5. Windows opens the Internet Protocol Version 4 (TCP/IPv4) Properties dialog box (shown in this example) or the Internet Protocol Version 6 (TCP/IPv6) Properties dialog box (which is similar). Normally, the Obtain An IP Address Automatically option button and the Obtain DNS Server Address Automatically option button will be selected.

6. Select the [Use The Following IP Address] option button. Windows selects the Use The Following DNS Server Addresses option button automatically. Type the addresses, and then click the [OK] button.

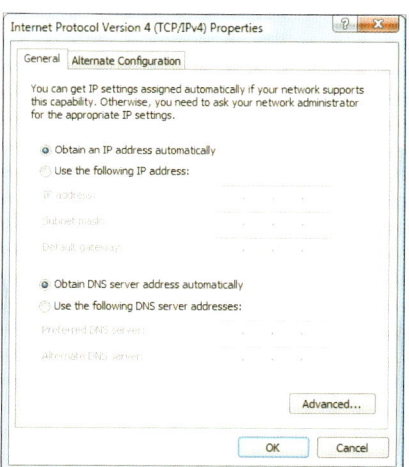

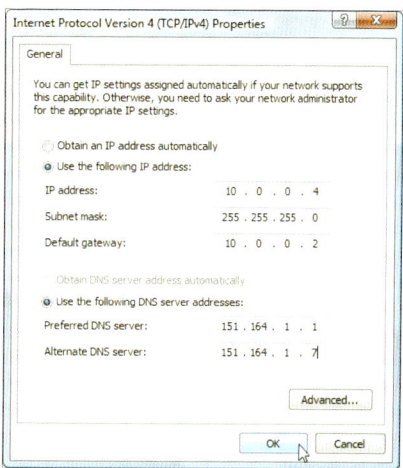

7. Windows closes the Internet Protocol Properties dialog box, returning you to the connection's Properties dialog box. Click the [OK] button to close the dialog box, and then click the [Close] button (the [X] button) to close the Network Connections window.

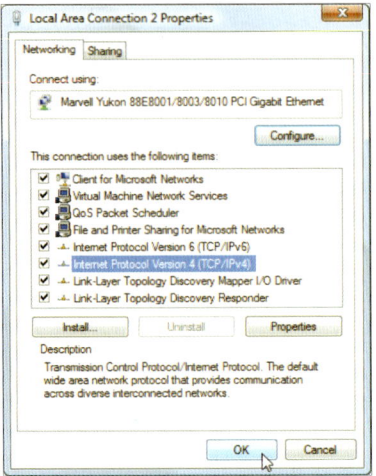

Understanding What IP Addresses Are   Note >>>

An IP address is a set of numbers that identifies your computer on the network. Windows Vista can use either Internet Protocol version 4 (IPv4) or the newer Internet Protocol version 6 (IPv6). At this writing, IPv4 is still predominant in many countries, but in others (such as China) IPv6 is gaining the upper hand.

An IPv4 address appears as four groups of decimal numbers separated by periods, with each number in the range 0–255. For example, 192.168.0.44 is an IPv4 address. Most likely, you will use IPv4 addresses if you need to configure your network.

An IPv6 address appears as eight groups of hexadecimal characters separated by colons.
For example, 08ac:0db8:85a3:08d3:1319:8a2e:0370:7334 is an IPv6 address.

SECTION 04 — Browsing and Using Folders on a Network

Once you've connected your computer to the network, you can browse the network to locate shared folders on it. Browsing lets you see all shared folders, but typically you will want to use only some of those folders regularly. You can map a network drive to such a folder to make your computer automatically establish a connection to it.

Browsing a Network

To see which shared folders are available on the network to which your computer is connected, you can browse the network—moving among the computers that are sharing folders and the folders they are sharing. Follow these steps:

1. Click the [Start] button, and then click [Network]. Windows opens a Network window. If a bar across the top of the window says "File sharing is turned off. Some network computers and devices might not be visible," turn on sharing by clicking the [bar], choosing [Turn On Network Discovery And File Sharing], and then going through User Account Control for the Network And Sharing Center feature.

2. Double-click the [computer] or [device you want to browse].

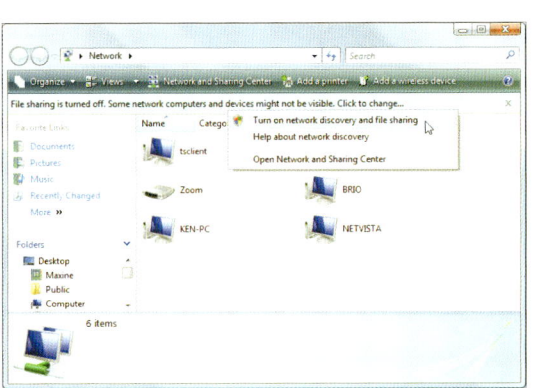

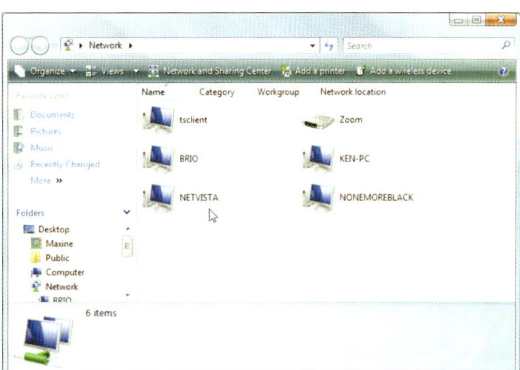

3. Windows Explorer displays the folders and devices shared by the computer or device. This example shows the network folders and network printers shared by a computer. Double-click the [folder you want to open].

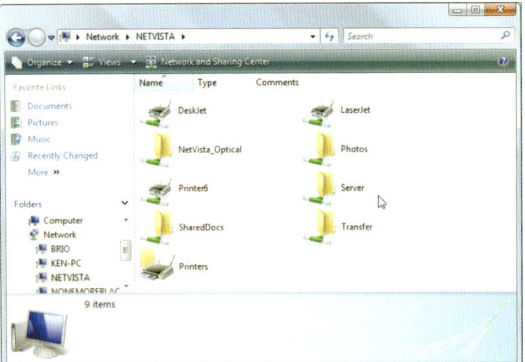

4. Double-click another folder if necessary to reach the folder or files you want. When you have finished browsing, click the [Close] button (the ![close] button) to close the Windows Explorer window.

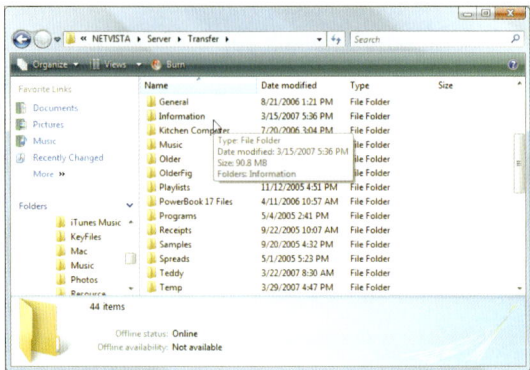

Mapping a Drive to a Network Folder

If you connect your computer regularly to the same network, you will probably want to map one or more drives to network folders so that you can access those folders easily.

To map a network drive, follow these steps:

1. Click the [Start] button, and then click [Computer]. Windows opens a computer window. Click the [Map Network Drive] button.

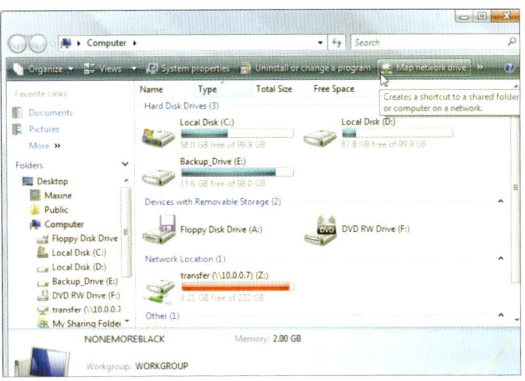

2. Windows opens the Map Network Drive dialog box. Verify the letter shown in the Drive drop-down list, and change it if necessary. Windows automatically chooses the last available drive letter—for example, Z—for the first network drive you map.

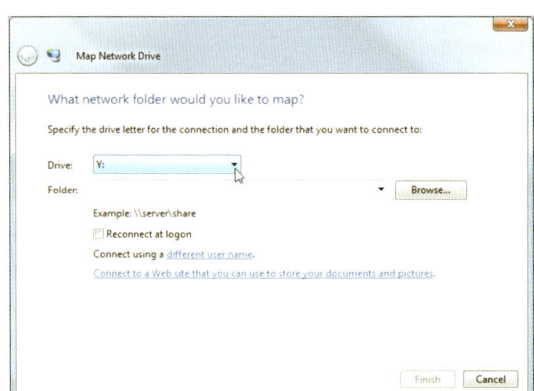

3. To tell Windows where the network folder is, click the [Browse] button. Windows opens the Browse For Folder dialog box. Expand the folder tree by clicking the [triangles on the left], select the [network folder] to which you want to map the drive, and then click the [OK] button.

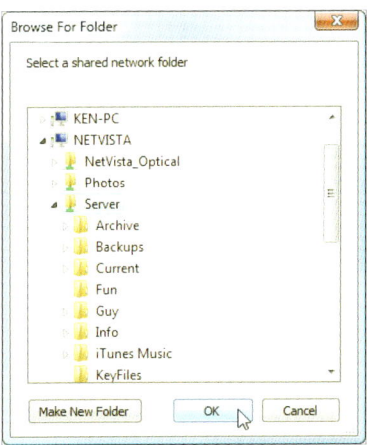

> **Choosing Whether to Make the Drive Mapping Permanent** Note >>>
>
> Normally, you'll want to make the drive mapping permanent, so that Windows maps the drive letter to the network folder whenever you log on. To make the mapping permanent, select the [Reconnect At Logon] check box in the Map Network Drive dialog box.
>
> However, you may sometimes want to map a drive only temporarily—for example, so that you can access an optical drive on another computer in order to install a program on your subnotebook. In this case, clear the Reconnect At Logon check box to make the drive mapping last only until you log out. (Alternatively, disconnect the network drive manually, as described in the next section.)

4. Typically, you will use your regular user name and password to connect to the network drive. However, if you need to use different credentials, click the [Connect Using A Different User Name] link. In the Connect As dialog box, type the user name and password, and then click the [OK] button.

5. When you've chosen all the settings you need, click the [Finish] button. Windows closes the Map Network Drive dialog box and opens a Windows Explorer window to the network folder. The drive also appears in the Network Location section of the Computer window. Click the [Close] button (the button) to close each window if you don't need them open.

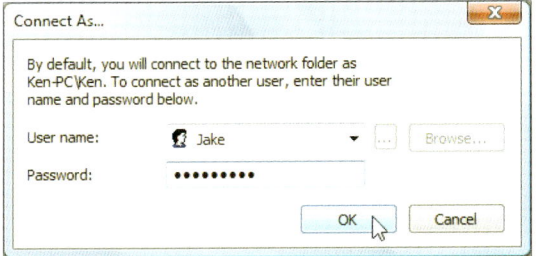

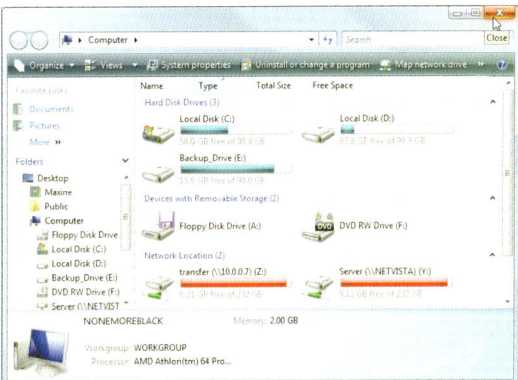

Disconnecting a Mapped Network Drive

Normally, you'll leave your permanent network drive mappings in place so that you can access the network folders to which they refer. But sometimes you may need to disconnect a mapped drive—for example, because the folder is no longer there.

To disconnect a mapped network drive, follow these steps:

1. Click the [Start] button, and then click [Computer]. Windows opens a Computer window. Right-click the [network drive], and then choose [Disconnect] from the context menu.

2. If Windows displays an Error dialog box telling you that there are files open on the drive, close any files open from the drive, or close any Windows Explorer window showing the drive. Then click the [Yes] button.

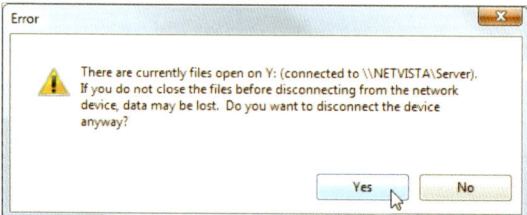

SECTION 05 — Sharing Files with Other Users

When you create files and store them within your user folders—for example, in your Documents folder or your Pictures folder—Windows makes them private, so that only you can see them. (But see the next Warning.)

Normally, this is what you want, for your private files, anyway. But you may also need to share files with other users. Windows lets you share files and folders either with other users of your computer or with other computers connected to the same network as your computer.

Sharing Files with Other Users of Your Computer

If you share your computer with other people, you may want to share some of your files with them. Windows provides an easy way to do so—by using the Public folders. Follow these steps:

1. Click the [Start] button, and then click your [user name].

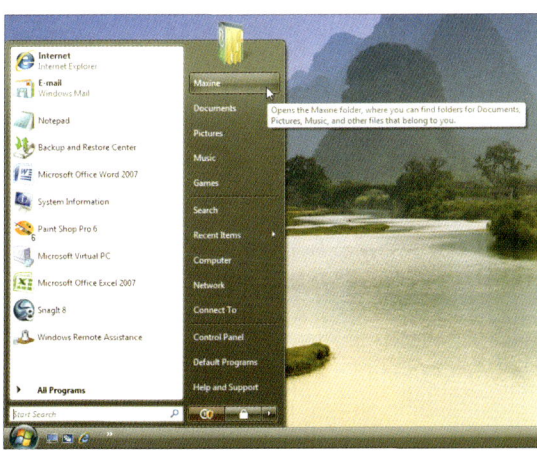

2. Windows opens a Windows Explorer window to your user folder. Click the [Public] link in the [Favorite Links] area. You may have to click the [More] link at the bottom of the displayed part of the Favorite Links list to reach the Public link.

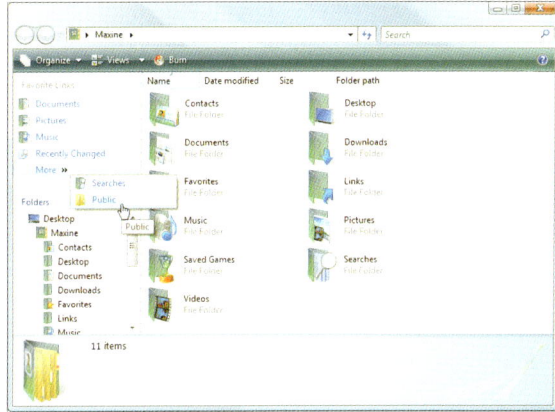

Administrator Users Can View Other Users' Files — Warning >>>

Even though Windows prevents each user from viewing another user's files, an Administrator can gain access to another user's files by going through User Account Control for the Edit Security feature.

This capability is to let an Administrator solve problems on the computer, but it also creates security issues for anyone who needs to keep his or her files private. (If you're the only Administrator user for your computer, there's no problem—nobody else can access your files.)

3. Windows displays the Public folder, which contains folders for different types of files: Public Documents, Public Downloads, Public Music, Public Pictures, and Public Videos. If you have Windows Vista Home Premium or Ultimate, there's a Recorded TV folder as well. Double-click the [folder you want to open].

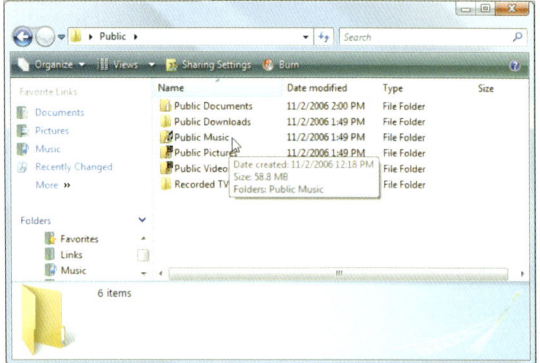

4. Windows displays the folder you double-clicked. You can then open, play, or work with existing files in the folder. You can add files to the folder by copying them or moving them to it. When you've finished using the folder, click the [Close] button (the [X] button).

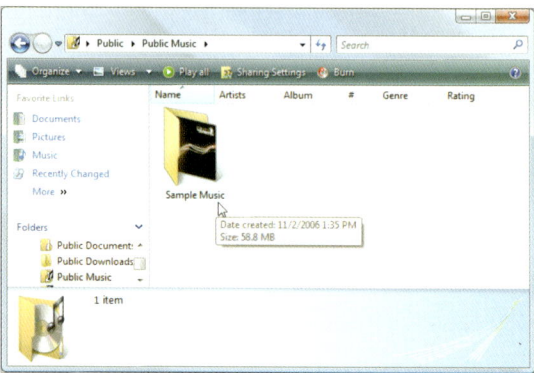

Sharing Files with Other Users of Your Network

As you saw in the previous section, you can easily share files with other users of your computer. But what you'll often need to do is share files with users of other computers on the same network as your computer.

To share files with users of other computers follow these steps:

1. Click the [Start] button, right-click [Network], and then click [Properties].

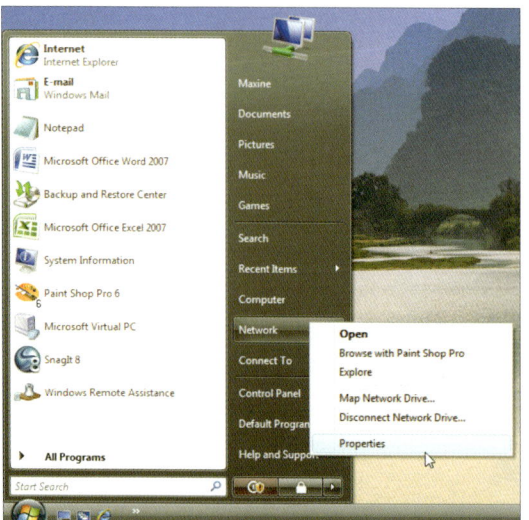

222

2. Windows opens a Network And Sharing Center window. In the Sharing And Discovery list, see if Network Discovery is Off rather than On. If it is off, click the [arrow at the right end of the Network Discovery line].

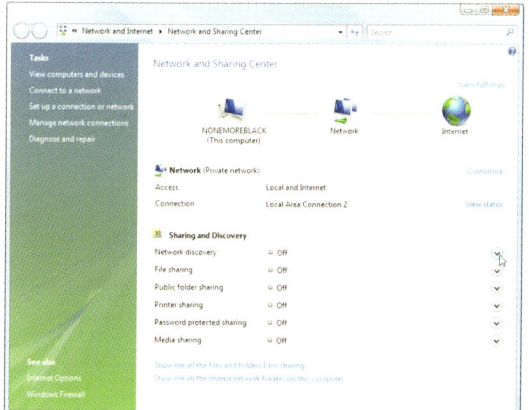

3. Windows displays the Network Discovery options. Select the [Turn On Network Discovery option] button, click the [Apply] button, and then go through User Account Control for the Network And Sharing Center feature.

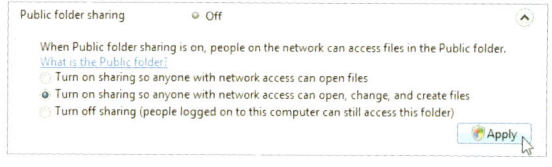

4. In the Sharing And Discovery list, click the [arrow at the right end of the Public Folder Sharing] line.

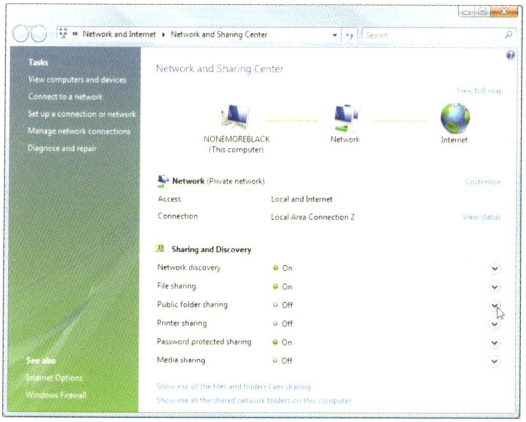

5. Windows expands the Public Folder Sharing options. Select the [Turn On Sharing So Anyone With Network Access Can Open Files] option button if you want others to be able to view your files but not change them. Select the [Turn On Sharing So Anyone With Network Access Can Open, Change, And Create Files] option button if you want others to be able to change your files. Click the [Apply] button, and then go through [User Account Control for the Network And Sharing Center] feature.

6. If you want to restrict access to your shared files to only people who have a user account on your computer (even though they may be using another computer on the network), make sure Password Protected Sharing is On. If the Password Protected Sharing line says Off, click the [arrow at its right end].

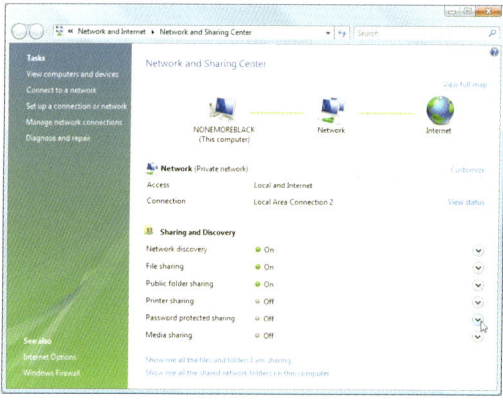

223

7. Windows expands the Password Protected Sharing options. Select the [Turn On Password Protected Sharing] option button, click the [Apply] button, and then go through User Account Control for the Network And Sharing Center feature.

8. Windows adds the words "(password required)" to the Public Folder Sharing line to indicate that Password Protected Sharing is on. Click the [Close] button (the 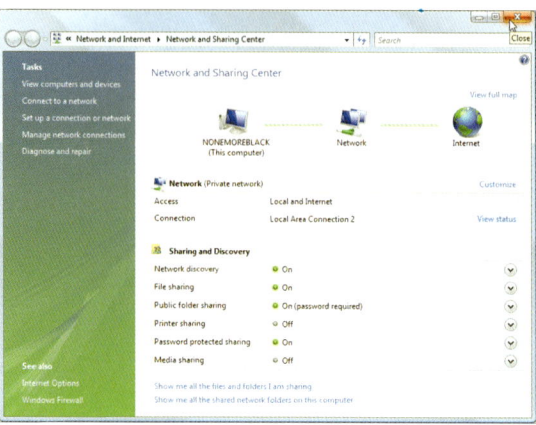 button) to close the Network And Sharing Center window.

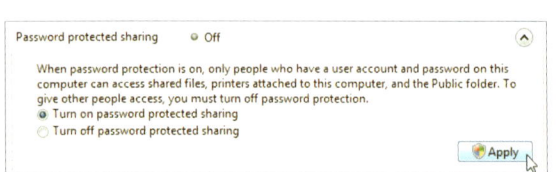

Changing Your Computer's Workgroup

Sharing works best if all the computers belong to the same workgroup (a group of computers). If the workgroup shown in the Workgroup readout is different from the workgroup on your other networked computers, change it as follows:

1. Click the Change Settings link in the System window, and then go through User Account Control for the Change Computer Settings feature.

2. Windows shows the Computer Name tab of the System Properties dialog box. Click the [Change] button.

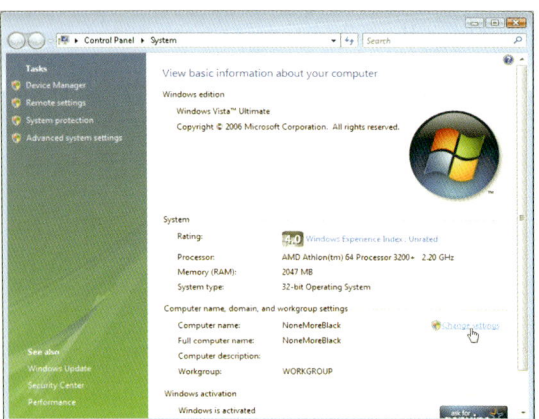

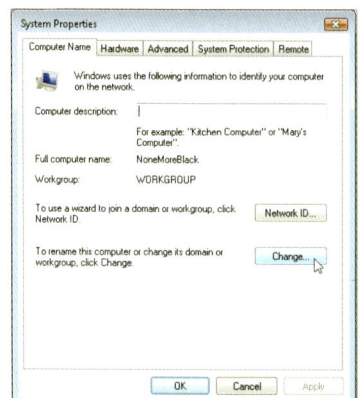

224

3. Windows shows the Computer Name/Domain Changes dialog box. Type the workgroup name in the Workgroup option button, and then click the [OK] button.

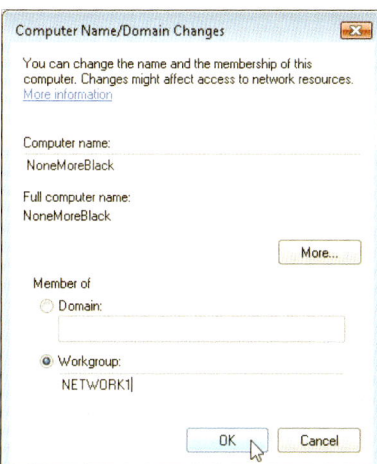

4. Windows shows a Computer Name/Domain Changes dialog box welcoming you to the new workgroup. Click the [OK] button.

5. Windows shows a Computer Name/Domain Changes dialog box prompting you to restart your computer. Close any open files and programs, and then click the [OK] button

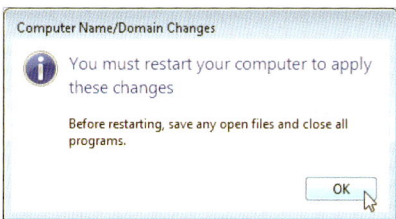

6. Windows shows the Computer Name tab of the System Properties dialog box again. Click the [Close] button.

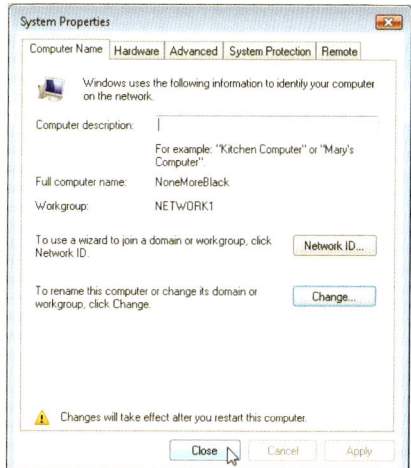

7. Windows shows a message box telling you that you must restart your computer. Click the [Restart Now] button.

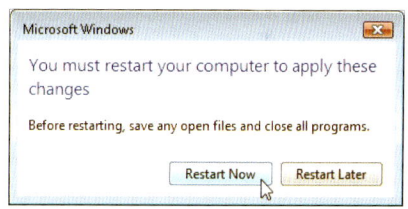

Chapter 9

Managing Hardware, Printers, and Fonts

The hardware is the physical devices that make up your computer—for example, a hard drive, a DVD drive, or a network card. Your computer probably came with most of the hardware you need, but you may need to add devices to get extra functionality. Windows requires a driver, or software component, that allows it to communicate with each hardware device. The driver tells Windows what the device does, what its capabilities are, and how to communicate with it. For example, if you install a printer on your computer, Windows needs a printer driver to be able to communicate with the printer.

SECTION 01

Installing Hardware Devices

Many modern hardware devices are designed so that you can install them—or remove them—while the computer is running rather than having to shut the computer down first and open its case. For example, you can insert a PC Card device in a laptop computer, or plug a USB device into either a laptop or a desktop, while that computer is running. Such devices are called hot-pluggable devices—you can plug them in while the computer is hot (running).

Connecting Hot-Pluggable Devices

When Windows detects that you've plugged in a new device, it tries to find a suitable driver automatically. If Windows finds a driver, installation is easy, as in these steps:

1. Log on to Windows as usual, and then connect the device to your computer. Windows detects the device and shows a pop-up message above the notification area.

2. If you want to see the details of what Windows is installing, click the pop-up message. Windows shows a [Driver Software Installation] dialog box that contains this information. Click the [Close] button.

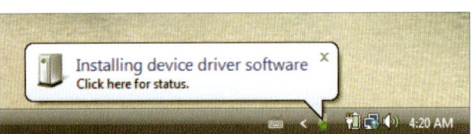

3. If you do not open the [Driver Software Installation] dialog box, Windows shows another pop-up message above the notification area when it has finished installing the device. You can now use the device.

If Windows does not find a driver for the device, see the section "Let's Go Pro! Providing a Driver Manually," later in this chapter.

228

Disconnecting Hot-Pluggable Devices

To remove a hot-pluggable device, follow these steps:

1. Look in the notification area for the [Safely Remove Hardware] icon. If it appears, you need to warn Windows that you are about to remove the hardware. Click the icon.

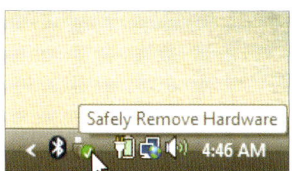

2. Windows shows a pop-up menu of devices you can remove.

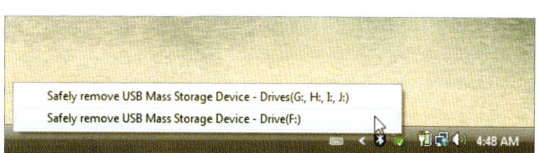

3. If you can identify the device you want to remove, click it. Windows shows the [Safe To Remove Hardware] dialog box. Click the [OK] button, and then remove the device.

4. If you can't identify the device, double-click the [Safely Remove Hardware] icon. Windows opens the [Safely Remove Hardware] dialog box. If you need more information to identify the device, select the [Display Device Components] check box.

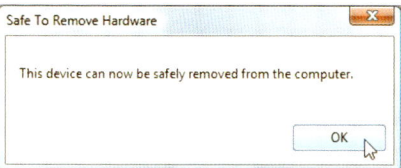

5. Select the device you want to stop, and then click the [Stop] button.

6. Windows shows the [Stop a Hardware Device] dialog box to confirm which device you're going to stop. Click the [OK] button.

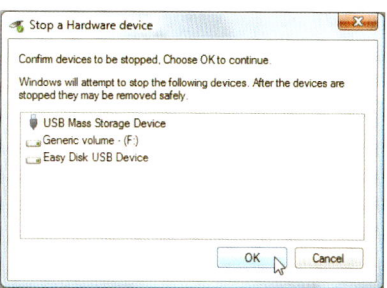

229

7. Windows stops the device and shows the [Safe to Remove Hardware] dialog box. Click the [OK] button, and then remove the device. Click the [Close] button to close the [Safely Remove Hardware] dialog box.

Installing a Non–Hot-Pluggable Device

As you've just seen, hot-pluggable devices are easy to install. But sometimes you'll need to install other devices—for example, a hard disk or a network card that uses a slot inside the computer. To install such devices, you must shut down Windows, power off the computer, disconnect the cables, and open the case.

Once you have installed the device, closed the case, and reconnected the cables, driver installation proceeds in the same way: If Windows can locate a driver, it installs it automatically. If not, Windows prompts you to provide a driver (see the section "Let's Go Pro! Providing a Driver Manually").

> **Windows May Finish Hardware Installation Before You Log On**   Note >>>
>
> When you install a non–hot-pluggable device in your computer, Windows may finish installing the driver before you log on to the computer. When this happens, it is not always obvious that the device has been installed successfully. Look for an icon above the notification area indicating that the device has been installed.

Removing a Non–Hot-Pluggable Device

To remove a non–hot-pluggable device from your computer, shut down Windows, power off the computer, and then disconnect the cables. Remove the device, close the case, reconnect the cables, and then restart the computer.

Let's Go Pro!

Providing a Driver Manually

If Windows is not able to find a suitable driver for a device you've connected, you must provide a driver manually. Follow these steps:

① Log on to Windows as usual, and then connect the device to your computer. Windows detects the device and starts the Found New Hardware Wizard. Click the [Locate and Install Driver Software] button, and then go through User Account Control for the Device Drive Software Installation feature.

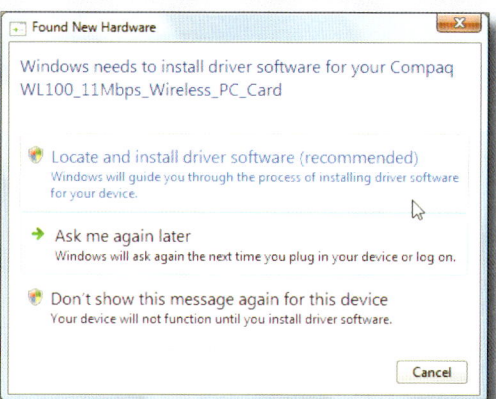

② The wizard hides its window and shows a popup message in the notification area while it searches for a suitable driver for the device.

③ If the wizard finds no driver, it prompts you to insert the disc that came with the device. If you have the disc, insert it, and let Windows search for the driver. If not, as in this example, click the [I Don't Have the Disc. Show Me Other Options] button.

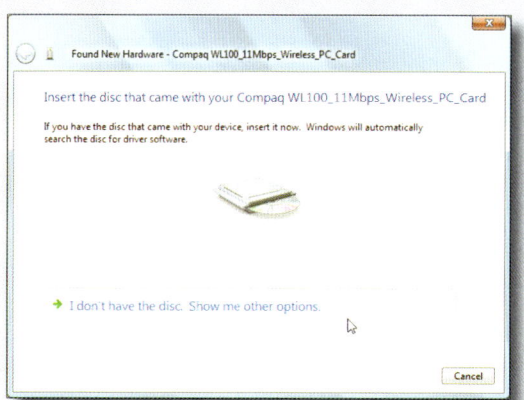

④ Wizard shows the [Windows Couldn't Find Driver Software for Your Device] screen. Click the [Check for a Solution] button.

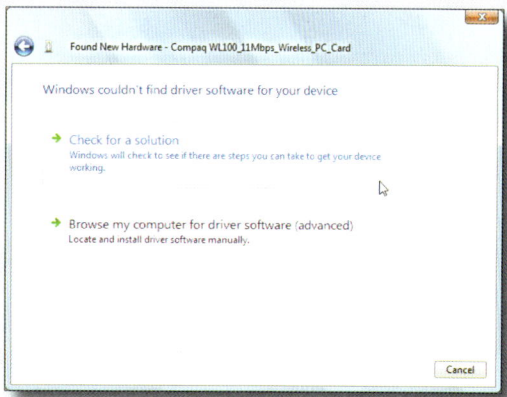

⑤ The wizard searches online for a solution. If it finds a suitable driver, the wizard installs it. If not, as in this example, it shows the [Windows Was Unable to Install Your Device] screen (where Device is the device's name). Click the [Back] button.

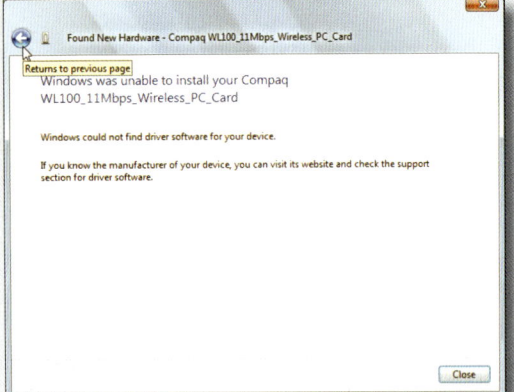

⑥ The wizard shows the [Windows Couldn't Find Driver Software for Your Device] screen again. Click the [Browse My Computer for Driver Software] button.

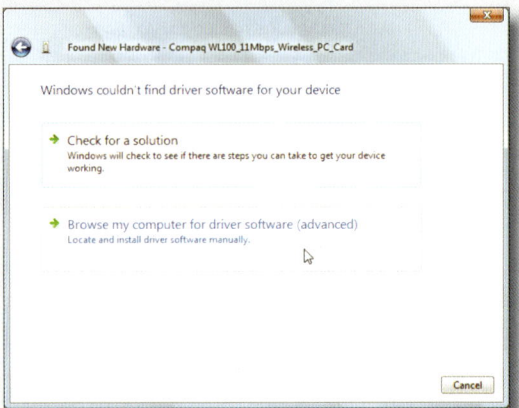

⑦ The wizard shows the [Browse for Driver Software on Your Computer] screen. Look at the [Search for Driver Software in This Location] folder. If necessary, change it by clicking the [Browse] button and using the [Browse for Folder] dialog box to choose the folder. Select the [Include Subfolders] check box. Then click the [Next] button.

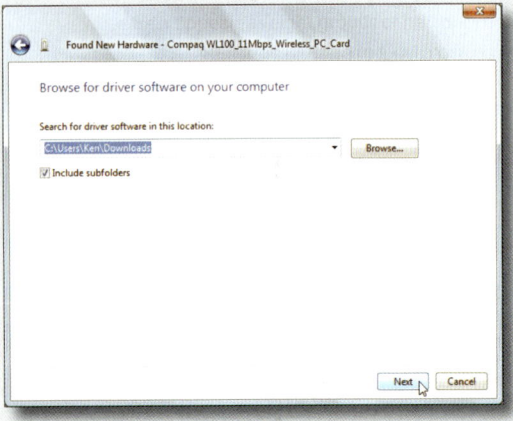

⑧ If the wizard shows a [Windows Security] dialog box saying that Windows can't verify the publisher of the driver, click the [Install This Driver Software] button if you're confident that the driver is safe.

⑨ Wait while the wizard installs the driver, and then click the [Close] button when it has finished.

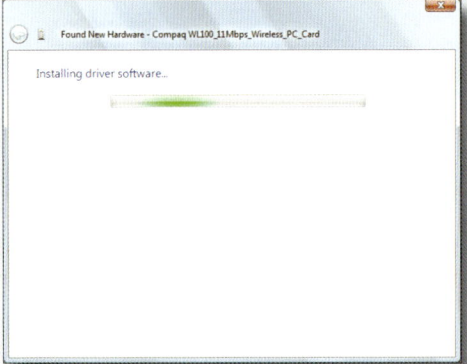

tip>>

Deciding Whether a Driver Is Safe

If the Found New Hardware Wizard shows a [Windows Security] dialog box, you'll need to decide whether the driver is safe. There's no hard-and-fast rule, but if the device is from a reputable manufacturer, and you've downloaded the driver from the manufacturer's Web site, the driver should be safe. However, if you've downloaded the driver from one of the many driver sites on the Web, it might contain malware (malevolent software), and you should probably not install it.

SECTION 02

Updating a Device Driver

Once you've found a suitable driver for each hardware device on your computer, you can normally continue using that driver until Windows Update offers you an updated driver. However, you may sometimes need to update a driver because a device is no longer functioning correctly.

To update a device driver, follow these steps:

1. Press <Windows> + <Break>. Windows opens a System window. In the left pane, click the [Device Manager] link, and then go through User Account Control for the Microsoft Management Console feature.

2. Windows opens Device Manager, which shows the hardware devices installed on your computer. Double-click the category of device you want to remove (unless the category is expanded already).

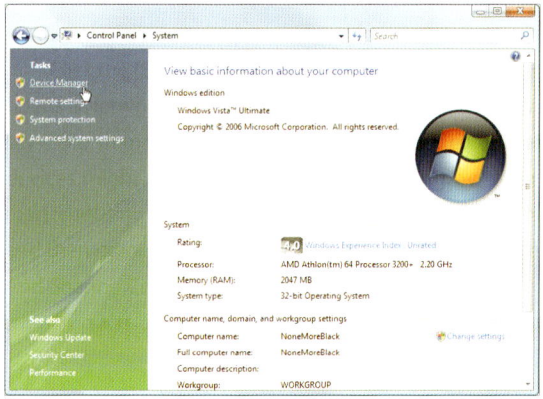

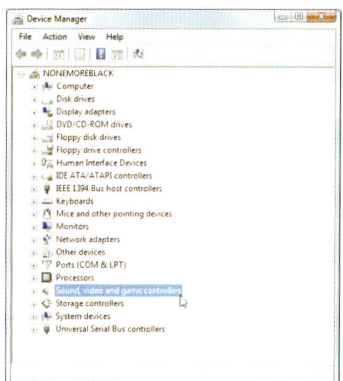

3. Right-click the device, and then choose [Update Driver Software] from the context menu.

4. Windows launches the Update Driver Software Wizard. Click the [Search Automatically for Driver Software] button.

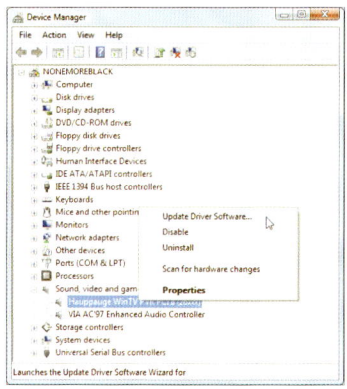

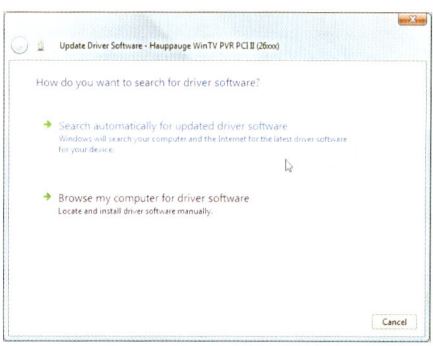

233

5. The wizard searches for a driver. If the wizard finds a driver, it installs it and then displays a screen telling you that it has done so. Click the [Close] button.

6. The wizard closes, returning you to Device Manager. Click the [Close] button (the button) to close Device Manager, and then click the [Close] button to close the System window.

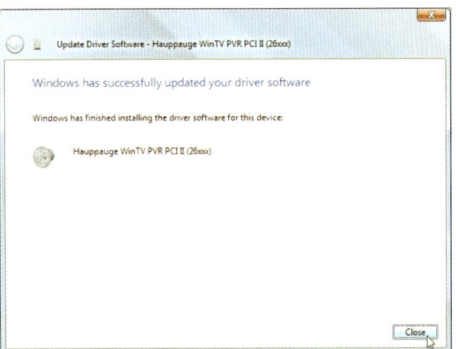

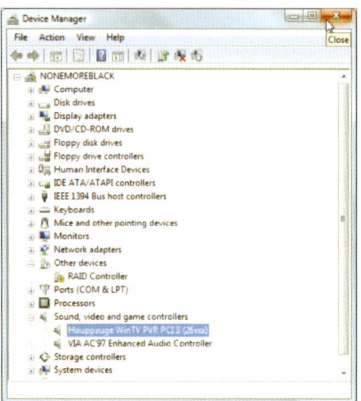

Rolling Back a Device Driver

Usually, each new device driver you install will make your computer more stable (or at least maintain its current stable state); some new device drivers may even provide additional features. But in some cases, you may find that installing a new device driver makes your computer unstable or removes features you need.

When this happens, you can roll back the driver, restoring the previous driver. Follow these steps:

1. Press <Windows> + <Break>. Windows opens a System window. In the left pane, click the [Device Manager] link, and then go through User Account Control for the Microsoft Management Console feature.

2. Windows opens Device Manager, which shows the hardware devices installed on your computer. Double-click the category of device you want to remove (unless the category is expanded already).

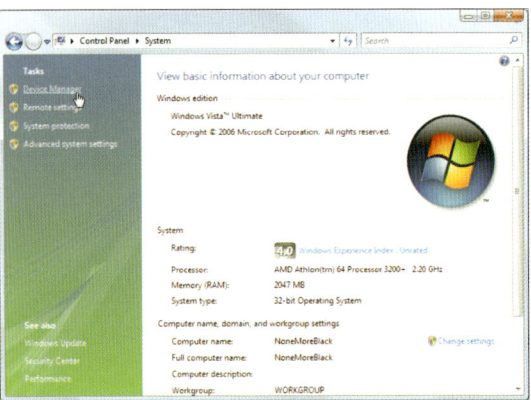

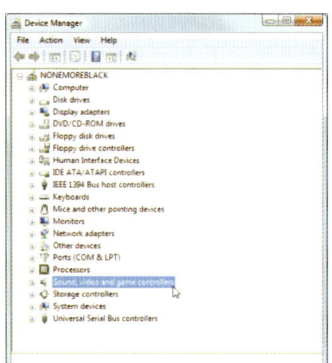

3. Right-click the device, and then choose [Properties] from the context menu.

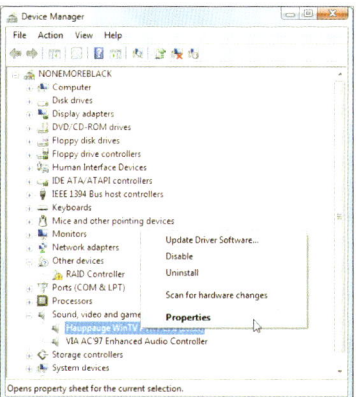

4. Windows opens the [Properties] dialog box for the device. Click the [Driver] tab to display its contents, and then click the [Roll Back Driver] button.

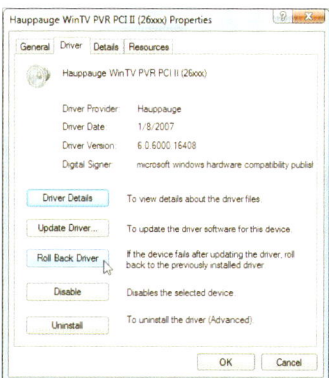

When the [Roll Back Driver] Button Is Unavailable   Note >>>

If there is no previous driver to which you can return, Windows makes the [Roll Back Driver] button dimmed and unavailable. You may find that the [Roll Back Driver] button is dimmed once you've rolled back one device driver—because no other previous device driver is available.

5. Windows shows the [Driver Package Rollback] dialog box. Click the [Yes] button.

6. Windows restores the previous driver and then returns the focus to the [Properties] dialog box. Click the [Close] button to close the dialog box, click the [Close] button (the ⊠ button) to close the [System Properties] dialog box, and then close the System window.

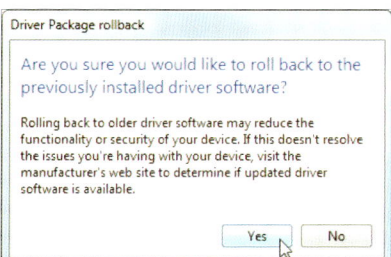

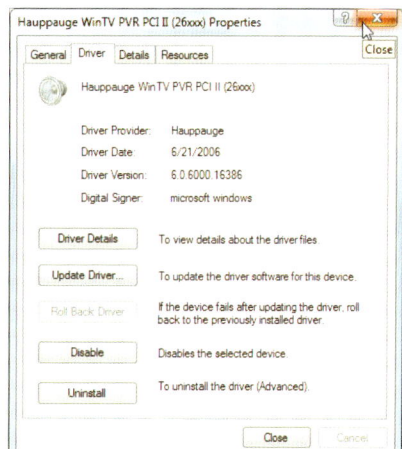

235

SECTION 03 — Installing a Printer

The device you're perhaps most likely to need to install on your computer is a printer, because almost no computer includes a printer (some do, but you must look hard), and most people still need to print documents.

You can install a printer either connected directly to your computer or connected to your network (if you have a network).

Installing a Printer Connected to Your Computer

To install a printer connected directly to your computer, follow these steps:

1. Connect the printer to the computer. Most modern printers use USB connections. Windows detects the printer and shows the message "Installing device driver software" above the notification area.

2. If Windows finds a driver for the printer, Windows installs the driver. If Windows cannot find a driver for the printer (as is often the case), it starts the Found New Hardware Wizard. Click the [Locate and Install Driver Software] button, and then go through User Account Control for the Device Driver Software Installation feature.

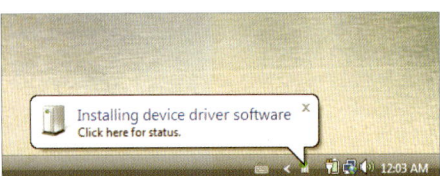

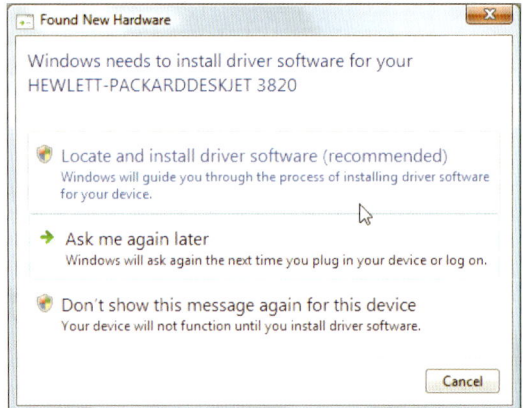

3. If the wizard prompts you to insert the disc that came with your printer, insert the disc, and allow Windows time to notice it.

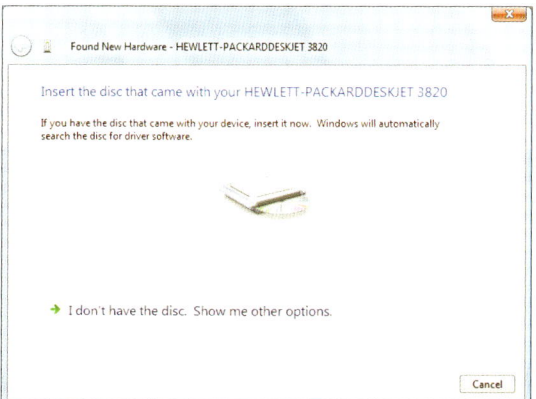

4. The wizard lists the drivers it has found on the disc. Click the driver you want to install. Make sure the lower-left corner of the window shows "This driver is digitally signed," which means that the driver has an audit trail you can follow if necessary. Click the [Next] button.

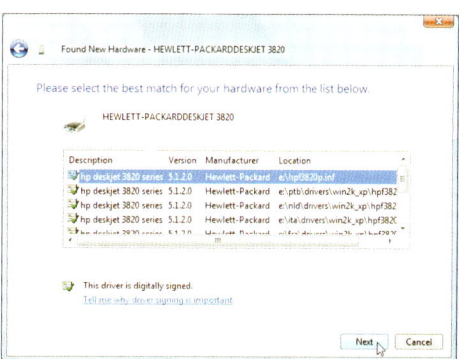

5. The wizard installs the driver software and then shows a screen telling you that the software for the device has been installed successfully. Click the [Close] button.

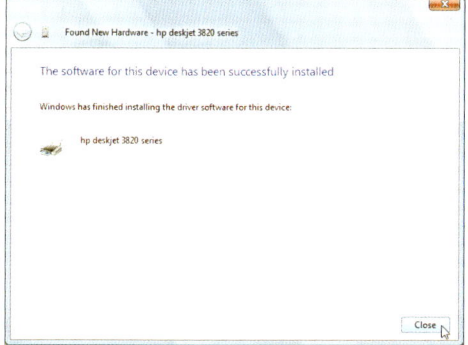

6. The wizard closes. Windows displays a pop-up message above the notification area telling you that your devices are ready to use. Click the [Close] button (the ✕ button).

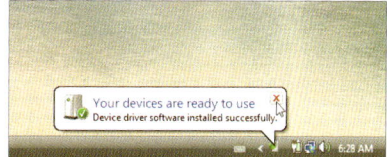

Connecting a Parallel Port Printer via USB — Note >>>

Although most modern printers use USB connections, some older printers use parallel-port connections. If your computer has a parallel port, simply connect the printer's cable to the parallel port. But if your computer, like many modern ones, doesn't have a parallel port, you can still connect a parallel-port printer by buying a parallel-to-USB cable. These are available from most major retailers.

Sharing a Printer

After setting up a printer on your computer, you can share it with other users of your network. Follow these steps:

1. Click the [Start] button, and then click [Control Panel]. In the Control Panel window, click the [Classic View] link if it does not already have a dot beside it. Then double-click the [Printers] icon.

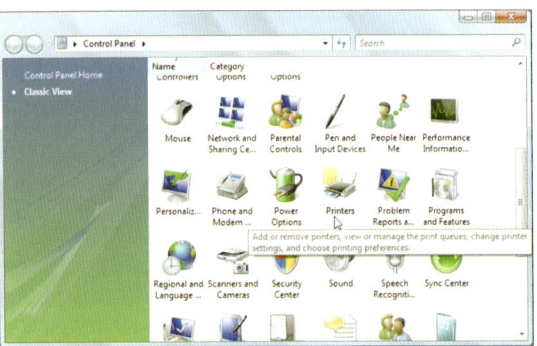

2. Windows opens a Printers window. Click the printer you want to share, and then click [Share] on the toolbar (you may have to click the [Display Additional Commands] button at the right end).

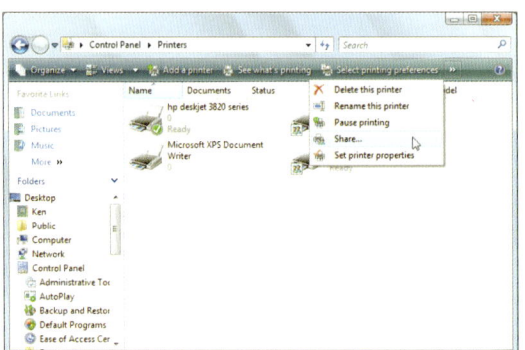

Identifying and Changing the Default Printer   Note >>>

Your default printer is the one with a green circle containing a white check mark. This is the printer that programs use unless you tell them to use another printer. To change the default printer, click the printer you want to make the new default, and then click the [Set as Default Printer] button on the toolbar.

3. Windows opens the printer's [Properties] dialog box with the [Sharing] tab at the front. Click the [Change Sharing Options] button, and then go through User Account Control for the Change Printing Settings feature.

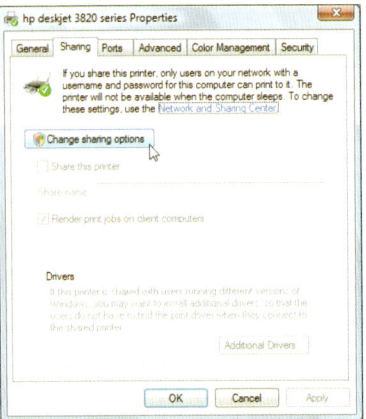

4. Windows enables the settings for sharing the printer. Select the [Share This Printer] check box. If needed, change the name in the [Share Name] text box. Select the [Render Print Jobs on Client Computers] check box. Click the [OK] button.

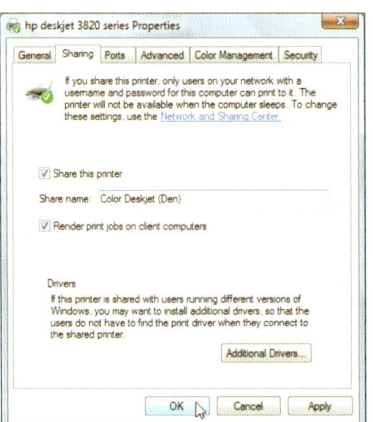

5. Windows closes the [Properties] dialog box. The printer appears in the Printers window with a symbol of two users to indicate that it is shared, as shown here. Click the [Close] button (the ✖ button) to close the Printers window.

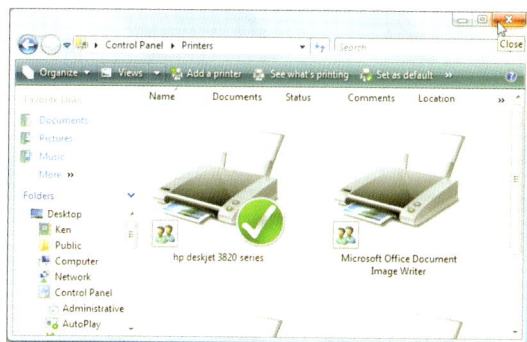

Installing a Printer Shared on the Network

Once you have shared a printer on the network, you can use it from another computer. To install the printer, follow these steps:

1. Click the [Start] button, and then click [Control Panel]. In the Control Panel window, click the [Classic View] link if it does not already have a dot beside it. Then double-click the [Printers] icon.

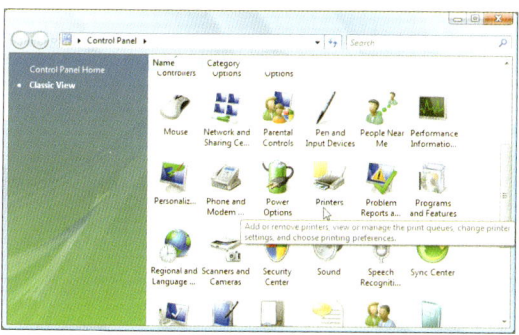

2 Windows opens a Printers window. Click the [Add a Printer] button on the toolbar.

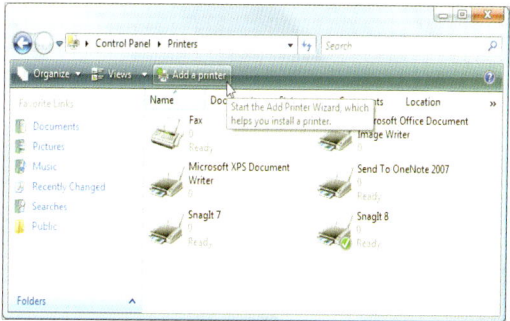

3. Windows starts the Add Printer Wizard. Click the [Add a Network, Wireless or Bluetooth Printer] button.

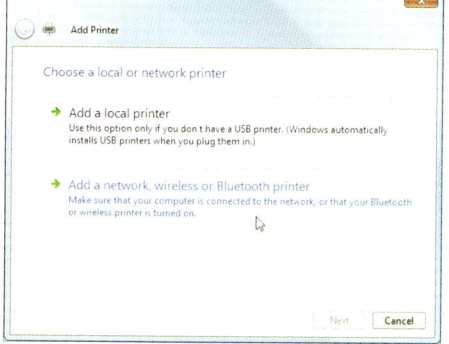

4. The wizard searches for available printers and displays a list of those it finds. If the printer is listed, click it and go to step 6. Otherwise, click the [Printer That I Want Isn't Listed] button.

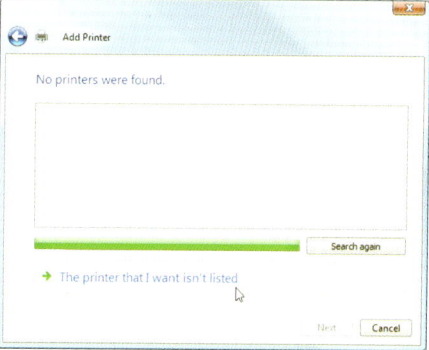

239

5. The wizard shows the [Find a Printer by Name or TCP/IP Address] screen. Select the [Browse for a Printer] option button, and then click the [Next] button.

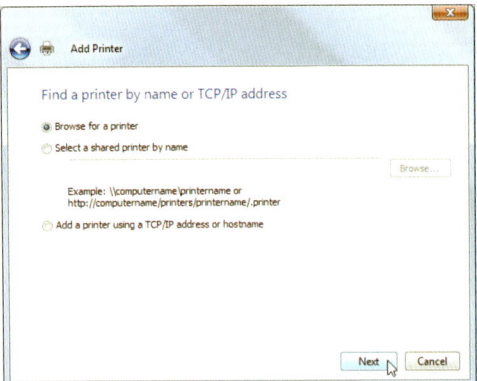

6. The wizard shows the [Please Select the Network Printer] screen, which lists the computers that are sharing printers. Double-click the computer that's sharing the printer.

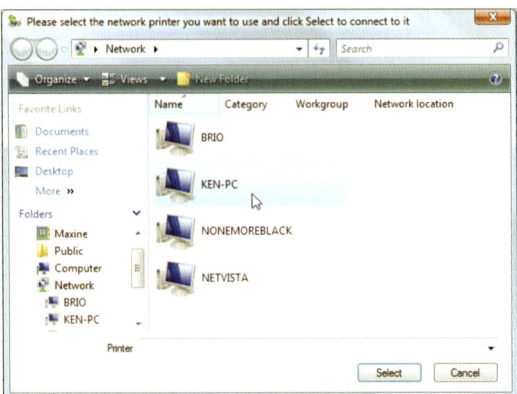

7. If Windows shows the [Connect To] dialog box for the printer, type your user name and password for that computer (not for the computer you're using). Select the [Remember My Password] check box. Click the [OK] button.

8. The wizard shows the printers that are available. Click the printer you want, and then click the [Select] button.

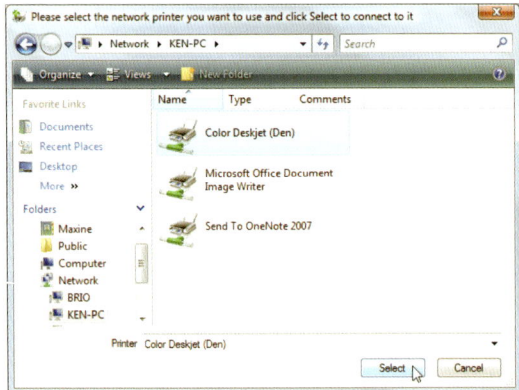

9. If the wizard shows the [Printers] dialog box telling you that you must install a printer driver, click the [Install Driver] button, and then go through User Account Control for the Printer Driver Software Installation feature.

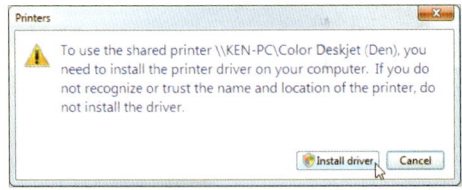

10. The wizard shows the [Type a Printer Name] screen. However, it prevents you from changing the printer name. Select the [Set as the Default Printer] check box if you want to use this printer as your default printer. Click the [Next] button.

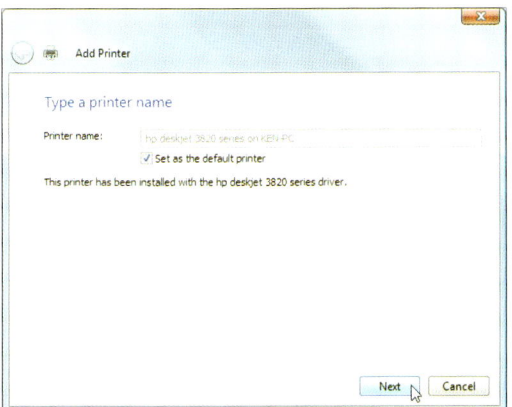

11. The wizard shows a screen saying that you've successfully added the printer. Click the [Print a Test Page] button to print a test page. Then click the [Finish] button.

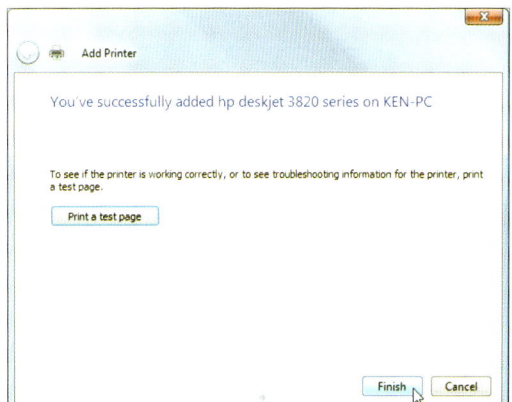

12. The wizard closes, and the printer appears in the Printers window. Click the [Close] button (the button) to close the Printers window.

Printing a Document

When you have installed a printer, you can print to it easily from any program. Follow these general steps, which use the WordPad program that is included with Windows:

1. Open the program, and then open the document you want to print. When you are ready to print it, press <Ctrl> + <P> or click the [File] menu, and then click [Print].

2. The [Print] dialog box opens. If necessary, choose the printer in the [Select Printer] box. The program uses your default printer until you change printers.

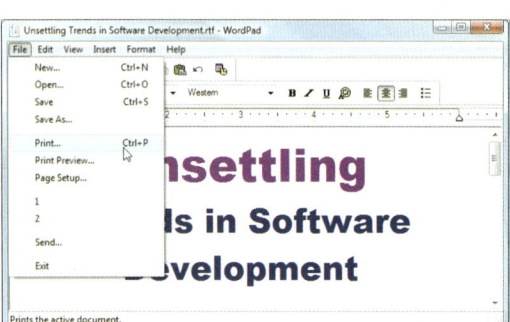

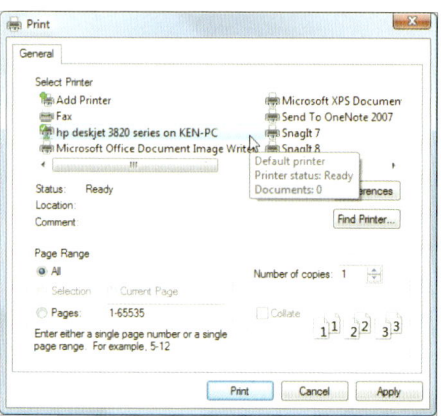

3. Choose other options as necessary. For example, choose to print only part of the document, or choose to print more than one copy. Then click the [Print] button.

4. The program sends the document to the printer, which prints it. If you have finished working with the document, click the [Close] button (the button) to close it.

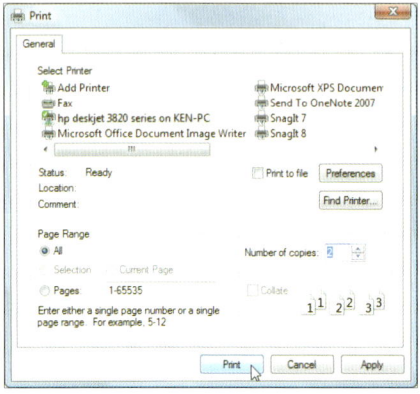

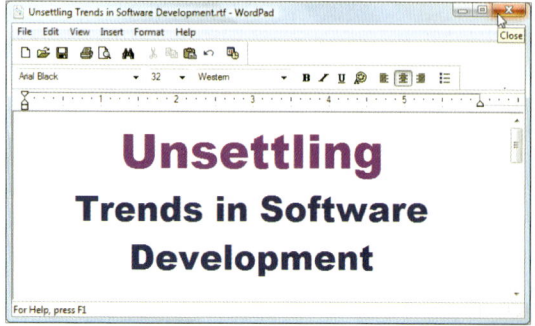

SECTION 04

Adding and Managing Fonts

Windows includes many fonts, or typefaces, that you can use freely to make the text in your documents appear readable, attractive, or both. In fact, Windows includes so many fonts that you may never need to install any extra fonts unless you have special needs, such as doing design work or page layout.

Viewing the Fonts on Your Computer

To examine the fonts installed on your computer, follow these steps:

1. Click the [Start] button, and then click [Control Panel]. In the Control Panel window, click the [Classic View] link if it does not already have a dot beside it. Double-click the [Fonts] icon.

2. Windows opens the Fonts window. To group the fonts, click the drop-down button next to the Font Type heading, and then click [Group]. (See the "Understanding the Font Types That Windows Uses" sidebar for an explanation of font types.)

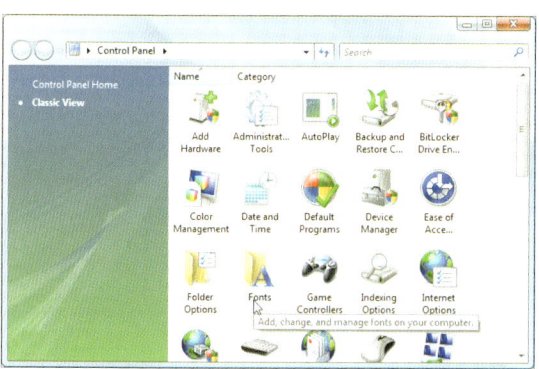

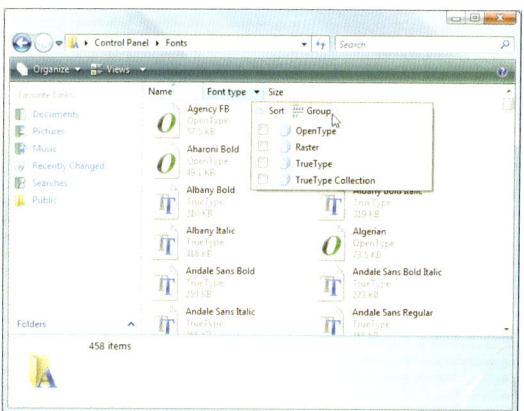

3. Windows groups the fonts by types. Here, the OpenType font type appears at the top of the list. To view a font, double-click it.

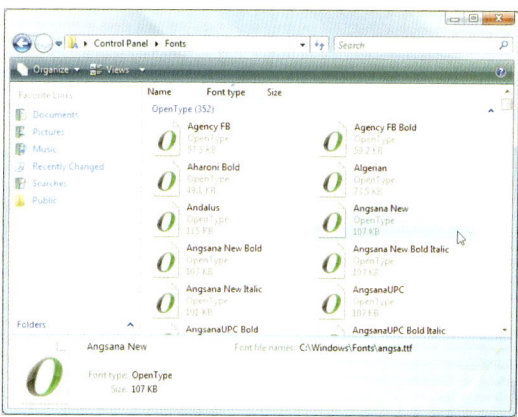

243

4. Windows opens a window showing the font's characters and a sample sentence at different sizes. Click the [Print] button if you want to print the font. Click the [Close] button (the 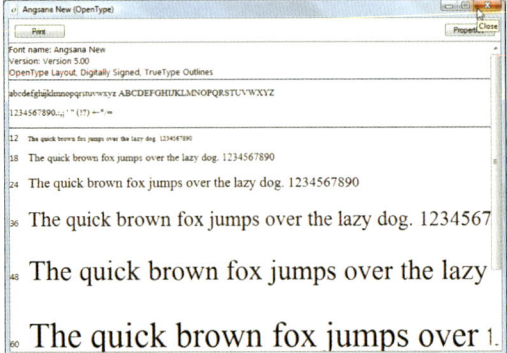 button) when you're ready to close the window. If you want to add or remove a font, leave the Fonts window open.

Understanding the Font Types That Windows Uses

Note >>>

Windows lets you sort fonts by four main font types:

Raster Font
A raster font is an older type of font that uses a picture for each character. Windows has only a few raster fonts, which are included for compatibility with older programs. Raster fonts may distort when enlarged or reduced.

TrueType Font
A TrueType font is a type of outline font—a font that Windows displays by creating the letters on the fly. The advantage of this approach is that Windows can enlarge or reduce the font to exactly the size needed.

TrueType Collection
A TrueType Collection is a group of related TrueType fonts.

OpenType Font
OpenType is the latest form of TrueType font. An OpenType font is an outline font.

Adding a Font

To add a font to your computer, you install it. Follow these steps:

1. With the Fonts window open, press <Alt>. Windows displays the menu bar. Click the [File] menu, and then click [Install New Font].

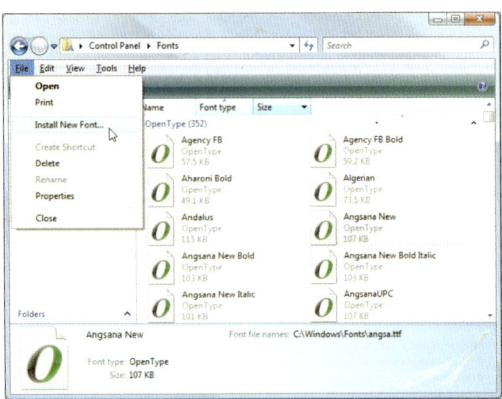

244

Chapter 09. Managing Hardware, Printers, and Fonts

2. Windows opens the [Add Fonts] dialog box. Use the Drives drop-down list and the Folders drop-down list as necessary to navigate to the folder that contains the fonts.

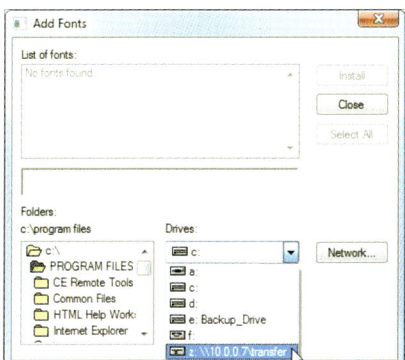

3. The [List of Fonts] box shows the fonts Windows has found in the folder. Make sure the [Copy Fonts to Fonts Folder] check box is selected. Select the fonts you want to install. For example, click the [Select All] button to select all the fonts.

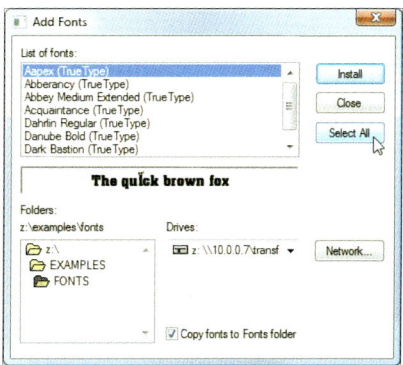

4. Click the [Install] button, and then go through User Account Control for the Windows Font Folder feature.

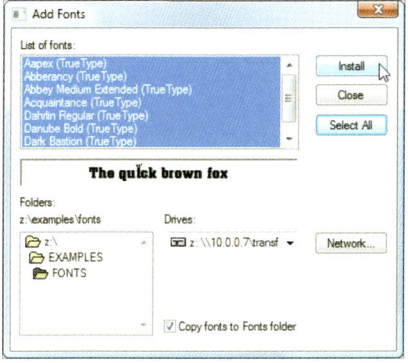

5. Windows installs the fonts. Click the [Close] button to close the [Add Fonts] dialog box.

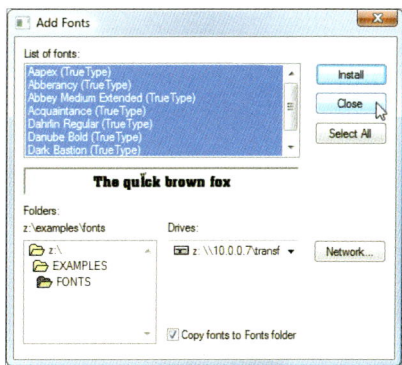

tip >>

Removing a Font

If you find you need only some of the fonts that are installed on your computer, you can remove those you don't need. You can delete fonts from the Fonts folder (select a font, and then press <Delete>), but what's usually easier is simply to move the fonts to another folder. That way, you can restore them to the Fonts folder if you find you need them.

245

Chapter | **10**

Securing Your PC and Windows

Connecting your computer to the Internet or to another network exposes it to security threats. Windows Vista provides essential security features—including automatic updates of Windows components, a firewall, malware protection, and Internet security—but you must make sure that these features are turned on for your computer. You may also need to configure them manually to ensure they give your computer the best protection possible. Besides, you may need to install antivirus software.

SECTION 01 Applying Essential Security Settings

Your first step in securing your computer is to make sure that Windows' most important security settings are turned on. These include the Windows Firewall, which secures network connections; the Windows Defender program, which protects against malevolent software; security options in Internet Explorer; and the User Account Control feature. You must also verify that the Automatic Updates feature is configured to check for updates.

When you first set up Windows Vista, the setup routine prompts you to Use Recommended Settings for security, as shown here.

If you do so, Windows applies the security settings that Microsoft recommends.

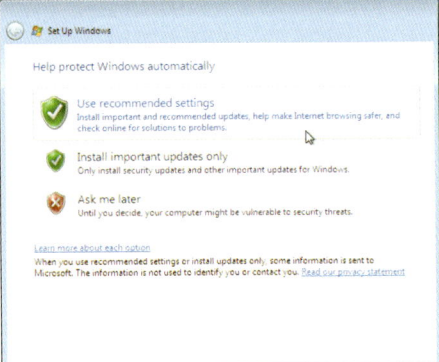

Understanding Windows' Five Security Essentials

These are the five essentials of the security settings:

- **Windows Firewall:** Windows uses Windows Firewall to secure each network connection on the computer. Windows Firewall does a fair job of protecting your computer from unwanted attentions.

- **Automatic Updates:** Windows automatically checks for updates every morning at 3 a.m., applies those it finds, and restarts your computer if necessary.

- **Malware Protection:** Windows runs the Windows Defender program, which attempts to protect your computer against malware (malevolent software). Windows expects you to install and run a third-party antivirus program as well as run Windows Defender.

- **Internet Security:** Internet Explorer comes configured to protect you against phishing and other attacks.

- **User Account Control:** Windows automatically turns on the User Account Control feature, which checks for an Administrator user's permission before performing any systemwide or otherwise sensitive Windows configuration change.

Applying the Recommended Security Settings

Microsoft's recommended security settings provide good protection for your computer—assuming that they're running. If someone (or malevolent software) has switched off one or more of the essential security settings, you may need to reapply it, as discussed here. In addition, you may need to install antivirus software, as discussed in Section 2.

To apply the recommended security settings, follow these steps:

1. Click the [Start] button, and then click [Control Panel]. If there is a dot next to [Control Panel Home] in the left panel, click the [Classic View] link. Then double-click the [Security Center] icon.

2. Windows opens a Windows Security Center window. Verify your security settings. Ideally, you want the following:
- Firewall   On
- Automatic Updating   On
- Malware Protection   On
- Other Security Settings   OK

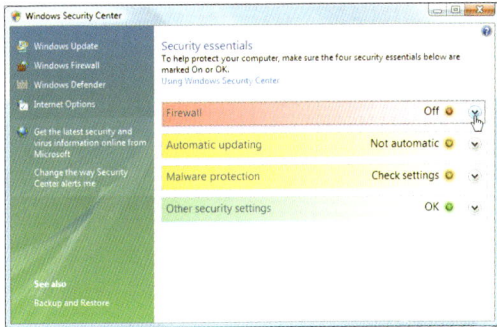

3. If the [Firewall] line reads [Off], click the button at its right end. Windows shows the Windows Firewall options. Click the [Turn On Now] button, and then go through User Account Control for the Security Center feature. Windows turns on Windows Firewall and closes the options area.

4. If the [Automatic Updating] line reads [Not Automatic], click the button at its right end. Windows shows the Automatic Updating options. Click the [Change Settings] button.

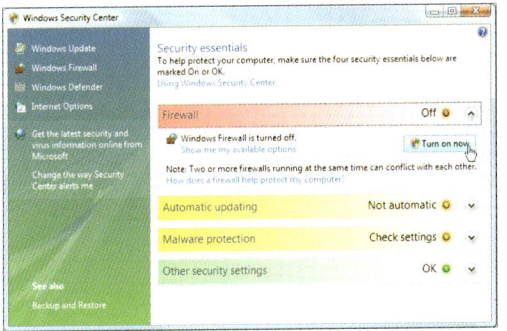

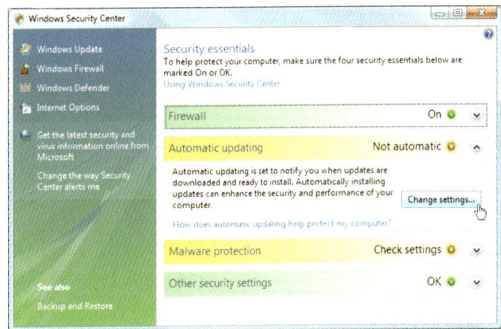

Installing Another Firewall May Turn Windows Firewall Off   Warning >>>

If you install an antivirus program such as Windows Live OneCare, it may turn Windows Firewall off and run its own firewall instead. This behavior is as intended, but it is confusing, because if you open Windows Firewall, it shows that it is not configured as recommended.

5. Windows shows the [Choose an Automatic Updating Option] dialog box. For best results, click the [Install Updates Automatically] button, and then go through User Account Control for the Security Center feature. Windows turns Automatic Updating on and closes the options area.

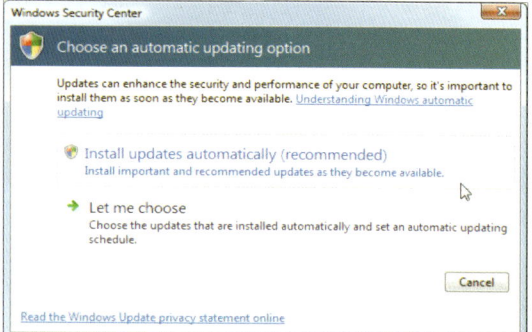

6. If the [Malware Protection] line reads [Check Settings], click the button at its right end. Windows shows the Malware Protection options. If the [Virus Protection] line shows [Not Found], follow the instructions in Section 2 for finding and installing an antivirus program.

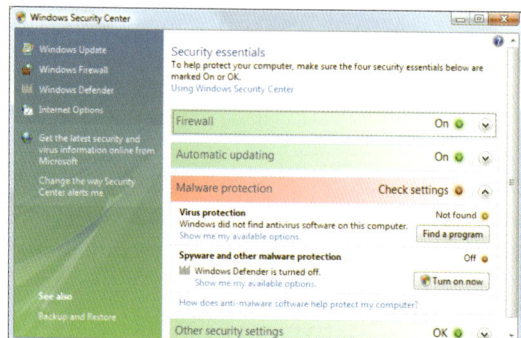

Applying Only Some Windows Updates   Note >>>

If you want to apply only some updates, see "Choosing to Apply Windows Updates Manually," later in this chapter.

7. If the [Spyware and Other Malware Protection] line reads [Off], click the [Turn On Now] button, and then go through User Account Control for the Security Center feature. Windows turns Windows Defender on.

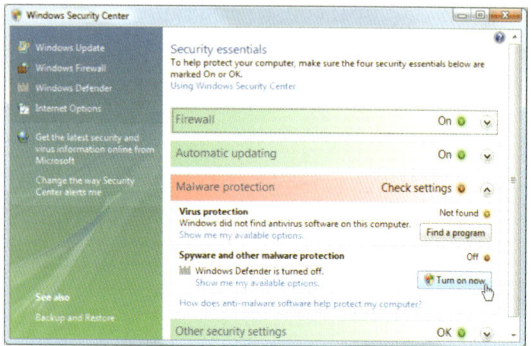

8. If the [Other Security Settings] line reads [Check Settings], click the button at its right end. Windows shows the Other Security Settings options. If the [User Account Control] line reads [Off], click the [Turn On Now] button.

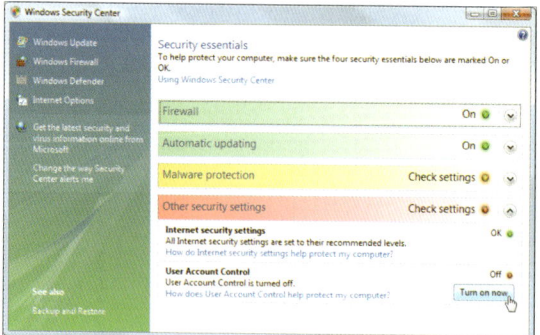

9. Windows shows a [Restart] dialog box. Save any unsaved work in other programs, and then click the [Restart Now] button to restart Windows.

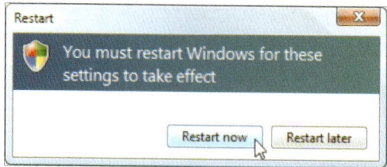

250

Let's Go Pro!

Configuring Windows Firewall to Allow a Program to Run

Windows Firewall is intended to protect your computer against malevolent software running. However, sometimes Windows Firewall may identify a legitimate program as a potential malefactor and prevents it from communicating across the network or Internet. When this happens, you can sometimes quickly unblock the program. Other times, you may need to configure Windows Firewall manually to allow the program to communicate.

● **Unblocking a Program That Windows Firewall Blocks**

By default, Windows Firewall alerts you when it blocks a program or a feature of a program, as shown here. Click the [Unblock] button if you want to unblock the program or feature. Click the [Keep Blocking] button if you want to continue the blocking.

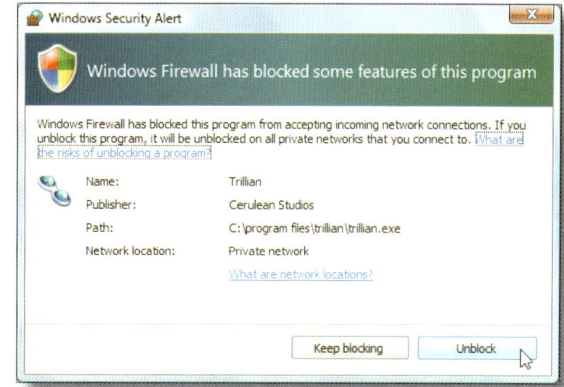

● **Allowing a Program Through Windows Firewall**

To allow a program to communicate through Windows Firewall, follow these steps:

① Click the [Start] button, click in the [Start Search] box, and then type **firewall**. Windows shows a list of matching items. Click the [Windows Firewall] item.

251

② Windows opens the Windows Firewall window. In the left panel, click the [Allow a Program through Windows Firewall] link, and then go through User Account Control for the Windows Firewall Settings feature.

③ Windows opens the [Windows Firewall Settings] dialog box with the Exceptions tab at the front. If the program you want to allow through Windows Firewall appears in the list box, select its check box. Otherwise, click the [Add Program] button.

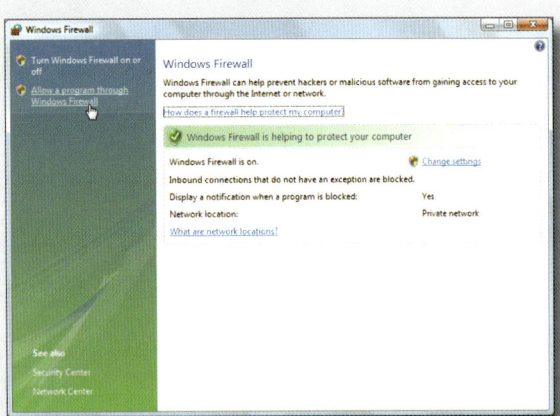

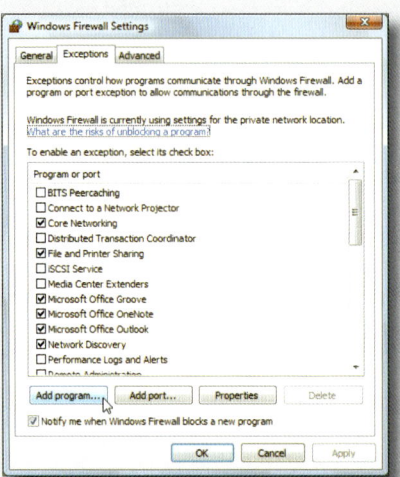

④ Windows opens the [Add a Program] dialog box. Select the program in the [Programs] list box, and then click the [OK] button.

⑤ Windows adds the program to the list on the Exceptions tab and selects the program's check box. Click the [OK] button to close the [Windows Firewall Settings] dialog box.

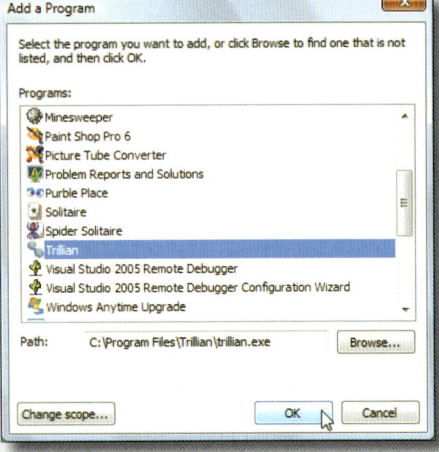

Allowing a Program That's Not Listed through Windows Firewall — Note >>>

If the program you want to allow through Windows Firewall doesn't appear in the list in the [Add a Program] dialog box, click the [Browse] button. The [Browse] dialog box opens. Navigate to the folder that contains the program, select the program, and then click the [Open] button. Windows returns you to the [Add a Program] dialog box, where it has added the program you selected to the Programs list.

SECTION 02

Installing an Antivirus Program

Microsoft strongly recommends that you use an antivirus program to help protect Windows Vista, your programs, and your data from unwanted attention. However, Windows Vista does not include an antivirus program.

Choosing an Antivirus Program

Your computer's manufacturer may have included antivirus software with Windows Vista. If you have paid for this antivirus software, it will be a full version, and presumably you will want to use it. But if the antivirus software is a free trial version, you will have an incentive to use it—because it is there—but you are not committed to it.

This section uses Microsoft's own antivirus software, OneCare, as an example. At this writing, there is a 90-day free trial that you can download from the Windows Live OneCare Web site (http://onecare.live.com), so you can try the program before you buy it.

You may prefer to use another antivirus program, such as McAfee Internet Security Suite, Symantec Norton Internet Security, Trend Micro PC-cillin Internet Security, or Computer Associates eTrust Antivirus. Some of these vendors offer free trial versions of their software.

The exact steps for installing and configuring other antivirus software programs are different, so if you choose another antivirus program, consult its documentation for instructions.

Never Use Two Antivirus Programs at Once — Warning >>>

You should only ever use one antivirus program at a time. This is because antivirus programs can cause problems with each other, either raising false alerts or compromising your PC's protection.

Before installing an antivirus program, uninstall any existing antivirus program on your computer. See Chapter 2 for instructions on uninstalling programs.

Installing Windows Live OneCare

To install OneCare, follow these steps:

1. Close all programs you're running. Click the [Start] button, and then click [Internet]. Windows opens an Internet Explorer window. Press <Alt> + <D> to activate the Address Bar, type **onecare.live.com**, and then press <Enter>.

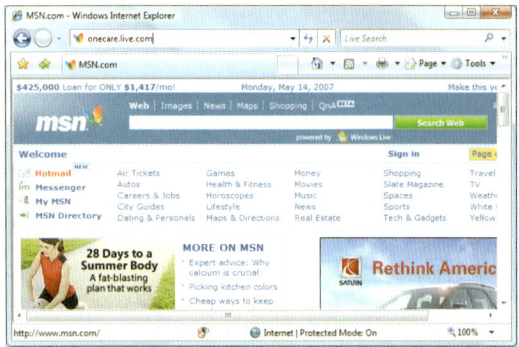

2. Internet Explorer shows the Windows Live OneCare Home page. Click the [Download the 90-Day Free Trial] button.

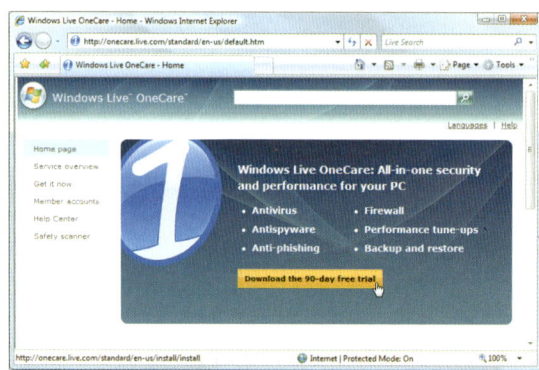

3. On the Windows Live OneCare Installation page, click the [Install Windows Live OneCare] link.

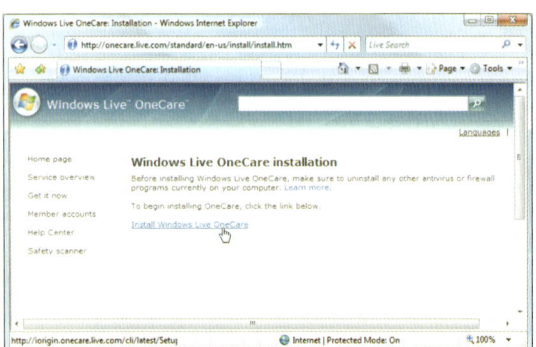

4. Windows shows a [File Download—Security Warning] dialog box. Click the [Run] button. Windows downloads the file and launches the installation routine. Go through User Account Control for the Windows Live OneCare feature.

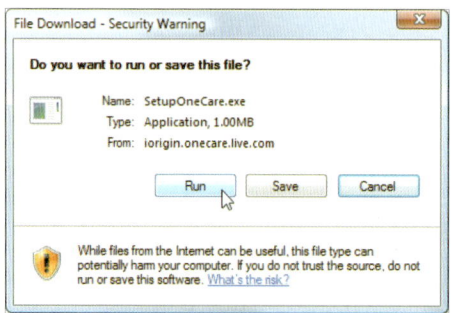

5. The installation routine shows the Windows Live OneCare Installation window. Select your language in the drop-down list. Click the links to read the OneCare feature summary, the Microsoft Online Privacy Statement, and the OneCare Privacy Supplement. If you want to continue, click the [Next] button.

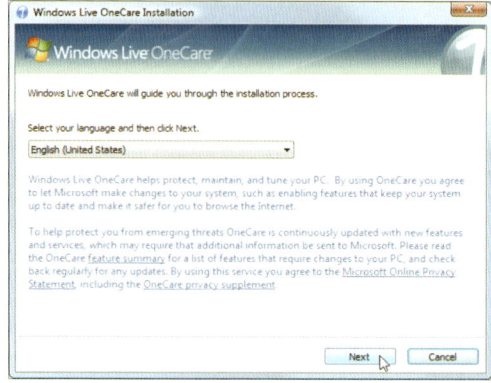

6. The [Terms of Use] screen appears. If the terms are acceptable, select the [I Accept the Terms of Use] option button, and then click the [Next] button.

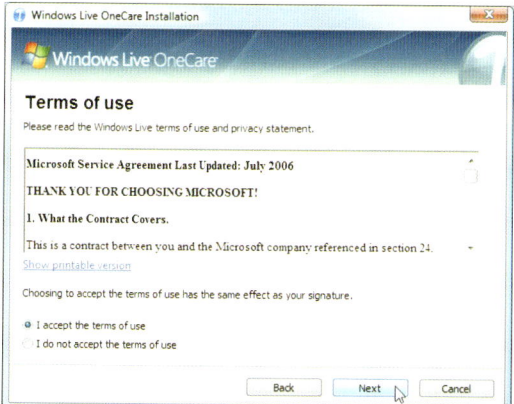

7. Wait while the installation routine downloads OneCare and installs it on your computer.

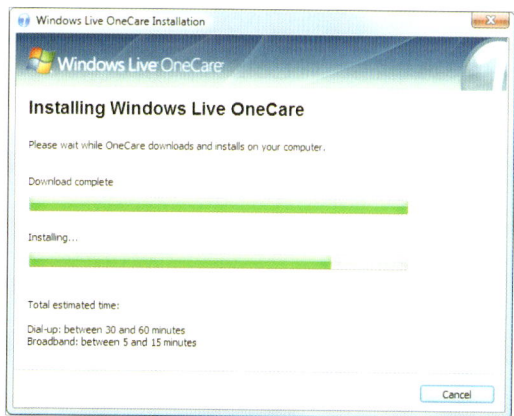

8. When installation is complete, OneCare scans for conflicting programs (in case you have not removed them). If all is well, the [Complete the OneCare Installation] screen appears. Select the [Restart Now] check box if you want to restart now. Click the [Finish] button.

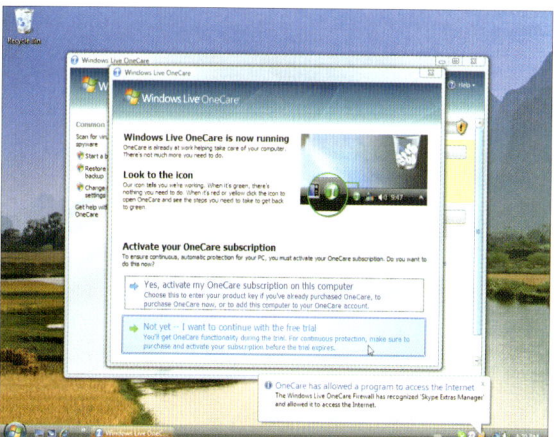

9. OneCare restarts your computer. After you log on, OneCare runs and displays an introductory screen. Click the [Not Yet—I Want to Continue with the Free Trial] button to start your free trial.

10. OneCare then opens its main window, which summarizes your computer's status and lists any actions you need to take. For example, in the following screen, you can click the [Turn On] button to turn on the Phishing Filter for all users (this is normally a good idea).

11. OneCare displays an icon in the notification area that gives you a traffic-signal indication of your computer's general status: green for good, amber for moderate, and red for a problem you must deal with. You can click the icon to display a menu that allows you to open the OneCare window.

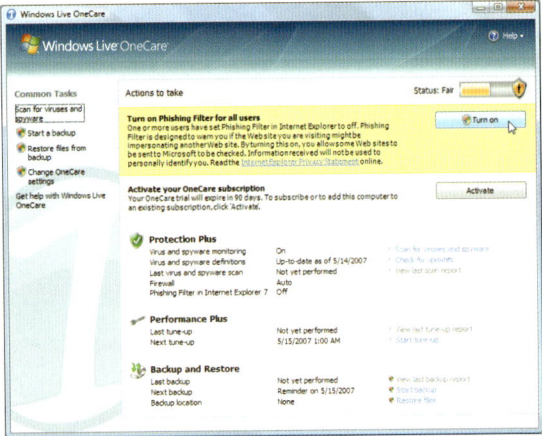

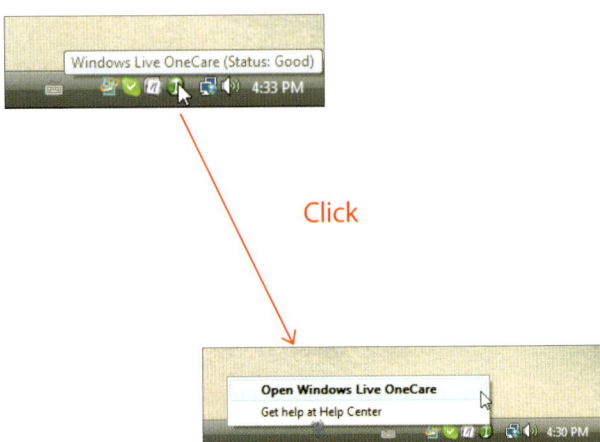

Click

Leaving Your Antivirus Program Running — Warning >>>

Normally, once you've installed an antivirus program on your computer, you leave it running so that it can detect (and, you hope, prevent) any problems. Therefore you do not exit an antivirus program or turn it off—you simply allow it to run in the background. Most antivirus programs display an icon in the notification area to allow you to easily monitor their status and open the program window.

SECTION 03 Keeping Windows Up-to-Date

As you saw at the beginning of this chapter, Window's setup routine encourages you to sign up for automatic updates for all new Windows components. Given that Microsoft frequently releases fixed and improved versions of Windows components, this is usually a good idea.

Applying Windows Updates Automatically

Windows makes it as easy as possible to apply Windows Updates automatically. If you allow Windows to use its default settings, and your computer has an Internet connection, Windows checks for updates at 3 a.m. every morning. If it finds updates, it downloads them, applies them, and then restarts your computer if that's necessary. After you log on again, Windows displays a pop-up in the notification area to let you know, as shown here. Click the pop-up message to see the details of the updates Windows applied.

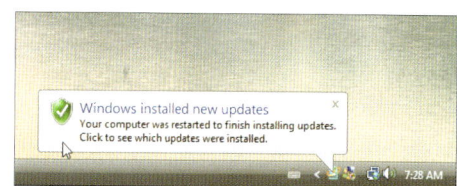

If you catch Windows in the process of applying automatic updates, Windows prompts you to restart your computer. To postpone the restart, choose the length of time in the [Remind Me In] drop-down list, and then click the [Postpone] button. Otherwise, click the [Restart Now] button to restart immediately.

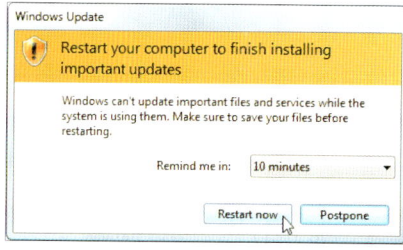

If Windows has already shut down in order to apply updates, allow it to finish, as instructed here.

> **Warning >>>**
> **Automatic Updates Can Cost You Unsaved Work**
>
> If you use Automatic Updates, save your work before you leave your computer at the end of the day. Otherwise, Windows closes the programs so that it can restart the computer, and you lose any unsaved changes. You cannot normally recover such lost material.

Choosing to Apply Windows Updates Manually

Instead of applying all Windows Updates automatically, you may prefer to apply Windows Updates manually. For example, you may find it inconvenient to have Windows restart your computer without consulting you in order to apply updates—especially because, if you have left unsaved documents open, these automatic restarts can cost you work and time.

To set Windows up so that you can apply updates manually, follow these steps:

1. Click the [Start] button, click [All Programs], and then click [Windows Update]. Windows opens the Windows Update window. In the left panel, click the [Change Settings] link.

2. Windows opens the Change Settings window. If you have a broadband Internet connection, select the [Download Updates but Let Me Choose Whether to Install Them] option button. If you have a dial-up connection, select the [Check for Updates but Let Me Choose Whether to Download and Install Them] option button.

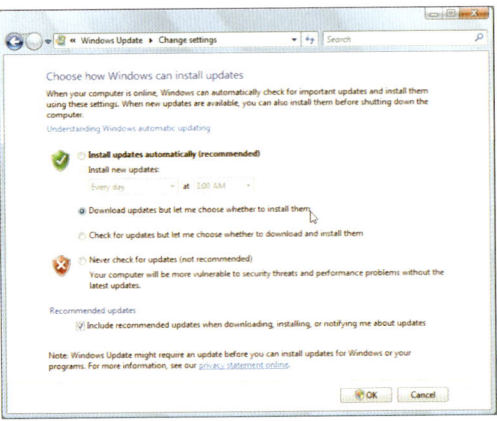

> **Note >>>**
> **Turning Off Checking for Updates**
>
> The Change Settings window also includes the [Never Check for Updates] option button, which you can select to prevent Windows from checking for updates. This is not normally a good idea, because it may leave your computer open to security threats against which updates would protect it. However, you can check for updates manually by clicking the [Check for Updates] link in the left panel of the Windows Update window.

3. Select the [Include Recommended Updates When Downloading, Installing, or Notifying Me about Updates] check box if you want to include recommended updates as well as critical ones. This is normally a good idea. Click the [OK] button, and then go through User Account Control for the Windows Update feature.

4. Windows returns you to the Windows Update window. Click the [Close] button (the button) to close the window.

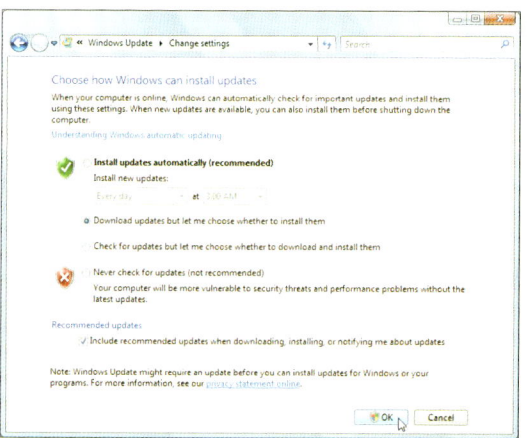

Applying Windows Updates Manually

Once you've configured Windows to notify you about updates, you will need to apply any available updates manually. Follow these steps:

1. Windows shows a notification-area pop-up message to let you know that updates are available. Click this message. Alternatively, click the [Start] button, click [All Programs], and then click [Windows Update].

2. Windows opens the Windows Update window. Examine the [Install Updates for Your Computer] readout. If there are updates, click the [View Available Updates] link.

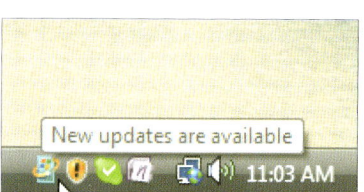

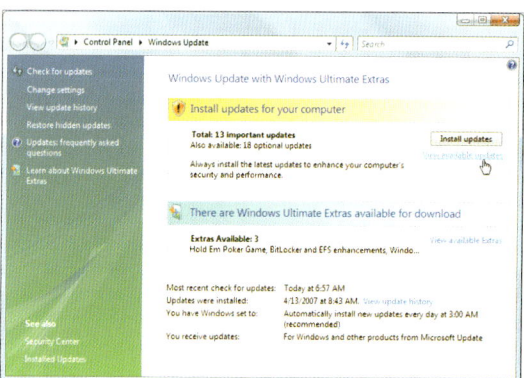

3. Windows opens the View Available Updates window. Select the check box for each update you want to apply, and then click the [Install] button.

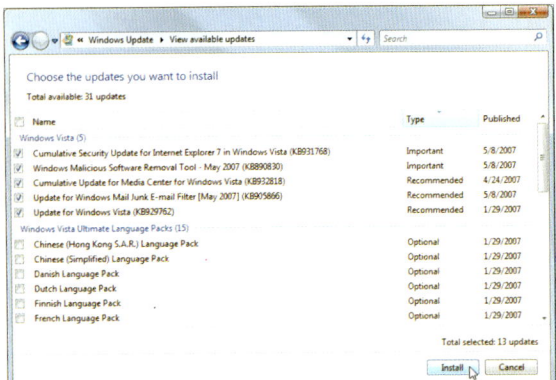

4. Wait while Windows creates a system restore point and installs the updates.

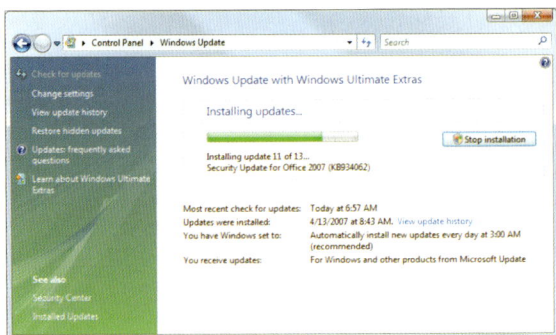

5. After installing updates, you may need to restart Windows. Click the [Restart Now] button.

Let's Go Pro!

Resetting Internet Security Settings Manually

At this writing, Windows Security Center sometimes fails to monitor your Internet security settings correctly. If Internet Explorer warns you that Protected Mode is not on, but Windows Security Center indicates that Internet security settings are OK, follow these steps.

① Click the [Start] button, and then click [Internet]. Windows opens Internet Explorer. Click the [Tools] button, and then choose [Internet Options]. The [Internet Options] dialog box opens. Click the [Advanced] tab, and then click the [Reset] button.

② Internet Explorer opens the [Reset Internet Explorer Settings] dialog box. Read the warnings. If they seem acceptable, click the [Reset] button.

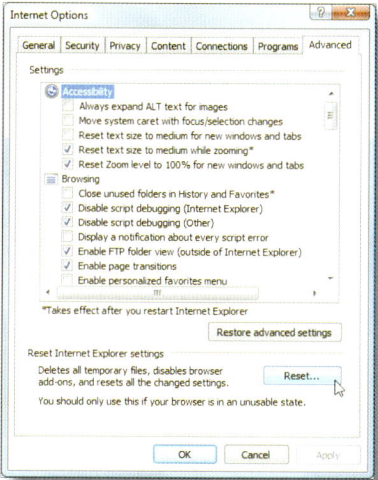

③ Internet Explorer opens a second [Reset Internet Explorer Settings] dialog box, which lists the settings being reset. Click the [Close] button.

④ Internet Explorer displays a dialog box telling you that you will need to restart Internet Explorer. Click the [OK] button to close the dialog box.

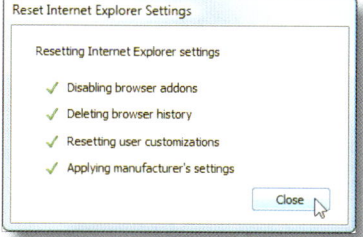

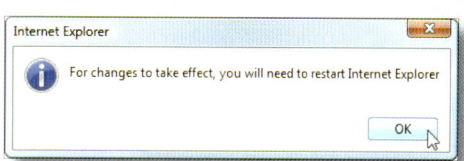

⑤ Click the [OK] button to close the [Internet Options] dialog box, and then click the [Close] button (the button) to close Internet Explorer. Click the [Start] button, and then click [Internet] to launch Internet Explorer again.

261

SECTION 04

Scanning for Problems with Windows Defender

As you saw at the beginning of this chapter, Windows includes a utility called Windows Defender designed to help protect your computer against malicious software.

Configuring Windows Defender

To configure Windows Defender so that it runs when you want it to, follow these steps:

1. Click the [Start] button, and then click [Control Panel]. If the Control Panel window opens in Control Panel Home view, click the [Classic View] link. Then double-click the Windows Defender icon.

2. Windows open the Windows Defender window. Click the [Tools] link.

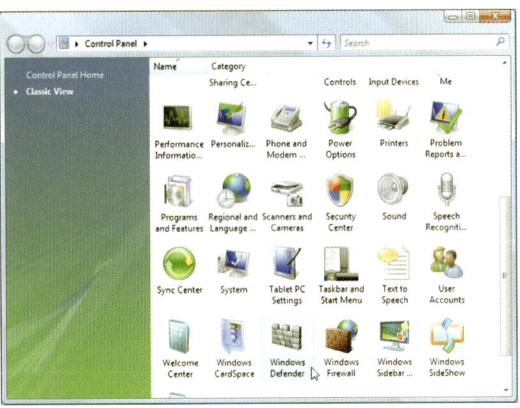

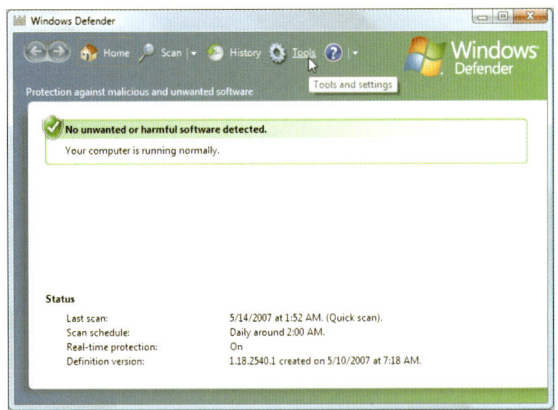

3. Windows Defender opens the [Tools and Settings] screen. Click the [Options] link.

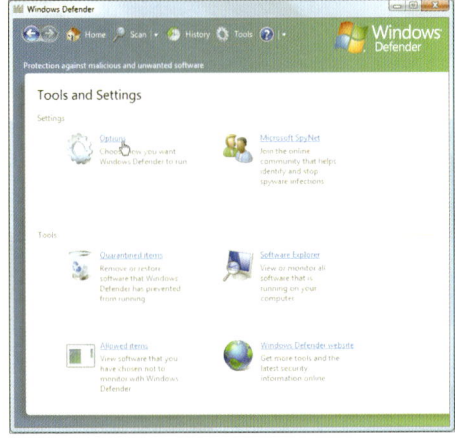

4. Make sure the [Automatically Scan My Computer] check box is selected. Choose the [Daily] item in the [Frequency] drop-down list, choose the time in the [Approximate Time] drop-down list (for example, 12:00 a.m.), and then select the type (Quick Scan or Full System Scan) in the [Type] drop-down list. Select the [Check for Updated Definitions Before Scanning] check box.

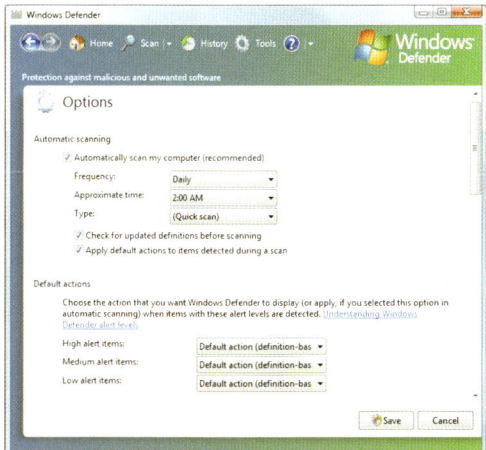

5. Normally, you will want to use Windows Defender's default actions for items it detects. Select the [Apply Default Actions to Items Detected during a Scan] check box. In the Default Actions area, leave each drop-down list set to Default Action (Definition-Based).

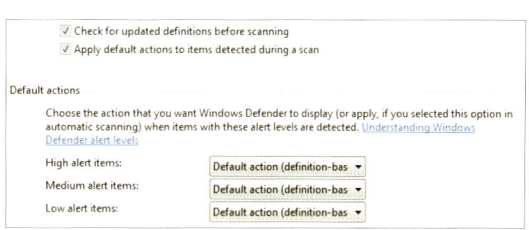

6. Scroll down the window, and then select the [Use Real-Time Protection] check box. In the [Choose Which Security Agents You Want to Run] area, select the check box for each agent you want to run. Usually, it is best to run them all. Leave the two [Choose If Windows Defender Should Notify You About] check boxes cleared, and select the [Only If Windows Defender Detects an Action to Take] option button.

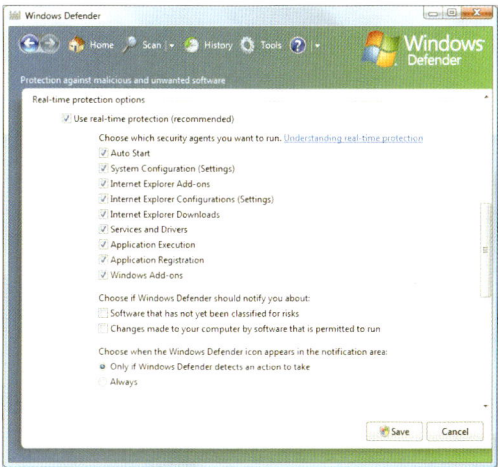

7. If necessary, choose advanced options. Normally you will want to select all five check boxes in the Advanced Options section. If you need to prevent Windows Defender from scanning a particular folder or file, click the [Add] button, use the [Browse for Folder] dialog box to select the folder or file, and click the [OK] button. Click the [Save] button, and then go through User Account Control for the Windows Defender feature.

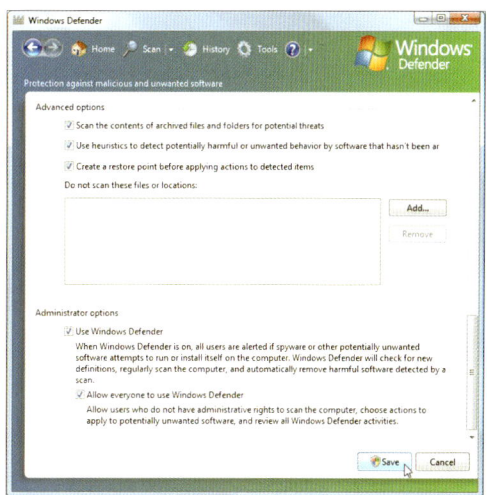

8. Windows Defender displays the [Tools and Settings] screen. Click the [Close] button (the ![close] button) to close Windows Defender.

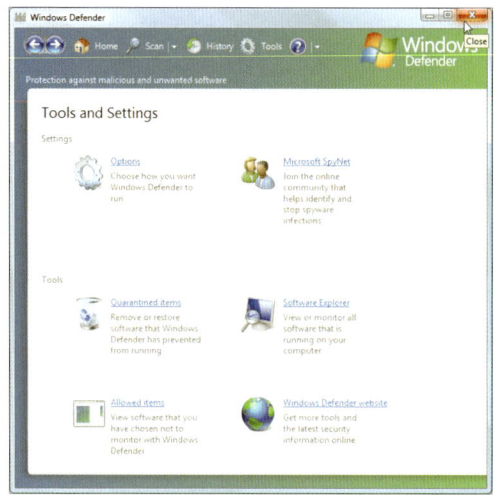

Running a Scan Manually

Normally, you leave Windows Defender running all the time on your computer. If Windows Defender identifies a problem, it notifies you; otherwise, it runs in the background, so you don't see it.

However, if you suspect a problem has occurred on your computer, you can also run a scan manually. Follow these steps:

1. Click the [Start] button, and then click [Control Panel]. If the Control Panel window opens in Control Panel Home view, click the [Classic View] link. Then double-click the Windows Defender icon.

2. Windows opens the Windows Defender window. Click the [Scan] drop-down button, and then choose [Quick Scan] or [Full Scan]. Normally, it is best to run a full scan if you suspect trouble—but because a full scan can take several hours, you may prefer to run a quick scan immediately and a full scan later (for example, at night).

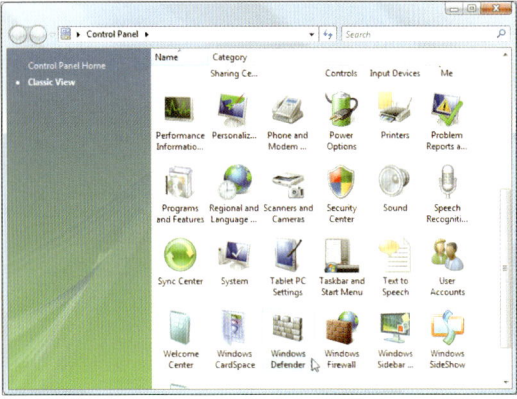

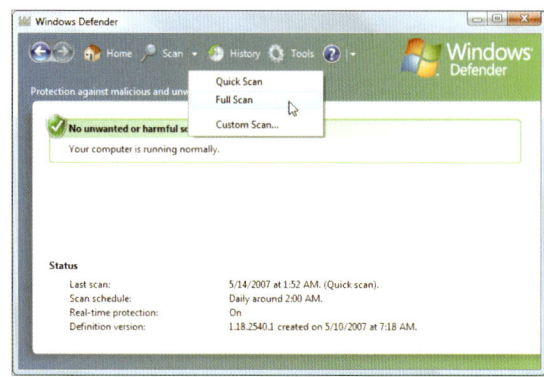

3. If possible, leave your computer alone while Windows Defender scans.

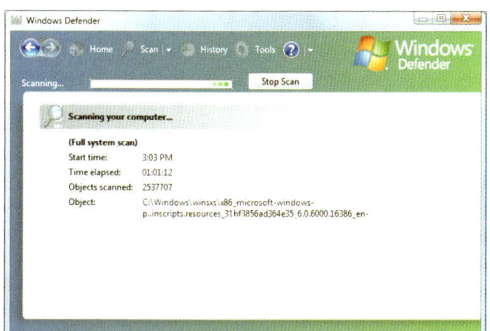

4. When the scan is over, deal with any problems that it has identified. If there are no problems, as in the example shown here, simply click the [Close] button (the button) to close the Windows Defender window.

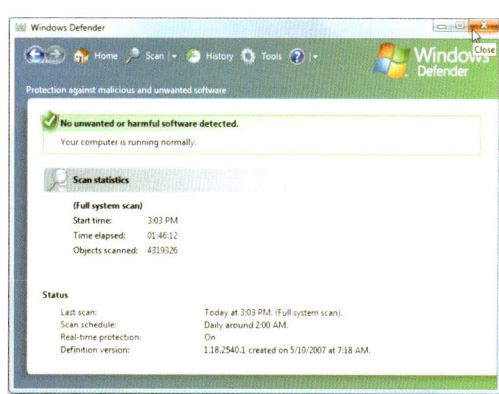

Chapter 11

Troubleshooting Problems

This chapter shows you how to deal with some of the most common problems that occur with Windows Vista. You'll learn how to get help via the Remote Assistance feature when you encounter a problem that you cannot solve yourself, how to use the System Restore feature, how to back up and restore data, and how to find solutions for Windows problems.

SECTION 01 — Getting Help via Remote Assistance

If you encounter a Windows problem that you cannot solve yourself, you can use the Remote Assistance feature to ask someone else to help you. Remote Assistance lets another person view your computer screen across a network or the Internet and chat with you to determine the problem and offer advice. If you trust the other person, you can even let this person take control of your computer so he or she can fix the problem directly.

Setting Up Remote Assistance

Before using Remote Assistance, set it up. Follow these steps:

1. Click the [Start] button, right-click the [Computer] entry, and then choose [Properties] from the context menu.

2. Windows opens a System window. Click the [Remote Settings] link in the Tasks panel on the left of the window, and then go through User Account Control for the System Remote Settings feature.

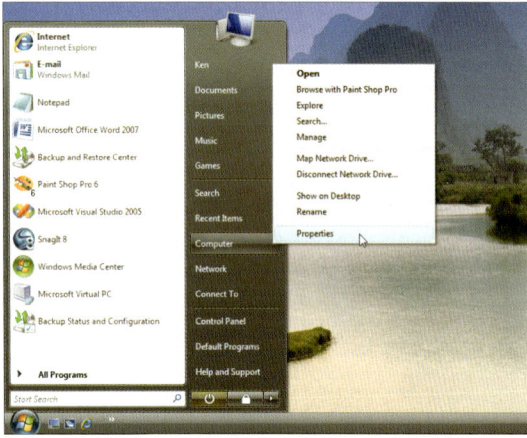

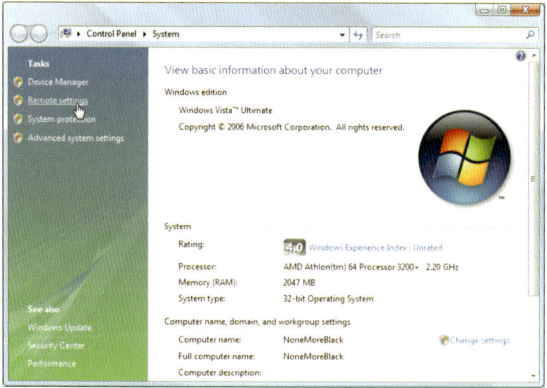

3. Windows opens the [System Properties] dialog box with the Remote tab at the front. Make sure the [Allow Remote Assistance Connections to This Computer] check box is selected, and then click the [Advanced] button.

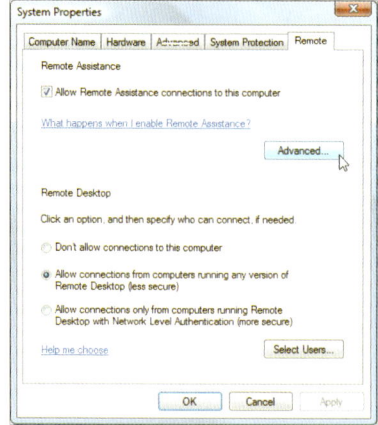

268

4. Windows opens the [Remote Assistance Settings] dialog box. Select the [Allow This Computer to Be Controlled Remotely] check box if you want your helper to be able to take control of the computer (with your permission).

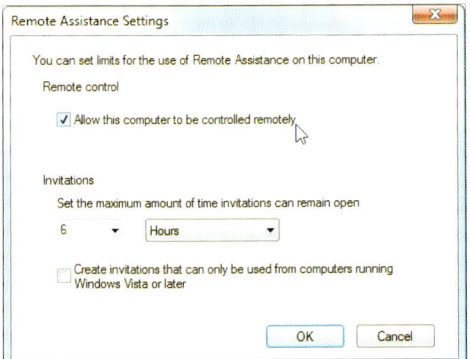

5. In the Invitations area, use the two drop-down lists to set the lifetime of each Remote Assistance invitation—for example, 90 minutes, 3 hours, or 2 days. A shorter invitation life is safer if you are confident your helper will respond quickly.

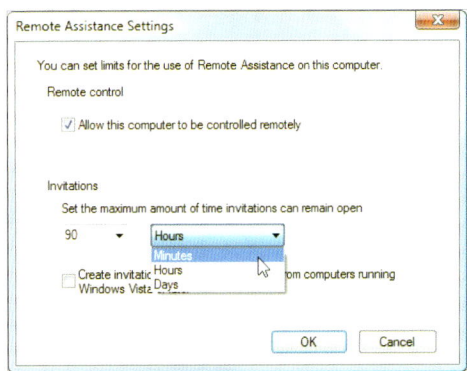

6. If you know all your helpers use Windows Vista rather than earlier versions of Windows, select the [Create Invitations That Can Only Be Used from Computers Running Windows Vista or Later] check box. Otherwise, clear this check box. Click the [OK] button.

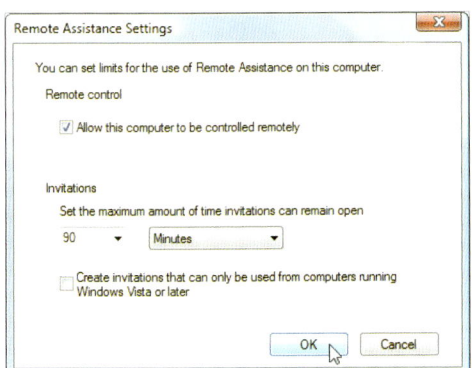

7. Windows closes the [Remote Assistance Settings] dialog box, returning you to the [System Properties] dialog box. Click the [OK] button to close this dialog box, and then click the [Close] button (the button) to close the System window. Your computer is now ready to send Remote Assistance invitations.

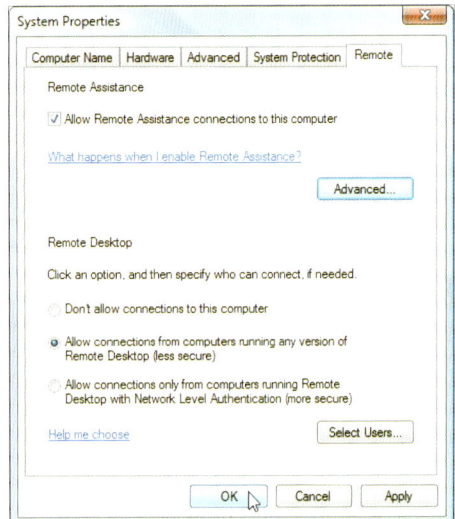

Sending a Remote Assistance Invitation

When you need help with a problem, send a Remote Assistance invitation to someone who can help you—for example, a friend or family member who's a computer expert. To send a Remote Assistance invitation, follow these steps:

1. Click the [Start] button, click [All Programs], click [Maintenance], and then click the [Windows Remote Assistance] item.

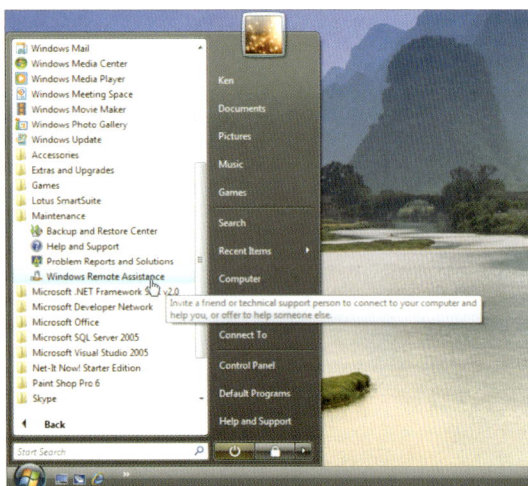

2. Windows launches the Windows Remote Assistance Wizard, which displays the [Do You Want to Ask for or Offer Help?] screen. Click the [Invite Someone You Trust to Help You] button.

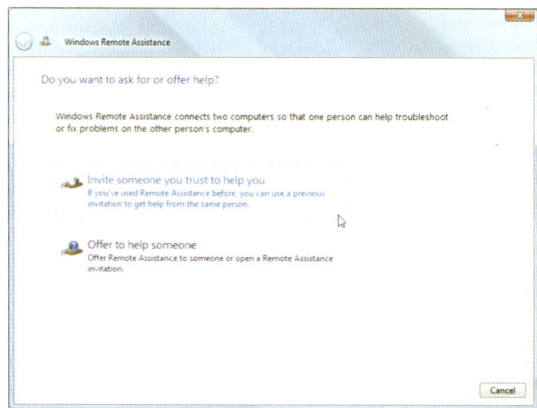

3. The wizard displays the [How Do You Want to Invite Someone to Help You?] screen. Click the [Use E-mail to Send an Invitation] button. (If you want to use a Web-based e-mail account, see the sidebar "Using a Web-Based E-mail Account to Send a Remote Assistance Invitation.")

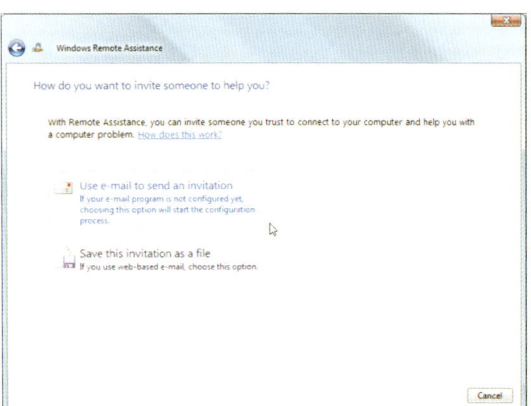

4. The wizard displays the [Choose a Password for Connecting to Your Computer] screen. Choose a password of six characters or more, type it in each text box, and then click the [Next] button.

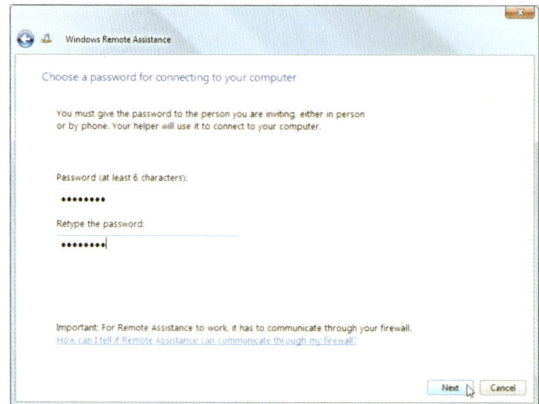

5. The wizard displays the [Starting Your E-mail] screen, opens your e-mail program, and starts a new message. Enter the recipient in the [To] box, type a personal note if necessary, and then send the message—for example, in Windows Mail, click the [Send] button.

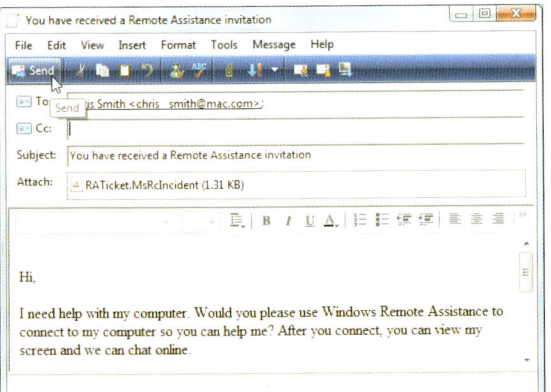

6. When your e-mail program has sent the message, the wizard closes itself and opens the Windows Remote Assistance window. This window shows the message "Waiting for incoming connection." You're now ready to receive assistance from your helper—but before the helper can connect, you must communicate the password to him or her. The best way to do so is via a telephone call or instant messaging. Never send the password along with the invitation, because anyone intercepting the invitation message can then masquerade as your helper.

Using a Web Based E mail Account to Send a Remote Assistance Invitation

Note >>>

To send a Remote Assistance invitation via a Web-based e-mail program (such as Hotmail or Gmail), follow the first two steps in "Sending a Remote Assistance Invitation." Then follow these steps:

1. On the [How Do You Want to Invite Someone to Help You?] screen, click the [Save This Invitation as a File] button.

2. The wizard displays the [Save the Invitation as a File] screen. Change the suggested file name or path but leave the file extension (.msrcincident) if it appears. Type a password in each text box, and then click the [Finish] button.

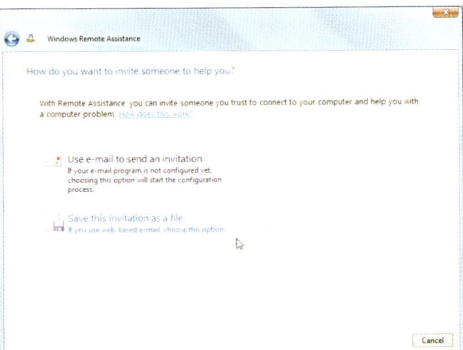

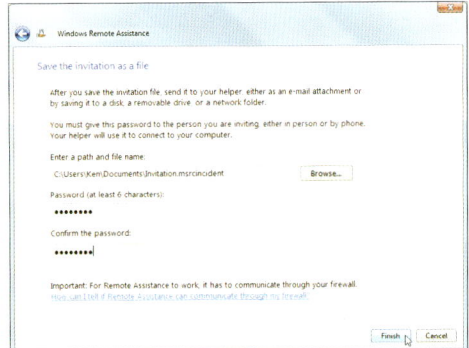

3. The wizard saves the file with the name and path you specified, closes, and opens the Windows Remote Assistance window to wait for a connection.

4. Open your browser (for example, click the [Start] button, and then click [Internet]), go to the Web-based e-mail service, create a message, attach the invitation file, and then send it.

Receiving Help via Remote Assistance

When your helper answers the Remote Assistance invitation, follow these steps:

1. Windows Remote Assistance window opens asking if you would like the helper to connect to your computer. Click the [Yes] button.

2. Remote Assistance establishes the connection. Your helper can now see your desktop. The Windows Remote Assistance window tells you so.

3. If your computer is using the Vista Aero user interface, Windows may change to the Vista Basic user interface and replace your desktop background picture or color with white. Windows displays the notification-area message shown here. Click the [Close] button (the [X] button) to close the message.

4. To chat with your helper, click the [Chat] button. Windows expands the Remote Assistance window to show the chat pane. Click in the text box, type a message, and then press <Enter> or click the [Send] button.

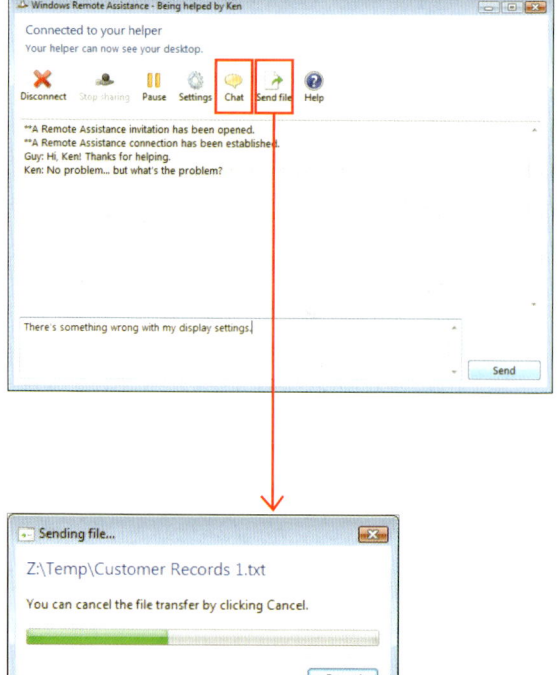

5. To send a file to your helper, click the [Send File] button. Windows displays an [Open] dialog box. Select the file, and then click the [Open] button. Windows prompts your helper to accept the file transfer; if your helper does, Windows transfers the file.

Chapter 11. Troubleshooting Problems

6. If you need to perform an action without your helper seeing (for example, you might shut a sensitive document), click the [Pause] button. Perform the action while Remote Assistance is paused, and then click the [Continue] button.

7. If your helper requests control of your computer, a Windows Remote Assistance window opens asking you whether you want to share control. Select the [Allow [Helper] to Respond to User Account Control Prompts] check box only if you trust the helper completely. Click the [Yes] button if you want to give your helper control.

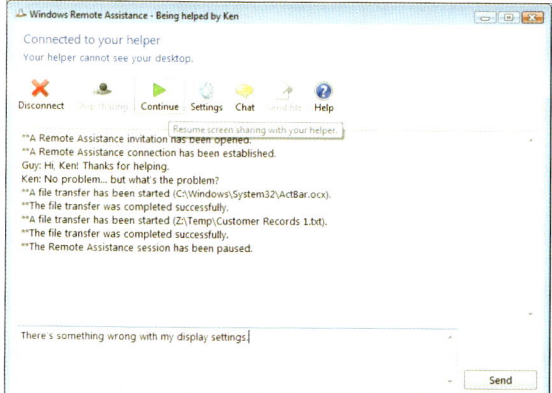

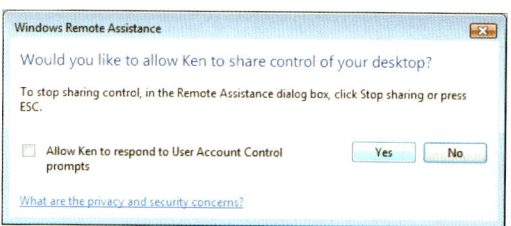

8. To reclaim control of your computer, click the [Stop Sharing] button.

9. To end the Remote Assistance session, click the [Disconnect] button. Windows displays a confirmation message box. Click the [Yes] button. Windows ends the Remote Assistance session and restores the Vista Aero interface if you were using it.

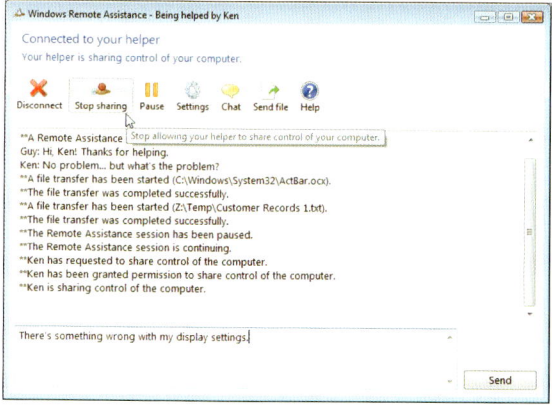

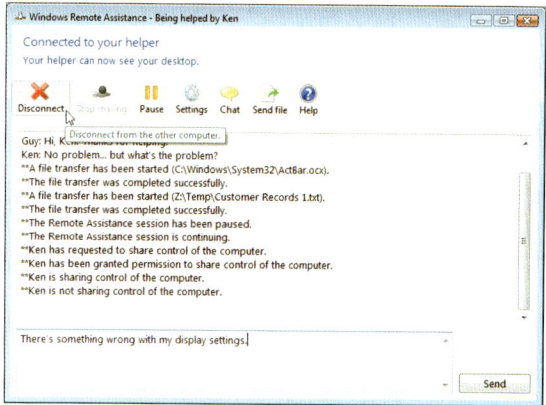

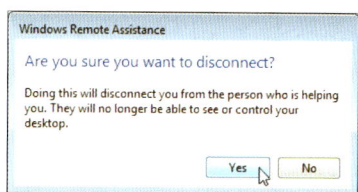

273

Let's Go Pro!

Giving Help via Remote Assistance

As you've seen, Remote Assistance makes it easy for you to ask for help. But you can also be the helper just as easily, as long as you have the Windows knowledge needed. To give someone help via Remote Assistance, follow these steps:

① When you receive the Remote Assistance invitation file in an e-mail, save it to a folder—for example, to your desktop. Then double-click the invitation file. Windows opens a Remote Assistance window. Type the password for the connection, and then click the [OK] button.

② Windows opens a Remote Assistance window and waits for the person who invited you to accept the connection.

③ When the other person accepts the connection, Remote Assistance shows you that person's desktop. You can click the [Fit to Screen] button to toggle between seeing the entire desktop in the Remote Assistance window or seeing it at actual size.

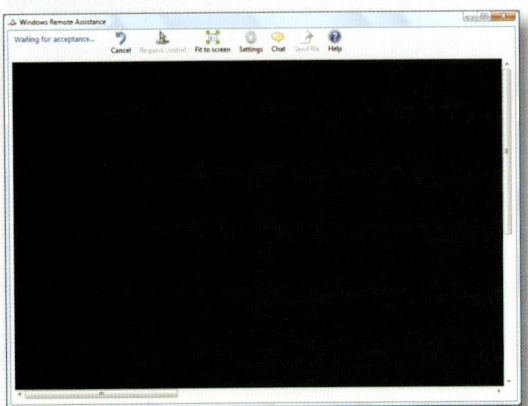

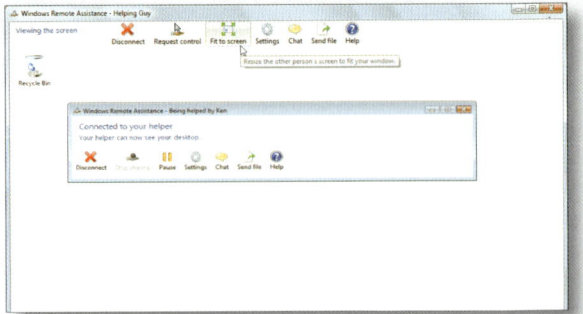

④ To chat with the other person, click the [Chat] button, type a chat message, and then press <Enter> or click the [Send] button.

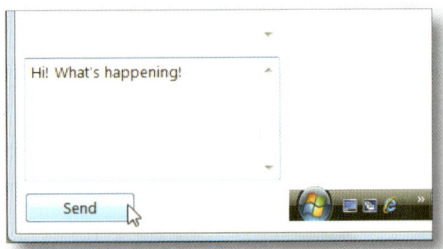

274

⑤ To send a file to the other person, click the [Send File] button, select the file, and then click the [Open] button. If the other person chooses to accept the file, the transfer starts.

⑥ To request control of the other computer, click the [Request Control] button. You will see Remote Assistance prompt the other user to give you control.

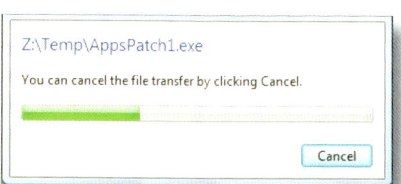

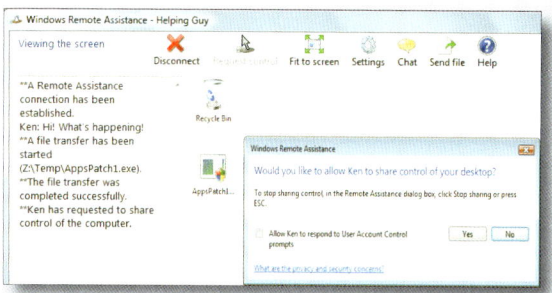

⑦ If the other user gives you control, you can then take actions on the remote computer by using your mouse and keyboard.

⑧ To release control of the other computer, click the [Stop Sharing] button.

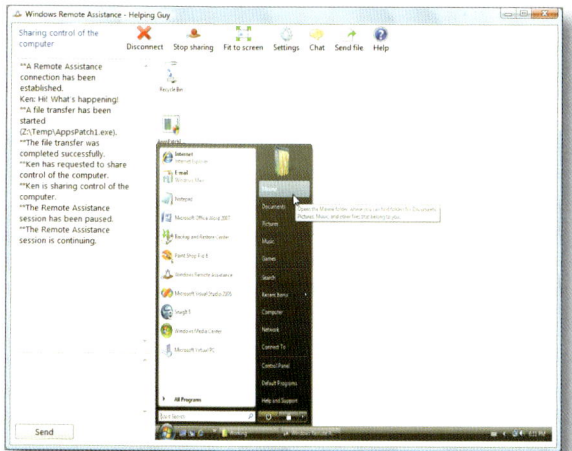

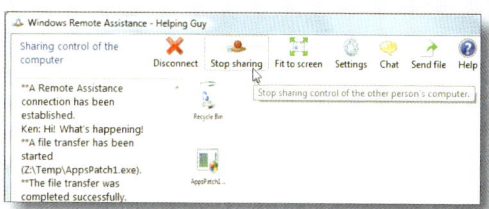

⑨ To end the Remote Assistance session, click the [Disconnect] button. Windows displays a confirmation dialog box. Click the [Yes] button.

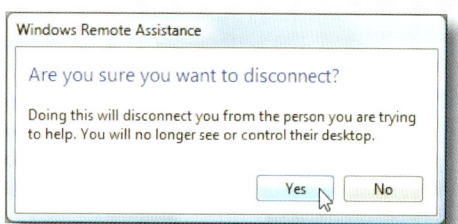

SECTION 02

Using System Restore

Installing software on your computer can make it unstable, so Windows Vista includes a feature called System Restore for saving your computer's configuration so that you can restore it to a previous state after things have gone wrong.

Saving Your Computer's Configuration with System Restore

Windows automatically saves your computer's configuration in a restore point once a day (provided that your computer is running) and before you install most programs and Windows Updates. This means that there are normally plenty of restore points available when you need to restore your computer.

However, you may want to create restore points manually before installing software or otherwise changing your computer—for example, so that you can give a restore point a descriptive name by which you can easily identify it. To create a restore point, follow these steps:

1. Click the [Start] button, right-click the [Computer] entry, and then choose [Properties] from the context menu.

2. Windows opens a System window. In the Tasks panel on the left, click the [System Protection] link, and then go through User Account Control for the System Protection Settings feature.

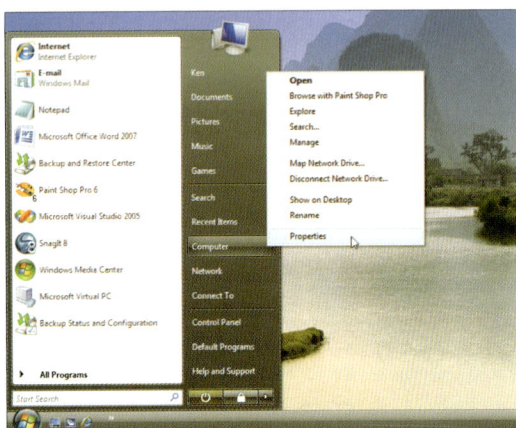

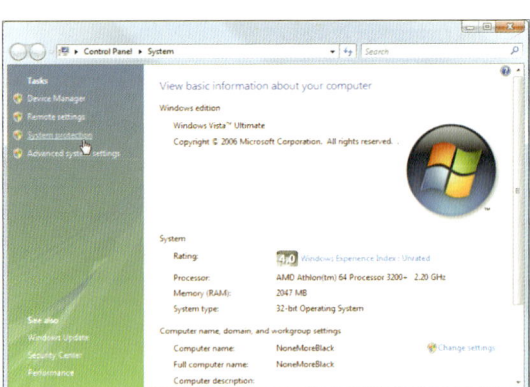

3. Windows opens the [System Properties] dialog box with the System Protection tab at the front. Click the [Create] button.

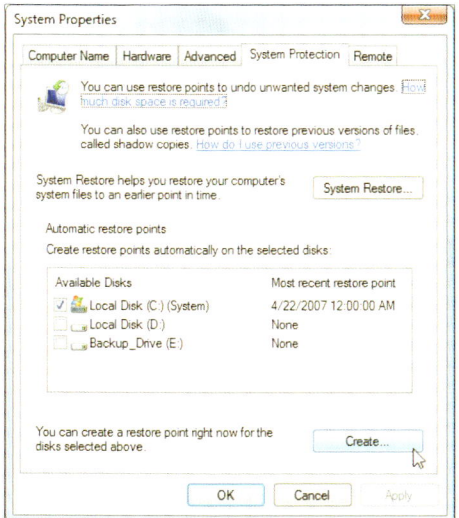

4. Windows opens the [System Protection] dialog box, which prompts you to create a restore point. Type the description you want to use for the restore point. You needn't type the date and time, because Windows adds these to the name. Click the [Create] button.

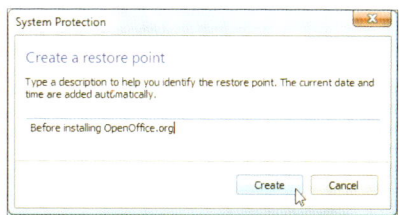

5. System Restore creates the restore point and then displays a message box telling you that it has done so. Click the [OK] button to close the message box, and then click the [OK] button to close the [System Properties] dialog box.

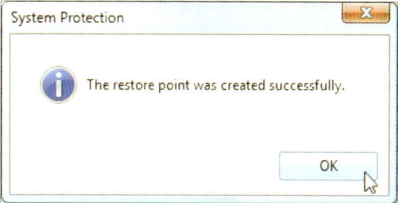

Restoring Your Computer to an Earlier Restore Point

To restore your computer to a restore point, follow these steps:

1. Close all running programs. Click the [Start] button, click [All Programs], click [Accessories], click [System Tools], and then click [System Restore]. Go through User Account Control for the Microsoft Windows System Restore feature.

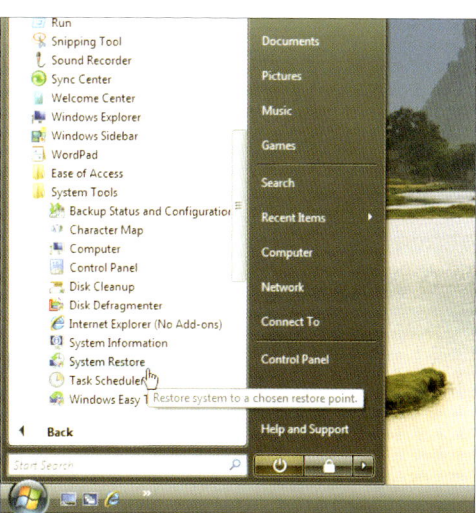

2. Windows launches the System Restore Wizard, which displays the [Restore System Files and Settings] screen. Select the [Recommended Restore] option button if the listed restore point is the one you want. Otherwise, select the [Choose a Different Restore Point] option button. Click the [Next] button.

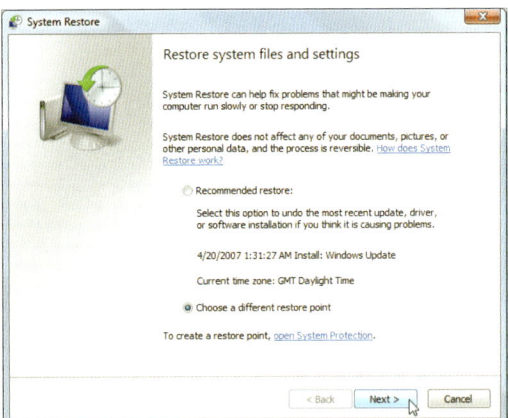

3. If you selected the [Choose a Different Restore Point] option button, the wizard displays the [Choose a Restore Point] screen. Select the [Show Restore Points Older Than 5 Days] check box if you need to see all restore points. Click the restore point, and then click the [Next] button.

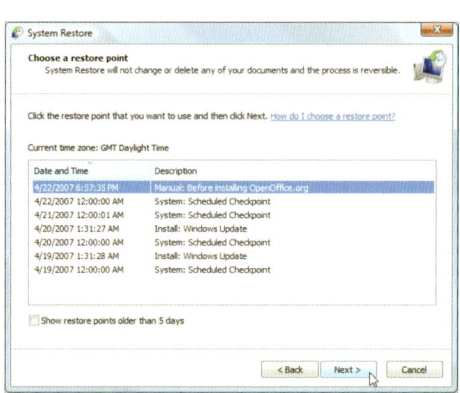

4. The wizard displays the [Confirm Your Restore Point] screen. Verify that the restore point is correct, and then click the [Finish] button.

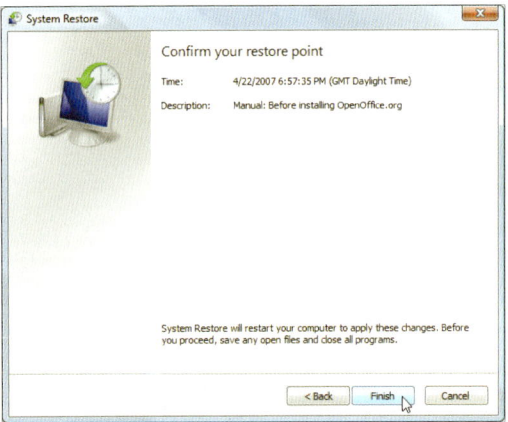

5. The wizard displays a confirmation dialog box. Click the [Yes] button. The wizard closes. System Restore restores your computer to the state saved in the restore point you chose and then restarts the computer.

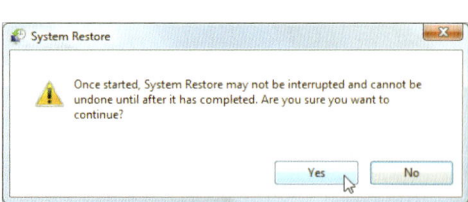

6. After you log on, you see a [System Restore] message box telling you that System Restore completed. Click the [Close] button.

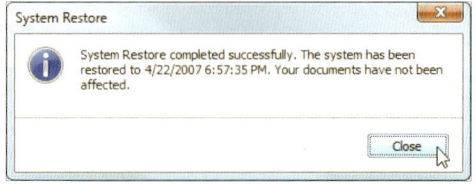

> **Running System Restore Again** — Note >>>
>
> After you restore your computer to a restore point, check that the computer runs correctly. If necessary, you can use System Restore again to restore your computer to a different restore point.

SECTION 03

Backing Up and Restoring Your Data

Computers are highly reliable these days, but you should still be prepared for your computer to go wrong at any time. This means you should back up any data files that you value so that you can restore them later if necessary.

Backing Up Your Files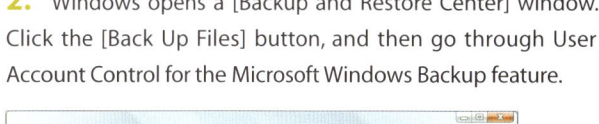

You can back up your files to a hard disk, optical disk (for example, a DVD), or a network. This example uses a hard disk, which is typically the easiest option. To back up your files, follow these steps:

1. Click the [Start] button, click [All Programs], click [Maintenance], and then click [Backup and Restore Center].

2. Windows opens a [Backup and Restore Center] window. Click the [Back Up Files] button, and then go through User Account Control for the Microsoft Windows Backup feature.

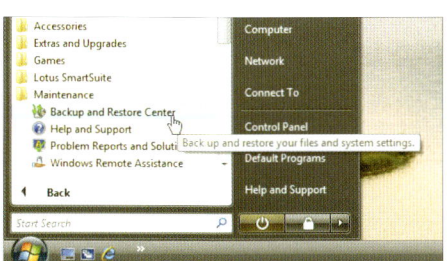

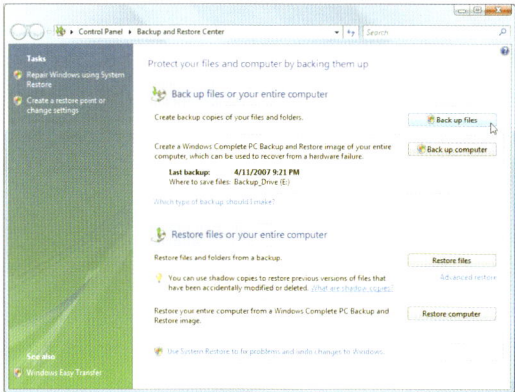

3. Windows launches the Back Up Files Wizard, which displays the [Where Do You Want to Save Your Backup?] screen. Select the [On a Hard Disk, CD, or DVD] option button and choose the drive, or select the [On a Network] option button and specify the path. Click the [Next] button.

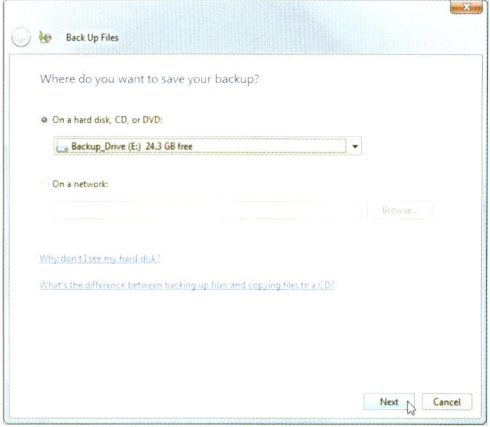

279

> **Backing Up Your Entire Computer** — Note >>>
>
> Windows Vista Ultimate Edition and Windows Vista Business Edition include the Complete PC Backup and Restore feature, which lets you back up your entire PC rather than just certain files. If you have Ultimate or Business, see Chapter 12 for instructions on using this feature.

4. The wizard displays the [Which Disks Do You Want to Include in the Backup?] screen. Select the check box for each disk you want to back up, and then click the [Next] button.

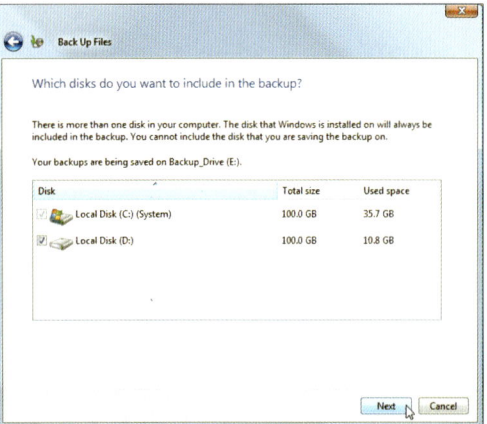

5. The wizard displays the [Which File Types Do You Want to Back Up?] screen. Select the check box for each file type you want to back up, and then click the [Next] button.

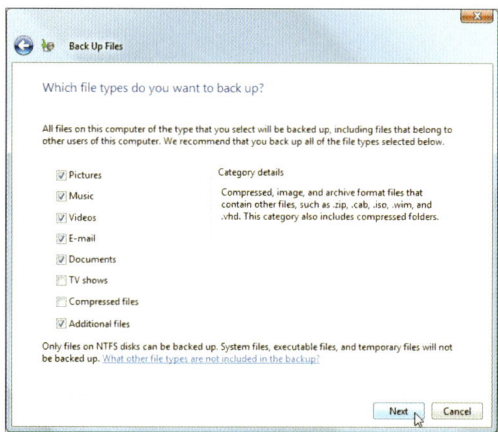

> **Keeping Down the Size of a Backup** — Note >>>
>
> If you have plenty of hard disk space, backing up all files may be the easiest option. But if disk space is short, consider omitting less valuable files. For example, TV shows recorded using Windows Media Center can take up a lot of space, so you might choose to exclude them from backups.

6. The wizard displays the [How Often Do You Want to Create a Backup?] screen. Choose the frequency in the [How Often], [What Day], and [What Time] drop-down lists, and then click the [Save Settings and Start Backup] button.

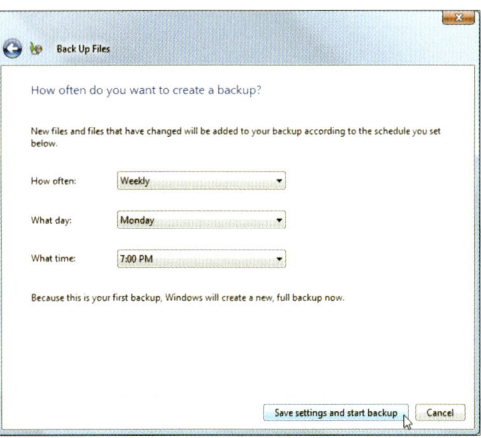

7. The wizard backs up the files, displaying a progress readout as it does so. When the backup has finished, click the [Close] button.

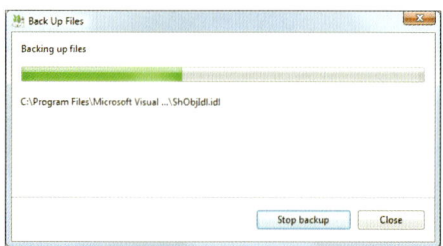

Restoring Your Files from Backup

To restore your files from backup, follow these steps:

1. Click the [Start] button, click [All Programs], click [Maintenance], and then click [Backup and Restore Center].

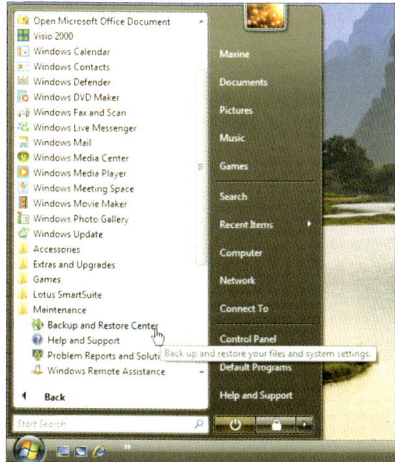

2. Windows opens a [Backup and Restore Center] window. Click the [Restore Files] button.

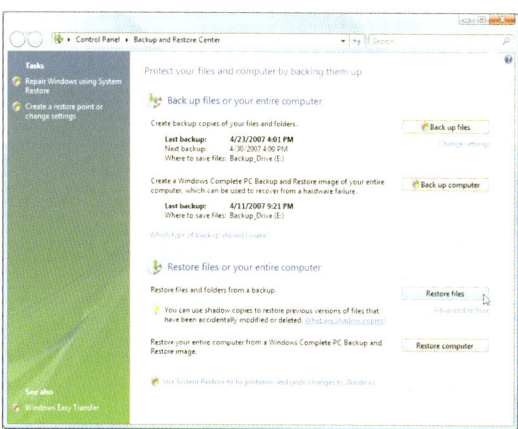

3. Windows launches the Restore Files Wizard, which displays the [What Do You Want to Restore?] screen. If you want to use the latest backup, select the [Files from the Latest Backup] option button. Otherwise, select the [Files from an Older Backup] option button. Click the [Next] button.

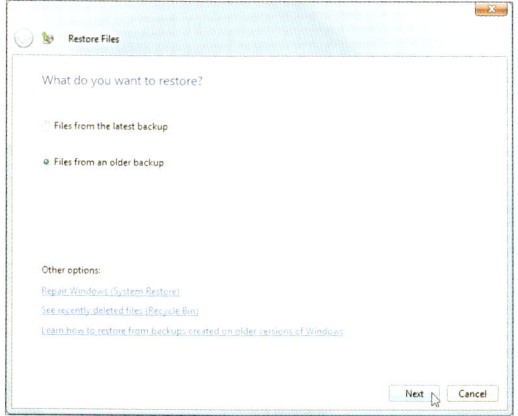

4. If you selected the [Files from an Older Backup] option button, the wizard displays the [Select the Date to Restore From] screen. Click the backup you want to use, and then click the [Next] button.

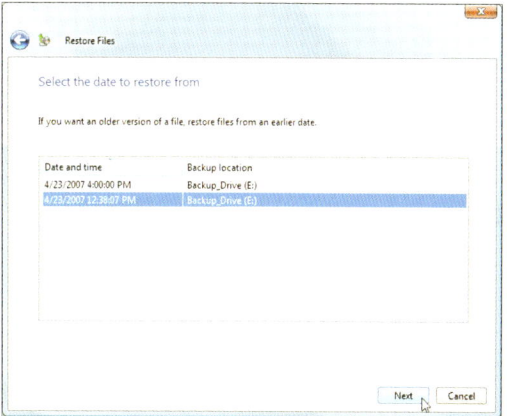

> **Recreating the Folder Structure in a Different Location** — Note >>>
>
> If you select the [In the Following Location] option button, you have two more options. Select the [Restore the Files to Their Original Subfolders] check box to re-create the folder structure in the folder you specify. If you select this check box, you can select the [Create a Subfolder for the Drive Letter] check box to create a separate subfolder for the drive. These two options are useful when you're restoring many files and folders and want to check them before replacing the originals with them.

5. The wizard displays the [Select the Files and Folders to Restore] screen. Click the [Add Folders] button. The wizard opens an [Add Folder to Restore] window.

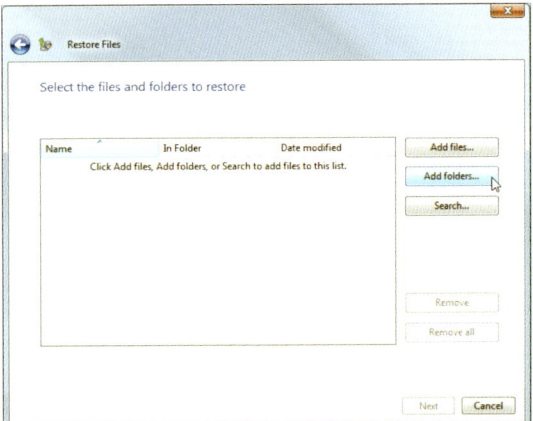

7. If necessary, add individual files by clicking the [Add Files] button and using the [Add Files to Restore] window. When you have finished, click the [Next] button in the wizard. The wizard displays the [Where Do You Want to Save the Restored Files?] screen.

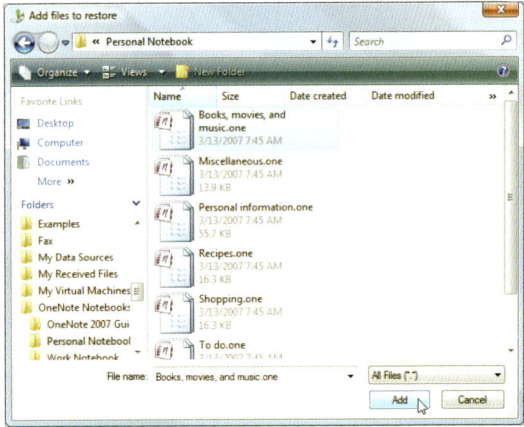

9. The wizard restores the files and then displays the [Successfully Restored Files] screen. Click the [Finish] button, and then check your files.

6. Click the folder, and then click the [Add] button. The wizard closes the dialog box and adds the folder to the Restore Files list.

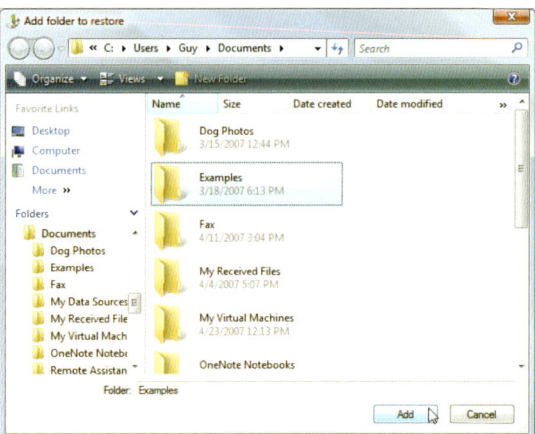

8. Select the [In the Original Location] option button if you want to overwrite the original files. Otherwise, select the [In the Following Location] option button, click the [Browse] button, and specify the folder. Click the [Start Restore] button.

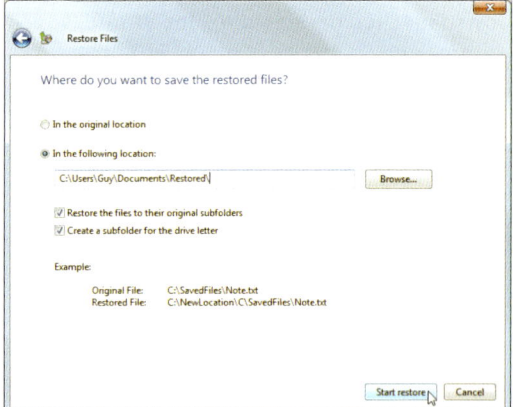

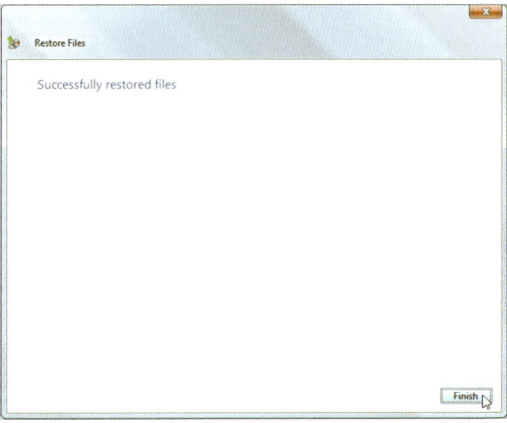

SECTION 04

Finding Solutions for Problems

Windows Vista includes a feature called Problem Reports and Solutions for finding fixes for problems that occur with your computer. Windows displays notification-area messages to tell you when it has found solutions, but you can also check for solutions manually.

Dealing with Automatic Notifications of Problems

Windows automatically notifies you when problems have occurred. When this happens, follow these steps:

1. Click the pop-up message that appears above the notification area.

2. Windows opens a window that gives brief information about the problem. Click the [View Problem Details] link.

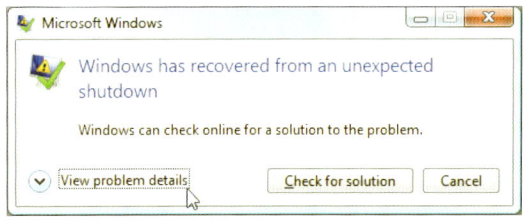

3. Windows displays the detail about the problem. If you want to check for a solution to the problem (as is usually a good idea), click the [Check for Solution] button.

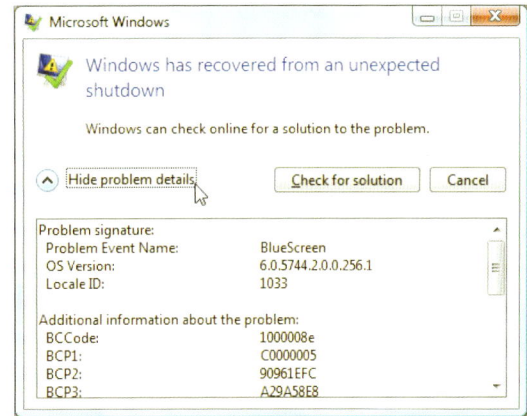

283

Checking for Solutions to Problems Manually

Windows automatically notifies you when problems have occurred. When this happens, follow these steps:

1. Click the [Start] button, click [All Programs], click [Maintenance], and then click [Problem Reports and Solutions].

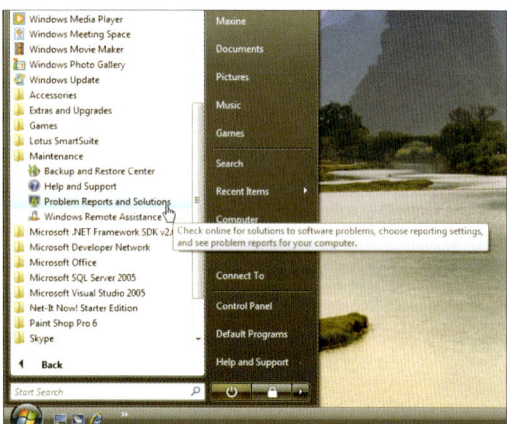

2. Windows opens a [Problem Reports and Solutions] window. To check for the latest solutions to problems, click the [Check for New Solutions] link.

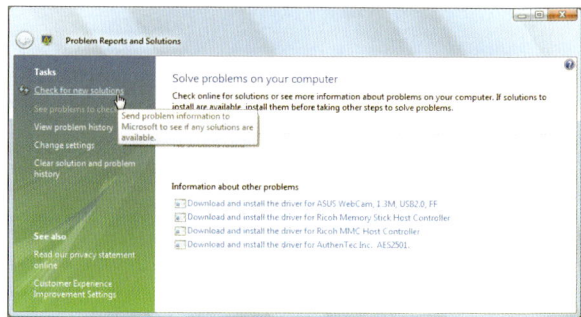

3. Windows checks for solutions to the problems of which it is currently aware.

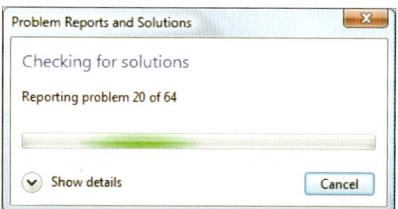

4. If Windows prompts you to send more information to solve a problem, click the [View Problem Details] button to show the details. If you decide to send the information, click the [Send Information] button. Windows sends the information.

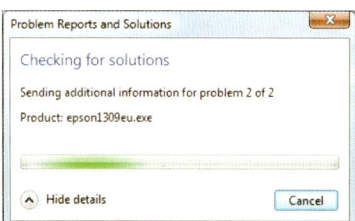

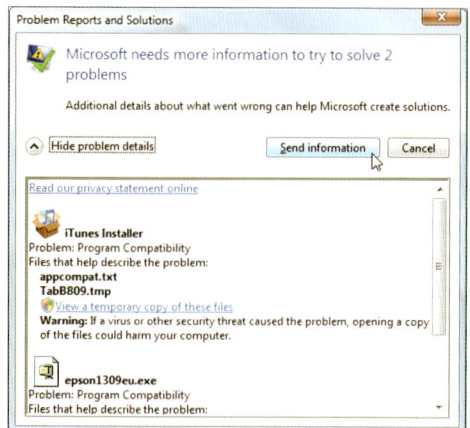

284

Chapter 11. Troubleshooting Problems

5. To install a solution, click it in the [Solutions to Install] list.

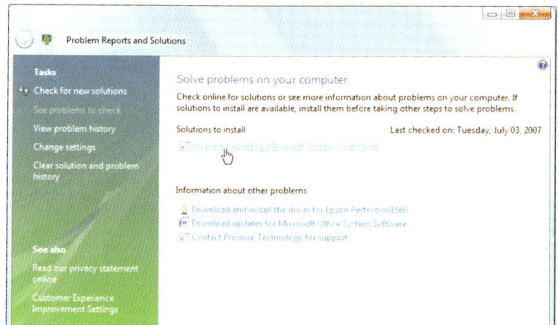

6. To learn about another item, click it in the [Information about Other Problems] list.

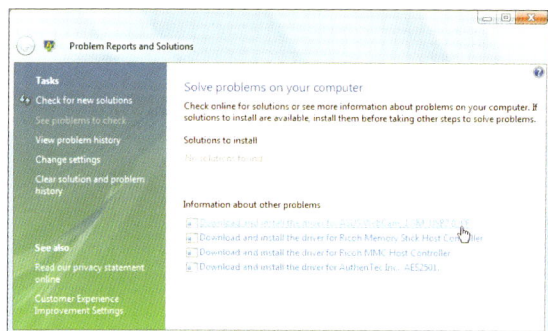

7. In the [Problem Reports and Solutions] window, read about the problem, and then click the [OK] button. Follow the instructions to deal with the problem.

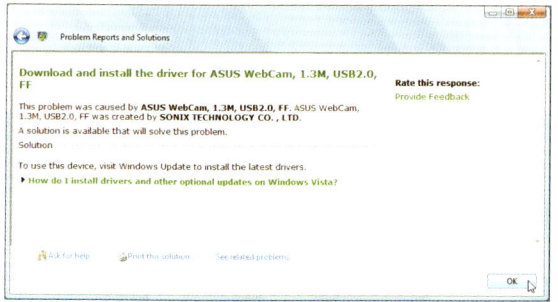

8. When you've finished checking problem reports and solutions, click the [Close] button (the ![] button) to close the [Problem Reports and Solutions] window.

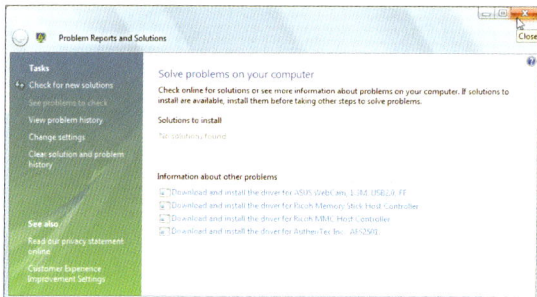

285

Let's Go Pro!

Closing a Program That Has Crashed

Sometimes a program stops responding to the mouse and keyboard. This means that you can't control the program directly anymore. To close it, you must use Windows Task Manager. Follow these steps:

① Right-click the clock in the notification area, and then choose [Task Manager] from the context menu.

② Windows opens the Windows Task Manager window. Click the [Applications] tab if any other tab is displayed. Click the application that is not responding, and then click the [End Task] button.

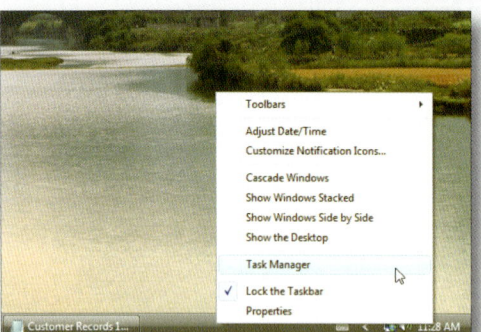

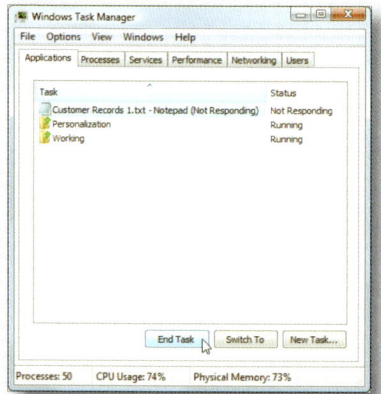

③ Windows opens a [Microsoft Windows] dialog box telling you that the program is not responding. Click the [Close the Program] button to close the program.

④ Windows changes the [Microsoft Windows] dialog box to tell you that it is checking for a solution to the problem. When Windows has finished checking, it closes the dialog box and the program that was not responding.

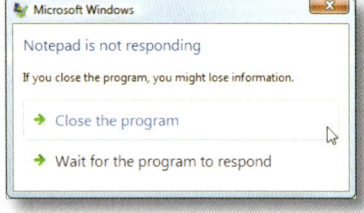

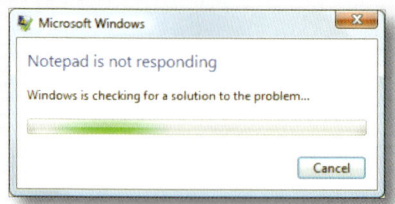

⑤ Click the [Close] button (the ⟨X⟩ button) on the Windows Task Manager window to close the program.

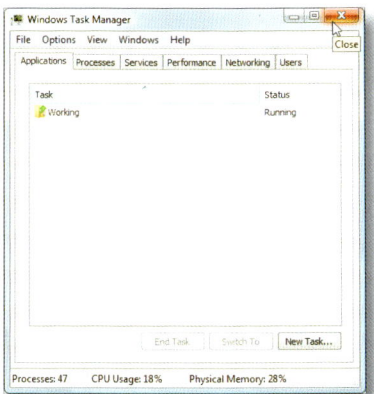

tip>>
Save Your Work Before Crashing a Program
Windows Vista runs each program in a separate area of memory, so when you have to close a program forcibly rather than normally, the closure shouldn't affect any of the other programs on the computer. In rare cases, however, the closure may cause problems with Windows itself. If this happens, you may need to restart your computer. For this reason, it's a good idea to save any unsaved work in any program before you crash another program—better safe than sorry.

Chapter | **12**

Using the Windows Vista Ultimate Features

This chapter shows you how to use the premium features that are included in Windows Vista Ultimate Edition and how to get extra Ultimate features that Microsoft makes available online. Remote Desktop lets you access your computer from another computer. Windows Complete PC Backup and Restore lets you back up all files on your PC and then restore it to its saved state after a disaster occurs. Windows Fax and Scan lets you send and receive faxes from your PC; you can also scan documents. Finally, BitLocker Drive Encryption lets you protect all the data on your computer using powerful encryption.

SECTION 01

Using Remote Desktop

Remote Desktop lets you control one computer from another computer across a network connection or across the Internet. Remote Desktop is included in Windows Vista Ultimate Edition, Windows Vista Business Edition, and Windows XP Professional Edition.

Remote Desktop runs on the computer that is being controlled, which is called the remote computer. The computer that is doing the controlling runs Remote Desktop Connection, which is included in all versions of Windows Vista and Windows XP. This computer is called the home computer.

Setting Up Remote Desktop

To set up the remote computer, follow these steps:

1. Press <Windows>+<Break>. Windows opens a System window. In the Tasks list in the left pane, click the [Remote Settings] link, and then go through User Account Control for the System Remote Settings feature.

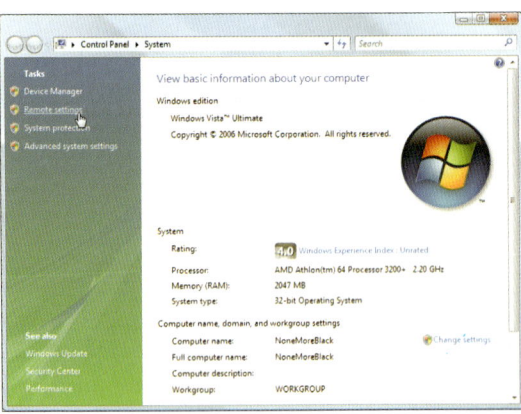

2. Windows opens the System Properties dialog box with the Remote tab at the front. Click In the [Remote Desktop] group box, select the second or third option button as needed, and then click the [Select Users] button. Windows opens the [Remote Desktop Users] dialog box.

① **Allow Connections from Computers Running Any Version of Remote Desktop:** Select this option button if you need to connect using a home computer running Windows XP or any other version of Windows than Windows Vista.

② **Allow Connections Only from Computers Running Remote Desktop with Network Level Authentication:** Select this option button if your home computer runs Windows Vista.

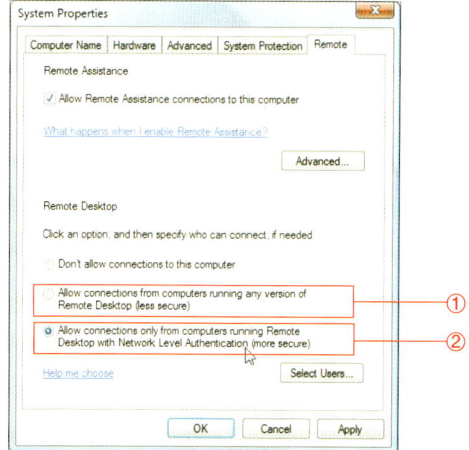

3. The [Remote Desktop Users] dialog box shows that the user account you're currently using already has right-click access. To add another user account, click the [Add] button. Windows opens the [Select Users] dialog box.

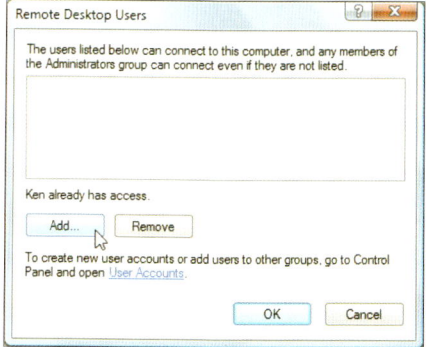

4. Type the user account name in the [Enter the Object Names to Select] box, and then click the [OK] button. Windows closes the [Select Users] dialog box and returns you to the [Remote Desktop Users] dialog box. Click the [OK] button to close this dialog box, and then click the [OK] button to close the [System Properties] dialog box.

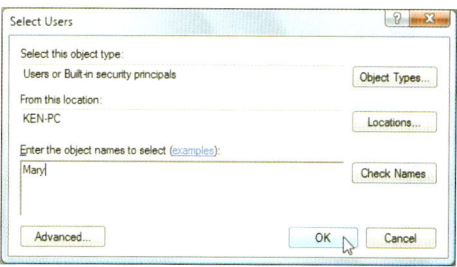

Setting Up Remote Desktop Connection

To set up Remote Desktop Connection on the home computer (the computer you will use to control the remote computer), follow these steps:

1. Click the [Start] button, click [All Programs], click [Accessories], and then click [Remote Desktop Connection]. Windows opens the Remote Desktop Connection window. Enter the remote computer's name or IP address in the [Computer] text box. You can type the name or IP address, choose a previously used item from the drop-down list, or click the [Browse for More] item in the drop-down list and use the [Browse for Computers] dialog box to select the computer.

2. Click the [Options] button. Windows displays the rest of the Remote Desktop Connection window.

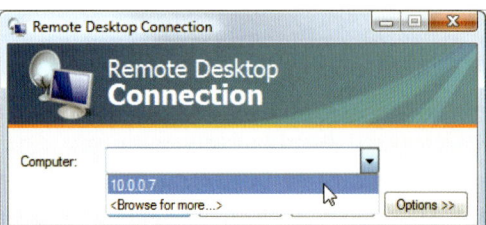

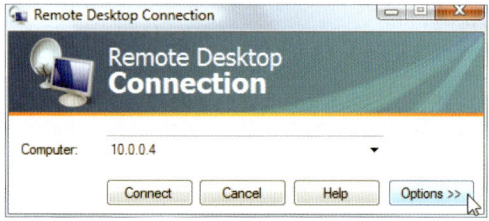

3. Click the [Display] tab, and then drag the Remote Desktop Size slider to set the resolution you want for the remote desktop. The default setting is Full Screen. Also choose the color quality—Highest Quality (32 Bit), True Color (24 Bit), High Color (16 Bit), High Color (15 Bit), or 256 Colors—and verify that the [Display the Connection Bar When in Full Screen Mode] check box is selected.

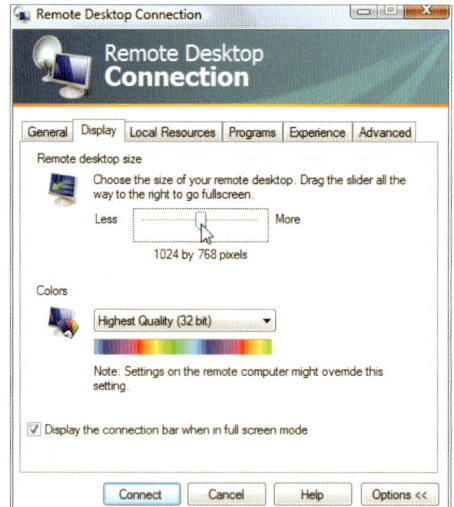

4. Click the [Local Resources] tab, open the [Remote Computer Sound] drop-down list, and then choose how to handle sound: Bring to This Computer (good for working over high-speed connections), Do Not Play (good for low-speed connections), or Leave at Remote Computer (good for when the remote computer is also at your desk and you can hear its speakers).

In the [Apply Windows Key Combinations] drop-down list, choose how to handle key combinations: On the Local Computer, On the Remote Computer, or In Full Screen Mode Only (usually the best choice). In the Local Devices area, select the [Printers] check box and the [Clipboard] check box if you want to share these devices with the remote computer.

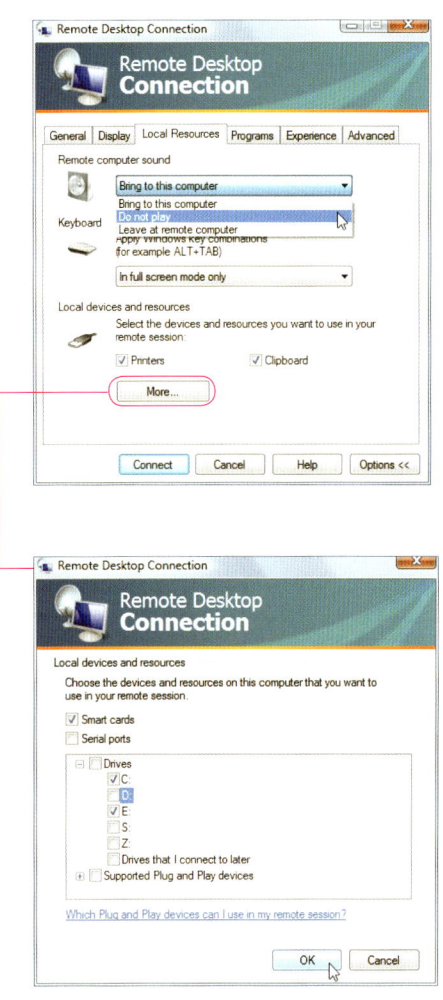

5. If you want to share drives or plug-and-play devices, click the [More] button, and then choose the devices in the [Local Devices and Resources] dialog box. For example, you might share a drive or a serial port. Click the [OK] button when you're done.

6. The Programs page lets you start a program automatically on connection, but this is a specialized need. Click the [Experience] tab, and then select your connection speed in the [Choose Your Connection Speed to Optimize Performance] drop-down list. The setting you choose selects and clears check boxes in the [Allow the Following] list. You can also select and clear check boxes manually to produce a custom configuration. Either way, verify that the [Reconnect If Connection Is Dropped] check box is selected.

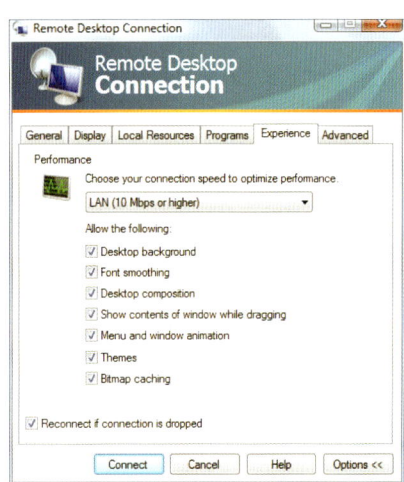

7. Click the [Advanced] tab, and then select [Warn Me If Authentication Fails] in the [Authentication Options] drop-down list.

8. Click the [General] tab, and then click the [Save] button to save these settings as your default Remote Desktop Connection configuration.

Connecting to Different Computers via Remote Desktop Connection — Note >>>

Remote Desktop Connection assumes that you'll want to connect to the same remote computer most of the time. When you click the [Save] button, it saves your current Remote Desktop Connection settings to its default Remote Desktop Connection file, which is named Default.rdp.

If you need to use different connections, click the [Save As] button and use the resulting Save As to save each computer's settings under a different name. You can then click the [Open] button and open the settings file for the computer you want to access.

If you use one connection more frequently than the others, name that connection Default.rdp so that Windows opens it by default.

Connecting to the Remote Computer and Working on It

Once you've chosen settings as described in the previous section, connecting to the remote computer is easy. Follow these steps:

1. If the Remote Desktop Connection window is already open, activate it. If it's not open, click the [Start] button, click [All Programs], click [Accessories], and then click [Remote Desktop Connection] to open the program with your default connection shown. Click the [Connect] button.

2. Remote Desktop Connection opens the [Windows Security] dialog box prompting you to enter your credentials for the connection. Type your user name in the top box and your password in the second box. Select the [Remember My Credentials] check box if you want to avoid typing the user name and password for this connection on this computer in the future. Click the [OK] button.

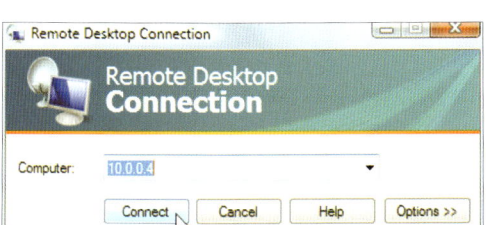

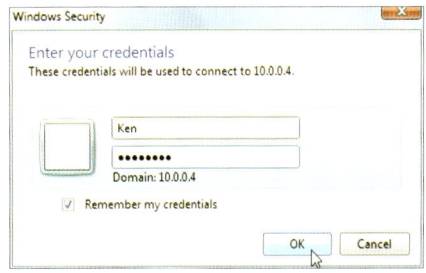

3. Remote Desktop Connection connects to the remote computer, logs you on, and displays its screen either in a window (as shown here) or full screen on your computer. Work on the remote computer using the mouse and the keyboard.

4. If you've established a full-screen connection, Windows displays the connection bar at the top of the screen. Click the [Minimize] button on the connection bar if you want to minimize the full-screen connection so that you can reach the home computer's desktop, or click the [Restore] button to switch it to a normal window. If you want the connection bar to hide itself when you're not using it, click the [Auto-Hide] button at its left end to withdraw the pin holding it in place.

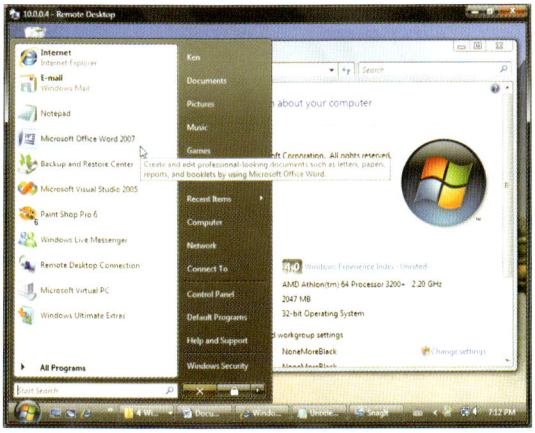

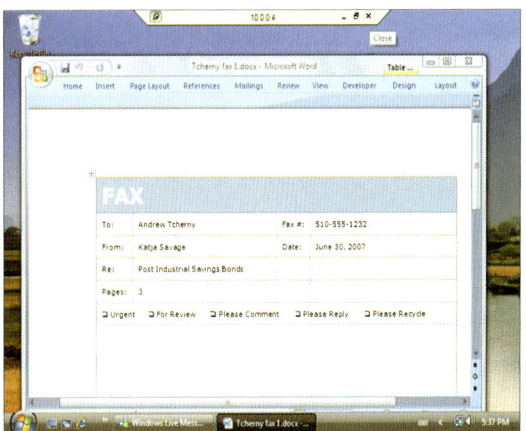

5. When you've finished working on the remote computer, click the [Start] button on that computer's screen, and then click the [Disconnect] button (the ![button] button). Windows disconnects your session.

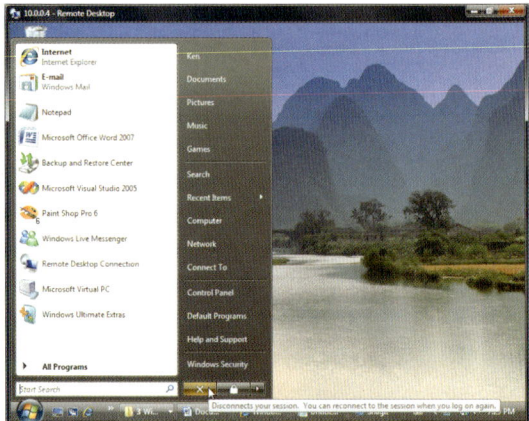

> **Working via a Remote Desktop Connection**   Note >>>
>
> Once connected to the remote computer, you can work more or less as normal using the mouse and the keyboard.
>
> Depending on the connection speed, you may experience a delay between taking an action and the computer registering it. If this delay is long enough to make working on the remote computer difficult, disconnect the connection, choose a lower connection speed on the Experience tab, and then connect again.

Let's Go Pro!

Getting Windows Ultimate Extras

Windows Vista Ultimate Edition includes several features that either do not appear in other versions of Windows Vista or appear in only some versions. But Microsoft also provides what it calls Windows Ultimate Extras—extra features that are available only for users of Windows Vista Ultimate Edition. To get these features, download them by following these steps:

① Click the [Start] button, click [All Programs], and then click [Windows Update]. Windows opens a Windows Update window.

② Click the [View Available Extras] link. Windows opens a View Available Updates window.

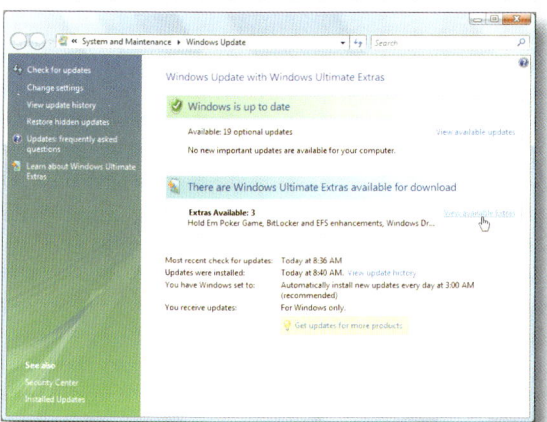

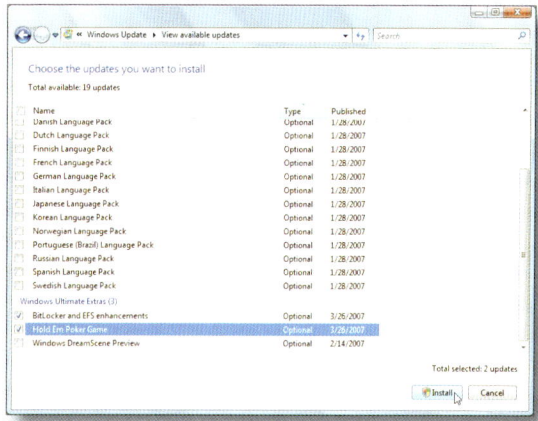

③ In the Windows Ultimate Extras areas, select the check box for each item you want to install. (If you want to install other updates as well, select the check box for each of them.) Click the [Install] button, and then go through User Account Control for the Windows Update feature. Wait while Windows downloads and installs the updates. When Windows Update has installed the updates, click the [Close] button (the [X] button).

④ To run the updates you have installed, use the Start menu as you would for any other program. To find the new programs, follow the yellow bars that the Start menu shows for new items and the folders that contain them, as on the System Tools folder, the BitLocker folder, and the BitLocker Drive Preparation Tool item in the next illustration.

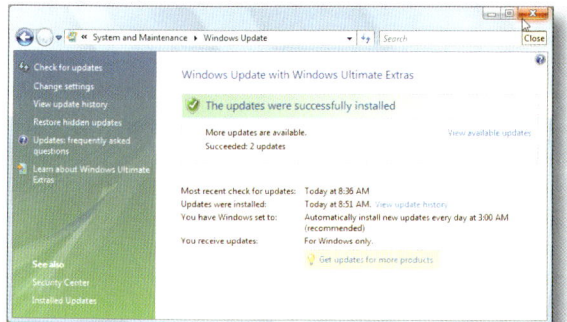

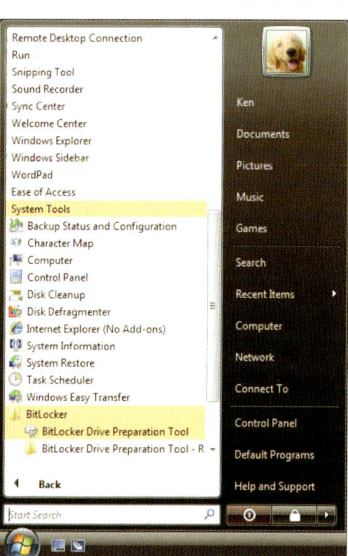

297

SECTION 02
Backing Up and Restoring Your Entire PC

Windows Vista is designed to be as reliable as possible, but even so, you should back up your computer so that you can restore it easily if something goes wrong. To back up your computer fully, you can use the Complete PC Backup and Restore feature included in Windows Vista Ultimate Edition and Windows Vista Business Edition.

Backing Up Your PC

To back up your PC using Complete PC Backup and Restore, follow these steps:

1. Click the [Start] button, click [All Programs], click [Accessories], click [System Tools], and then click [Backup Status and Configuration]. Windows opens a Backup Status and Configuration window. Click the [Complete PC Backup] button in the left pane.

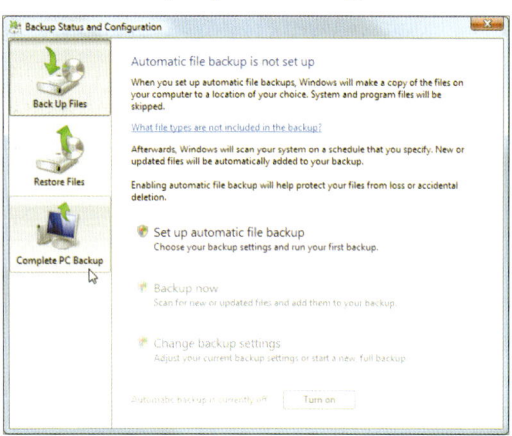

2. Backup Status and Configuration displays the Complete PC Backup tab. Click the [Create a Backup Now] link, and then go through User Account Control for the Microsoft Windows Backup feature.

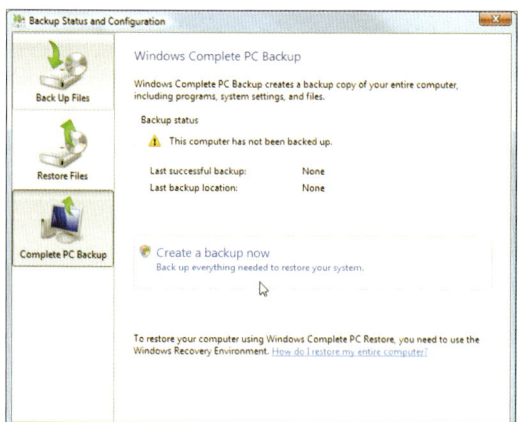

3. Windows launches the Windows Complete PC Backup Wizard, which searches for available backup devices and then displays the [Where Do You Want to Save the Backup?] screen. Select the [On a Hard Disk] option button if you want to use a hard disk, and then select the hard disk in the drop-down list. Generally, a hard disk is the best option, because hard disks have much greater capacity than DVDs. However, if you want to use DVDs, select the [On One or More DVDs] option button, and then verify that Windows has selected the correct DVD drive in the drop-down list. (Unless you have multiple recordable DVD drives, Windows should always select the correct drive.) Click the [Next] button.

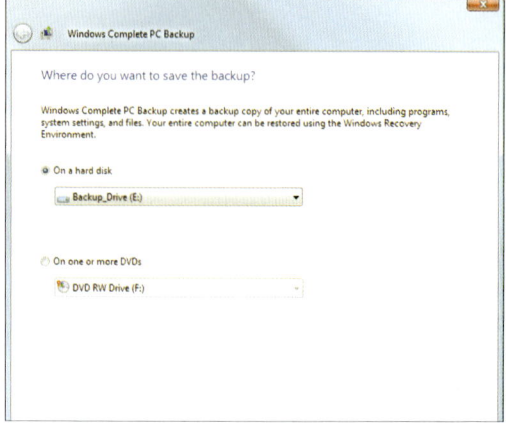

4. The wizard displays the [Which Disks Do You Want to Include in the Backup?] screen. Select the check box for the disk or disks you want to include in the backup. Verify that there is enough space on the backup disk you chose—the wizard warns you if there is not. Click the [Next] button.

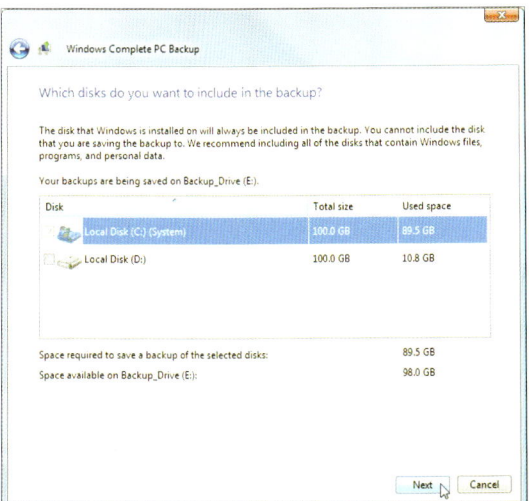

6. The wizard displays the dialog box shown next while it creates the backup.

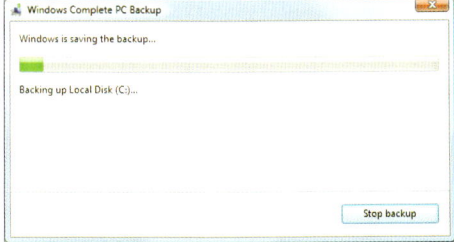

5. The wizard displays the [Confirm Your Backup Settings] screen. If all the settings are correct, click the [Start Backup] button.

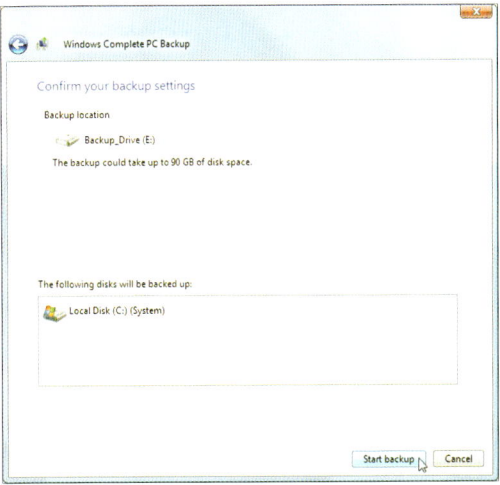

7. When the wizard displays a dialog box containing the message [The Backup Completed Successfully], click the [Close] button. The wizard closes, and your backup is complete. Click the [Close] button (the ▨ button) on the Backup Status and Configuration window.

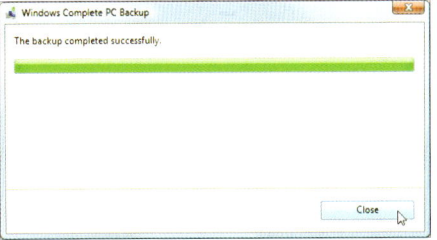

Restoring Your PC Using a Full Backup

To restore your PC using Complete PC Backup and Restore, follow these steps:

1. Insert the Windows installation DVD in your computer's optical drive, and then restart your computer. When your computer prompts you to "Press any key to boot from CD or DVD," press any key (for example, press <Spacebar>). Windows loads files and then opens the Install Windows screen.
In the [Keyboard or Input Method] drop-down list, select the language you want to use for the restore procedure. For example, choose [US] to select the U.S. English keyboard layout. Click the [Next] button.

2. Windows opens the Install Now screen. Click the [Repair Your Computer] link.

3. Windows opens the [System Recovery Options] dialog box. In the list box, click the entry for your operating system. (If this is the only entry, Windows will have selected it already.) Then click the [Next] button.

4. Windows opens the second [System Recovery Options] dialog box. Click the [Windows Complete PC Restore] link. Windows scans for backup disks and then opens the [Restore Your Entire Computer from a Backup] screen.

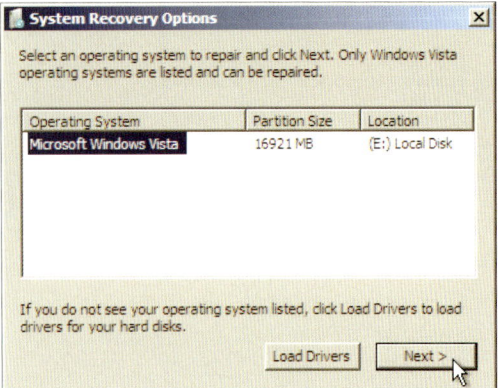

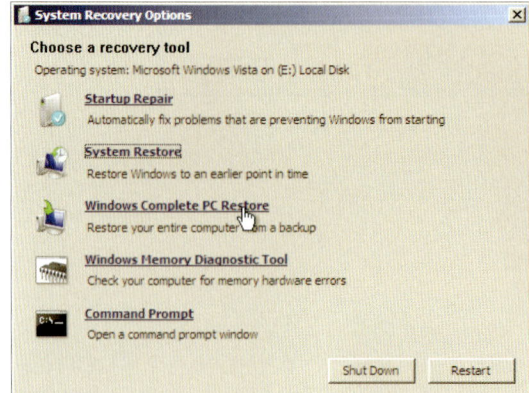

5. If Windows has chosen the correct backup, leave the [Restore the Following Backup] option button selected, and then click the [Next] button. Otherwise, select the [Restore a Different Backup] option button, click the [Next] button, choose the backup on the [Select the Location of the Backup] screen, and then click the [Next] button.

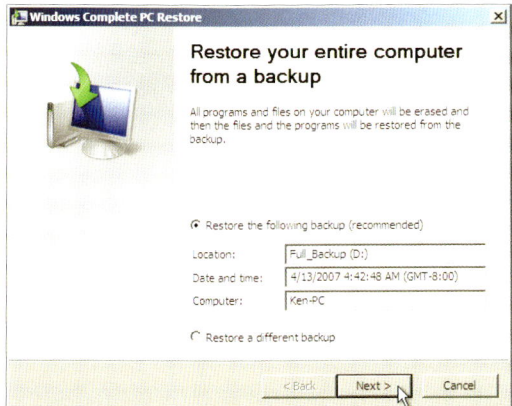

6. Whichever backup you choose, Windows displays a confirmation screen. Verify the settings chosen. If you want to reformat your computer's disk and restore its partitions according to the backup, select the [Format and Repair Disks] check box. Normally, it is best to leave this check box cleared. Click the [Finish] button. Windows displays a final confirmation dialog box.

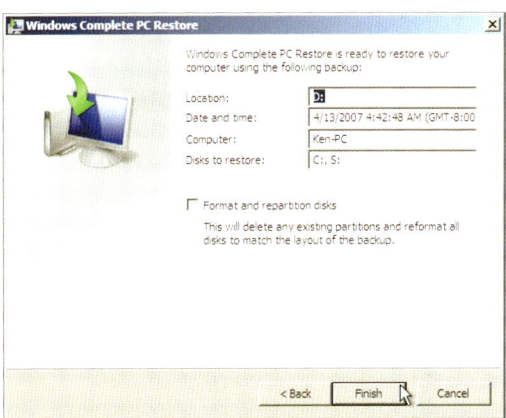

7. Select the [I Confirm That I Want to Erase All Existing Data and Restore the Backup] check box, and then click the [OK] button.

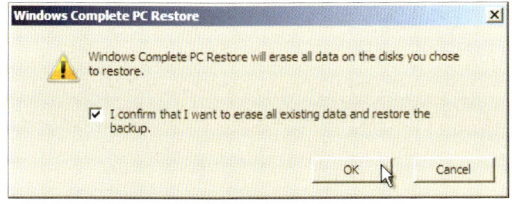

8. Windows begins the restoration process, displaying a progress readout as it does so. When the restoration completes, Windows restarts your PC. You can then log on as usual.

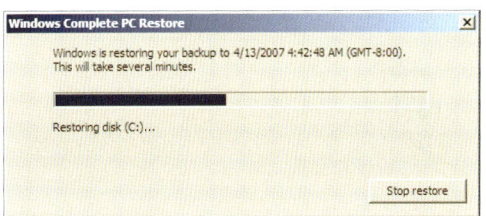

SECTION 03 — Faxing with Windows Fax and Scan

If you have Windows Vista Ultimate Edition or Windows Vista Business Edition, you can use the Fax and Scan feature to send and receive faxes. This feature is not included in Windows Vista Home Basic Edition or Windows Vista Home Premium Edition.

Launching and Setting Up Windows Fax and Scan

Before you can send faxes with Windows Fax and Scan, you must configure it. Follow these steps:

1. Click the [Start] button, click [All Programs], and then click [Windows Fax and Scan]. Windows opens the [Windows Fax and Scan] window. Click the [New Fax] button.

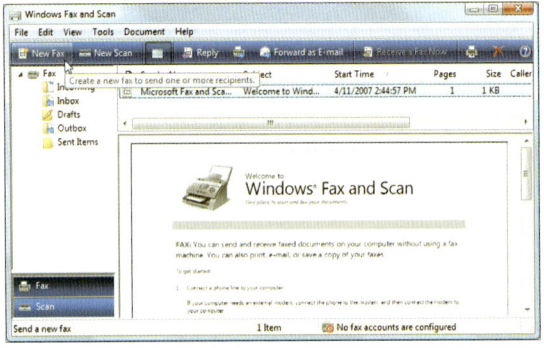

2. Windows Fax and Scan launches the Fax Setup Wizard, which displays the [Choose a Fax Modem or Server] screen. To use your computer's fax modem, click the [Connect to a Fax Modem] button.

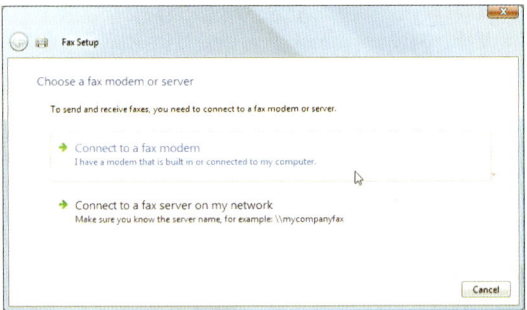

3. The wizard displays the [Choose a Modem Name] screen. Type the name for the fax modem, and then click the [Next] button.

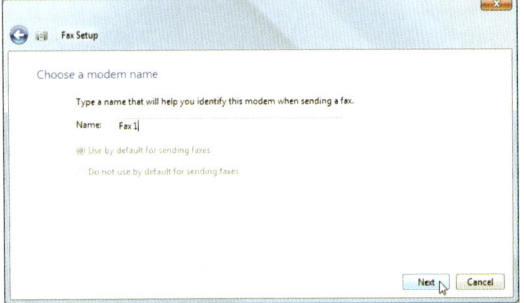

4. The wizard displays the [Choose How to Receive Faxes] screen. Click the [Answer Automatically] button if you want Windows Fax and Scan to answer incoming calls automatically after five rings. Click the [Notify Me] button if you want to answer calls yourself and receive incoming faxes manually.

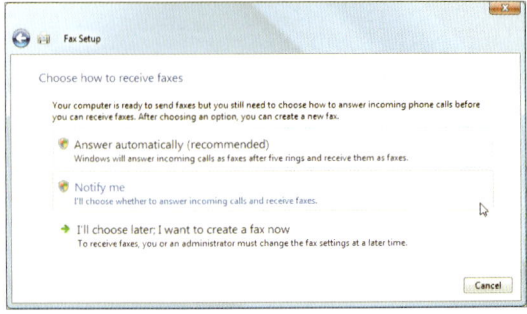

5. Go through User Account Control for the Windows Fax and Scan feature. Windows may display a [Windows Security Alert] dialog box such as that shown next telling you "Windows Firewall has blocked some features of this program." Click the [Unblock] button, and then go through User Account Control for the Windows Firewall feature.

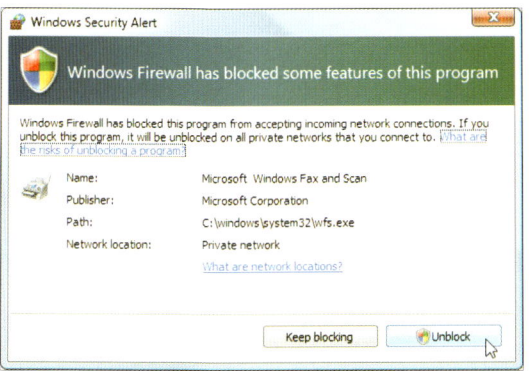

6. Windows Fax and Scan displays a New Fax window. If you want to create a new fax now, go to step 2 in the next section. Otherwise, click the [Close] button (the button) on the New Fax window, and then return to Windows Fax and Scan when you want to send a fax.

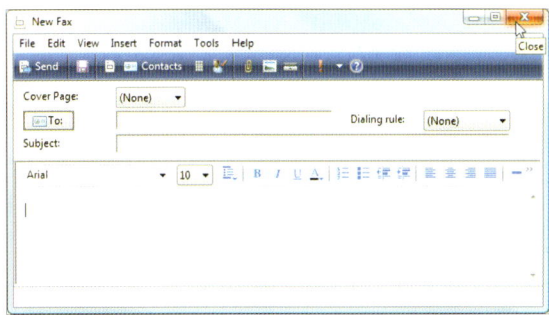

Creating and Sending a Fax

You can send a fax either directly from Windows Fax and Scan or by printing it from a program such as Microsoft Word, as discussed in the next section. To send a fax from Windows Fax And Scan, follow these steps:

1. Open Windows Fax and Scan, and then click the [New] button. Windows Fax and Scan opens a New Fax window. If you want to include a cover page, choose it from the [Cover Page] drop-down list. If not, choose "(none)" in the list. This example uses no cover page. Enter the recipient's name in the [To] box.

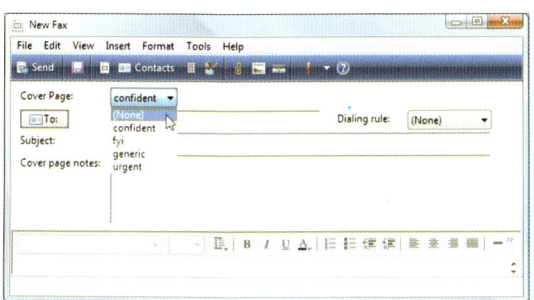

2. Either click the [To] button, choose the recipient in the [Select Recipients] dialog box, and then click the [OK] button, or simply type the recipient's fax number.

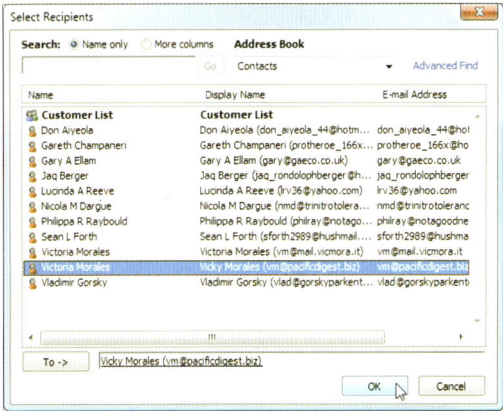

3. If you will need to use a dialing rule, select it in the [Dialing Rule] drop-down list. For example, you might need to dial 9 for an outside line.

4. Type the fax's subject in the [Subject] box, and then compose the fax text in the main box. Use the formatting controls to apply any formatting that is needed. For example, you may need to create bulleted lists or numbered lists. When the fax is complete, click the [Send] button.

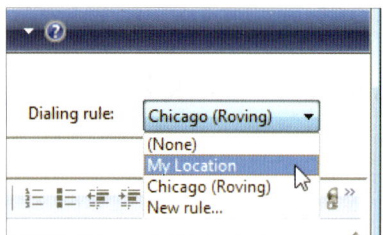

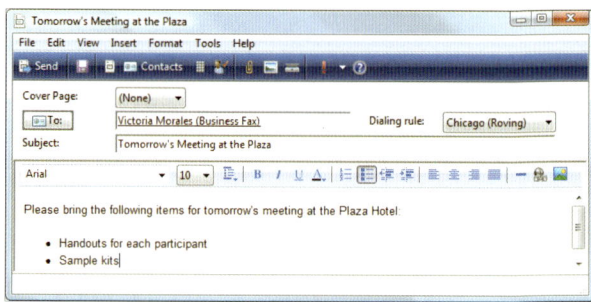

Sending a Fax from Another Program

To send a fax from another program, follow these steps:

1. Open the program as usual, and then open an existing document in it or create a new document. Issue a [Print] command. For example, click the [Office] button, and then click [Print].

2. The program opens the [Print] dialog box. In the [Name] drop-down list or [Printer] drop-down list (depending on the program), select the [Fax] item.

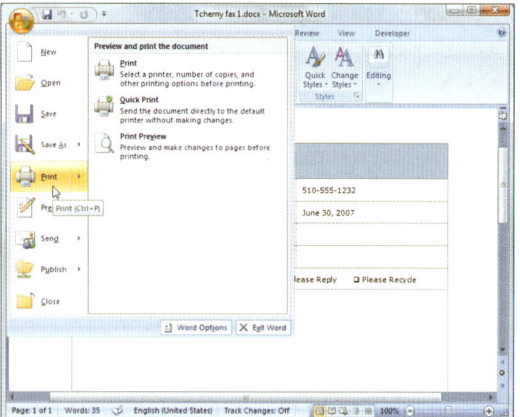

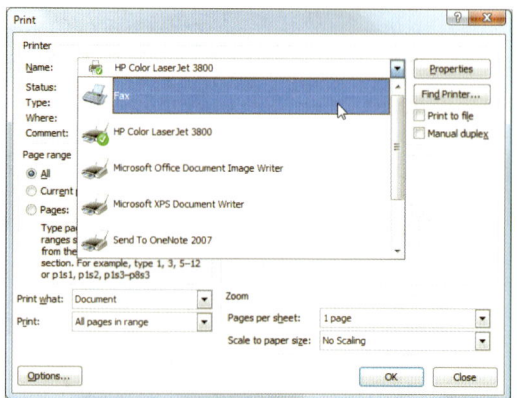

3. Choose any other printing options needed (for example, you might choose to include only part of the document), and then click the [OK] button.

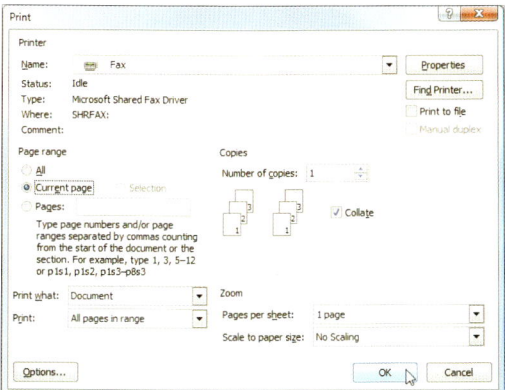

4. The [Print] dialog box closes, and Windows opens a New Fax window with the document attached as a graphic. Address the fax as described in the previous section, and then click the [Send] button.

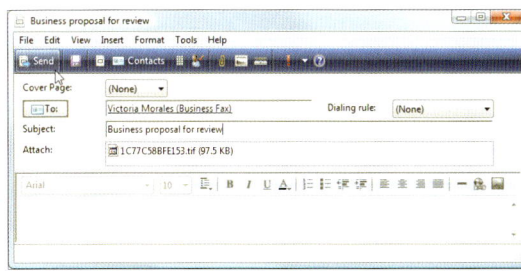

Receiving a Fax

If you have chosen to receive faxes automatically, Windows Fax and Scan automatically answers incoming calls after five rings, as shown here.

1. If you have chosen to receive faxes manually, Windows Fax and Scan prompts you to answer an incoming call.

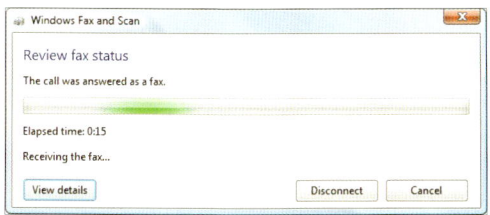

2. Click the balloon in the notification area to start receiving it. To view a fax you have received, double-click its item in the Inbox.

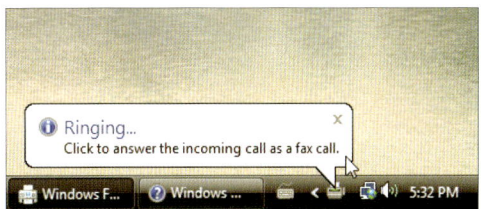

SECTION 04
Encrypting Your Drive with BitLocker

BitLocker is a feature that lets you encrypt your computer's entire hard disk to protect it against prying eyes. BitLocker provides strong protection that is normally required only in business, government, or military settings rather than home settings. BitLocker is included only in Windows Vista Ultimate Edition, not in any other edition of Windows Vista.

Preparing to Run BitLocker

BitLocker is complicated to set up—but not impossible. If your computer does not have suitable hardware, you may need to upgrade it. And if your hard disk is not set up in a suitable way for BitLocker, you may need to change its configuration. In some cases, you may need to reinstall Windows Vista—but if you use BitLocker Drive Preparation Tool, this should not be necessary.

To use BitLocker, your computer must have either a Trusted Platform Module (TPM) version 1.2 or later chip built in or a USB flash drive attached. BitLocker uses the TPM chip or the USB flash drive to store its encryption and decryption key. Windows warns you if your computer doesn't have a suitable TPM chip for BitLocker.

Understanding How BitLocker Works — Note >>>

Before you implement BitLocker, it's important that you understand a little about what BitLocker does and how it works. This knowledge will help you decide whether using BitLocker is a good idea for your computer and help you avoid running into problems.

Instead of the one *partition*, or volume, that Windows normally uses, BitLocker requires two partitions:

- **System Partition:** This is the partition that contains the Windows Vista operating system and all your files. This partition acts like a system partition normally does except that it is encrypted (which a system partition normally is not). This partition needs to be large enough to contain all your program files and data files as well as the operating system.
- **Active Partition:** This is an unencrypted partition that BitLocker uses to start the computer and to access data on the encrypted partition. The active partition must be at least 1.5GB, but it doesn't have to be large. You should not store your own files on this partition—instead leave this partition to Windows.

Both partitions must use the NTFS format. Windows Vista uses NTFS by default, so this should not be a problem. If you use BitLocker Drive Preparation Tool, it creates a suitable extra partition for you.

Creating an Active Partition with BitLocker Drive Preparation Tool

To run BitLocker, make sure you've downloaded BitLocker Drive Preparation Tool from the Windows Ultimate Extras service. See "Let's Go Pro!," earlier in this chapter, for instructions.

To set up an active partition using BitLocker Drive Preparation Tool and then turn on BitLocker, log on using an Administrator account, and then follow these steps:

1. Close any running programs, and then click the [Start] button, click [All Programs], click [Accessories], click [System Tools], click [BitLocker], and then click [BitLocker Drive Preparation Tool]. Go through User Account Control for the BitLocker Drive Preparation Tool feature, read the license agreement, and then click the [I Accept] button if you accept the terms. Windows displays the [BitLocker Drive Encryption] dialog box. Click the [Continue] button.

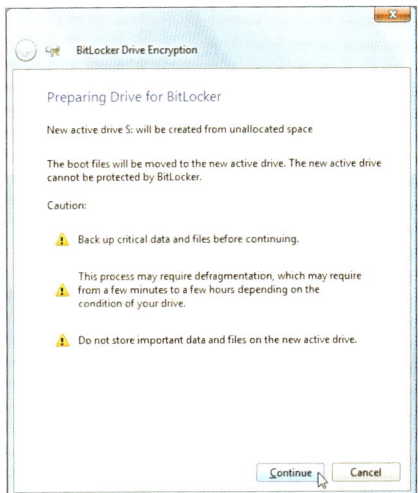

Caution >>

Backing Up Your Data

Before using BitLocker Drive Preparation Tool, back up your data in case a problem occurs.

2. The dialog box shows progress readouts as the BitLocker Drive Preparation Tool shrinks your C: drive, creates an active drive, and prepares the drive for BitLocker. Click the [Finish] button.

3. BitLocker Drive Preparation Tool prompts you to restart your PC. Click the [Restart Now] button.

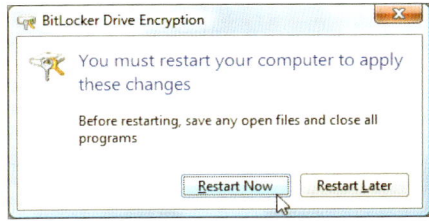

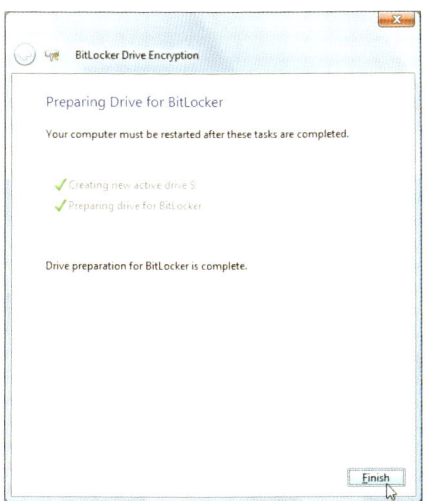

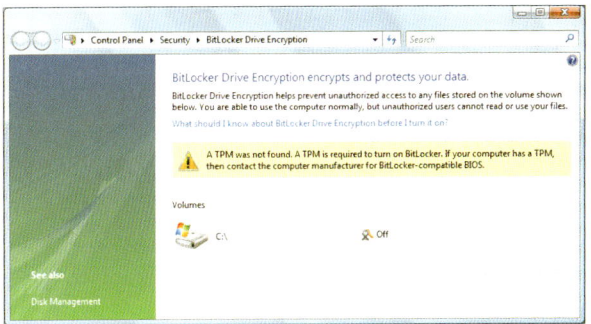

4. Windows restarts your PC. Log on to Windows as usual. Windows then opens the BitLocker Drive Encryption window.

5. If the window shows the message "A TPM was not found," as in the example shown here, you will need to use a USB key drive to store the encryption and decryption key. Click the [Close] button (the ██ button) to close the BitLocker Drive Encryption window, and then follow steps 6 through 12. If the [Turn On BitLocker] link appears, go to step 13.

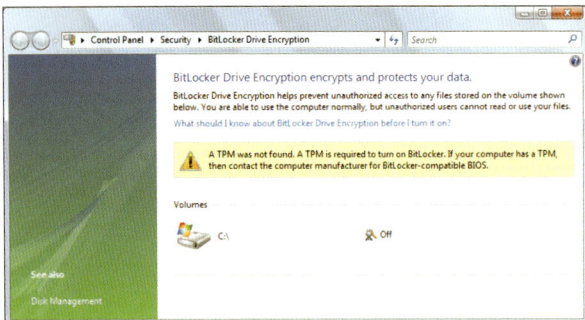

6. Press <Windows> + <R> to open the [Run] dialog box. Type **gpedit.msc** and then press <Enter> or click the [OK] button.

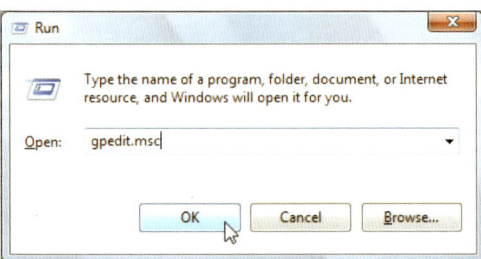

7. Go through User Account Control for the Microsoft Management Console feature. Windows opens a Group Policy Object Editor window. Under the Local Computer Policy object, click the triangle next to the Administrative Templates item to expand its contents. Then click the triangle next to the Windows Components item to expand its contents. Under the Windows Components object, click the [BitLocker Drive Encryption] item to display its contents in the right pane. Then double-click the [Control Panel Setup: Enable Advanced Startup Options] setting to open the dialog box for the setting.

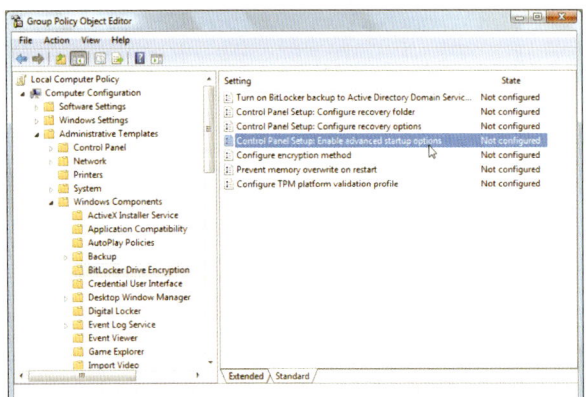

8. Near the top of the Setting tab of the dialog box, select the [Enabled] option button. Windows makes the controls in the main list box available. Verify that the [Allow BitLocker without a Compatible TPM] check box is selected, and then click the [OK] button to close the dialog box. Click the [Close] button (the ██ button) to close the Group Policy Object Editor window.

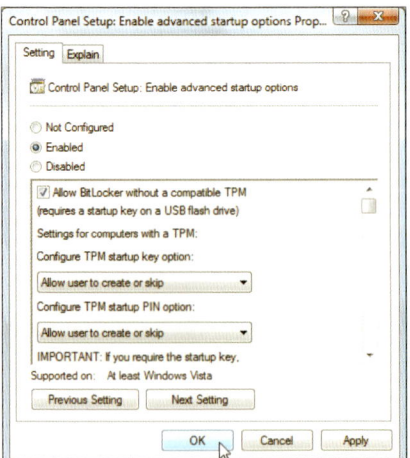

9. Press <Windows> + <R> to open the [Run] dialog box. Type gpupdate /force and then press <Enter> or click the [OK] button. Windows opens a Command Prompt window, runs the command (which forces an update to your computer's group policy), and then closes the Command Prompt window.

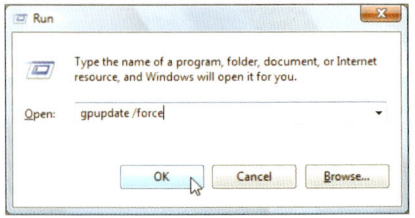

10. Click the [Start] button, type BitLocker in the [Search] box, and then click the [BitLocker Drive Encryption] item in the [Programs] list.

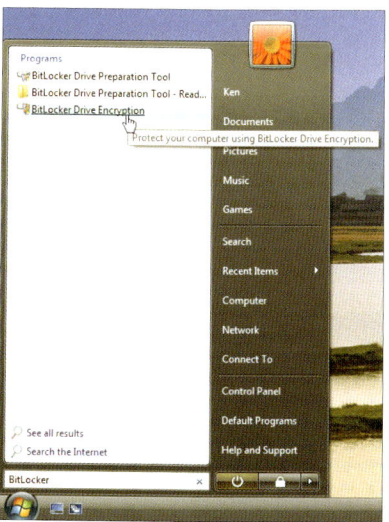

11. Go through User Account Control for the BitLocker Drive Encryption feature. Windows opens the BitLocker Drive Encryption window. The [Turn On BitLocker] link now appears. Click the [Turn On BitLocker] link.

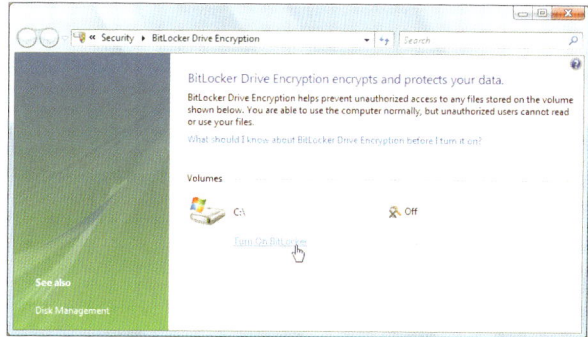

12. Windows launches the BitLocker Drive Encryption Wizard, which displays the [Set BitLocker Startup Preferences] screen. Click the button for the option you want to use:

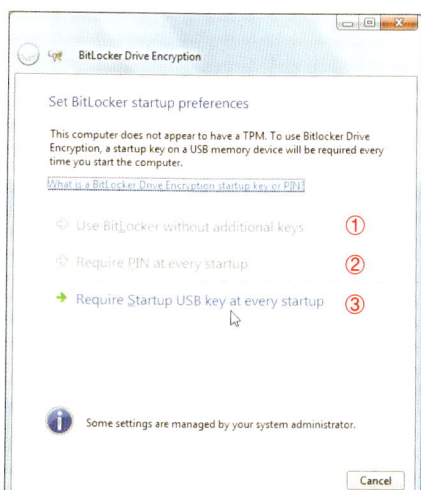

① **Use BitLocker without Additional Keys** Click this button if you want to use the BitLocker encryption key stored on your computer's TPM to encrypt your disk. This option is not available if you're using a USB key.

② **Require PIN at Every Startup** Click this button if you want to use both the BitLocker encryption key stored on your computer's TPM and an extra personal identification number (PIN) that you must enter each time you start your computer. This setting provides the greatest security but is not available if you're using a USB key.

③ **Require Startup USB Key at Every Startup** Click this button if you're using a USB key to implement BitLocker, as in the example shown. You must insert the USB key each time you start your computer. By keeping the USB key separate from the computer, you implement effective security. The wizard displays the [Save Your Startup Key] screen.

13. Insert your USB key (if you haven't inserted it already), click the drive in the list box, and then click the [Save] button. The wizard displays the [Save the Recovery Password] screen.

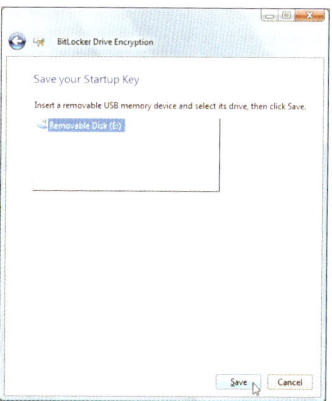

14. Save your BitLocker recovery password in any or all of the three ways available: to a USB drive, to a folder, or by printing it to paper. When you have done so, click the [Next] button.

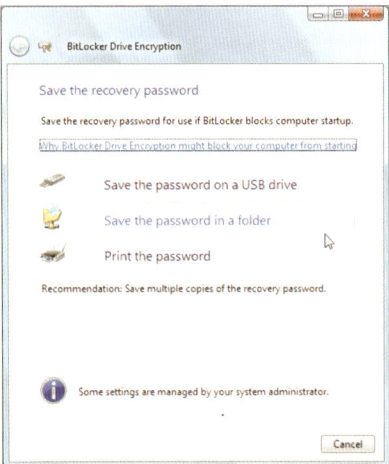

15. The wizard displays the [Encrypt the Volume] screen. Verify that the wizard has chosen the correct volume to encrypt, and make sure the [Run BitLocker System Check] check box is selected. Then click the [Continue] button.

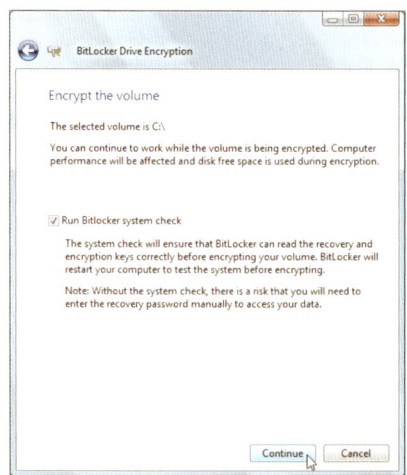

16. The wizard displays the [Computer Must Be Restarted] dialog box. Make sure the USB key is still inserted in the USB port, and check that the optical drive contains no CD or DVD. Then click the [Restart Now] button to restart your computer and allow BitLocker to encrypt your computer's hard disk.

17. When Windows restarts, log on as usual. BitLocker then runs automatically and encrypts your hard disk. You can work during this process, but the encryption runs faster if you allow BitLocker to work uninterrupted

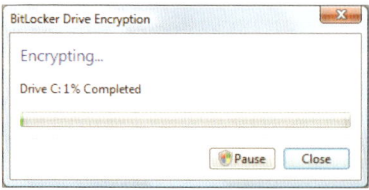

18. After you've installed BitLocker, you must provide the PIN (if you chose that option) or the BitLocker USB key (if you chose that option) whenever you start your computer. The following illustration shows the prompt for a USB key.

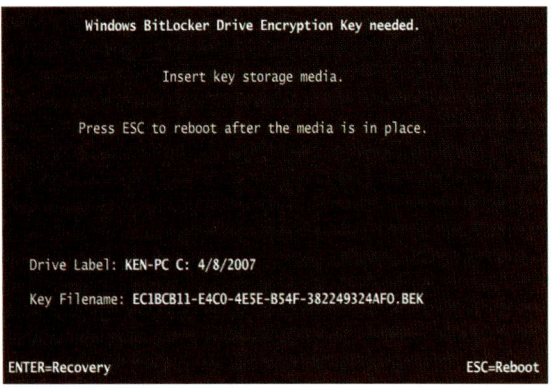

19. If you do not have your USB key, you can press <Enter> to access BitLocker's Recovery mode, in which you enter the BitLocker password on the screen shown here.

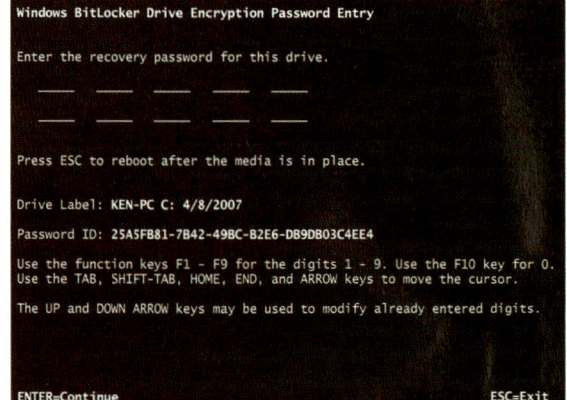

Let's Go Pro!

Turning Off BitLocker Drive Encryption

Normally, once you've implemented BitLocker on a computer, you'll leave it on so that your computer remains protected. But if you need to remove BitLocker—for example, so that you can give the computer to someone else—follow these steps:

① Click the [Start] button, type BitLocker in the [Search] box, and then click the [BitLocker Drive Encryption] item in the [Programs] list. Go through User Account Control for the BitLocker Drive Encryption feature. Windows opens the BitLocker Drive Encryption window. Click the [Turn Off BitLocker] link

② Windows opens a [BitLocker Drive Encryption] dialog box. Click the [Decrypt the Volume] button.

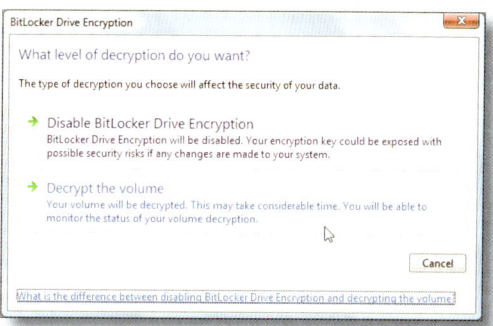

③ BitLocker starts decrypting the hard drive and displays an icon in the notification area. You can hover the mouse pointer over the icon to display a progress indicator. To get a constant readout, click the notification-area icon. Windows displays a [BitLocker Drive Encryption] dialog box.

④ Click the [Close] button if you want to close the dialog box rather than leave it open.

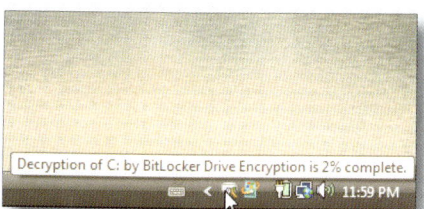

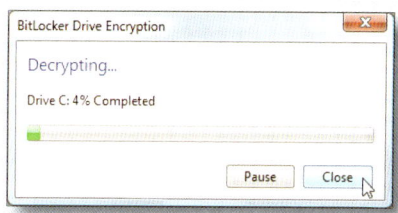

Index >>>

A

Activating Windows	18
Active Partition	306
Activity Viewer	119
Advanced Search	76
Antivirus Program	253
Appearance Settings	99
Attach a file	153
Automatic Updates	248, 257

B

Backup and Restore Center	279
Bit rate	178
BitLocker	306
BitLocker Drive Encryption	309
BitLocker Drive Preparation Tool	307
Burning Audio CDs	184

C

Cascade Windows	35
Change Desktop Icon	88
Change Your Picture	106
Check Compatibility Online	11
Closed Wireless Network	212
Combined Network	201
Compatibility Settings	45
Computer-based E-mail	146
Copy To Folder	64
Copying via Drag and Drop	68
Crash program	286
Create A Password Reset Disk	111
Create New Account	108
Create Password	109
Customize Start Menu	107

D

Default.rdp	295
Delete Account	110
Delete Command	69
Desktop	30
Desktop Background	86
Desktop Toolbars	96
Device Driver	233
Device Manager	234
DHCP	199, 214
Dial-up Connection	128
Display Settings	84
DVD	187

E

Emoticon	164
Extract Compressed (Zipped) Folder Wizard	79

F

Favorites	140
Favorites Center	142
Files	54
Folders	54
Font Types	244
Fonts	243
Forward message	151

G

Gadgets	37
Get More Gadgets Online	39
Google's Cookie	139

H

Home page	139
Hot-Pluggable Devices	228

I

Internet Explorer	132
Internet Security Settings	261
Internet Service Provider(ISP)	124
IP Address	214

Pv4	215	Product Key	15
IPv6	215	Program Compatibility Wizard	47

K

Keyboard Layout	22

Q

Quick Launch Toolbar	33

L

Lock button	25
Lock The Taskbar	93
Log Off button	26
Logging On to Windows Vista	20

R

Recycle Bin	69
Remote Assisatance	268, 274
Remote Assisatance Invitation	270
Remote Desktop	290
Remote Desktop Connection	292
Reply message	151
Restart	27
Restore Down	36
Restore Point	277
Restrictions Windows	114
Rips CD	178
Roll back	234

M

Malware Protection	248
Maximize button	36
Media Library	173
Minimize button	36
Modem	125
Move To Folder	66
Moving via Drag and Drop	68

S

Screeen Refresh Rate	85
Screen Saver	103
Search Box	74
Search Result Window	75
Sending message	151
Sharing a Printer	238
Sharing Files	221
Sharing Music	186
Shortcuts	81
Show Hidden Icons	33
Show Windows Side by Side	36
Show Windows Stacked	36
Shut Down	27
Shut Down Option	23
Sidebar	37
Signature	154
Sounds	97
Start Menu	31
Switch User	24
System Partition	306
System Restore	276

R

Network Adapters	198
Network Cable	198
Network Drive	218
Network Switch	198
Non-Hot-Pluggable Devices	230
Notification Area	33, 95

O

Parental Controls	113
Password Reset Wizard	112
Personalization Windows	84, 86
PIN	310
Pin To Start Menu	34
Playlist	181
Power button	26
Power Options	105
Printer	236
Problem Reports and Solutions	283

Index >>>

T

Tabs	134
Taskbar	32, 92
Taskbar and Start Menu Properties	94
Theme Settings	91

U

Unpin From Start Menu	34
URGE online music service	175
USB flash drive	204
USB key	310
User Account Control	43, 50, 248

V

Vista Aero	6, 99
Vista Basic	99
Vista Recommended minimum specification	10

W

Web-based E-mail	146, 156, 271
Webcam	166
Window Color And Appearance	99, 101
Windows Complete PC Backup	298
Windows Complete PC Restore	300
Windows Defender	262
Windows Explorer	54, 58
Windows Fax and Scan	302
Windows Firewall	248
Windows Flip	35
Windows Flip 3D	35
Windows Live ID	160
Windows Live Messenger	157
Windows Live OnCare	254
Windows Live Search	137
Windows Mail	147
Windows Media Center	191
Windows Media Player	170
Windows Photo Gallery	56
Windows Security Center	249
Windows Sidebar Properties	41
Windows Task Manager	286
Windows Ultimate Extras	297
Windows Update	297
Windows Upgrade Advisor	10
Windows Vista Bussiness Edition	7, 290
Windows Vista Enterprise Edition	7
Windows Vista Home Basic	6
Windows Vista Home Premium	6
Windows Vista Starter Editon	6
Windows Vista Ultimate Edition	7, 288
Windows XP	10, 290
Wired Network	198
Wireless Network	201, 202
WordPad	242
Workgroups	224

Z

Zipped folders	78